MEDIA RESEARCH METHODS

MEDIA RESEARCH METHODS

Measuring Audiences, Reactions and Impact

Barrie Gunter

SAGE Publications
London • Thousand Oaks • New Delhi

SAGE Publications Ltd
6 Bonhill Street
London EC2A 4PU

SAGE Publications Inc
2455 Teller Road
Thousand Oaks, California 91320

SAGE Publications India Pvt Ltd
32, M-Block Market
Greater Kailash - I
New Delhi 110 048

British Library Cataloguing in Publication data

A catalogue record for this book is
available from the British Library

ISBN 0 7619 5658 1
ISBN 0 7619 5659 X (pbk)

Library of Congress catalog card number available

Typeset by SIVA Math Setters, Chennai, India.

CONTENTS

CHAPTER 1 Evolving Theoretical Background
of Media Research   1

CHAPTER 2 Overview of Media Research Methodologies:
Audiences   22

CHAPTER 3 Overview of Media Research Methodologies:
Media Output   55

CHAPTER 4 Measuring Media Usage and Exposure   93

CHAPTER 5 Measuring Affective Responses to Media   135

CHAPTER 6 Measuring Cognitive Responses to Media:
Attention and Comprehension   163

CHAPTER 7 Measuring Cognitive Impact of Media   190

CHAPTER 8 Measuring Behavioural Impact of Media:
From Association to Causation   236

References   280

Index   308

CHAPTER I

EVOLVING THEORETICAL BACKGROUND OF MEDIA RESEARCH

The purpose of this book is to examine the range and variety of research methodologies used in a number of different media research contexts. It is not a methodology handbook designed to show readers how to utilize particular research techniques or a book of best practice with regard to specific quantitative or qualitative methods. Such books are already plentiful. It is concerned with the different research orientations that media scholars have used over the years in relation to principal areas of enquiry. For the purposes of this book, distinctions have been made between: analysis of media output; analysis of media audiences and their consumption of media; analysis of audience evaluative or affective responses to media; analysis of cognitive involvement with, processing and interpretation of media; and analysis of media effects, at the cognitive level and at the behavioural level. In each of these areas of media research, however, a range of different research methodologies have been applied. Sometimes, these methodologies simply represent different techniques for measuring social phenomena. On other occasions, the application of specific methodologies reflects deeper divisions among media scholars in respect of their theoretical or philosophical orientations. This book attempts to describe the methodologies that have been applied in connection with key areas of media enquiry, but goes beyond mere description to examine the advantages and disadvantages of specific methodologies, technically in the sense of their ability to collect relevant and meaningful data, and epistemologically in the sense of their ability to yield a comprehensive understanding of media-related phenomena.

A proper understanding of media research and the way it has been carried out cannot emerge without some consideration of the theoretical background of different approaches to media analysis. While this book does explore issues relating to the practicalities of 'doing media research', this kind of analysis cannot effectively take place divorced from any consideration of the theoretical underpinnings of media research methods. The specific mechanical aspects of studying the media that are chosen by media scholars are generally determined by a theoretical view of the nature and production of media output or of the way individuals interact with and respond to the content with which they are provided by the media. Over the years, media research has borrowed from and been dominated by theories deriving from such disciplines as anthropology, linguistics, sociology, political science and psychology. Different perspectives on the study of the media have emerged historically in response not only to the findings of empirical enquiries, which changed ideas about the way people respond to the media, but more often and more significantly as a result of paradigm shifts within social science research more generally. In order to establish a conceptual framework within which to present, review and critique media research methodologies, therefore, it is important to examine these conceptual changes and the dominant epistemological premises of research and ontological assumptions about humankind that shaped scientific thinking throughout the history of the modern mass media.

Littlejohn (1983) presented a meta-theoretical scheme that, at least for heuristic purposes, is useful for providing some order to the theoretical perspectives underlying the multitude of theories, models and approaches in communication research. This two-dimensional scheme presented a descriptive framework that distinguished broad epistemological premises and ontological assumptions related to communication research. Research in this realm was conceived to derive from one of two epistemological positions. The first of these is characterized by the assumption that human beings are surrounded by a physical, more or less completely knowable world. This is called 'World View I'. According to Littlejohn,

> This tradition is based on empiricist and rationalist ideas. It treats reality as distinct from the human being, something that people discover outside themselves. It assumes a physical, knowledge reality that is self-evident to the trained observer. Discovery is important in this position; the world is waiting for the scientist to find it. Since knowledge is viewed as something acquired from outside oneself. (1983: 20–1).

The second characteristic is the serious doubt in human capability for acquiring such positivistic knowledge of an 'objective' world. Knowing is seen as interpreting, an activity everybody is assumed to be engaged in. This hermeneutic position is termed 'World View II'.

> This tradition takes a different turn by relying heavily on constructivism, viewing the world in process. In this view people take an active role in creating knowledge. A world of things exists outside the person, but the individual can conceptualise these things in a variety of useful ways. Knowledge therefore arises not out of our discovery but from interactions between knower and known. For this reason perceptual and interpretive processes of the individuals are important objects for study. (Littlejohn, 1983: 21)

The second dimension of Littlejohn's scheme, that of ontology, deals with the nature of phenomena communication researchers seek to know. Essentially, there are two ontological positions to be found in communication research, labelled (1) the 'non-actional' position and (2) the 'actional' position. Both positions are characterized by typical assumptions concerning the concept of man, the concept of human action as well as the concept of human interaction.

Non-actional theory 'assumes that behavior is determined by and responsive to past pressures. Covering laws are usually viewed as appropriate in this tradition, active interpretation by the individual is downplayed' (Littlejohn, 1983: 22). A further elaboration on this approach was offered by another writer. 'The *non-actional approach* normally reduces the material under investigation to empirically (objectively) observable events that can be identified and tested intersubjectively, scientific efforts are made to relate empirically observed phenomena in order to formulate hypotheses. In the case of human action, directly observable are overt *behavioural responses*; as factors playing an overt behaviour (observed) external influences, i.e. *behavioural stimuli*, are taken' (Hunziger, 1988: 72, cited in Recnkstorff and McQuail, 1996).

Actional theory, instead, assumes 'that individuals create meanings, they have intentions, they make real choices. The actional view rests on a teleological base, which says that people make decisions that are designed to achieve goals. Theorists of the actional tradition are reluctant to seek covering laws ... instead, they assume that people behave differently in different situations because rules change from one situation to another' (Littlejohn, 1983: 22).

Hunziger sums this position up succinctly. 'The *action-theoretical approach* postulates that human social action is based on *subjective meanings* ("subjectivesinngebung"). Research efforts are made to understand these subjective meanings as well as the underlying motives and the social means within which social actions take place. The problem of *verstehen* is due to the fact that neither motives, nor orientations or perspectives of the actors can be investigated directly' (1988: 73).

The combination of both dimensions – the epistemological and the ontological – of communication research, thus allows the discrimination of four theoretical perspectives underlying contemporary communication research: (a) the behaviouristic; (b) the transmissional; (c) the interactional; and (d) the transactional perspective (see Figure 1.1).

MAJOR THEORETICAL PERSPECTIVES

A number of broad theoretical perspectives have emerged that have played an important part in shaping dominant modes of thinking within

Figure 1.1   Classification of Theoretical Perspectives on Communication Research

		Ontological position	
		Non-actional theory	Actional theory
Epistemological position	'World View I' (physical, knowable reality; self-evident to trained observer)	Behaviouristic perspective Transmissional perspective	
	'World View II' (social construction of reality)	Interactional perspective	Transactional perspective

the social sciences during the 20th century. Each approach is linked to a particular tradition in social theory and provides a distinctive model of human nature and paradigm for investigating it. These perspectives also reflect the hermeneutic framework discussed in the first part of this chapter. Three traditions in particular can be singled out as having a profound influence on thinking about the role and impact of the mass media: (1) positivism; (2) interpretive social science; and (3) critical social science.

Positivism

This approach is based on the early 19th century philosophical school of thought founded by Auguste Comte and later developed by Emile Durkheim. The type of research associated with this paradigm tends to be quantitative in nature, using experiments, surveys and statistics. Positivist empirical researchers search for objectivity in measurement and utilize predominantly numerical forms of measurement to understand social phenomena. The overriding objective is to prove or disprove hypotheses and ultimately to establish universal laws of behaviour through the use of numerically defined and quantifiable measures analogous to those used by the natural sciences.

According to one writer: 'Positivism defines social science as an organised method for combining deductive logic with precise empirical observations of individual behavior in order to discover and confirm a set of probabilistic causal laws that can be used to predict general patterns of human activity' (Neuman, 1994: 58). In the context of understanding social behaviour, quantitative methodologies provide techniques for exploring the causes of behaviour. The focus is placed upon what can be observed. Research techniques are used through which observable phenomena can be quantified and classified. The main goal of positivistic social science is to explain causal relations between these observable phenomena.

Positivism does not believe in absolute determinism. Causal laws are probabilistic. Such laws may be true for large groups of people or situations, but not to an equal degree for everyone or everything. Scientific laws allow for predictions to be made. Thus, if event X occurs, there may be a certain probability that event Y will follow. But event Y may not always occur. Scientific explanation is *nomothetic* – it is based on universal laws. Laws of human behaviour should be universally valid. In applying the efficacy of laws, people pass through a deductive process, collecting facts and testing them against hypotheses or predictions. Distinctions are made between truth and falsehood, through the acquisition of knowledge which enables one to determine if a particular state of affairs or a relationship between events can be proven.

Explanations of human behaviour must comply with and be supported by the facts. Furthermore, for a law to become established, it must be *repeatedly* supported by facts – the notion of replication. Facts are obtained through empirical research techniques which tend usually to collect quantitative statistical data or measures of observable events, objects and behaviours. In the process the researcher must remain detached from the data collection exercise. Positivistic social research is based upon objective measurement and not intuition or subjective judgements.

Interpretive social science

Interpretive social science contrasts with positivism by switching attention from the external and observable to the internal factors or forces that move people. The origins of this perspective have been identified with the writings of Max Weber, a German sociologist. According to Neuman '.... interpretive social science is also related to *hermeneutics*, a theory of meaning that originated in the nineteenth century but is largely found in the humanities (philosophy, art history, religious studies, linguistics, and literary criticism). It emphasizes a detailed reading or examination of *text*, which could refer to a conversation, written words or pictures. The reading is to discover embedded meaning' (1994: 61).

It is believed that people convey subjective experience through texts. Close inspection of such texts will reveal insights into a person's inner feelings and motives. There are several varieties of interpretive social science, including hermeneutics, ethnomethodology and qualitative social research. Researchers who follow this paradigm often use participant observation or field research. These techniques require that researchers spend numerous hours in direct personal contact with those being studied. They analyse transcripts of conversations or study videotapes of behaviour in extraordinary detail, analysing non-verbal as well as verbal communications among those under investigation.

The data collected by qualitative research methods are impressionistic rather than numerically defined. In a media research context, for instance, the raw data may comprise media texts or transcripts of conversations people have held about media content, rather than numerically scored responses given to mutiple-choice questionnaires. The researcher uses rigorous and detailed methods to gather large quantities of qualitative data in the form of specific details. In comparison, a positivist researcher uses pre-structured techniques that constrain the way people can respond verbally or behaviourally, but often obtains data from larger numbers of individuals or greater amounts of media output than would the follower of interpretive social scientific approaches. An interpretive researcher may spend a year living with a dozen people to get an in-depth understanding of their lives. A positivist using quantitative empirical methods would rather obtain data from 1200 individuals in an interview taking just a few minutes.

The interpretive approach argues that social researchers should study meaningful social action not just the external or observable behaviour of people. Social action is action to which people attach subjective meaning – activity with a purpose or intent. The interpretive approach holds that social life is based on social interactions and socially constructed meaning systems. People possess an internally experienced sense of reality. This subjective sense of reality is crucial for explaining human social life.

Social reality is based on people's definitions of it. Positivists assume that everyone shares the same meaning system; they take it as a given that we all experience the world in the same way. The interpretive approach says that people may or may not experience social reality in the same way. An interpretive approach assumes that multiple interpretations of human experience, or realities, are possible.

Interpretive researchers want to discover what actions mean to the people who engage in them. They think that it makes little sense to try to deduce social life from abstract logical theories that may not relate to the feelings and experiences of ordinary people. Individual motives are crucial to consider even if they are irrational, emotion-laden and contain false facts and prejudices. Interpretive researchers value common sense as a way to interpret the world, while positivists would generally dismiss common sense for being 'unscientific'.

Positivists believe that social theory should be similar to natural science theory with deductive axioms, theorems and interconnected causal laws. Interpretive research focuses on the experiences of individuals and is less concerned with drawing wide general statements about human nature. Good evidence in positivism is observable, precise and independent of theory or values. Interpretive social science in contrast sees the unique features of specific contexts and meanings as essential for understanding social meaning.

Interpretive researchers rarely ask objective survey questions, aggregate the answers of many people, and claim to have something meaningful. Instead, each person's interpretation of the survey question must be placed in a more personal, idiosyncratic context (e.g. the individual's previous experiences or the survey interview situation), and the true meaning of a person's answer will vary according to the interview or questioning context and how that situation is perceived by individual respondents. Moreover, because each person assigns a somewhat different meaning to the question and answer, according to the followers of the interpretive tradition, combining answers only produces nonsense.

Critical social science

In many ways, the critical social science approach concurs with the criticisms the interpretive approach directs at positivism. It does not agree with interpretive social science entirely, however. Criticial social science has its origins in the thinking of Karl Marx and is thus underpinned by notions of social class struggles. Like the interpretive approach, critical social science identifies a crucial shortcoming in positivism in its failure adequately to represent personal interpretations people place upon social phenomena. In addition, critical social science adds a socio-economic and political dimension to the equation by identifying specific sociopolitical motives with positivism, which is regarded as an approach to scientific enquiry that is aligned with dominant political and socio-economic forces in society. At the same time, critical researchers criticize the interpretive approach for being too subjective and relativist.

For the critical social scientific researcher a principal aim of research is to reveal, explain and understand power structures and relationships within society. The media are identified as powerful sources of social control, themselves controlled by social, cultural and political elites. Such establishment institutions can utilize the media to promulgate specific values, beliefs and opinions, maintaining their own position vis-à-vis less powerful groups within society. Through exposing these manipulative processes and the mechanisms through which they operate, researchers hope to empower the less powerful by enabling them to recognize these processes and hence to challenge them. The media provide a stereotyped representation of external reality which needs to be recognized for what it is. However, this reality is a constantly changing and evolving entity which thus needs to be constantly monitored. The critical social science approach argues that social reality has multiple layers. Behind immediately observable surface reality lie deep structures or unobservable mechanisms. Only with effort can deep structures be exposed.

Critical social science uses the idea of false consciousness to explain its position on common sense. This is taken to mean that people are fooled or mistaken and act against their own true best interests as defined in objective reality. This concept is meaningless in interpretive social science because it implies that a social actor uses a meaning system that is false or out of touch with objective reality. The interpretive approach says that people create and use such systems, and that researchers can only describe such systems, not judge their value.

The critical social science approach says that social researchers should study subjective ideas and common sense because these shape human behaviour although they are full of myth and illusion. A complete critical social science explanation does several things. It demystifies illusion, describes the underlying structure of conditions, explains how change can be achieved, and provides a vision of a possible future. Critical theory does more than describe the unseen mechanisms that account for observable reality; it also critiques conditions and implies a plan of change.

Positivism believes in absolutes, while interpretive social science believes in relativism. Thus, for positivists, general, abstract rules about external reality can be determined that explain social phenomena and in respect of which a broad consensus of recognition can be established among people. For interpretivists, no such universal rules or principles can be established; individuals have unique and idiosyncratic perceptions of the world. These individual differences should be emphasized over any attempt to uncover universal truths about social phenomena. Positivism assumes that there are incontestable facts about social reality on which all rational people agree. The interpretive approach sees the social world as made up of generated meaning, with people creating and negotiating meanings that they take to be facts. The critical approach adopts a slightly different position again, acknowledging in partial agreement with positivists that the world contains material conditions upon which certain broad consensus beliefs can be attained, but at the same time, due account must be given to variations in the meanings individuals from different communities may attach to the same social phenomena.

One branch of critical social science is *feminist research*, which is carried out by people, usually women, who hold a feminist self-identity. Multiple research techniques may be used by this approach. The overriding feature of feminist methodology is its attempt to give voice to women and to correct the male-oriented perspective that has predominated in the development of social science.

Many feminist researchers argue that positivism is consistent with a male point of view; it is objective, logical, task-oriented, and instrumental. It reflects a male emphasis on individual competition, on dominating and controlling the environment, and on the hard facts and forces that act on the world. Women emphasize accommodation and gradually developing bonds. They see the social world as an interconnected web of human relations full of people linked to one another by feelings of trust and mutual obligation. This perspective tends to use softer, qualitative research techniques and case study approaches to investigating social scientific questions.

Postmodern research

This is an approach that began in the humanities and has roots in the philosophies of existentialism and the ideas produced by Heidegger, Nietzsche, Sartre and Wittgenstein. It goes beyond the interpretive and critical social science perspectives in an attempt to transform social science radically. Extreme postmodernists reject even the possibility of a science of the social world. They distrust systematic empirical observation and question whether knowledge is generalizable or accumulates over time. Postmodernism rejects 'modernism', the assumptions and beliefs that arose in the Enlightenment era of Western history. Modernism relies on logical reasoning, is optimistic about the future, believes in progress, and has confidence in technology and science. Postmodernism rejects the use of science to predict and to make policy decisions. Postmodernists oppose those who use positivist science to reinforce power relations.

Postmodernism shares with critical social science the goal of demystifying the social world. Its approach is to deconstruct or tear apart surface appearances to reveal the internal hidden structure. It distrusts abstract explanation and holds that research can never do more than describe, with all descriptions equally valid. In postmodernism a researcher's description is neither superior nor inferior to anyone else's.

CONVERGENCE OF PERSPECTIVES

Widespread agreement is emerging within media research for a process of cross-fertilization to begin between empirical sociology or psychology approaches and cultural or critical approaches. McQuail (1985: 131) registered the increased importance of critical theory for media sociology: '... the trend towards more qualitative, intensive research ... stimulated by the cross-fertilization between media sociology and humanistic, now often semiological approaches'. A similar view was propounded by one American writer who was severely critical of American sociological theories and methods. He envisaged: 'a convergence of quantitative and qualitative research' in order to realize the 'potential for accurate description and explanation of the significance of communications in all contexts' (Lull, 1985: 219–20). Blumler et al. (1985: 271), also appealed for sociologists 'to work toward convergences with other paradigms' including ones 'that ostensibly would seem altogether incompatible with our own'.

Then, scholars from the humanistic cultural studies tradition have become aware of the need for both traditions to sacrifice some of their sacred cows. Criticizing the reluctance among critical scholars to face audience questions empirically, Jensen (1986: 2–3) argued that 'there is at present a need for a theory of reception which is both critical and empirical' and discussed 'how different, qualitative and quantitative research designs may contribute to answering the general question of what media do to people and vice versa'.

Despite the widespread agreement about the importance of cross-fertilization between the two paradigms, very few have been able to articulate a way forward. There is clearly a need to find an appropriate hybrid approach given the limitations of each of the others. As Katz and Liebes (1986: 4–5) remarked: 'Some of us are studying the texts of popular culture while others are studying their effects on audiences .... The former ... don't know anything about the audience, and the latter ... don't know anything about the texts'.

EVOLVING RESEARCH PARADIGMS IN MEDIA RESEARCH

Media research has evolved over time, in part reflecting paradigm shifts and the evolution of analytical models in the wider social sciences. In the course of this process, significant changes have occurred in conceptions of the media's roles and influences in society. These theoretical developments have also underpinned changing fashions in research methodologies. This phenomenon can be illustrated by the changing notions of the audience across the past five decades.

During the period between the first and second world wars there was a broad consensus among researchers that the media exercised a powerful and persuasive influence. Underpinning this opinion were several developments. First, the 1920s and 1930s witnessed the emergence of mass audiences on an unprecedented scale as a function of the growth and establishment of the press, films and radio. Second, a view emerged that urbanization and industrialization of society had produced a volatile, unstable and alienated public susceptible to manipulation. Third, this mass urbanized public was regarded as being easy prey to persuasive messages, especially as conveyed via mass communications, primarily because individuals lacked a firm and stable anchor point, traditionally associated with more settled and mutually supportive rural communities. Fourth, there was a cynical observation that the mass media had been used to brainwash people during the two world wars and played a part in the rise of fascism in Europe during the inter-war years. As a result of these observations, the media came to be regarded as potentially powerful propaganda agencies capable of shaping public opinion and behaviour (Curran et al., 1987).

One critique of the role of the mass media in contemporary culture emanated in the 1940s from the Marxist dominated Frankfurt School. This school of thought espoused a pessimistic conception of the audience, which was shaped by a reaction to the breakdown of German society into fascism at that time. This breakdown was attributed in part to the loosening of traditional ties and structures and was seen as leaving people atomized and exposed to external influences, especially to the influence of mass propaganda of powerful leaders, the most effective agency of which was the mass media.

This pessimistic view of mass society stressed the conservative and reconciliatory role of 'mass culture' for the audience. Mass culture offered a dominant ideology or point of view on the world and left little room for alternatives or individual idiosyncracies to surface. Implicit here was a 'hypodermic' model in which the media were seen as having the power to 'inject' a repressive ideology directly into the consciousness of the masses. Thus, mass audiences were pictured as more or less helpless victims of manipulation and exploitation by capitalist media devoted to purveying 'false consciousness', meaning essentially the loss of any sense of class identity and solidarity (Hart, 1991; Jay, 1973; Rosenberg and White, 1957). The victimized working classes were unable to defend themselves against propaganda and manipulation, because of their lack of education and their experience of mindless and exhausting labour from which mass culture was a relief.

Writing of this thesis, Katz and Lazarsfeld (1955: 16) noted: 'The image of the mass communication process entertained by researchers had been, firstly, one of "an atomistic mass" of millions of readers, listeners and movie-goers, prepared to receive the message; and secondly ... every message [was conceived of] as a direct and powerful stimulus to action which would elicit immediate response'.

C. Wright Mills (1951, 1956) elaborated on the extreme dependence and vulnerability of the ordinary person in the face of the monopoly media and advertising industry. The media were attributed the power to create extreme dependence in respect of the basic psychic needs for identity and self-realization. The mass audience was part of a process of control and homogenization by the media. Real differences associated with class were concealed without being resolved.

The emigration of the leading members of the Frankfurt School (Adorno, Marcuse, Horkheimer) to America during the 1930s led to the development of a specifically 'American' school of research in the 1940s and 1950s. The Frankfurt School's 'pessimistic' thesis of the link between 'mass society' and fascism, and the role of the media in cementing it, proved unacceptable to American researchers. The pessimistic thesis proposed too direct and unmediated an impact by the media on their audiences. The proposition that all intermediary social structures between leaders/media and the masses had broken down, did not reflect the pluralistic nature of American society – it was sociologically naïve. Certainly, the media have social effects, but these were not all-powerful, nor did they act directly upon audiences.

Any links between the media and audience had to be demonstrated. American researchers thus developed a quantitative and positivist methodology for empirical media research (at that time focusing on radio audiences) into the 'sociology of mass persuasion', as a reaction to the critical social theory and qualitative analysis of the Frankfurt School.

Both the 'optimistic' (American) and 'pessimistic' (Frankfurt) paradigms embodied a shared implicit theory of the dimensions of power and influence through which the powerful (leaders and communicators) were connected to the powerless (ordinary people, audiences). Operating within this paradigm, the different styles and strategies of research may then be differentiated in terms of two perspectives: one, message-based studies, which moved from an analysis of the content of messages to their effects on audiences; and two, audience-based studies which focused on the social characteristics environment and, subsequently, needs which audiences derived from, or brought to, the message.

The American empirical school

The 'hypodermic' model of media influences promulgated by the Frankfurt School from the 1930s encouraged the development of research methodologies designed to test the extent of such influences. The notion that the mass media could serve as effective propaganda vehicles which could carry persuasive messages to mass audiences, shaping their political and social values and behaviours, led to a series of 'campaign' studies in the 1940s and 1950s. These studies were designed to measure the potency of media messages in relation to shaping political and consumer behaviours. Following the thinking of the Frankfurt School, the media were seen as potential agents of remote control, possessing the ability to persuade individuals to change their attitudes and behaviour. Media effects were assumed to be direct, immediate and total. Within the USA, an empirical, positivistic school of enquiry into media effects became established in which the assumptions of the Frankfurt School were tested.

The post Second World War American mass communication research made a three-dimensional critique of the pessimistic mass society thesis, reflecting the arguments that informal communication played only a minor role in modern society, that the audience was a mass in the simple sense of an aggregation of socially atomized individualism and that it was possible to equate directly content and effects.

Sociologist Robert Merton argued that media research had previously been concerned almost wholly with the content rather than the effects of propaganda. While this work had been useful in identifying the nature of some of the appeals and rhetorical devices used by propagandists, it had not really shed much light on the actual processes of persuasion. Effects of media materials were too often inferred rather than demonstrated. An analysis of media content alone was insufficient to prove specific effects upon audiences (Merton, 1946). Certainly, the characteristics of the message were important in relation to the kinds of influences that might be propagated upon audiences. Specific message features could serve as triggers to particular audience responses because they had links with specific audience beliefs or values. Media messages, however, do not act upon audiences in a vacuum. Audiences place their own interpretations upon these messages in the light of their pre-existing knowledge, values and opinions, and the expectations that are placed upon them by their surrounding social and cultural milieu in regard to their general conduct and behaviour. This analysis of media effects failed to have any widespread influence upon scholarly thinking at that time, although a notion did emerge among some media theorists that media effects were not invariably direct, but often operated via mediators, in the form of 'opinion leaders'. The shaping of public opinion then had an important interpersonal component whereby some groups might be directly cognizant of and reactive to media messages, while others were influenced, in turn, by messages relayed by the latter individuals (Katz and Lazarsfeld, 1955).

Media effects and media uses

Research carried out within this positivist paradigm explored two different avenues of relationship between the media and the public. One line of enquiry comprised an assessment of the nature of links between media messages and different types of audience response. The other line of enquiry focused on the ways in which audiences used the media and on the motivational forces that shaped patterns of media consumption. Research into media effects has been influenced predominantly by behaviourist psychology. Its primary interest has been with establishing how the behaviour of audiences is affected by the contents of media messages. This perspective yielded a substantial body of research during the 1960s and 1970s, particularly on topics such as the effects of media violence. During the 1980s, the behaviourist paradigm became modified so as to reflect the growing recognition of the importance of 'cognitive' processes in the media-effects relationship. Under this revised theoretical model, media messages were regarded as having effects only if they could first penetrate the cognitive information-processing systems of media consumers and influence beliefs and attitudes or long-term world knowledge stores.

Research into patterns of media use and consumption by audiences has been largely structural and functional in orientation, focusing on the social and psychological characteristics of audiences. 'Cognitive' elements eventually surfaced within this perspective, but reflected the conceived mediating role of individual needs or expectations regarding the media and their contents. Thus, media consumers were thought to use the media deliberately and selectively, choosing to consume particular types of content because of the personal needs they were expected to gratify.

Degree and type of media effects

As the debate about media effects continued over the post Second World War decades, differences of opinion emerged among members of the scholarly community concerning the nature and potency of media effects. A fundamental reassessment of the mass media during the late 1940s, 1950s and early 1960s gave rise to a new academic orthodoxy – that the mass media have only a very limited influence. A classic work that embraced this conclusion was produced by Klapper (1960), who wrote that 'mass communications do not serve as a necessary and sufficient cause of audience effects' (p. 8). In this thesis there was a reassessment of the mass public's susceptibility to influence. A succession of empirical enquiries, using experimental laboratory and social survey techniques, demonstrated that people tended to expose themselves to, understand and remember communications selectively, according to prior dispositions. People, it was argued, manipulated – rather than were manipulated by – the mass media. The empirical demonstration of selective audience behaviour was further reinforced by a number of uses and gratifications studies which argued that audience members are active rather than passive and bring to the media a variety of different needs and uses that influence their response to the media.

Underpinning this view about the lack of media influence was a repudiation of the mass society thesis on which the presumption of media power had been based. The view of society as being composed of isolated and anomic individuals gave way to a view of society as a honeycomb of small groups bound by a rich web of personal ties and dependencies.

Stable group pressures, it was concluded, helped to shield the individual from media influence. This stress on the salience of small groups as a buffer against media influence was often linked to a diffusionist model of power.

Not all behaviourally oriented media-effects theorizing has concluded that the mass media's influences are muted. Even from the earliest days of research into media effects, there was an underlying concern, which frequently surfaced, that the media had effects upon their consumers, not all of these effects were for the good, and that some groups were more susceptible than others. There was special concern reserved for children and young people, who were believed to be especially susceptible to media influences. This was particularly worrying in regard to harmful effects that media might exert on vulnerable young media consumers (Klapper, 1960).

A steady flow of research publications emerged during the 1950s and 1960s on media effects, and much of this work focused on demonstrating the degree to which youngsters might respond in socially undesirable ways to media content. Most of these media-effects studies placed most attention on measuring audience responses and considered audiences as 'exposed' to the influences of media content. The impact of the media might be manifest in terms of attitudinal change in response to persuasive messages, the learning of behavioural patterns that might later be reproduced under appropriate conditions, and direct emotional or behavioural reactions to specific media depictions or portrayals.

Much early effects research followed the experimental approach in which communication conditions were manipulated in the search for general lessons about how better to communicate or to avoid harmful consequences. An early example was the war-time research programme into film as a motivational and training tool for recruits (Hovland et al., 1949). The appeal of, and response to, portrayals of violence and related phenomena in the media have mainly been investigated within this tradition. The Payne Fund studies of the early 1930s into the effects of film on youth (e.g. Blumer, 1933) provide the first example of such research. Many studies of elections, beginning with Lazarsfeld et al.'s (1944) classic study of the 1940 US presidential election have sought to relate media content to subsequent audience behaviour, in this case in the context of voting.

A series of laboratory-based psychological studies in the 1960s yielded a substantial body of evidence on the alleged harmful behavioural effects of audience exposure to media violence. In this context, emphasis was placed upon violent portrayals in films and television programmes, with behavioural effects being measured almost exclusively among children and university students. These studies attempted to pin down, by way of stimulus – response, imitation and learning theory approaches, applied under laboratory conditions, the small but quantifiable effects of media content on human behaviour.

Albert Bandura and Leonard Berkowitz were among the foremost exponents of this style of research. They focused on the message as a simple, visual stimulus to imitation or 'acting out'of media portrayals and attended to the consequences, in terms of violent behaviour and delinquency, of the individual's exposure to media portrayals of violence, of 'filmed aggressive role models'.

Use and gratifications

When the results of empirical studies indicated that the media were not as efficient as had been assumed, the focus shifted to address the question 'why not?'. The answer seemed to lie in two concepts: selectivity and interpersonal relations, processes which intervene between the communicators and the audience so as to diminish the direct impact of media messages.

This research stream is still classified by many writers as part of the 'behavioural' audience research tradition. It differs from the behavioural-effects research grounded in behavioural psychology in that it is more concerned with the way audiences use the media than in simply how they might respond to media content. While members of the media audience are regarded, in one sense, as victims waiting to be altered in some way beyond their control, as a function of their exposure to media content, this alternative perspective regards audiences as having volition and being able to determine which media they use and which media content they choose to consume (Blumler and Katz, 1974).

This alternative orientation focused upon the subjective motives and interpretations of media users. In this connection, Katz (1959) argued that this approach crucially assumed that even the most potent of mass media content cannot ordinarily influence an individual who has no 'use' for it in the social and psychological context in which he lives. The 'uses' approach assumes that people's values, their interests and their social roles are pre-potent and that people selectively fashion what they believe from what they read, see and hear in the mass media.

Katz and Lazarsfeld (1955) invented the concept of 'two-step flow' to account for the way in which media messages passed through opinion leaders before reaching the population at large; consequently, media effects could no longer be seen as direct and immediate; they were relayed through mediators in a process requiring a certain amount of time. Both exposure to and perception of media content came to be seen as highly selective, governed by the attempt by the individual to avoid cognitive dissonance. Consequently, the intended or anticipated audience response could be resisted or re-interpreted if the message challenged the preconceived opinions of the audience. Once the audience had been restored to a position of power and liberated from the chains of passivity, it became natural to focus on the ways in which audiences play an active role in selecting and experiencing media content.

Pioneering work was conducted even before the Second World War, and continued during the war-time years. This research was most interested in the motives underpinning readers' and listeners' use of newspapers, magazines and radio (e.g. Cantril and Allport, 1935; Lazarsfeld and Stanton, 1941; Waples et al., 1940). Gratifications studies tried to explain listeners' experiences of quiz programmes and daytime serials (Herzog, 1944; Warner and Henry, 1948). However, the tradition was not developed, and its practitioners were largely ignored, until the late 1960s when the overwhelming focus on campaign effects petered out. Since then, 'uses and gratifications' research has concerned itself with '1) the social and psychological origins of 2) needs, which generate 3) expectations of 4) the mass media or other sources, which lead to 5) differential patterns of media exposure (or engagement in other activities), resulting in 6) need gratification and 7) other consequences' (Katz et al., 1974: 20).

Until the mid-1980s the 'uses and gratifications' tradition represented no deviation from the empirical methodology of the social science paradigm. Even Rosengren et al. (1985) in their state-of-the-art review of gratifications research hardly offered any studies outside the framework of logical positivism. As well as these aspects of media sociology, there was also the vast body of research on the role of the media as initiators or legitimators of violence – falling within the general category of behaviourist social psychology – research that focused on measurable, individual-level effects, the short-term establishment or change of attitudes or behaviour rather than on long-term, institutional or societal effects (e.g. the power to define the public agenda, to justify the status quo, and to exclude alternative versions by shaping unfavourable images of oppositional movements). The uses tradition was subsequently developed through research into the effects of media violence and prosocial content, especially where children are concerned (Rosengren and Windahl, 1989).

A distinctive movement within the tradition also crystallized from research into the motives for media choice and the perceived gratifications obtained from the use of different media content (Rosengren et al., 1985). The definition of the 'uses and gratifications' approach as strictly 'behavioural' has been questioned, however, since its main emphasis is on the social origins of media gratifications and on the wider social functions of media, for instance in facilitating social contact and interaction or in reducing tension and anxiety.

Weaknesses in the empirical behaviourist tradition

There is a problem in the sociological paradigm with the concept of *interpersonal relations*. Katz and Lazarsfeld (1955) reported that 58 per cent of the changes in political opinion were made 'without any remembered personal contact, and were, very often, dependent upon the mass media' (quoted by Gitlin, 1978, in Wilhoit and de Bock, 1978: 73–112). However, when combined with the percentages of personal influence in fashion and consumer attitudes (which were high), this major result for understanding the formation of public opinion becomes invisible, the general conclusion being that two-step flow *is* the process of media effect.

Gitlin demonstrated, using Katz and Lazarsfeld's own data, that the factor of 'interpersonal relations' is inoperative or much reduced in effect, with respect to the change of political attitudes: the media do work directly upon public consciousness. The 'hypodermic' theory of powerful effects thus seems to have been resurrected. What is really at issue, however, is a need for sociological media research to reconceptualize the notion of interpersonal relations, not to abandon it.

The role played by interpersonal relations is simply not reducible to mechanistic solutions such as the two-step flow. However, such a reduction or simplification is the only way in which a behaviouristic approach can make the concept researchable, i.e. quantifiable. Interpersonal relations need to be broken down into discrete steps called 'intervening variables' to be researched within this paradigm.

A media theory which wants to understand how social meanings are formed, changed and reinforced through complex interactive processes, must rethink interpersonal relations in qualitative terms as the formative forces in the individual's socializing environment, profoundly affecting identity, behaviour and attitudes. According to Gitlin (1978, in Wilhoit and de Bock, 1978: 73–112), 'thirty years of methodological research on "effects" of mass media have produced little theory and few coherent findings'. There were, however, early signs that this was beginning to change. Katz (1980) noted a new generation of scholars in the 1970s who were branching out in new directions. In studying the role of media in socialization processes, agenda setting and imparting knowledge, more recognition was given to media influence in a wider social and cultural context and more sophisticated ideas were beginning to emerge about how media consumers processed and acted upon information from the media.

The cultural indicators research of the 1970s and 1980s, for example, focused on the way the mass media function as linkages between culture and other societal systems (Rosengren, 1985). For Rosengren, however, a project that attempts to synthesize the study of culture, socialization and mass media is inconceivable unless it builds on a firm quantitative foundation. Such rigid and dogmatic adherence to a purely quantitative methodology, according to some writers (Schroder, 1987), may continue to limit the insights and value of findings which derive from this positivistic perspective.

The critical paradigm

During the 1970s an alternative approach to the study of mass media surfaced. This perspective derived from a hinterland between the social sciences and humanities. Its principal exponents had worked in the emerging fields of cultural studies and literary or film criticism (Fiske and

Hartley, 1978; Newcomb, 1976, 1978) A few sociologists also contributed (Schudson, 1978, 1984; Gitlin, 1978). These media analysts have leaned on European theoretical traditions, in particular, the political thinking of Marx, Althusser and Gramsci, the cultural studies theories of Habermas, Raymond Williams and Stuart Hall, and psychoanalytic theories.

Scholars within the Marxist and neo-Marxist critical tradition challenged the limited effects model and methodologies of the positivistic empirical behaviourism perspective. Many critical tradition scholars dismissed totally any empirical communications research. They argued that the media were ideological agencies that played a central role in maintaining class domination. Research studies in the empirical tradition were theoretically limited and therefore useless.

Gitlin (1978) was critical of empirical research and suggested an alternative approach grounded more in critical theory, but measuring the ideological impact of media on audiences. He envisaged the mass media as repressive agents of mass deception – in line with the Frankfurt School – whose role is to compensate working people for a lack of freedom and drudgery in their own lives through distracting entertainment and messages which condition them to accept the status quo. The method used to analyse media messages is the qualitative tool derived from literary or semiotic theories, adding systematic scrutiny to what might otherwise easily lapse into impressionable introspection. The objective is to account for the manifest and latent meaning communicated by the media, the meaning supposedly being 'injected' into the minds of members of the audience. The result is an ideological effect, namely the shaping of individual consciousness in accordance with the ideological properties inherent in media texts. According to this perspective, therefore, the media are once again regarded as powerful influences because even audience selectivity in content consumption and discussion of media content with others cannot totally preclude the ideological impact of the media upon individuals.

The cultural studies perspective differs from the traditional critical studies perspective in placing greater emphasis on the interpretive capabilities of audiences. Although this school of thought rejects the stimulus – response behavioural effects model of media influences, it is equally critical of the notion of an all-powerful mass media system on an ideological level.

A further theoretical development in the form of social action theory evolved from this cultural studies school, with a basis also in sociology. This theory represented a further attempt to understand audience behaviour and to contribute to the debate on media impact. A methodological arm of this new school, called reception theory, emerged to facilitate empirical enquiry into media influences. According to Jensen and Rosengren (1990: 222): 'Drawing on methods of analysis-cum-interpretation from the literary tradition and the conception of communication and cultural processes as socially situated discourses from cultural studies, *reception analysis* can be said to perform a comparative reading of media discourses and audience discourses in order to understand the process of reception'.

Reception analysis is effectively the audience research arm of modern cultural studies, rather than an independent tradition. It strongly emphasizes the role of the 'reader' in the 'decoding' of media texts. It has claimed for the audience a power to resist and subvert the dominant or hegemonic meanings offered by the mass media. It is characterized by the use of qualitative and ethnographic methods (Morley, 1992; Seiter et al., 1989).

The origins of the reception approach are mixed, drawing about equally on critical theory, textual and literary analysis and work on popular culture. A key founding text was Hall's (1973, 1980) seminal article 'Encoding and decoding in the television discourse' which offered a model emphasizing the fact that the meaning of media messages was reconstituted by their 'readers' according to their own life experiences and knowledge, which often sharply diverge from the perspectives of those who produce and transmit messages. The emphasis was thus placed on 'differential decoding', and early attempts to demonstrate this concept focused on different interpretations placed on media content by audience members from different social classes or with different political affiliations.

Thus initial attempts at 'empirical' demonstration of Hall's ideas showed that media messages could be read or 'decoded' in different ways by different audience groups and also in ways that were different from the meanings intended by media producers (Morley, 1980). As decoding research proceeded during the 1980s, further evidence emerged that media messages were essentially 'polysemic', or had multiple meanings, and were therefore open to different possible interpretations (Liebes and Katz, 1986, 1989, 1990).

The other main strand of the culturalist approach involves a view of media use as in itself a significant aspect of everyday life. Media use practices can only be understood in relation to the particular social context and experience of a subcultural group (Bausinger, 1984). Media reception research emphasized the study of audiences as 'interpretive communities' (Lindlof, 1988). This concept refers to shared outlook and modes of understanding, often arising out of shared social experiences.

WHICH PERSPECTIVE?

Early theorizing about the mass media concluded that the media can exert powerful effects upon mass publics. While this view was challenged by later empirical researchers, the latter nevertheless failed to reach a consensus view about media effects. Some adopted the opinion that the media have minimal effects, while others signalled selective influences that were dependent upon the types of content to which audiences were exposed. The idea of minimal impact can easily become confused, however, with the maintenance of the status quo. What may appear as a zero impact may in fact be profound but not readily detectable.

Media scholars who adopted a different perspective on media effects criticized the empiricist approach to explaining and demonstrating media effects for misunderstanding the true nature of the media and their role in society. The media shape ideologies, and such influences cannot be detected in simplistic laboratory experiments or one-off surveys of public opinion.

A temporary re-emergence of the powerful media hypothesis occurred among critical studies scholars, but this soon became tempered by a modified interpretivist school of thought which accorded to audiences an ability to select meanings from media content that did not necessarily concur with those intended by media producers. The critical tradition faced a problem in understanding how media messages are produced so as to acquire the hegemonic function they attribute to media texts and thus to lead people astray. Evidence of the polysemic qualities of media contents also causes difficulty for the critical analysts' position on all-powerful media effects.

Audience members may, of course, gradually digest media messages over time, but their influence will be moderated by the cultural identity to which these individuals adhere. Social and cultural values are established primarily through interpersonal relations with other members of the community. It is important, even within the critical tradition, to examine how the audience actually selects, perceives, decodes and makes sense of media content. A more complex empirical methodology is needed than that supplied by the behaviourist tradition to shed light on such matters. Despite their oppositional stance and mutual criticism, the critical and empirical positivistic perspectives face similar problems in advancing their causes to provide a better understanding of how people use and respond to the mass media. This observation is succinctly summed up by one writer as follows:

> Differences between the pluralist and critical schools about the power of the mass media, at the level of effectiveness, are to a certain extent based on mutual misunderstanding (notably an over-literal acceptance by some Marxist commentators of polemical generalizations about the lack of media influence advanced by some empirical researchers). This misunderstanding has been perpetuated by the tendency for researchers in the two traditions to examine the impact of the mass media in different contexts as a consequence of their divergent ideological and theoretical preoccupations. (Curran et al.: 61)

Throughout this book, evidence will be examined from the positivist social science perspective that has dominated so much media research as well as from other philosophical approaches to the study of social phenomena. Since the beginning of the 1980s, media research has witnessed a steady convergence of theoretical orientations and methodological approaches, particularly in respect of the analysis of media content, media audiences, and audiences' interpretations of meanings conveyed by media. Positivists have recognized the necessity to adopt methodologies that are more effective at representing and measuring audiences' involvement with and interpretations of media content within a model that is more sophisticated than a basic stimulus – response concept. Meanwhile, critical and interpretivist researchers have acknowledged that in order properly to understand audiences, it is necessary, at least some of the time, to obtain data directly from them. Before turning to specific areas of media analysis, the next two chapters provide broad overviews of key methodologies that have been applied to the analysis of media output and the analysis of media audiences. Later chapters then examine methodologies that have been applied to measure media audiences, immediate audience reactions to media content, and the longer-term impact of media on audiences.

CHAPTER 2

OVERVIEW OF MEDIA RESEARCH METHODOLOGIES: AUDIENCES

The history of media research has been characterized by changing fashions in methodologies over time. As with other fashions, however, preferred methodologies have come into and gone out of vogue at different times. A key determining factor underpinning the prevalent methodologies of any research era is the dominant paradigm or theoretical perspective of the time. Chapter 1 discussed the major schools of thought within the social sciences that have influenced media research. A broad distinction emerged between positivist social science and more critical and interpretive approaches. In methodology terms, these alternative paradigms have emphasized specific types of research procedure.

Positivist social science has been concerned with elucidating patterns of media usage and effects, and it places significant weight on research which provides quantitative measurements of media-related phenomena. These measurements are deemed to be best achieved through survey and experimental methodologies. Critical and interpretivist perspectives are more concerned with understanding how people interact with and make sense of the media through reference to various communities which represent membership or reference groups from which they derive their values and standards. These things can be difficult to quantify and may be better understood through qualitative methodologies, typified by ethnomethodological approaches such as field observations and focus group or in-depth interview procedures.

The application of each of these methodological perspectives will be examined in this book in relation to different realms of media research, including: (1) measurement of media exposure; (2) attention to media; (3) affective responses to media; (4) cognitive processing of media; (5) impact of media; (6) the output of media; and (7) the production of media.

Before discussing the methodologies that have been applied by media researchers working in each of these areas of media investigation, however, this chapter will present a broad overview of the key methodologies. It will describe the basic principles of each methodology, its strengths and weaknesses, and the kinds of data that it can yield. This overview is designed to provide a general frame of reference for the reader in conceptualizing media research methodologies and to supplement the theoretical frame of reference to media research perspectives provided in Chapter 1.

In the present discussion of methodologies, therefore, distinctions will be made between quantitative and qualitative approaches to data collection in connection with the analysis of audiences. The next chapter will examine quantitative and qualitative research into media output.

QUANTITATIVE VERSUS QUALITATIVE APPROACHES TO AUDIENCES

Under the quantitative research heading are subsumed methodologies theoretically framed by a positivist, empirical social scientific approach to measurement. The principal methodological tools of the trade comprise surveys and experiments in which behavioural phenomena are quantified and measured numerically. Qualitative research embraces methodologies that are theoretically framed by critical or interpretivist social science paradigms that emphasize interpretation over measurement. The principal techniques in audience research comprise in-depth interviews, often conducted in a focus group format, and ethnographic approaches based on observation. The principles of quantitative and qualitative methodologies can also be applied to the study of media production practices and media output. Surveys have been conducted among media professionals, and ethnographic approaches have been applied to the study of media organizations. Media output has been examined by quantitative content analysis procedures and by qualitative, linguistic and discourse analysis procedures (see Berger, 1993). We begin this overview of media audience research methodologies with surveys.

QUANTITATIVE AUDIENCE RESEARCH

Surveys

The growth of survey research has led to significant development in methodological practice. Survey research today has advanced markedly on the simplistic procedures that characterized the earliest surveys, with major developments having occurred in sampling methods, questionnaire design and the management of respondents, data collection and analysis procedures. Mounting a survey is no simple matter. It is not just a matter of asking a group of people a few questions. It requires much planning and a high level of skill in its administration to ensure that valid and usable data are obtained. The current chapter will not provide a detailed analysis of the mechanics and conventions of running surveys. Helpful 'how to do it' handbooks have been published elsewhere (Babbie, 1990; Fink, 1995a,b; Oppenheim, 1992). Instead, our interest here will centre on the way surveys have been used. A more detailed account of surveys is provided in Chapter 8, which examines research into the behavioural effects of the media.

Types of survey

There are a number of different types of survey. They can be distinguished in terms of their purpose, the way they are administered to respondents, and the time span over which they are carried out. As noted earlier, this book does not purport to be a methodology handbook for those wishing to know how to practise different kinds of social scientific research. It is a book about the major research methods that have been used by media researchers to investigate a number of key media research issues. Nevertheless, in setting the scene, it is important for readers to understand the major forms that this methodology can take.

In drawing up a broad taxonomy of survey research, therefore, it is convenient to differentiate surveys along three dimensions:

1. the purpose of the survey
2. the form of administration
3. the time span of the research.

These three distinguishing factors are often mutually interdependent in that a decision in respect of one set of criteria can influence decision making in respect of one of the other two sets of criteria.

The purpose of the survey

Surveys can be used either to describe phenomena or to explain them. Descriptive surveys document a particular state of affairs regarding public opinion or behaviour or population characteristics at one point in time. Public opinion polls, for example, provide information about the current status of people's attitudes on a specified topic. This may concern their opinions about government performance, the suitability for leadership of a president or prime minister, or the departure of a favourite soap opera star. Descriptive surveys are also used by media industries to measure the size or composition of their audiences.

Surveys that have an explanatory purpose do not restrict themselves to the collection of purely descriptive data, but obtain measurements of variables between which relationships can be analysed. For example, a survey may assess levels of product purchase and the extent to which these are linked to exposure to a recent advertising campaign for that product. Surveys can be used to measure whether people's decisions to change their voting preferences in an election are connected to their exposure to political messages in the media. Survey research has also played a prominent part in the ongoing debate about the effects of media violence. Researchers have explored degrees of association between self-reported aggressive tendencies of respondents and their self-reported television viewing patterns.

The form of administration

Surveys collect data through questionnaires and interview schedules. The main forms of questionnaire administration are by post, telephone interview, personal interview and group administration.

Postal surveys Postal surveys involve mailing questionnaires to a predefined sample of respondents. Respondents are required to complete the questionnaire on their own and return it by post in a pre-paid, addressed envelope. Questionnaires may sometimes be placed at respondents' homes for return by post when filled in. Questionnaires may also be included with a newspaper or magazine bought by the respondent and returned by post. Incentives are usually provided to encourage respondents to complete and return their questionnaire. Such incentives may involve money, gifts, or entry into a prize draw.

Postal questionnaires must be self-explanatory and easy to follow, because respondents are not guided through the instrument by the researcher or an interviewer. They should be kept fairly short, and researchers should avoid packing large numbers of questions onto a single side.

Postal surveys can cover wide geographic areas at a fairly low cost. They are advantageous for reaching respondents in remote locations to which it would be difficult and expensive to send an interviewer. These surveys also provide complete anonymity so that respondents may be more likely to reply honestly to sensitive questions. The weakness of this type of survey is that the researcher has no control over the way respondents complete the questionnaire. It is not possible to be certain whether it was completed by one person or by more than one person. If the respondent encounters a question that is difficult to understand, there is no researcher on hand to explain its meaning and purpose. There is also no control over the rate at which respondents reply. The postal survey provides the slowest response rate of any survey methodology. Furthermore, the respondents who do reply may differ demographically from the original contact sample and no longer represent the population from which they were drawn.

Telephone surveys Telephone surveys involve the use of trained interviewers who phone respondents who have usually been selected at random from telephone number listings. Some telephone surveys are conducted with members of pre-specified groups who may be unlikely to respond to postal questionnaires and are difficult to access through personal interviews, such as politicians, businessmen or journalists.

Telephone surveys offer more control over respondents than do postal surveys and generate higher response rates. Data collection is immediate, and this facilitates a rapid turn-around of results. Telephone interviews must be kept short. Thus, studies requiring in-depth probing would probably not use this data collection method. There are also limitations to the types of questions that can be asked in a telephone interview. For example, multiple-choice questions offering a number of potential response options work better in a personal interview, when the response options can be shown to the respondent on a show card. In a telephone interview, the options must be read out after the question, and the respondent must hold those options in memory while deciding which one to choose. Telephone surveys were once regarded as limited because their samples did not represent the population at large. These days, however, telephone penetration is so widespread that this is no longer an issue.

Personal interviews Personal interviews can take place at a research centre, in the street or in the respondent's home or place of work. There are two basic types of interview: *structured* and *unstructured*. In a structured interview, the interviewer generally works from a questionnaire or interview schedule in which questions are asked in a predetermined order and most questions supply respondents with a range of possible answers. In an unstructured interview, broader, open-ended questions are asked to which respondents provide answers in their own words. These are either written down verbatim or audio-recorded for later transcription and interpretation. There is also a degree of freedom accorded to the interviewer to introduce new, previously unscheduled, questions to follow up on specific remarks made by the respondent.

In the case of personal, one-on-one interviews conducted in an office or in the respondent's home, there is a great deal of control over the data collection process. Respondent selection can be tightly managed, and response rates are 100 per cent once respondents have been recruited. Personal interviews can last for up to an hour and allow ample time to collect detailed data on specified topics. Data turn-around is not customarily as rapid as with telephone interviewing, but the increased use of computer-assisted interviewing procedures whereby respondents' answers to pre-structured questions are entered directly into a portable personal computer by the interviewer have helped to speed up data processing significantly.

Interviews conducted in the street, shopping centres or airport lounges require the interviewer to intercept people in transit between one location and another. Interviewers must identify potential respondents on the basis of their external appearance and, through the use of a filter question, quickly determine if they fit a particular quota. These interviews must be kept short because respondents do not usually welcome intrusion from research interviewers.

Group administration Group administration is a procedure that combines aspects of the postal survey and personal interview. Respondents are recruited to attend sessions at specified locations at which they complete a questionnaire. These sessions may take place in a hotel conference suite, theatre setting or classroom. Group-administered surveys allow quicker turnaround of data collection and higher response rates than postal questionnaires. While interviewers are present, respondents complete the questionnaire themselves. However, if they have any problems with the questions, there is a qualified person on hand to assist them.

Time span of the research

The third major distinguishing characteristic of surveys is whether they are conducted at one point in time or are repeated over two or more occasions. The first type of survey is referred to as a *cross-sectional survey* and the second is a *longitudinal study*. Cross-sectional surveys represent the most frequently used type of field research. They provide snapshots of the status of public opinion, knowledge and understanding, or behaviour, at a given point in time. They may comprise purely descriptive accounts of population characteristics, or provide explanatory analyses of relationships between variables such as media usage and behaviour.

Longitudinal research is much rarer. It involves the collection of data at different points in time. Sometimes, the data are collected from distinct samples and on other occasions from the same group of people. There are three types of longitudinal study: trend studies, cohort analysis, and panel studies.

Trend studies   This is the most common type of longitudinal study in mass media research. A trend study samples different groups of people at different times from the same population. This form of analysis is often used at times of elections. Samples of respondents are surveyed before, during and at the end of election campaigns to establish their voting intentions and attitudes associated with candidates and their policies. Such studies reveal short-term or long-term patterns in public opinion and behaviour. They can detect changes in opinion over time and link such changes to specific media events or to information from respondents about their levels of media usage.

In trend studies, researchers can either generate their own data or use data from secondary sources that may have been originally constructed for other purposes. In using secondary data sources, however, it is important to ensure that the underlying data obtained at different points in time were derived from the same or very similar forms of questioning and comparable sample bases. Any changes to question wording or significant fluctuations in sample composition would probably render the data from different surveys non-comparable.

Cohort analysis   A *cohort* is any group of individuals who are linked in some way or who have experienced the same significant life event within a given period. Usually the significant life event is birth, in which case the group is called a *birth cohort*. Cohorts can also be identified in terms of education (e.g. all children who started school at age five in a given location, in a given year), marital status (e.g. all people who got divorced in 1990) and so on. Any study in which there are measures of some characteristics of one or more cohorts at two or more points in time is a cohort analysis. Cohort analysis attempts to identify a cohort effect. Are changes in the dependent variable due to aging, or are they present because the sample members belong to the same cohort?

Suppose that a sample of five-year-old children in a community watch television for two hours a day, whereas a group of eight-year-olds watch for four hours a day. Are these differences in viewing level a function of the age of the children or are they caused by some other difference between the two samples. One way of finding out would be to follow both groups over the next three years and to observe whether the five-year-olds increase their viewing levels as they approach eight years of age. If they do, then the results would signal something about an age-related television viewing pattern.

Cohort analysis is a flexible technique that can indicate whether changes in attitudes or behaviour are affected by maturation or other social and cultural factors. Its major disadvantage is that the specific effects of age, cohort, and period of analysis are difficult to untangle through purely statistical analysis of cohort data. Differences between groups surveyed at different points in time may be a function of variations in the nature of the samples surveyed on those occasions. Controlling for the effects of such factors can be difficult, especially when using secondary data bases over which the researcher has no direct control.

Panel studies   The measurement of the same sample of respondents at different points in time represents a panel design. Panel studies can reveal information about both net change and gross change in the dependent variable. Panel studies can make use of postal questionnaires, telephone interviews or personal interviews. Television networks, advertising agencies and marketing research companies use panel studies to track changes in consumer behaviour. Panel studies can reveal shifting attitudes and patterns of behaviour that might go unnoticed with other research approaches.

Depending on the purpose of the study, researchers can use either a *continuous panel*, consisting of members who report specific attitudes or behaviour patterns on a regular basis, or an *interval panel*, whose members agree to complete a certain number of questionnaires or other instruments (e.g. diaries) only when the information is needed. Panel studies produce data suitable for sophisticated statistical analysis and enable researchers to predict cause – effect relationships.

There are problems associated with panel studies, however. Panel members can be hard to recruit because people may be reluctant to commit themselves to repeated surveys. Panel erosion means that the membership of the panel can change over time, as members drop away. This shrinkage has implications for the continuing representativeness of the panel. Another issue is the extent to which panel members gradually become conditioned or primed to the task after repeat surveys, with the nature of their responses being altered purely as a function of repeat interview experiences.

Experiments

Experiments have been used in media research for at least half a century. Most published experimental research has been concerned with quantifying the effects of television, although there have been experimental studies conducted with radio and print media. Theoretically, experimental methodologies are primarily influenced by behavioural psychology.

An experiment is a form of quantitative research. It begins with a hypothesis about a likely outcome following an event or set of events, or about a relationship or set of relationships between two or more quantifiable variables. An experiment usually involves modifying something in a particular situation. It concludes by comparing outcomes in situations with and without the modification. In the context of media research, an experiment will create a set of conditions under which a group of individuals is exposed to a media stimulus and are then invited to respond in some way. The conditions are set in such a way that the media content can be said to have caused a particular kind of audience response to occur. Thus, for example, if one wished to test a hypothesis about a behavioural effect upon an audience of watching a media depiction of violence, a minimum of two situations would be created in which different audience groups would watch either a violent or non-violent portrayal. Subsequently, both groups would be placed in another situation in which there is an opportunity to behave aggressively. The research hypothesis might predict that those individuals who were exposed to the media violence will behave more aggressively than those who were shown non-violent media material. Quantitative measurements would be taken to establish, objectively, whether this prediction was borne out by the observed behaviour of the two sets of individuals.

To prove causation, however, it is essential to demonstrate convincingly that other potential causes of the measured response can be effectively discounted. It is for this reason that experiments usually take place in artificial laboratory conditions in which conditions of media exposure, media content and audience response(s) can be controlled by the investigator.

Compared with other social science research techniques – both qualitative research and quantitative research of the kind embodied by surveys – experimental research is the best equipped for testing causal relationships. This advantage stems from the fact that the researcher can manipulate and control the conditions under which individuals are observed to behave. In methodologies that depend upon the self-reports of respondents, regardless of whether these reports are given in open-ended interviews or pre-structured questionnaires, there is little or no opportunity for the investigator to determine the conditions under which the experiences upon which respondents are reporting occurred in the first place.

There are many media research issues that can be studied with experiments. Essentially, though, only those research questions that let the investigator manipulate conditions are appropriate. Thus, questions about the behavioural, attitudinal or knowledge effects of the media can be studied via experiments, but will tend to take the form of trying to establish the impact of specific media outputs which can be thoroughly analysed for their relevant informational content and for which conditions of exposure to audiences can be controlled in advance. Experiments attempt to establish cause and effect relations between variables. This method controls the time-order of presentation of variables to make sure that the (hypothesized) cause precedes the measured effect. An experiment allows the researcher to control for other possible causes of the variable under investigation.

In an experiment, the researcher has control over the environment, variables and individuals under study. Laboratory research allows isolation of specific potential causal factors. Levels of exposure of individuals to particular conditions can be controlled and their effects measured systematically in a precise quantitative fashion. Another important facet of an experiment is that the conditions under which it is run, the manipulations that are carried out, and the variables that are quantified are clearly spelled out, making it possible for others to repeat the exercise should they wish to do so.

An experiment comprises a number of parts or stages. At the outset, the researcher creates a situation or enters into an ongoing situation, and then modifies it. For instance, if the experiment is conducted under artificial, laboratory conditions, then the researcher has to create a set of conditions that in some sense mimic, at least partially, some real-world situation. In an investigation of the impact of certain presentation features on audience members' memory for the content of a televised news programme, the researcher may produce a specially edited sequence of pre-recorded television news materials to isolate particular features. A second sequence may be produced in which a different set of features is isolated. Two groups of viewers are randomly assigned to watch one or the other of these two news sequences and are subsequently tested for their memory of the news stories presented. If one group fares better than the other, then one explanation could be that specific presentation features enhanced or impeded information uptake. This explanation is only valid, however, if other possible explanations can be discounted. For example, it could be that one group of viewers was more intelligent or more knowledgeable than the other. Alternatively, there may have been presentation features other than those manipulated by the experimenter which affected retention of news content, and that these features differed between the two sets of materials presented to each group. Thus, the two news sequences had not been properly controlled for differences in production.

In mounting an experiment, therefore, there are a number of factors that need to be carefully defined and procedures that should be carefully followed to ensure that accurate and valid explanations of cause – effect relations are produced. The first factor an experimenter needs to define is the 'independent variable'. This is the treatment or manipulation of conditions which represent what the researcher modified within the environment in which individuals are observed and tested. The second key factor is the 'dependent variable', which represents the measurable outcome of the experimental manipulation. Thus, in the example given above, the independent variable was the particular version of the news sequence presented. The dependent variable, or measured outcome, was the extent and accuracy of news recall by members of each audience group.

To get around the possibility of pre-existing differences between groups which could account for later differences in their performance, there are two important steps a researcher can take. Upon dividing a sample of individuals into groups, who will be assigned to different experimental conditions, the assignment is conducted on a random basis. This procedure reduces the probability of biases in the nature of the groups. Random assignment of experimental subjects to groups increases the likelihood that each group will contain individuals with equal measures of specific characteristics. In some studies, however, researchers will adopt a slightly different strategy of 'matching' groups in which quotas will be fixed to control the rate of allocation of individuals to groups on the basis of specific characteristics. For example, a researcher may wish to ensure that there are equal numbers of males and females per group. Thus, while the selection of males or females for each group will be done randomly, this random assignment process will only operate within and not across the sexes. Males will be randomly allocated to a particular group until 50 per cent of the places available in that group have been filled. The remainder will be allocated to randomly selected females.

Another important mechanism of control of differences between groups prior to the experimental treatment being implemented is to conduct a 'pre-test'. The researcher measures the dependent variable(s) more than once. The pre-test is the measurement of the dependent variable prior to the introduction of the treatment. Afterwards a 'post-test' is conducted to measure the dependent variable after the experimental conditions have been implemented.

An experiment generally, though not always, comprises more than one group of respondents. In a typical design, one or more groups will be exposed to one or more treatments, while at least one group, designated the 'control' group will not be exposed to these treatments.

Types of experimental design

In understanding how experiments work and therefore how they can be applied to the study of media, it will be useful to review some of the main types of experimental design. There are a number of variations in experimental designs. The essence of an experiment is to measure the effect upon a group of media consumers of a media stimulus (i.e. television programme, movie, magazine or newspaper article). As noted already, to establish a cause – effect relationship it is necessary to compare the reactions of the 'treatment' group (i.e. the group of consumers receiving the media stimulus) with a 'control' group of consumers who did not receive that stimulus. In the very simplest experimental design, two groups, an experimental group and a control group, are compared in their behaviour (or attitudinal or cognitive) responses following the exposure of the experimental group to a media stimulus. The control group does not receive the stimulus.

In a slightly more complex design, both groups may be assessed in terms of critical cognitive, attitudinal or behavioural responses prior to the media stimulus being presented to the experimental group. Then both are assessed for a second time after media exposure has occurred. In the simple design the experimental and control groups are compared once only on post-media-exposure measures to see if they differ in their responses. In the second design, experimental and control groups are again compared on post-exposure measures. However, pre-exposure measures also establish the extent to which these two groups already differed in critical measures prior to the presentation of the media stimulus to the experimental group (see Clifford et al., 1995). The main types of experimental design are summarized below.

Classical experimental design

This design can also be described as a *pre-test – post-test with control group* design. It comprises random assignment of cases to groups, a pre-test and a post-test, an experimental group and a control group. An example would be a study of the effects on viewers' attitudes of violence in a film. Here two groups of individuals are randomly assigned to either a group that watches a movie with violence or a movie with no violence. Both groups complete a questionnaire before and after viewing the movie which asks about their attitudes towards violence. The aim is to find out if attitudes shift to a greater extent among the violent-movie group than among the non-violent-movie group.

Pre-experimental designs

It is not always possible for the researcher to adopt a classical experimental design because circumstances will not allow the strict requirements of that experimental format to be followed. Thus, it may not be possible to assign subjects at random to different conditions or treatments. Instead, the researcher must settle for a compromise between the methodological precision of the pre-test – post-test with control group format and the reality of the data collection opportunity that presents itself. Hence, studies are run that omit pre-tests or the use of control groups.

One-group post-test-only design   This design has only one group, a treatment and a post-test. A group of individuals may be shown a violent movie and then given an attitude test afterwards. There is no way of telling whether the movie had any influence upon attitudes as distinct from other (untested) factors.

One-group pre-test – post-test design   This design has one group, a pre-test, a treatment and a post-test. Viewers may be given an attitude test, watch a violent movie, and then complete the attitude test again to measure any changes contingent upon movie watching. This is better than the previous design because respondents are compared against themselves. But it lacks a control group and leaves open the possibility that attitude change might be a consequence of something other than the movie.

Quasi-experimental and special designs

These designs make identifying causal relationships more certain than do the pre-experimental designs. Quasi-experimental designs help researchers test for causal relationships in a variety of situations where the classical design is difficult or inappropriate. They are called *quasi* because they are variations on the classical experimental design. Some have randomization but lack a pre-test, some use more than two groups, others substitute many observations of one group over time for a control group.

Two-group post-test-only design   In this case, two groups are run with subjects randomly assigned to each condition. The experimental group is distinguished by receiving the experimental treatment. The groups are tested just once, after the presentation of the experimental treatment to the experimental group. The random assignment reduces the chances that the groups differed before treatment, but without a pre-test a researcher cannot be sure. This design is weaker than one that uses a pre-test stage because it makes no attempt to discover pre-treatment differences between experimental and control group subjects on the key measures under investigation. Any post-treatment differences between the two groups could therefore be explained, at least in part, by pre-experiment differences between them.

Post-test only with control group   This is a slightly different version of the two-group post-test only design in that only one group receives the experimental treatment while the second group acts as a control and receives no treatment. Once again, though, no pre-testing is done. Instead, the post-test performance of the experimental group is compared with the performance of the controls in a one-time-only measurement stage.

Solomon four-group design   Even with a pre-test design, measurement issues can arise. There is a possibility, for instance, that a pre-test may influence the way subjects respond during the experimental treatment because the initial test stage gives away clues as to the purpose of the experiment or gives subjects an opportunity to practise a relevant skill. The Solomon design offers a way of controlling for this possible effect. Respondents are randomly assigned to four groups, two of which receive a pre-test and two of which do not. All groups then undergo the treatment. Here two groups (one with pre-test and one without pre-test) undergo one version of the treatment, while the other two groups undergo the second version, or receive no treatment and serve as controls. All groups are then post-tested. If the groups who were pre-tested differ in their post-test performance from those who were not pre-tested, the researcher can then conclude that the pre-test itself did influence post-test results.

Factorial designs

The designs presented up to this point can accommodate the manipulation of one independent variable or 'treatment' variable. However, media researchers are often interested in investigating two or more independent variables within the same study, both for their separate effects and for the way they might interact with each other. For example, in exploring factors that influence the display of aggression, one might be interested in finding out how much the effects of annoying someone or showing them a violent film clip will cause them to react aggressively. In this case, a subject sample would be randomly allocated to one of four possible conditions: prior annoyance plus violent film clip; prior annoyance and no violent film clip; no prior annoyance and violent film clip; and no prior annoyance and no violent film clip. This is known as a factorial design, in which each independent variable (annoyance, showing violent footage) is called a factor.

Repeated measures designs

The designs examined so far require the random allocation of subjects to distinct treatments. This type of experiment can become very resource hungry if many different independent variables are investigated in the same study. One solution to this problem is to use a repeated measures design, in which the effects of multiple manipulations are studied with the same group of people, instead of recruiting a different group on each occasion. The effects of these different manipulations are assessed by monitoring and quantifying changes in the subjects' performance each time a treatment is applied. Since each subject acts as their own control, fewer subjects in total are needed.

   This design has proven to be sensitive to detecting the effects of different treatment applications, but does suffer from carry-over effects, where the effects of one manipulation may still be present when the next manipulation is presented. There is also a greater likelihood that subjects will become aware of the purposes of the experiment, as they experience a range of different treatments. This second-guessing of the purpose could affect the way they behave.

There are two variations on the repeated measures design that can be distinguished. In one case, repeated measures are taken on either side of a single treatment or manipulation of circumstances, and, in the other, repeated measures are taken following repeated treatments.

Interrupted time series With this design, a researcher uses one group and makes multiple pre-test measures before and multiple post-test measures after the treatment. For example, a community might experience the introduction of television for the first time, and a researcher might be interested in finding out what impact this made on people's leisure activities. Leisure pursuits could be measured over several years prior to television and then over a similar period afterwards to compare differences. It would also be necessary, however, to know whether other changes in addition to the introduction of television had taken place during these years.

Equivalent time series design This is another one-group design that extends over a time period. Instead of one treatment, it has a pre-test, then a treatment and post-test, then treatment and post-test, then treatment and post-test and so on. Following the above television example, there might initially have been only one channel in a community, then after two years a second channel, and then a couple of years later two more. The impact of increasing amounts of television on the behaviour of the community could then be tracked.

Advantages and disadvantages of experiments

The principal aim of experimental methodologies is to establish the existence of cause – effect relationships between measured variables. Whether casual links between social phenomena can ever be conclusively demonstrated is a debatable point. While the positivist social science perspective would argue that such links can be proven, other schools of thought, taking on a more critical or interpretivist perspective to social science analysis, would challenge this viewpoint.

What is generally agreed upon, even by positivistic media researchers, is that there are certain methodologies, particularly ones that rely on self-report studies such as surveys, focus groups or in-depth interviews, that cannot conclusively demonstrate cause – effect relationships because the researcher typically has very little control over the research environment (Bailey, 1994; Neuman, 1994; Wimmer and Dominick, 1994). The data with which the investigator works when using these methodologies are often long-removed from the time and place of occurrence of the behaviours or phenomena on which they report. Experimentation is different. The experimenter is usually present on the scene when the data are collected and exercises considerable control over the sequence of events and the environment in which they occur. This degree of control over conditions enables the experimenter to attempt to establish causation rather than mere correlation between variables. The causation and control elements of experimentation represent its two major strong points.

Experiments do not represent a perfect, unflawed methodology, however. They have been criticized on a number of levels in respect of the content of their analysis of the impact of television and other media on audience knowledge, attitudes and behaviours (Cook et al., 1983; Stipp and Milavsky, 1988). There are certain disadvantages to experimental research that have always posed problems for investigators using this approach.

First, experiments tend to be carried out in artificial environments. Experiments try to shed light on real-world phenomena by manipulating them under artificial laboratory conditions where greater control can be exerted over the independent and dependent variables under examination as well as over other possible confounding variables. The problem with this approach is that it raises a question about the generalizability of the results beyond the very precise conditions under which the experiment took place. The way individuals behave in laboratory experiments may be quite different from the way they would normally behave in the natural environment.

It is important with an experiment, therefore, to question the *external validity* of its results. External validity is the ability to generalize experimental findings to events and settings outside the experiment itself. If a study lacks external validity, its findings hold true only in the experimental situation – and nowhere else. What are the different aspects of external validity? One question to ask is whether the experimental situation is like the real world. To what extent does it depart from everyday reality in certain key respects? In media research, are the research stimuli typical of the media content to which individuals would be exposed in real life? In many media experiments the stimuli are created by the experimenter or are taken out of context and are not representative of normal media output. Media stimuli might comprise short clips from movies or television programmes. The action that is shown is selected because its intrinsic content is expected to maximize the likelihood of a desired behavioural response among viewers. Such short sequences may be removed from the original story context that is vital to the way members of the audience would ordinarily make sense of them under natural viewing circumstances. Sometimes, the sequences are actually produced by the researcher using laboratory film or video equipment which lack professional broadcast quality and depict specially-contrived events designed to facilitate a particular response.

Similarly, are the actions or behaviours measured in the experiment like those that occur in the real world? In much research on the behavioural effects of the media, for example, researchers have frequently created artificial behaviour measures, especially when studying the effects of media violence on audience aggression. While there are sound ethical reasons for adopting this kind of procedure, the responses measured in experiments often fail to resemble what would be more generally seen as 'aggressive behaviour'. The laboratory creates a special social environment all its own with the usual social sanctions against behaving in particular ways (e.g. aggressively) suspended.

According to Comstock (1998: 25):

> Experimental research often focuses on some element of content or technique of production (often called a 'form' element). The intended inference is that these vary in their effect on attention, cognition or behaviour. The generalisability problem arises because the power of the research design to examine these elements means that they occur in isolation or in the specific context of the video used in the research. There is only limited surety that their effects do not depend on an interaction that may be missing in other contexts or that in other contexts an interaction may occur that will alter their effects.
>
> Experimental research also employs a setting that in many respects will be artificial and different from the circumstances in which viewing normally occurs. Exposure is likely to be short term, set apart from other video stimuli, and in strange surroundings not of one's choosing. The measure of subsequent behaviour may restrict options: constraints that ordinarily govern behaviour, such as the possibility of retaliation if aggression or hostility is expressed after exposure, implied with these factors, may exaggerate effects.

A further major problem faced by experiments is *experimenter bias*. In this case, the individuals participating in an experiment pick up clues about the hypothesis being tested or the goal of the experiment and produce the responses they think the experimenter wants them to produce. An experimenter may unwittingly reveal the purpose of the study, leading his subjects to conform to his or her wishes during the experiment. Laboratory experiments often require individuals to pay special attention to particular types of media content to a greater degree than they would normally. Their responses may therefore be much more pronounced under such conditions than one might find in connection with ordinary media usage conditions in their own lives. This weakness can be counteracted by using a 'double-blind' procedure. In this design, the person who assigns subjects to experimental and control groups is not the same as the person who runs the experiment itself. The latter person is 'blind' to the particular treatment condition that is operating with specific subjects. Since they do not know how the subjects ought to respond according to the experimental hypothesis, they cannot provide any clues in accordance with that set of expectations.

Methodological gaps

Ward and Greenfield (1998) identified a number of methodological gaps in experimental research, which they illustrated through reference to work on television and gender roles. These gaps, however, can equally be applied to other fields of media effects research. Seven method gaps were noted by these two writers.

First, experimental research has studied a fairly limited range of real-world materials. More use could be made of popular mainstream television programmes as stimuli. Situation comedies, drama and soap operas are among the most watched programmes on television but are seldom used as sources of research materials. This applies to research on television and violence, television and gender roles, and other areas. Where portrayals that are used in experiments differ significantly from the more typical portrayals of television, will any effects measured in response to them necessarily be representative of the kinds of effects one might find in connection with mainstream television portrayals?

Second, researchers conducting experiments tend to select the materials to be presented as stimuli, rather than respondents being given a choice. Under ordinary viewing conditions, viewers choose their own favourite programmes and have their opinions about preferred characters. Research has shown that well-liked and admired people are more potent role models. Insofar as television characters and personalities are an extension of the real-life social environment (Meyrowitz, 1985), this principle might hold for television as well. Preliminary evidence suggests that liking and familiarity do influence viewers' perceptions (e.g. Brown and Schulze, 1993). For example, Miller and Reeves (1976) found that 3rd and 6th graders who were familiar with female television characters with non-traditional occupations were more accepting of girls' aspiring to them.

How might variables such as liking and familiarity be addressed experimentally. Ward and Greenfield (1998: 80) offered a suggestion.

> One approach would be to use liking as an independent variable in a two-factor analysis of variance. Suppose, for example, that one were interested in exploring the effects on adolescent viewers of stereotypes about men's and women's ability to nurture. One might first select a set of eight clips from situation comedies of varying popularity among adolescents. In half of these clips, the female would be depicted as the nurturant one (the traditional image); in the other half, the male would be the nurturant one (a nontraditional image). During testing sessions, experimenters would first ask participants to rank the programs from which the stimuli had been selected to determine the most and least favored for each participant. These rankings would then be used to assign program stimuli to participants using a 2 by 2 design in which liking is crossed with traditionality. Thus, Group 1 would see four clips depicting traditional images of nurturers from their more favored shows. Group 2 would see four clips depicting traditional images of nurturers from their least favored shows. In the same way, Groups 3 and 4 would see clips depicting nontraditional images of nurturers from their more favored and least favored programs, respectively. Actual stimuli would vary from person to person in the same experimental group; what would be held constant would be the participants' evaluations of the stimuli.

Experiments could do more to examine the differential effects of genre, format or formal features. Would the same type of portrayal occurring in a music video, cartoon, drama or sit-com have different effects?

A further gap exists in relation to developmental differences in the way media consumers respond to specific media stimuli. Comparisons are needed across age groups to outline developmental trends in how specific stimuli affect viewers at different ages. There may be particular developmental periods during which viewers are especially vulnerable to stereotypical or counter-stereotypical portrayals (Durkin, 1985).

A fifth gap concerns knowledge about the contrasting impact of underrepresentation versus misrepresentation of people in various social categories. Many of the existing paradigms that study television's representation of particular groups focus on the influence of stereotypical versus non-stereotypical portrayals. However, content analyses have shown that certain groups are not only misrepresented but also underrepresented (Greenberg and Brand, 1994; Signorielli, 1989, 1993). Experiments would be an excellent tool for exploring the differential impacts of misrepresentation and underrepresentation on viewers' perceptions of the target group. Given the already demonstrated effects of positive versus negative or stereotypical portrayals, the main question here would be as follows: Are group members perceived as less important, competent, or powerful when they are minimally represented on television or when they are presented yet depicted negatively or stereotypically?

A sixth methodological gap concerns the nature and impact of viewers' individual perceptions of the stimuli presented. Many of the experimental studies present in the literature have examined cultivation or imitation as the mechanisms of effects, assuming that viewers would adopt the attitudes or imitate the behaviours in the content presented. However, because a segment's impact is likely to vary based on viewers' interpretations of it, research also needs to consider the role of viewers' individual perceptions.

Evidence comes from a study of undergraduate perceptions of male – female interactions in four clips from situation comedies (Ward and Eschwege, 1996). Here, no more than 40 per cent of the participants agreed that any one theme, from a choice of five, was the dominant message of the scene viewed. Thus, given the complexity of actual network content, it should be expected that individual viewers often would see the same material differently and that the effects of this content would vary based on these interpretations (Gunter, 1988).

Even if viewers did interpret a given material in the same way, some might choose to accept the messages inferred whereas others might be offended by or even reject them. Content is likely to be interpreted in a way that reinforces one's existing views and perspectives. Moreover, because differential interpretations are likely to mediate other variables, researchers can use subjects' interpretations as mediating variables to explore their impact on related social attitudes and behaviours.

The final methodological gap identified by Ward and Greenfield (1998) was the testing of the effects of television content that is presented in multiple media. Although almost all research on television addresses the medium in isolation, television is part of an interlinked multimedia environment that includes super-systems built around the same characters and stories (Kinder, 1991). Not only can viewers see their favourite characters on television, they can buy the T-shirts, play the video games, read the comic books, and see the films in which the characters appear. Do viewers believe and identify more with characters they have encountered in several media? Do they see them as more realistic and like themselves?

Quasi-experimental research

Experiments conducted in the laboratory suffer from being conducted in controlled, artificial surroundings in which stimulus materials rarely resemble the nature of media consumption experiences in the real world. These characteristics pose problems of external validity and the generalizability of laboratory findings to the real world. Methodological discussions regarding research on the effects of television, for instance, often contrast the advantages of laboratory experiments for making causal inferences with the advantages of more naturalistic, ecologically valid field studies. Laboratory experiments are designed to answer the question '*Can* television affect viewers?' whereas field studies are designed to answer the question '*Does* television affect viewers as they use it over time in day-to-day life?'.

One solution to the problem of ecological validity for experiments conducted in the laboratory is to conduct experiments, if possible, in more naturalistic surroundings. Such *quasi-experiments* require researchers to take advantage of circumstances in the real world that allow the systematic measurement of media effects. There are two basic categories of real-world experiment:

1. those in which the researcher manipulates a set of conditions in a real-world environment;
2. those in which the researcher takes advantage of some naturally occurring event or change of circumstances, the effects of which can be measured.

The first type of study is often referred to as a *field experiment* and the second type is called a *natural experiment* (see MacBeth, 1998).

In field experiments, researchers also often study pre-existing groups, but in this case they assign different groups (e.g. preschool classes) to different television viewing 'diets' (e.g. prosocial programmes versus cartoons versus no television). The groups may be observed first during a baseline period to establish their similarity, and then again after the exposure period. An example of the first type of study would be an experiment in which the research is interested in the effects of television programmes on viewers' aggressiveness. In a cable television environment in which the flow of television programmes into people's homes could be controlled by the supplier, it would be possible to create two separate groups: one that receives violence-containing programmes and another that receives a violence-free television diet. Over a number of days or weeks before, during and after this treatment, the viewers could be monitored by someone in their family for any mood or behaviour changes that occur as a result of this television diet manipulation (see Gorney, Loye and Steele, 1977).

In natural experiments, researchers take advantage of a naturally occurring change in the availability of television reception to assess the impact of this change on viewers. For example, a pre-existing group with access to television may be compared with another pre-existing group that has less or no television reception. Or, a pre-existing group may be studied before television reception first becomes available and then again after some period of use, usually a relatively longer-term period of months or years. The group experiencing change in the availability of television may be contrasted with other similar groups whose exposure does not change over the same interval (Williams, 1986).

According to Cook et al. (1990: 492), experiments are 'any experimenter-controlled or naturally occurring event with rapid onset (a "treatment") whose possible consequences are to be empirically assessed'. Two major categories of experiments exist. In randomized experiments, participants are assigned to treatments at random, whereas 'quasi-experiments primarily depend on self-selection or administrative decisions to determine who is to be exposed to a treatment'. Cook et al. pointed out, 'It is generally easier to implement quasi-experiments than randomized experiments in many of the field settings where causal conclusions are needed'. They defined a field setting as any one 'that respondents do not perceive as having been set up for the primary purpose of conducting research'.

When making causal inferences is the researchers' primary concern, random assignment to groups is the method of choice. However, it is rarely possible in randomized experiments to manipulate more than a few independent variables, and so randomized experiments can test hypotheses about the independent and interactive effects of only a small number of manipulated variables. The complexities of real life typically involve many more relevant factors, most or all of which also operate in quasi-experiments.

QUALITATIVE AUDIENCE RESEARCH

Quantitative methodologies are designed to yield numerically-scored data about media audiences, media-related behaviour and reactions, and the impact of the media. While they provide procedures that can enable large quantities of data to be collected across large numbers of individuals or for the testing of causal hypotheses, they do so by placing artificial constraints on research respondents, either in the way such individuals are required to think about and report upon their personal experiences or in the way their actual behaviour is operationally defined and measured. We turn now to research methodologies that allow respondents to converse freely about their media experiences, choosing their own answers, their own language and terminology, and even their own questions. We also examine techniques that permit the collection of data about naturally occurring behaviour, unconstrained in any way by the researcher.

Focus groups

Focus groups were first used in the 1940s. At that time, military psychologists and civilian consultants used group interviews to determine the effectiveness of radio programmes designed to boost army morale (Libresco, 1983; Merton, 1987; Morgan, 1988). They were largely eschewed by academic media researchers, but became established as a marketing research tool used by commercial research agencies during the 1950s and beyond. During the 1980s, however, with the emergence of critical and interpretive media research perspectives, focus groups were adopted by academic researchers within these traditions as an audience research tool which was believed to be better able than more quantitative methodologies to represent their theoretical views about the ways audiences respond to the mass media (Merton, 1987; Morgan, 1988).

The methodology involves bringing together a group or series of groups of individuals to discuss an issue in the presence of a moderator. The moderator ensures that the discussion remains on the issue at hand, while eliciting a wide range of opinions on that issue. There are many different conditions under which group discussions can be held. The decisions taken by researchers concerning the size and composition of the group, form of questions asked, setting and in-built checks for consistency and honesty or accuracy of responses can all affect the nature and quality of the data. There is potentially much diversity in the way focus groups can be employed (Lunt and Livingstone, 1996).

In the beginning, CBS research director Paul Lazarsfeld introduced sociologist Robert Merton to the use of the method to guide the interpretation of data gathered from people pressing buttons to indicate positive and negative emotional reactions to radio programmes. After listening to a programme and evaluating it on a continuous basis while listening, respondents participated in a group discussion, where they were able to elaborate in their own words on the ratings they had given.

Lazarsfeld had been invited by the US Office of Facts and Figures to test responses to several radio morale programmes. The method was used, in this context, to examine responses to the use of radio as a means of persuading people to pledge war bonds. Merton was impressed by the way the focus group interview could concentrate the respondent's attention on a particular issue or topic. Intrigued by the technique, Merton subsequently worked with Patricia Kendall to develop its methodology further (Merton and Kendall, 1946). Merton later published a classic text about the technique called 'The Focused Interview' (Merton et al., 1956). Despite these efforts, the focus group was rarely used in academic social science research in the 1950s.

Academic researchers adopted more exclusively quantitative methods as part of broader changes in social scientific practice. Focus group interviews instead found a place within commercially oriented market research, where they became an established form of data collection (Bartos, 1986; Hayes and Tathum, 1989; Morgan, 1988; Morrison, 1998). During the 1970s and 1980s there was a gradual shift in attitude towards the use of focus groups in the academic social sciences. It became established as an effective alternative form of research into media audiences to quantitative methodologies.

Merton, of course, had regarded focus groups as a supplementary stage in questionnaire design or experimental study. The purpose of this qualitative methodology was to inform quantitative research methods, which were still regarded as the principal components of any legitimate social scientific study. Not only could focus groups assist with questionnaire design for large-scale surveys, they could also clarify aspects of research stimuli or the measurement of their effects in experimental studies. Thus, the focus group was essentially subordinate to quantitative methods.

Effective application

Focus group procedures generally include having a trained and practised facilitator ask a small group of individuals a series of open-ended questions. The moderator may use a single standard set of questions, asking each one in turn, to stimulate discussion and conversation during a given session. He or she may use this same set of questions during successive sessions, thus enabling comparisons to be made between the answers given by different groups of interviewees. The questions may be more or less standardized depending upon the needs of the research and the inclination of the investigator.

Often, researchers employ a tactic called the *extended focus group*. This procedure includes a questionnaire administered to participants prior to the group session. The questionnaire generally includes material that will be discussed during the focus group session. Information from this questionnaire may assist both group members and the moderator. The questionnaires allow the participants to develop a commitment to a position before any group discussion begins (Sussman et al., 1991). Information from these pre-group questionnaires may help to ensure that the moderator draws out minority opinions as well as more dominant majority ones (Wimmer and Dominick, 1994).

One of the most difficult tasks of a moderator is controlling dominating respondents while simultaneously encouraging passive group members.

This must be accomplished without embarrassing or completely shutting down the dominating participants. If a moderator can successfully establish a rapport with the group in general, this will help in efforts to encourage even quiet members to participate.

Most researchers who use focus group techniques acknowledge that group influences can distort individual opinion. Some opinion may be more extreme and some may be less verbalized than others because of the group effect (Morgan, 1988; Sussman et al., 1991). Having some idea about how individuals thought about certain topics before the group sessions allows the investigator to gauge this group effect. This is not to say that material obtained during the group session is false. Quite the contrary, the opinions voiced during the session, even those that contradict pre-group questionnaires, merely demonstrate the impact of group dynamics. Additional information, confirmation or refutation of beliefs, arguments, discussion and solutions heard during the group session shape participants' thinking. What results is a collective understanding about issues discussed during the group session.

It is important not to lose sight of the fact that focus group data are *group data.* They reflect the collective notions shared and negotiated by members of the group. Individual in-depth interview data, in contrast, reflect the views and opinions of a single person, shaped by the social process of living in a particular culture or society.

The setting should be as informal as possible. The moderator usually has a discussion schedule or list of key points to check off. The discussion can be videotaped or audiotaped. Resulting tapes are transcribed. This can be difficult, however, if the conversation is flowing and different respondents talk across one another. Careful note-taking by the moderator is therefore also needed to keep track of who is speaking (Bertrand et al., 1992). Some researchers may also choose to videotape sessions. Often, a group session will include a person, other than the facilitator, designated to take notes. This note taker frequently is the individual responsible for transcribing the tape-recording or audio portion of the videotape. The transcriptions and session notes will serve as the data set for analysis of the focus group interviews. These transcripts represent textual data and can be organized and analysed using content analysis strategies.

Researchers must consider whether to use groups who know each other or those who are relative strangers, and whether groups should be constituted from members of the same or mixed categories (e.g. all male, all female versus mixed male – female; one age group or mixed age groups). Merton originally used relative strangers of diverse socio-economic categories. Other researchers have opted for groups composed of relatives or close friends (e.g. Liebes and Katz, 1990). Merton favoured the one-shot design, while others have preferred to use repeat meetings of the same group (Burgess et al., 1991).

While for many years, focus groups were seen as a supplement to surveys, increasingly in academic circles they are regarded and used as a viable stand-alone research technique (Livingstone and Lunt, 1996). They have been adopted by the critical and interpretivist schools of media analysis and identified as a 'new' and alternative form of audience research to positivist empirical approaches (Jensen, 1991). The critical approach emphasizes the social aspects of the research context. The research itself is questioned if it is context bound and therefore restricted to the context in which it was undertaken in terms of the relevance of its findings.

For Burgess et al., interviewees gain from participation in group discussions as well as researchers. They used a procedure in which respondents were interviewed repeatedly with the same group of people, to enable the group 'to create a unique culture, with its own history, humour, preoccupations and concerns' (1991: 503). Indeed, for many researchers, a balance has to be achieved between participant and research interests (e.g. Schlesinger et al., 1992).

It is critical to the focus group interview that researchers do not predetermine responses and that they allow the opportunity for unanticipated issues to arise. Most moderators work within a broadly standardized format with a schedule of topics or issues that, for the purposes of group comparability and coverage of theoretical concerns, must be addressed by participants.

One often-cited qualitative study by Morley (1980, 1981) has been widely credited with the re-emergence of the focus group methodology in the context of a cultural studies approach to studying the mass media. He used 27 homogeneous groups of between 3 and 13 people in a comparative design that covered variation in social class, educational level and political affiliation. His analysis of focus group discussions following the current affairs television programme *Nationwide*, revealed how audiences with different socio-economic backgrounds make different 'readings' of current affairs programmes, thereby opening up the path for many other investigations into diversity in audience reception.

There is a key difference between the way the mass audience and its relationship with the media were conceptualized in the Merton – Lazarsfeld era and today. Merton, Lazarsfeld and others studied audience response to mass media in order to understand the mass diffusion processes that lead to attitude and opinion formation. Contemporary theories of the audience are more concerned with the way that active audiences contribute to the negotiation and construction of meanings (Livingstone, 1990). Audiences do not comprise a vacuum to be passively filled by media messages. Instead, audiences must be conceived as being psychologically active in their use of the media and the way they react to media content. Viewers, listeners and readers place their own interpretations on media content that are influenced by the social communities to which they belong or with which they identify. Many different meanings can be obtained from the same media output by media consumers who have different backgrounds and bring different analytical perspectives to bear upon their readings of specific media texts (Lunt and Livingstone, 1996).

Qualitative approaches such as focus groups are regarded by their proponents as having greater ecological validity than quantitative methodologies such as surveys or experiments. For some researchers, the focus group discussion is regarded as a simulation of the spontaneous conversations that occur among people in their natural environments. This point has been made with particular force in relation to focus group research involving members of the same family (Liebes and Katz, 1990).

Whether focus groups produce ecologically-more-valid data than surveys or experiments, however, is a debatable point. Certainly, the presence of other group members can prompt a range of different remarks about a topic through encouraging respondents to speak from their individual social or material positions defined by their respective cultural backgrounds. Even when groups comprise demographically-homogeneous memberships, a range of opinions can emerge. Furthermore, after a time, a group identity may emerge once participants realize they share certain values and attitudes, thus enabling a consensus view also to emerge (Morley, 1980). However, it is important not to lose sight of the fact that, in most focus group research, respondents know they are participating in a research exercise, and that individuals will differ in their willingness to disclose certain thoughts and feelings in front of people they may not know very well, if at all. Variations in the skills level of moderators can also make a difference to the way the group discussion is conducted. The moderator has an important role to play not only in keeping the conversation flowing, but also in ensuring that the group does not become dominated by one forceful personality.

Some critical and interpretive social science researchers have also been critical of the way some of their colleagues have utilized focus groups. Jordin and Brunt (1988), for example, criticized Morley's work as exemplifying the use of the focus group according to the 'survey model', seeing individual interviewees as individual representatives of real-world social groups (rather than as a real-world social group in and of itself) and correlating the opinions expressed within the group with the social category of those group members.

While, for Morley, the group context reminds participants of their social identities, Radway (1984) used the focus group to investigate the broader 'interpretive community' where participants' routine social interpretations are of primary interest. For her, the group is primarily collective rather than taxonomic in nature. Radway showed how the critical and social response to popular literature might be mediated through the network of community members centred on a bookshop, where the shop functions as a focus for a discursive community. Radway used focused interviews to elaborate this interpretative community and to show the interweaving of critical responses to texts and the construction of a social network.

Research on audience response to audience discussion programmes on television used focus groups to see how arguments were raised and set against each other (Livingstone and Lunt, 1996). The focus group was seen as a device that allowed people to discuss issues abstracted from their social identities, as informed by Habermas' (1989) concept of the public sphere (a public space for the disinterested discussion of topics affecting the public good). As such, a focus group is used to simulate some of the processes of public opinion formation, where public opinion is understood as the outcome of rational critical debate or negotiation, rather than as the agglomeration of individual attitudes (Fraser, 1990). In this context, individuals may be seen to continually reposition themselves in relation to the circulation of discourses.

> Most of the researchers currently using focus groups would agree with Merton's implicit praise for the technique as providing valid and rich data that engages the subjects fully on a given topic. However, many would challenge Merton's relegation of focus group methods to a secondary position relative to surveys and experiments. (Lunt and Livingstone, 1996: 89)

Certainly focus groups cannot test or establish cause – effect relations. Further, they are so small and generally recruited in such a way that they lack representativeness. This means that their results cannot be generalized to the population as a whole. For some researchers, therefore, focus groups are regarded as belonging to early exploratory stages of research. This view is not held universally. Evidence has emerged that focus groups can yield data that are comparable to survey findings or which are consistent with such findings (see Morrison, 1998).

The criticism concerning the validity of focus group data can be challenged, however. For some researchers, the focus group emphasizes the social nature of communication and does not reduce social scientific research to the study of the individual. This is an important consideration in the context of media research, where mechanical conceptions of media effects are giving way to more social, semiotic and diffusion-based conceptions of media process (Lunt and Livingstone, 1996).

How are focus group data to be interpreted? Often, the researcher adopts a literary criticism approach of becoming immersed in the material, producing a thematically ordered account supported by material quoted from transcripts. There are problems with this approach in that many of the utterances made by participants in a group discussion do not represent responses to specific questions or prompts, but form part of a free-flowing conversation where several themes may be addressed simultaneously.

Hoijer (1990) criticized the analytic approach which selects exemplars to illustrate points that were made. These examples may not represent all the views offered, unless selected through some systematic scheme or methodology. Hoijer advocated the use of content analysis applied to the transcripts of group discussions.

Curran (1990) noted that interpretative analysis typically makes implicit frequency claims for the distribution of analytic themes. He argued that these should be made explicit and tested through a combination of interpretation with quantitative techniques. Increasingly, researchers are attempting to develop complex, thematic analysis of transcripts that combines interpretative sensitivity with systematic coding (Hoijer, 1990; Kepplinger, 1989; Liebes and Katz, 1990; Livingstone and Lunt, 1996). In addition, new forms of computer-based ethnographic coding are being developed to process the resulting data (Bertrand et al., 1992; Fielding and Lee, 1991).

Observational research

Whereas other qualitative research methods rely primarily on verbally articulated responses, observational research collects data on non-verbal behaviour. Although observational research is subsumed under the heading of 'qualitative' research, it does collect quantitative data as well. For example, non-verbal behaviours, once categorized and individually defined, can be counted for their frequencies of occurrence. However, they tend to be freely occurring behaviours rather than responses that are constrained by the investigator.

Typology of observational research

Observational research can be divided into a number of different types according to three main criteria: (1) whether the observer participates or not in the activities of the observed individuals; (2) whether observations are structured or unstructured; and (3) whether the observed behaviour occurs in a natural or artificial setting.

A further feature of observational research concerns the degree of structure imposed upon the environment under observation by the researcher (see Figure 2.1). Thus, the investigator can count the frequency with which certain behaviours occur or certain things are said, by imposing an *a priori* or gradually emerging coding scheme on the observed events. An alternative approach is for the researcher to adopt an unstructured procedure in which no particular behaviours are identified or classified. Instead, a note is made of any behaviour that occurs.

Figure 2.1   Degree of Structure of Observational Setting

		Natural setting	Artificial setting
Degree of structure imposed by observer	Unstructured	Completely unstructured field study	Unstructured laboratory study
	Structured	Structured field study	Completely structured laboratory study

Source: Bailey, 1994: 247.

In procedural terms observational research can be differentiated into participant or non-participant types. The participant observer is a regular participant in the activities being observed. Thus, a researcher interested in studying the way people use their television set may spend time in the household of the individual being observed (e.g. Lull, 1982, 1985). It is usual practice, however, for the researcher not to disclose at the outset the real purpose of the research. In that way, the researcher's presence is less likely to influence the behaviour of primary interest. A non-participant observer does not participate in the activities being observed. In this case the observer may be hidden from view while observing the behaviour of others or may analyse behaviour that has been filmed or videotaped by a camera placed unobtrusively at the location where the behaviour occurred (e.g. Gunter et al., 1995). Thus, observations may be either covert, with the individuals being observed unaware that they are being watched, or overt, with the observer clearly visible.

In a structured observational study, the observers classify and quantify behaviours according to a predefined scheme. Effectively, they conduct a content analysis of the activities occurring in front of them, recording the different types of behaviour that occurred, the types and number of individuals involved, and possibly also details about the environment in which they occurred in those cases where observed individuals may move from one location or setting to another. In an unstructured observational study, the observer writes down comments about the events that took place, unconstrained by a predefined analytical framework.

Observational research is usually carried out in the field. In other words it monitors and classifies the way people behave in their natural environments. There have been studies that have used observational measures to analyse behaviour in laboratory conditions. These have usually examined the behaviour of respondents either during or subsequent to exposure to media content. On some occasions, observational techniques are used within an experimental methodology as one mechanism for collecting data on media effects (e.g. Bandura et al., 1963a and b).

In a natural setting it is difficult for the researcher who wishes to be covert not to act as a participant. If the researcher does not participate, there is little to explain his or her presence, as he or she is very obvious to the actual participants, can affect their behaviour and can, in effect, change a natural setting into an unnatural one. Unlike a less structured study in which the observer can attempt to remember what occurs during the day while posing as a participant observer and then record these general impressions in privacy at night, structured observation requires counting frequencies. These numbers generally must be recorded immediately, an act difficult to perform during participant observation without arousing suspicion. Thus, structured studies in the natural setting tend to be non-participant studies.

In an artificial environment, non-participant observation is more readily accommodated. Many artificial laboratory settings are equipped with one-way mirrors, so that a non-participant can observe the research subjects from the next room. This form of observational analysis has often been used in research, conducted on children and television, that is concerned with either the degree of attention children pay to the screen or with the behavioural effects of watching specific types of film or television portrayal. In this case, observational analysis represents one aspect of an experimental study.

Indirect observation

Much observational research involves direct observations of ongoing behaviour. The researcher witnesses events first hand as they occur and does not have to rely on a secondary account of behaviour. However, cases can arise where this is not possible. The researcher may deliberately choose to avoid being at the scene for fear of influencing events. On these occasions methods of indirect observation can be used. These often take the form of using a hidden camera to record events. The video footage can then be analysed later at the researcher's convenience.

The best examples of this sort of work have been studies of the way people behave at home in front of their television set. Several observational studies using photographic or video evidence have been conducted from the mid-1960s onwards and provided evidence of the amount of time viewers remain in front of the television while it is switched on, and the differential degrees of attention they pay to different types of programming (Allen, 1965; Bechtel et al., 1972; Collett and Lamb, 1986; Gunter et al., 1995).

Box 2.1 Types of observational study

Completely unstructured field studies

These studies take place in a natural setting, use participant observation (in most cases), and have very little structure imposed upon the setting by the observer. Instead, the observer attempts to become a part of the subculture or culture he or she is studying. This approach is characterized by what is often called the ethnographic method. The purpose of the ethnographic method is simply to describe a particular culture. The goal is to provide a broad descriptive account of the setting, language, customs, rules and so on. Generally this requires that the researcher becomes a participant observer.

Completely structured observation

These studies take place in a laboratory setting rather than in the natural environment. Structured observation of this sort attempts to test hypotheses. The instrument of measurement is a checklist of items to be observed rather than a questionnaire. In order for the different groups observed at different times to be comparable in terms of observational categories, it is necessary that these groups be as identical as possible. This is done by standardizing the laboratory so that laboratory conditions are identical at all times. While it may be possible in some observational studies to assign people randomly to groups, often this is not done.

Semi-structured study

A researcher wishing to capture the rigour and ability to quantify that is afforded by the structured study, but not wishing the accompanying artificiality, might conduct a study in a natural setting using a structured observational instrument. This structured field study methodology combines the advantages and disadvantages of the other techniques. The greatest advantage for some researchers is that the observer can become immersed in the culture being observed. However, the natural world of the observed is being transformed by the artificial structure being imposed upon it rather than being analysed in terms of its own natural structure. There may be some concerns also about reactivity whereby the people observed in the study, knowing they are being observed, behave differently from normal. The presence of the observer may bias their responding.

Unstructured laboratory study

One of the chief advantages of an observational study in which no structural set of categories is used is that it allows the persons being observed to structure the situation, and allows the observer to learn to view the world through his or her host's eyes. Such unstructured observation is very useful in natural settings, but generally requires a relatively long period. If a group of people are placed in an artificial environment, such as a room with a one-way mirror, they certainly are not likely to carry on day-to-day activities that would give a clue to their culture. Further, they cannot be kept in this confined environment for very long. A few unstructured studies have been conducted in a laboratory setting. These include studies in which children are observed in controlled play settings and allowed to play freely.

Advantages and disadvantages of observational research

Observational research is a superior technique to survey research, experimentation and focus groups for collecting data on non-verbal behaviour. While focus groups and surveys are useful for obtaining data on people's opinions about different things, they are less accurate indicators of how individuals actually behave in specific situations. Experiments provide powerful methodologies for analysing cause – effect relationships involving media and behaviour, but the behaviour measures are often contrived and far removed from behaviours typical of people in their everyday reality. An observer on the scene, however, can discern ongoing behaviour at it occurs. The observer can make field notes that record salient features of the behaviour, or may even record behaviour in its totality via videotape.

While the survey questionnaire is a rather artificial and restrictive instrument limited to a relatively small number of previously chosen questions, the observational method allows in-depth study of the whole individual. Investigators frequently use the observational method in preliminary studies. Many times a researcher plans to conduct a survey but is relatively unfamiliar with his or her respondents and is not sure which questions are appropriate or necessary. By conducting a preliminary observational study, the researcher can discover the appropriate characteristics for study, including some behaviours of which the respondent may not be aware.

Another major advantage of much observational research is that behaviour takes place in its natural environment. Some proponents of observational research feel that observation is less reactive than the other major data-collection techniques (Johnson, 1975). Experiments and surveys can cause bias in the data they measure through the techniques they use to generate responses from those being investigated. Observation is not so restrictive.

As with other methodologies, however, even observational research suffers from a number of disadvantages. First, the researcher has a lack of control over the behaviour of the people being observed and over the environment in which observed behaviour occurs. This means that any given observed pattern of behaviour could have been caused by a number of factors, some of which were visible at the time and others invisible. Explaining why certain observed behaviour occurred when it did and in the way it did can therefore be difficult.

There are measurement problems with observational research. Non-participant observation that uses a predefined framework for classifying and quantifying behaviour provides a structure to behavioural analysis that facilitates ease of data collection. Relatively unstructured approaches adopted more often by participant observers lack the same level of precision. Moreover, to preserve his or her anonymity, the participant observer must not be seen making field notes in the presence of those being observed. Thus, the observer must write up his or her observations after each field observation session. There is greater scope for inaccuracies to creep into the data when observations are not catalogued immediately.

Observational studies tend to use smaller samples than surveys, though generally larger samples than either focus groups or experiments. Even so, probability sampling frames tend not to be deployed, meaning that most samples in observational studies cannot be regarded as representative of the populations under study.

One practical difficulty faced by observational research can be gaining entry to the environments targeted for study. Observational research in a media context has often been used to study media production processes.

This work requires obtaining entry to media organizations, newsrooms, and production locations. Some organizations or departments within organizations are reluctant to allow unlimited access to media researchers. Where access is restricted, this will also limit the amount of detail the researcher is able to obtain about the organization's internal operations.

CONCLUDING REMARKS

The history of media *audience* research has been characterized by a number of shifts in methodological fashions that can be mapped onto changing patterns of theoretical modelling and explanation of audience involvement with media and media effects upon audiences. The waxing and waning of theoretical emphases, driven in turn by dominant episte-mologies and their associated sociopolitical ideologies, have brought different methodologies into vogue at different times.

Early concerns in the first part of the 20th century that the mass media, in the form of newspapers, radio and films, could exert powerful effects upon the general public, led researchers to utilize methodologies, as they became available, to attempt to demonstrate links between media messages and public opinion. There was repeated failure to empirically verify powerful media effects derived from research that utilized questionnaire-based surveys. Instead, an alternative view was proffered that the media do not act directly upon the public, but only indirectly via mediators in the form of opinion leaders (Katz and Lazarsfeld, 1955; Lazarsfeld et al., 1944). Other methodologies, championed by other schools of thought, were utilized, however, to indicate that there may be occasions when the media can exert direct effects upon members of the audience, especially younger members.

A series of experimental studies, led by behavioural psychologists such as Leonard Berkowitz and Albert Bandura, in the 1960s, produced pub-lished results that were interpreted to show that children could be encour-aged directly to mimic film portrayals and that young adults could be invited to deliver what they believed to be a painful stimulus to another person in laboratory contexts after exposure to film violence. These media effects, however, were less easy to demonstrate outside the laboratory. Other epistemological schools of thought were entirely dismissive of such empirical research, which was believed to ignore the areas where the real potency of media influences could be found – namely in the promulgation and maintenance of dominant ideologies (Barker and Petley, 1997; Gauntlett, 1995; Murdock, 1989). It should be noted though, that even among some positivistic empiricists, this view had surfaced some years earlier, with the media being conceptualized to reinforce existing behavioural systems more than change them (Klapper, 1960).

The 'discovery' by critical social scientists of qualitative audience research at the turn of the 1980s led to a further change of methodological fashion. Qualitative methodologies such as in-depth interviews or focus group discussions had actually been introduced much earlier, with the important work of Paul Lazarsfeld and Robert Merton in the 1940s. Although used continually by Merton during the next two decades, focus groups were eschewed by most media researchers in the academy, during an era when quantitative survey and experimental methods were in the ascendancy. The failure of these methodologies to provide satisfactory explanations of media effects, after more than 30 years, encouraged the search for an alternative perspective. This new perspective took the form of methods that allowed a deeper analysis of audiences' involvement with and responses to media than quantitative methods would permit. There was a growing recognition that audiences should be allowed to express their thoughts and feelings about media content in their own terms and that qualitative methodologies were best equipped to facilitate this type of investigation (Morley, 1980). Even quantitative researchers began to exhibit a conceptual and theoretical shift away from purely behaviourist explanations of media impact towards cognitive models that embraced notions of interpretation by audiences on media content. This meant that investigations of media involvement and media impact needed to generate not just numerical data, but also text-based data. Modes of analysis were needed that could facilitate systematic analyses of media 'texts' and those 'texts' produced by members of the audience when asked to describe in their own words their experiences with media (Hoijer, 1990). The challenge for researchers who use this approach is to devise analytical techniques in which the rules and procedures are clearly apparent and can be repeated by anyone else. Otherwise, the outcome will comprise little more than the application of highly personalized 'readings' of media or of audiences' conversational narratives about media. In the end, however, progress is most likely to derive from a combination of quantitative and qualitative research techniques in which the verbal and physical behaviours of audiences can be allowed to occur in as close to their natural form as possible, but assessed through systematic and reliable procedures that permit the testing of specific theories about media and audiences.

CHAPTER 3

OVERVIEW OF MEDIA RESEARCH METHODOLOGIES: MEDIA OUTPUT

This chapter shifts attention from the audience to the media themselves. So far, this book has examined methodologies that have been used by media scholars to investigate media audiences. Audience research has embraced studies of the way audiences use media, the degree to which they engage with media during exposure, audiences' cognitive and affective reactions to media content, and finally, the short- and longer-term effects media can have on audiences. Throughout much of this work with audiences, researchers have found it necessary to consider the nature of media content. In some audience studies, the nature of the media and their content has been considered only in a very global fashion. In others, audience responses to specific media content sequences have been measured. Some media audience researchers have compared reactions of media consumers to different types of media content. In these cases, however, distinctions have often been made between only two or three different types of media stimuli. More ambitious audience studies have gone as far as to devise more elaborate systems for the differentiation and classification of media content, especially where it is recognized that audiences themselves can make refined and often quite sophisticated distinctions between media reports, depictions and portrayals (e.g. Gunter, 1995a; Hodge and Tripp, 1986). However, it is rare that audience studies have represented the full range, complexity, and diversity of media output. The only way to recognize and represent media output fully is to develop methodologies that address media content directly to reveal the full array of meanings it can convey. In this chapter, we look at methods of media output analysis.

CONTENT ANALYSIS

Content analysis can be traced back to the Second World War when allied intelligence units monitored the number and types of popular songs played on European radio stations. According to Wimmer and Dominick (1994: 163), 'By comparing the music played on German stations with that on other stations in occupied Europe, the allies were able to measure with some degree of success, the changes in troop concentration on the continent'. Similar exercises took place in the Pacific theatre, where American intelligence monitored communications between Japan and its various island bases.

Apart from these specific military applications, techniques similar to content analysis were identified to be in use during the first half of the

20th century, largely to monitor social and economic trends (Beniger, 1978). As early as 1910, Max Weber had suggested launching an exercise to monitor press coverage of social and political issues alongside surveying public opinion on various issues – an early form of agenda-setting research. However, this ambitious project never materialized. Other early uses of content analysis were directed at verifying the authenticity of historical documents. These studies were concerned mostly with counting words in documents of questionable origin and comparing their frequencies and patterns of occurrence with the same words in documents whose authenticity had been verified.

After the 1940s, content analysis evolved methodologically and was used by academic researchers to study a wide range of media issues. As well as being deployed as a stand-alone research technique, it also came to be used in partnership with other research methodologies including surveys, experiments and certain qualitative methodologies, such as observational research and the analysis of focus group transcripts. The first attempt to define the technique conceived of content analysis as 'a research technique for the objective, systematic, and quantitative description of the manifest content of communication' (Berelson, 1952: 18). This view of content analysis prevailed and underpinned this type of research for the next three decades. Berelson's definition, however, has been criticized for a number of reasons:

- It is restricted to purely quantitative analysis (Huber, 1989; Kracauer, 1952; Lasswell, 1949).
- It is concerned with manifest content only.
- It is purely descriptive instead of yielding data from which one might infer influences of media content on audience perceptions of social reality (Krippendorf, 1980; Merten, 1995).

Later authors offered a number of further definitions of this methodology and its aims. According to Walizer and Wienir (1978), content analysis is any systematic procedure devised to examine the content of recorded information. Krippendorf (1980) defined it as a research technique for making replicable and valid references from data to their context. Kerlinger (1986) suggested that content analysis is a method of studying and analysing communication in a systematic, objective and quantifiable manner for the purpose of measuring variables.

Kerlinger's definition involves three concepts that require elaboration. First, content analysis is *systematic*. This means that the content to be analysed is selected according to explicit and consistently applied rules. There must be uniformity in the coding and analysis procedures. Only one set of guidelines is used throughout the study, to which all coders must adhere.

Second, content analysis is *objective*. In other words, the researcher's personal idiosyncrasies and biases should not enter into the findings. If replicated by another researcher, the analysis should yield the same results.

Operational definitions and rules for classification of variables should be explicit and comprehensive enough that other researchers who repeat the process will arrive at the same decisions and same results. Unless a clear set of criteria and procedures is established that fully explains the sampling and categorization methods, the research does not meet the requirements of objectivity, and the reliability of the results may be called into question.

Third, content analysis is *quantifiable*. The goal of content analysis is the accurate representation of a body of messages. However, purely quantitative features may not only be of importance. More qualitative factors may reveal more about meanings conveyed by media. The emphasis upon the quantitative has been increasingly challenged as the value and insights provided by positivist empirical research have been challenged by critical and interpretivist paradigms. Can content analysis ever be truly 'objective' in the sense of being devoid of all value judgements? Is a purely quantitative assessment necessarily the most useful in understanding the nature of media content?

Increasingly, there are arguments being raised for media output analysis to include techniques that do more than simply describe and count surface events in the media. Instead, greater value is believed by some writers to accrue from using measures that can identify meanings conveyed by media texts (Fowler, 1991; Krippendorf, 1980), or make empirically-verifiable inferences about the potential impact of media content upon individuals, groups or society as a whole (Gunter, 1985a; Hodge and Tripp, 1986). Counting and quantifying needs to be supplemented by interpretive procedures that can define the weight of a media message in terms of its potential impact upon the audience. Ascertaining the frequency with which certain social groups or social behaviours appear can reveal important information at one level about the motives or agenda of media producers or cultivation effects upon audiences. But frequency of occurrence is not all. Sometimes, infrequent, but highly salient or significant, events can have the greatest impact on the audience.

Continuing this debate, Merten (1996) raised two problems with content analysis. First, can it serve as an instrument for inquiry into social reality? Second, to what extent is content analysis contaminated by 'reactivity'? The latter means the effect of differences of viewpoint among coders in the way a coding frame is applied to the analysis of media content. This problem may become especially pronounced where more subjective, evaluative measures are taken.

Observation and interviewing are regularly-used techniques for the analysis of social reality. Through these techniques it is possible for researchers to record and catalogue occurrences within a social environment, translating them either into verbal accounts or numerical measurements of whatever behaviour occurred. Thus, a kind of symbolic representation of social reality is created (Merten and Teipen, 1991).

This approach is supposed to preserve the pertinent and significant elements of social reality, albeit in another form. However, this perfect representation may not in fact be achieved. Textual representations of social reality, for example, need further transformation before they truly become *data*. While in textual form, social reality has in fact been transferred into an alternative symbolic reality, represented by the text itself. A further stage of processing is needed before the symbolic representation of social reality is converted into data. Content analysis is a secondary instrument for recording social reality when used in tandem with interviewing or observational analysis. Thus, a model can be created in which we begin with social reality. This is transferred via observational analysis or depth interviewing into a symbolic reality (text). The latter is processed further through content analysis and is then converted into a set of data (Merten, 1996).

In the interviewing situation, the social reality to be recorded is gathered by a verbal question – answer procedure; in the observation situation by the direct presence of the observer and his/her simultaneous translation activities. In both cases, inevitably, a verbal or non-verbal communication process results. In the use of mailed questionnaires, the interviewer is not present, so that reactive influences caused by this person's presence are excluded. But the respondent, in completing the questionnaire, may lack guidance or structure concerning the meaning of the questions. In such cases, respondents will construct their own 'self-made' meaning (considering what the absent interviewer would suggest as the correct meaning). In this situation of the generation of expectations, a type of para-social interaction develops (Horton and Wohl, 1956) or, in methodological terms, reactivity may emerge.

With interview and observation instruments, the problem of reactivity is well-known and much research has been conducted around it (e.g. Jabine et al., 1984; Loftus et al., 1985). In contrast, content analysis is still considered a non-reactive instrument because texts are understood as some type of fossilized reality. The assumption is that content analysis may be an 'objective, systematic and quantitative description of the manifest content of communication' (Berelson, 1952: 18) is, from this perspective, no more than seductive hope (Merten, 1996).

Texts may be social realities in their own right. This may mean that during the act of coding them, they may invoke in coders sets of beliefs or attitudes which can bias the way the coding takes place. Three distinct semiotic levels have been identified at which this kind of problem can become evident (after Pierce, 1931):

- A syntactic level, at which a sign S is defined solely in terms of its relation to its means of representation (M);
- A semantic level, at which S is defined in terms of a two-fold relation to M and the reference to an object (O);
- A pragmatic level at which S is defined in terms of a three-fold relation to M, O and the user (interpretant, I) of the sign: S = (M,O,I).

Social reality, then, as recorded in texts, may be reactive only if variables inherent in the text interfere with social variables of the coder, i.e. the interpretant. Merten (1996) offers a schematic representation of how these different levels might function or interact to facilitate reactivity during content analysis (see Figure 3.1).

Cell 1 contains all purely *syntactic* techniques of content analysis. For example, frequency analyses of letters, words or sentences (Zipf, 1932) are of this type. Cell 2 contains all those content analyses on a syntactical basis, which require semantic rules, i.e. word analyses (Johnson, 1944). Cell 3 contains the classical *denotative* level. Content analyses here are purely semantic ones; the coding procedure requires only a semantic identification of a text (themes) or part of a text (key words) according to a semantic term or category in a lexical manner and causes, therefore, no reactivity. For instance, theme analyses, the most common type of content analysis are found here (Berelson, 1952).

Cell 4 contains the use of syntactical structures by a recipient. For instance, readability analyses based on the length of sentences (Flesch, 1951) are of this type. Because of the pragmatic activity of a recipient, these procedures are reactive, that is, different recipients may state a different readability ease. Cell 5 contains content analyses which require the communicative competence of a coder to identify *connotative* meanings, for example, the analysis of values (Osgood et al., 1957). This is possible only by referring to the value system of the coder and activates therefore a specific type of social structure so that reactivity may arise.

Cell 6 contains all purely *pragmatic* analyses which relate to either the intention of the communicator of a text or the *effects* that text may have on some recipient. Content analyses of this type require from the coder, in a specific sense, "to take the role of the other" (Mead, 1934) so that, again, a virtual communication process must be catalyzed to obtain information about intentions or effects. All types of *communication* effect analyses are found here and also contain the most reactivity. (Merten, 1996: 68–69)

Figure 3.1 A Schematic Representation of Media Text Analysis Perspectives

		Coder		
		Syntactics	Semantics	Pragmatics
Text	Syntactics	**1** Syntax	**2** Syntactic semantics	**4** Syntactic pragmatics
	Semantics		**3** Denotative semantics	**5** Connotative pragmatics
	Pragmatics			**6** Pragmatics pragmatics

Source: Merten, 1996: 69.

Content analyses conducted under conditions in which coder evaluation or reactivity may arise cannot be objective. It is best to develop measures designed to attain content analytical validity. Merten critically appraises a methodology developed by Kepplinger and Staab (1992) called Action – Evaluation analysis. This technique was designed to analyse the evaluation of political action of a person by other persons or journalists, by standardizing action and evaluation procedures in arguments through an Action – Evaluation Matrix.

From the perspective of content-analytic methodology, this technique possesses two closed category systems and shows a certain similarity with the interaction process analysis of Bales (1950). The coding procedure, therefore, is very easy; the coder, first, categorizes the reported action according to the nine possible states of action and, second, codes the evaluation by a second person or the writer of an article or moderator of a television report.

A closer look reveals some shortcomings in this procedure. While the interaction process analysis of Bales (1950) uses a category system that is theoretically deduced from Parson's (1968) structural-functional theory, Kepplinger and Staab developed their categories without reference to any theory, apparently for the sake of simplicity. This results in a number of unanswered questions, however. What reason accounts for the definition of exactly twelve categories of evaluations? What consideration explains the fact that the number of positive and negative evaluation categories is not the same? And what reason explains why some action categories – e.g. 'information about success' – may be self-evaluative? But the main objection against this technique lies in the fact that the coder must assess evaluations, therefore acting on the pragmatic level and evoking high degrees of reactivity. For example, a statement such as 'actor X *justifies* his action Y' is – according to the matrix – a positive one. But the statement 'The accused actor X justified his deceitful behaviour' is by no means positive. In a test of the Kepplinger – Staab model, Merten (1996) found that the evaluative categories did not yield consistent results when applied by coders to evaluate political arguments. Different content profiles emerged from coders whose own political positions tended to bias the way they applied this coding scheme.

How is content analysis used?

The central thrust of content analysis is to provide a descriptive account of what a media text (i.e. film, TV programme, advertisement, newspaper report, magazine feature) contains, and to do so in a fashion that can be reproduced by others. In its purely quantitative form, content analysis should therefore be objective, systematic and replicable. However, the applications of content analysis can go beyond simple description. Early on, content analysis was regarded as being able to provide insights into the intentions or objectives of media content producers and into the potential impact of content on audiences (Berelson, 1952). Much later, Wimmer and Dominick (1994) identified five main purposes of content analysis:

1. describing patterns or trends in media portrayals;
2. testing hypotheses about the policies or aims of media producers;
3. comparing media content with the real world;
4. assessing the representation of particular groups in society;
5. drawing inferences about media effects.

Despite the debate about the efficacy of purely descriptive content analysis *per se*, it continues to be widely used as a research technique crossing a range of contexts. The varying applications of this methodology are discussed in more detail in the sections that follow.

Describing patterns and trends in media portrayals

A number of studies have explored specific categories of content in the media such as depictions of violence, sexual behaviour, health-related behaviour, political coverage, gender-roles, and other social groups. Some of this work has attempted to produce general profiles of the way these things are presented across a medium as a whole, while others have focused upon their depiction within specific genres of media content.

Any content analysis begins with the selection of content for description. This entails an initial decision about the medium from which content will be obtained, then the construction of a sampling frame to select the media output to be analysed. The latter might comprise the selection of publications or broadcasts covering specified time periods, or the selection of subsections or portrayals from these media products for closer analysis. An analysis of newspaper coverage of a topic requires the researcher to decide which newspapers will be covered, which editions of those newspapers will be selected, and how topics will be identified within the selected publications. The analysis of television content requires the definition of basic units of analysis (e.g. portrayals within programmes or programmes themselves) and the creation of an analytical framework that will further classify attributes of content of interest in the research.

Once the medium has been chosen, the selection of issues, transmissions and dates follows. At this point, the time period over which the analysis takes place and the issues or transmission dates selected will depend upon the nature of the topic and research questions linked to that topic under consideration. Interest may centre on the general status of media coverage given to political, economic or industrial issues over the previous few weeks or months. In this case, a sampling frame will be devised for the selection of media content, probably in a random or quasi-random fashion, and a coding frame will be applied to assess coverage throughout that time period (e.g. Glasgow Media Group, 1976).

Alternatively, the research may be concerned with the way the media covered a specific event such as a war (Morrison, 1992a; Morrison and Tumber, 1988), a major industrial accident (Rubin, 1987), an election (Siegelman and Bullock, 1991), or a civil disturbance (Halloran et al., 1970). In such cases, sampling of media content will be intensively concentrated on those limited spells during which such events occurred.

Descriptive analyses of television violence

One of the most heavily researched media topics has been the depiction of violence. Most of this work has focused upon the way violence is shown on television. The earliest descriptive studies with television were undertaken in the 1950s (Smythe, 1954). The use of content analysis to measure violence on television usually begins with the setting up of an 'objective' statement of what is meant by violence. Violence is usually defined in broad terms. Accompanying this definition is a frame of reference which specifies how and where that definition should be applied in the assessment of programmes. This instructional frame of reference is given to teams of trained coders who watch samples of programmes recorded from television and count up incidents which match the definition of violence drawn up for the purposes of the analysis. This enables researchers to produce a quantitative assessment of the 'amount' of violence on television in terms of the numbers of violent incidents or events catalogued by coders.

The aim of such analysis is to yield an indication of the extent and location of particular classes of incident or event in television programmes. This research methodology attempts as far as possible to exclude any element of subjective judgement about violent television portrayals. All violence tends to be treated the same way by a content analysis, regardless of the type of programme or dramatic context or setting in which it occurs. Thus, cartoon violence, for example, is treated no differently than violence occurring in a contemporary drama series. Traditionally, content analysis researchers define the intensity of violence in a programme in terms of the numbers of certain kinds of incidents it contains, rather than in terms of the nature of those incidents. This type of measurement does not, of course, reflect the way in which viewers might respond to violence on television.

Research on viewers' perceptions of television violence has shown that viewers differentiate between violent portrayals on the basis of the context in which they occur, the form of violence displayed, and the types of characters involved as perpetrators or victims of violence (Gunter, 1985a). The important objective in content analysis, however, is consistency and reliability of assessment across different coders (Krippendorf, 1980; Wimmer and Dominick, 1994).

Even within the content analysis perspective, it is possible to utilize different definitional terms of reference. Content analysis methodologies can vary in terms of the definitions of violence they use, the way in which they sample programmes, and the degree of detail they obtain about violence on television. Most content analysis, however, places emphasis on the specification of profiles and structures of programmes' content. With regard to the measurement of television violence, the commonality in the application of this technique lies in the objective counting of incidents that match a single normative definition of violence.

Violence definitions Definitions of violence for content analysis purposes have varied around a common theme. The longest-running content analysis study of violence on television, conducted between the late 1960s and mid-1980s by Gerbner and his colleagues at the University of Pennsylvania, used a single normative definition of violence: 'the overt expression of physical force (with or without a weapon) against self or other, compelling action against one's will on pain of being hurt or killed, or actually hurting or killing' (Gerbner, 1972: 31). Further specifications were made that the incidents must be plausible and credible, but that no idle threats should be included. However, violent accidents or natural catastrophes, whose inclusion in dramatic plots was reasoned by Gerbner to be technically non-accidental, were included (Gerbner and Gross, 1976).

A Canadian study reported by Williams et al. (1982: 366) used Gerbner's definition but enhanced it with further specifications: '... Must be plausible and credible; no idle threats, verbal abuse, or comic gestures with no credible violent consequences. May be intentional or accidental; violent accidents, catastrophes, acts of nature are included'. More recent definitions of violence for content analysis purposes have tried to specify in more detail the kinds of incidents to be counted.

In a Finnish study, television violence was defined as: 'actions causing or designed to cause harm to oneself, or to another person, either physically or psychologically, including implicit threats, non-verbal behaviour, and outbursts of anger directed towards animals, and inanimate objects' (Mustonen and Pulkkinen, 1997: 173). These researchers also included portrayals of the mere victims of violence, if the connection between violent behaviour and a victim's injuries was clearly established. Antisocial activities with no aggressive connotations, such as deceit and theft; or mere negative affective or hostile reactions unaccompanied by physical injury or damage, were excluded from the analysis as well as verbal reports of violence.

Major American and British studies of television violence harmonized to some degree their definitions of violence to emphasize physically-harmful behaviour, while excluding accidental violence caused by natural disasters, unless these occurred as a consequence of some deliberate act of aggression on the part of a perpetrator intent on doing harm.

The National Television Violence study was funded over three years (1994–97) by the National Cable Television Association in the USA. This study developed an elaborate methodology that assessed not just the quantity of violence depicted on American television, but also the nature of violent portrayals and contexts within which violence occurred (Potter et al., 1996; Wilson et al., 1996).

The study developed a definition of violence that embodied three concepts: the notion of credible threat of violence, the overt occurrence of violent behaviour, and the harmful consequences of unseen violence (see Box 3.1). The idea of credible threat covered situations where an individual threatened another in such a way that there was a realistic likelihood that violence would follow, with the perpetrator having the clear means to carry out such action. The harmful consequences of unseen violence covered scenes where someone is depicted suffering some kind of pain or discomfort and indeed actual physical damage may be shown, and where other clues from the story-line establish that they were a victim of violence.

Much emphasis was placed on the context in which violence occurred, and an elaborate framework of analysis was created to enable a comprehensive classification of violence in terms of a range of attributes: its dramatic setting, motivational context, graphicness, rewards and punishments, severity of consequences for victims, physical form, and the nature of the perpetrators and victims. All these factors were rationalized in terms of their significance as possible mediators of audience response to media depictions of violence as signalled by published research literature on media effects (Wilson et al., 1996).

Box 3.1   Definitions of television violence

National Television Violence Study, USA (1994–97)

'Violence is defined as any overt depiction of a credible threat of physical force or the actual use of such force intended to physically harm an animate being or group of beings. Violence also includes certain depictions of physically harmful consequences against an animate being or group that occur as a result of unseen violent means.'

University of Sheffield Television Violence Study, UK (1995–96)

Violence defined as 'any overt depiction of a credible threat of physical force, or the actual use of physical force, with or without a weapon, which is intended to harm or intimidate an animate being or a group of animate beings. The violence may be carried out or merely attempted, and may or may not cause injury. Violence also includes any depiction of physically harmful consequences against an animate being (or group of animate beings) that occur as a result of unseen violent means' (Gunter and Harrison, 1998: 52).

Units of analysis

The unit of analysis is the entity that is counted in a content analysis. It is the smallest element of such an analysis, but it is also one of the most important. In written content, the unit of analysis might be a single word or symbol, a theme, or an entire article or story. In television and film analysis, units of analysis can be characters, behavioural actions, or entire programmes. Specific rules and definitions are required for determining these units and to ensure agreement between coders in their identification and cataloguing.

Some researchers have analysed media content simply in terms of the major themes that have been featured. In an investigation of the extent to which films released in Britain between 1945 and 1991 were characterized by crime themes, Allen et al. (1997) assigned films to one of ten genre categories (western, crime, war, romance, fantasy, sex, farce, adventure, drama, other) on the basis of details provided in film synopses. This analysis had two parts. The presence of crime content in each synopsis was assessed by examining it for mentions of a crime, criminal or the criminal justice system. Then, the film genre was classified according to the ten genre categories. In the case of crime films, allocation to this category meant that the 'primary focus of the narrative is on the causes or consequences of illegal activities, central characters include criminals, victims and those who work in the criminal justice system (e.g. private eyes, amateurs, police, courts, gangsters)' (Allen et al., 1997: 92).

In the National Television Violence Study, units of analysis were defined at more than one level. Whereas previous television violence content analyses had focused on counting violent acts, this study went beyond that level to include more global measures of violence that represented better the context features of violence. Three levels of measurement were devised: (1) the PAT; (2) the scene; and (3) the programme. A PAT represented an interaction between a perpetrator (P), an act (A), and a target (T). A sequence of PATs, either continuous and uninterrupted or separated by brief cutaways or scene changes, might comprise a violent scene and afforded an opportunity to examine relationships between discrete acts. Finally, the researchers argued that larger meanings could be conveyed by the pattern of violence considered as a whole within a programme, which could only be effectively interpreted when analysed alone with the context in which it was presented in the programme.

In addition to counting incidents or actions, other units of analysis that are often coded include the actors who perpetrate actions in fictional output or sources of information in the context of news. It is particularly insightful in the case of news to analyse the sources of quotes, comments or other material (Lasorsa and Reese, 1990). An analysis of the attributes of actors or characters in fictional media content, for example, can yield evidence about the proportional representation of different social groups. In news or factual output, analysis of the use of different types of information source can provide evidence of balance, neutrality, thoroughness and impartiality of reporting. This form of analysis may examine the range of sources used, which groups, organizations or institutions they represent, and the context (interview, official meeting, press conference) in which they appear. The analysis can also examine the kind of information sought and obtained from different sources and whether there was any indication of the status of the source (Ericson et al., 1991).

Analyses of news and factual media output has revealed frequent biases in the kinds of sources relied upon. Official sources frequently dominate, especially in the context of news of national or international importance (Brown et al., 1987; Giffard, 1989; Herman and Chomsky, 1988). The news media exhibit a tendency to rely on a fairly narrow band of experts to put events in context. These individuals tend to be male and are drawn from academia, journalism, think-tanks or are retired former members of a relevant profession (Cooper and Soley, 1990).

Sampling issues

Once the body of content to be considered has been specified, the researcher has to determine how much of that content to analyse. In some instances, the universe may be small enough to be analysed in its entirety. More often, researchers must sample a subset of content from that total universe which, is itself, too large to be analysed in full.

Sampling in content analysis often takes place in more than one step. A first step might be to specify which content sources are to be sampled. For example, in a study of newspaper coverage, the first step is to decide which newspapers are to be analysed at all. Then a decision must be taken about how many editions of each newspaper to analyse and over what period of time. A further step then may be to decide how much or which parts of the newspaper to analyse. At this level, one has to consider how many stories to analyse and how they should be identified. Finally, the analyst will consider whether there are specific story ingredients that need to be measured.

There are some rough guidelines for sampling. Stempel (1952) drew separate samples of 6, 12, 18, 24, and 48 issues of a newspaper and compared the average content of each sample size in a single subject category against the total for the entire year. He found that each of the five sample sizes was adequate and that increasing the sample beyond 12 issues did not significantly improve upon accuracy.

In television, Gerbner et al. (1978) demonstrated that, at least for the purpose of measuring violent behaviour, a sample of one week of autumn programming and various sample dates drawn throughout the year produced comparable results. As a general rule, however, the larger the sample the better – within reason, of course. If too few dates are selected for analysis, the possibility of an unrepresentative sample is increased. Larger samples, if chosen randomly, usually run less risk of being atypical.

Research into the depiction of violence on television in Britain adopted two distinct sampling frameworks. In an initial content analysis study, a four-week sample was drawn covering eight television channels. Programmes were video-recorded across four seven-day periods, beginning

Monday and ending on Sunday. In a second study a 28-day sample was drawn from ten television channels to produce four composite weeks, with Monday selected from one week, Tuesday from a second week through to Sunday from a seventh week. In this case, programmes were video-recorded across 28 weeks over a nine-month period, rather than just four weeks over a five-month period as in the first study (Gunter et al., 1996; Gunter and Harrison, 1998).

The question of content sampling was an issue looked at very closely by the National Television Violence Study. This study analysed a far larger sample of programme output from a larger number of television channels than any previous American content analysis study. In total the project sample covered programming broadcast throughout the day. What distinguished this research, however, was its use of a random sampling frame to select programmes for analysis over a period of 20 weeks each year. The programmes were chosen with a modified version of the equal probability of selection method. Two half-hour time slots (defined by hour of day and day of week) were randomly selected for each channel during each week that sampling occurred. Once a time slot was selected, the *TV Guide* was consulted and the programme corresponding to that time slot was entered into a scheduling grid several days before the target week of programming began. This procedure was run until a full composite week of programmes for each channel had been compiled.

Testing hypotheses about message producers

Some content analysis studies have gone beyond the description of surface features of media output to infer from that material certain characteristics, motives or ideologies of the producers and organizations that lie behind the content. In some instances, certain types of content are expected to be produced by media organizations believed to have agendas of their own with respect to the shaping or manipulation of public opinion. Very often, therefore, content analysis under this heading has focused upon classifying and quantifying the dominant features of media news output. It is assumed here that media organizations have their own political agenda that is catered for in the news treatment they provide. In the entertainment sphere, however, content analysis studies have attempted to identify hidden agendas linked to marketing campaigns. Programmes may contain characters who are little more than marketing vehicles for spin-off merchandise.

Illustrating the different political or ideological agendas of newspapers, Lacy, Fico and Simon (1991) found that prestige newspapers more often reported both sides of a controversy than did mass appeal, large circulation newspapers. In the marketing context, Eaton and Dominick (1991) found that cartoons built around characters merchandised as toys (e.g. G.I. Joe) had larger casts and contained more violence than did cartoons whose characters were not used in toy merchandising. In a broadcast news context, Soderland et al. (1989) compared the gender of anchors and reporters on private and government-operated stations in Canada and found that females were far more likely to serve as anchors on the government stations.

Comparing media content with the real world

Under this heading, content analysis research is conducted to compare the extent to which media depictions of events, groups and objects match their frequency and nature of occurrence in real life. In this regard, some researchers have examined subjects such as the depiction or reporting of crime. Does the crime coverage given by newspapers reflect the kinds of crime that occur most often in the real world (Davis, 1951)? Does the rate of involvement in crime of different demographic or social groups in fictional content on television reflect their actual involvement in crime in reality? Content analyses of peak-time television output in the USA, for example, have indicated that there are consistent patterns of group involvement in crime, whereby some demographic groups tend to be relatively more often portrayed as victims of crime. Furthermore, their involvement in crime on television far outweighs the real-life likelihood of being victimized (Gerbner and Gross, 1976; Gerbner et al., 1977, 1978, 1979). Other studies have compared television's portrayal of the world of work (De Fleur, 1964) or of industry (Trujillo and Ekdom, 1987) with real-world statistics on how prevalent they are in reality. De Fleur, for example, reported that certain occupations were over-represented on television, while others were virtually or completely absent.

Assessing the image of particular groups

Many content analysis studies have concentrated on accounting for the appearance or visibility of social groups in the media. Comparisons are then made between their frequency of occurrence in the world of television and their representation in the population in reality. Thus, studies have investigated the relative frequencies with which men and women, members of different age groups, ethnic minority groups, disabled groups, or occupational groups are depicted in leading roles or any roles at all, as compared with their representation in the population in the real world.

This type of research has indicated, for example, that men and women are not equally represented in leading roles, nor do they tend to occupy the same types of dramatic roles in television fiction. The way each gender tends to be portrayed is believed by some writers to promote or reinforce gender-related stereotypes (Furnham and Bitar, 1993; Furnham and Voli, 1989; Livingstone and Green, 1986; Long and Simon, 1974; see also Gunter, 1997b for review). Television has also been found to under-represent the elderly as compared with their number in real life (Gunter, 1998; Harris and Feinberg, 1977; Kubey, 1980).

In many cases, studies of this sort are conducted to assess changes in media policy towards these groups, particularly where such policies affect the extent to which members of these various groups are employed by the media industries. Such research is also carried out to investigate potential, subtle messages that may be conveyed by the mass media about these groups, especially where such messages are unflattering.

Content analysis as a basis for effects research

Although content analysis itself is a purely descriptive form of research that cannot directly explain media effects, it has been used in combination with other methodologies in studies designed to measure the impact of media on audiences.

The extensive work conducted by Gerbner and his colleagues throughout the 1970s and early 1980s into so-called cultivation effects of television is perhaps the best example of this sort of research. This research used both content analysis of prime-time network television and secondary analyses of public opinion survey data in an attempt to demonstrate the possibility that television could shape public perceptions of social reality. The content analysis was limited to dramatic entertainment programmes. News, documentaries, variety and quiz shows, and sports were excluded. One-week samples of television output were analysed for most years, limited to programmes transmitted between 7.30 and 11.00pm every evening and between 8.00am and 2.30pm at weekends. The definition of violence used in this research was presented earlier in this chapter. It emphasized incidents resulting in the infliction of injury or suffering, but largely ignored the context in which incidents occurred. Using this definition, trained coders recorded such features as the frequency and nature of violent acts, the perpetrators and victims of violence, and the temporal and spatial settings in which acts occurred. From certain combinations of these measures, Gerbner derived the 'Violence Profile', which purported to represent an objective and meaningful indicator of the amount of violence portrayed in television drama.

The Violence Profile itself comprised two sets of indicators: the Violence Index and the Risk Ratios. The amount of violence occurring on television was represented by the Violence Index. Essentially this index represented the percentages of programmes containing any violence at all, the frequency and rate of violent episodes per programme and per hour, and the number of leading characters involved in violence either as aggressors or victims.

The Risk Ratios signified a character's chances of involvement in violence in television drama programmes and, once involved, the likelihood of positive or negative consequences for them. The Risk Ratios also represented a composite of more than one measure: the Violence – Victim Ratio, which denoted the chances of being an aggressor or a victim, while the Killer – Killed Ratio denoted the risk of killing or being killed. Both ratios were catalogued within each dramatic and demographic category for a wide spectrum of character types.

Gerbner compared the patterns of involvement in violence of different social groups and more poignantly the patterns of outcome of involvement among these groups. The relative extent to which different groups were represented as aggressors or victims conveyed messages to the audience about the distribution of power among social groups, and was believed to transfer across to viewers' perceptions of the relative positions of these groups in the real world. Furthermore, by comparing 'television world' statistics with 'real world' statistics for the prevalence of violence, Gerbner concluded that the television world was a far more violent place than the real world and that heavy doses of exposure to this dramatically violent environment could cultivate exaggerated perceptions of violence in everyday reality.

Reporting findings for the mid- and late 1980s, Gerbner (1985, 1992) reported that children were today born into a symbolic world, presented by television that teaches lessons about society that may be quite different from those learned 'through parents, school or the church. The world experienced through the stories conveyed by television; this ubiquitous medium determines the issue agendas of young people.'

EXPERIMENTAL RESEARCH ON MEDIA OUTPUT

Some studies of media output have focused upon the idiosyncratic features of a particular medium in more direct relation to the impact that it might have on audiences. For instance, in the case of newspapers and magazines, analyses describe and articulate factors such as typography, layout, and makeup that may affect reader comprehension or enjoyment. In television, taxonomies of format features have been devised, in which programmes are analysed in terms of shot duration, pace of editing, scene location, camera angle, use of special effects, dialogue and so on, to shed more light on the complexities of audience reactions to programme content. In each case, a form of content analysis has been conducted to identify media-related features that have implications for effects upon media consumers. Often, these studies employ experimental paradigms in addition to purely descriptive analyses of media output.

Typography and makeup research

A type of content research that has been carried out with print media entails measuring the effects of news design elements – specifically typeface and page makeup – on readership, reader preferences, and comprehension. By means of this approach, researchers have tested the effects of different typography and makeup elements, including amount of white space, presence of paragraph headlines, size and style of type, variations in column width, and use of vertical or horizontal page makeup.

The experimental method is often used. Subjects are assigned to one or more treatment groups, exposed to an experimental stimulus (typically in the form of a mock newspaper or magazine page), and asked to rate what they have seen according to a series of dependent variable measures. Among the dependent variables that have been rated in such studies are the informative value of a publication, interest in reading a publication, image of a page, recall of textual material, readability, and general preference for a particular page.

Siskind (1979) used a nine-point, 20-item differential scale with such adjective pairs as 'messy – neat', 'informative – uninformative', 'unpleasant – pleasant', 'easy – difficult'. She obtained a general reader preference score by having subjects rate a newspaper page and summing their responses to all 20 items. Other studies have measured reader interest by using the rating scale technique or the 0–100 'feeling thermometer'. Comprehension and recall are typically measured by a series of true/false or multiple-choice questions on the content that is being assessed.

Haskins and Flynne (1974) conducted a typical design study to test the effects of different typefaces on reader interest in the women's section of a newspaper. They hypothesized that some typefaces would be perceived as more feminine than others and that headlines in such typefaces would create more reader interest in the page. The authors showed an experimental copy of a newspaper prepared specially for the study to a sample of 150 female heads of household: one sub-sample saw a version of the paper with headlines in the women's section printed in Garamond italic (a typeface experts had rated as feminine), while a second group saw the same page with Spartan Black headlines (considered to be a masculine typeface). A third group served as a control and saw only the headline copy typed on individual white cards. The subjects were asked to evaluate each article for reading interest. Additionally, each woman was shown a sample of ten typefaces and asked to rate them on a semantic differential scale with 16 adjective pairs.

The researchers discovered that typeface had no impact on reader interest scores. In fact, the scores were about the same for the printed headlines as they were for those typed on white cards. Analysis of the typeface ratings revealed that readers were able to differentiate between typefaces: Garamond Italic was rated as the second most feminine typeface while Spartan Black was rated most masculine, thus confirming the judgement of the expert raters.

Studies of page layout have been used to help magazine editors make decisions about the mechanics of editing and makeup. Click and Baird (1979) have provided a summary of more pertinent research in this area. A few of their conclusions were:

1. Large illustrations attract more readers than small ones.
2. Unusually shaped pictures irritate readers.

3. A small amount of text and a large picture on the opening pages of an article increases readership.
4. Readers do not like to read type set in italics.
5. For titles, readers prefer simple, familiar typefaces.
6. Readers and graphic designers seldom agree about what constitutes superior type design.
7. Roman type can be read more quickly than other typefaces.

Recent technological and makeup innovations have sparked renewed research interest in this area. In particular, the advent of *USA Today*, with its ground-breaking illustrations and use of colour has prompted several studies. Two studies by Geraci (1984a,b) compared the photographs, drawings, and other illustrations used by *USA Today* with those in traditional papers. Click and Stempel (1982) used seven front-page formats ranging from a modular page with a four-colour half-tone (the format favoured by *USA Today*) to a traditional format with no colour. Respondents were shown a slide of each page for 15 seconds and were asked to rate the page using 20 semantic differential scales. The results indicated that readers preferred modular pages and colour.

More recent studies have continued along these lines. Smith and Hajash (1988) performed a content analysis of the graphics used by 30 daily newspapers. They found that the average paper had one graphic per 17 pages compared to *USA Today*'s average of 1.3 graphics per single page. The authors concluded that the influence of *USA Today* has not been overwhelming. Utt and Pasternak (1989) found that the influence of *USA Today* was more evident on the front page design of American dailies. Most papers had increased their front page use of colour, photos, and informational graphics. Bohle and Gracia (1987) used the experimental method to gauge reader response to colour half-tones and spot colour usage in newspaper design. Their results indicted that colour made a newspaper page more appealing, pleasant, and powerful, but had little effect on readers' evaluations of a paper's importance, value, or ethical quality.

The impact of graphics on reader understanding and comprehension has also been examined, and the studies have had fairly consistent results. Kelly (1985) found that embellished graphic presentations of data (as commonly used by *USA Today*) were no better than unembellished graphics in helping readers retain information. Ward (1992) investigated whether using a sidebar graphic illustration along with a news story aided comprehension. He found that bar charts, tables, and an adorned bar chart were less effective than a straight side-bar story that accompanied the main story in aiding comprehension. Pasternak and Utt (1990) found that readers look to 'infographics' for both content and design reasons and, though many readers found them appealing, a substantial proportion still had trouble understanding them.

Readability research

How easy is it for readers to follow newspaper stories? Whether or not readers can understand what they are reading, find it interesting and are able to read it without feeling they are being required to make a lot of effort could make a difference to whether they will return to read that publication again (Dale and Chall, 1948). Research has been conducted into the readability of newspapers and other printed media to establish how comprehensible its written style is likely to be found by readers. Several formulas have been developed to determine objectively the readability of text. These formulas attempt to measure the comprehensibility of the language used and the clarity associated with the text's grammatical structure. One of the best known formulas is the Flesch Reading Ease Formula (Flesch, 1951). This requires the researcher to systematically select 100 words from the text, determine the total number of syllables in those words (wl), determine the average number of words per sentence (sl), and compute the following equation:

Reading ease = $206.835 - 0.846wl - 1.015sl$
The score is compared with a chart that provides a description of style (such as 'very easy') or school grade level for the potential readership.

Another measure of readability is the Fog Index, which was developed by Gunning (1952). To compute the Fog Index, researchers must systematically select samples of 100 words each, determine the mean sentence length by dividing the number of words by the number of sentences, count the number of words with three or more syllables, add the mean sentence length to the number of words with three or more syllables, and multiply this sum by 0.4. Like the Flesch Index, the Gunning formula suggests the educational level required for understanding a text. The chief advantages of the Fog Index are that the syllable count and the overall calculations are simpler to perform.

McLaughlin (1969) proposed a third readability index called SMOG Grading (for Simple Measure for Gobbledygook). The SMOG Grading is quick and easy to calculate: the researcher merely selects ten consecutive sentences near the beginning of the text, ten from the middle, and ten from the end, counts every word of three or more syllables, and takes the square root of the total. The number thus obtained represents the reading grade that a person must have reached to understand the text. McLaughlin's index can be quickly calculated using a small, easily measured sample. Although the procedure is related to that of the Fog Index, it appears that the SMOG grade is generally lower.

Taylor (1953) developed yet another method for measuring readability called the Cloze Procedure. This technique departs from the formulas listed above in that it does not require an actual count of words or syllables. Instead, the researcher chooses a passage of about 250–300 words, deletes every fifth word from a random starting point and replaces it with a blank, gives the passage to subjects and asks them to fill the blanks with what they think are the correct words, and counts the number of times the blanks are replaced with the correct words. Nestvold (1972) found that Cloze Procedure scores were highly correlated with readers' own evaluations of content difficulty. The Cloze Procedure was also found to be a better predictor of evaluations than several other common readability tests.

Although they are not used extensively in print media research, readability studies can provide valuable information. For example, Fowler and Smith (1979), using samples from 1904, 1933 and 1965, found that text from magazines had remained constant in readability, but that text from newspapers had fluctuated. For all years studied, magazines were easier to read than newspapers.

Hoskins (1973) analysed the readability levels of Associated Press and United Press International wire copy and found that both services scored in the 'difficult' range; the Flesch indexes indicated that a 13th- to 16th-grade education was necessary for comprehension.

Fowler and Smith (1982) analysed delayed-reward content (national affairs, science, medicine, business and economy) and immediate-reward content (sports, people, newsmakers and movies) in *Time* and *Newsweek*. In general, delayed-reward items were found to be more difficult to read than immediate-reward items. Smith (1984) also found differences in readability among categories of newspaper content, with features and entertainment more readable than national–international or state and local news. Smith also noted that three popular readability formulas did not assign the same level of reading difficulty to his sample of stories.

Porter and Stephens (1989) found that a sample of Utah managing editors consistently underestimated the Flesch readability scores of five different stories from five different papers. They also found that the common claim that reporters write front-page stories at an 8th-grade level was a myth. The hard news stories they analysed were written at an average 12th-grade level.

Television narrative analysis

Experimentalists studying comprehension and memory for media content have devised and utilized methods of content classification. These methods are designed to identify critical features of narratives that may influence audience processing and uptake of information from that content. Much media effects research has characterized media content in fairly global terms. Thus, studies may investigate the impact of television programmes without distinguishing features within a production that may have been critical to facilitating the effects observed.

Some researchers have developed procedures for characterizing content within programmes in a systematic way, within the requirements of an experimental research framework. Collins (1983) conducted 'event analyses' (after Omanson, 1982) of television programmes in order to identify pieces of content and the relations between them. The results of event analyses are then used to obtain ratings of the programme and to generate items for comprehension testing.

Event analysis was used on programme plots. This analysis can identify plot-essential content items and relations between them. Event analyses are designed for deriving the structure of narratives, rather than fitting narrative content to predetermined, idealized story structures. Using this form of analysis, the researcher prepares lists of events to give to groups of mature viewers. These viewers are then asked to select those events without which the plot could not be effectively retold.

A more detailed level of analysis has been used by other researchers (Gibbons et al., 1986; Lorch et al., 1987). Based on propositional analysis (Kintsch and van Dijk, 1978), they analysed stories into 'idea units' such that each unit expressed a single idea or action. An event in the Collins analysis might subsume more than one unit. Memory for different types of units could then be compared without confounding the amount of information with the variable of interest.

Analysis of television formats

As well as analysis of narrative structures, other systems of classification have been devised to classify television productions in terms of their presentational features. Watt and Krull identified and developed a system of programme format analysis guided by Information Theory (Shannon and Weaver, 1949). Their work defined a number of specific production format attributes that were later used in experimental studies on audience comprehension and reaction (Krull and Watt, 1975; Krull, Watt and Lichty, 1977; Watt and Krull, 1974, 1975, 1976). This system of format analysis identified several major variables.

Shot complexity is the randomness of the apparent distance between the camera and the objects in view. Coders are required to assess if the camera is showing a close-up, medium or long shot and to depress a push button as long as each kind of shot lasts. A mini computer is used to keep track of the number of coders' responses and to perform complexity calculations after coding is completed. The range of values for shot complexity is continuous from zero, indicating that the camera showed only one kind of shot, to 1.5, indicating that the camera showed an even balance of long, medium and close-up shots. The purpose of this variable is to determine the effect of changing the camera's view of a scene.

Set complexity is the randomness of visual duration of physical locations in a programme. Coders are required to determine which of the shooting locations (or sets) that appear in a programme is in view and to depress a push button assigned to the location. The procedure of computing complexity scores from the raw data is analogous to that for shot complexity. If a programme contains only a few sets, set complexity scores are low; if a programme contains many sets, each appearing for about the same amount of time, set complexity is high. The purpose of this variable is to see the effect of adding locations for action. As number of sets increases, so too does viewer processing load.

Visual interaction complexity is the randomness of characters' making audible sounds. Coders are required to press a push button when a particular character makes an audible sound (not just speech). The complexity of the interactions (its randomness) is determined by means of the entropy calculations. The objective of this variable is to see the effect of spreading dialogue (and other audible behaviour) among a number of characters.

Modal complexity is the randomness of the programme's message being carried by the visual or verbal track. Coders already are required to press push buttons to assess the amount of verbalization to score verbal interaction complexity. Modal complexity is determined by indexing coders' responses in a different way. Rather than keeping the amount of verbalization of different characters separated, modal complexity is computed by aggregating the total amount of audible behaviour produced by all characters and comparing that with the total amount of time during which there is no verbalization. The purpose of this variable is to see the effect of presenting information both visually and verbally. If a programme's action is presented visually only, viewers can understand the action just by paying visual attention. If the action is presented aurally only, viewers can understand just by listening – or it may alternate between these two modes.

Visual presence of speakers is the extent to which characters speaking are shown on screen. Coders score programmes by pressing one of four push buttons to signify many speaking characters on screen, one character on screen, one character off screen, and many characters off screen (Husson and Hughes, 1981). An index, formed from the raw scores, has high values if there are many characters speaking and visible. The index has low scores if many characters are speaking off screen.

Visual – verbal congruence is the number of instances per unit of time that the object referred to by verbalization is present on the screen. Coders assess whether segments of verbalization have a visible, concrete referent and press a push button to record each occurrence of such verbalizations. Congruence is most likely to increase when characters speak about physical objects; congruence is most likely to decrease when characters issue verbalizations that deal with abstract and therefore non-visible concepts.

Using these variables, researchers have measured the production complexity of television programmes. Much of this research has been carried out with educational programmes made especially for children, such as *Sesame Street* and *Mister Rogers' Neighborhood* (Watt and Welch, 1983). Such analyses classify the visual and auditory complexity of programmes. Such data may then be subsequently linked to children's abilities to understand and learn from the programme's educational content.

Analysis of children's television formats

Another aspect of television format analysis, often conducted within an experimental paradigm, has focused upon the varying formats adopted by television programmes aimed at children. In many instances, researchers have been concerned with establishing the kinds of formal features that make up programmes that are important in relation to attracting and maintaining audience attention, often with the aim of establishing the most effective educational formats for television programmes oriented towards younger audiences.

Huston and her colleagues (1981) analysed the formal features of children's television programmes in the USA. They compared the production characteristics of animated and non-animated programmes, and the ways that formal features would vary with the intended audience for the programme or with the intended goals of the production (e.g. educational or entertainment). Two samples of children's programmes were selected from Saturday morning, weekday prime-time and daytime educational programming, taken mostly from the Public Broadcasting Service. The format analysis catalogued the pace and range of physical activity depicted in each programme, the number of scene changes and the tempo or speed of scene change. The analysis also coded the use of special visual and sound effects, and the use of music and loud noises. These features were labelled as 'perceptually salient', meaning that they were likely to be key ingredients responsible for attracting young viewers' attention to the screen.

Perceptually salient features, as such, tended to be characteristic of entertainment programmes on mainstream television, though even some educationally oriented programmes mimicked these techniques. Within educational programmes, however, it is vital that formal features enhance the educational objectives. The use of child dialogue is beneficial to maintaining the attention of child viewers, songs can also enhance learning of certain educational messages, and camera work can be utilized to draw attention to specific areas of content. Long camera zooms and slow presentation can emphasize important content and give young viewers sufficient time to process the information being presented.

Linguistic codes within children's programmes

In addition to production techniques and formal features that involve largely non-verbal content, the nature of the verbal language used in television programmes is important to audience learning and impression formation. The analysis of the language used in children's television, for instance, can help us to understand television's linguistic conventions and how they interact with each other. This kind of analysis is also important in the context of understanding how effectively children are likely to be able to learn from programmes. As with formal features, the types of linguistic codes used in programmes may be adjusted to suit different types of audience or different production objectives.

In a pilot study of the linguistic structure of children's programmes, Rice (1979) analysed 25 categories of linguistic characteristics across six programmes. The programmes included animated stories with a great deal, moderate amounts of, or no dialogue, a situation comedy, and educational programmes differing in age of intended audience (i.e. *Mister Rogers' Neighborhood* and *The Electric Company*). Three sets of linguistic descriptors were coded. *Communication flow* consisted of measures of length, variability, rate, and repetition of utterances. *Language structure* contained measures of grammatical completeness, descriptive qualifiers, and stressed single words. *Meaning content* variables included selective prominence given to specific language features, non-literal meanings, explicit instructions, novel words and immediacy of reference.

Distinctive patterns of language usage were evidenced in the two educational programmes. *Mister Rogers' Neighborhood*, the educational programme for pre-school children, contained a moderate amount of dialogue, avoided the use of words with non-literal meanings, but did use techniques designed to place emphasis on single words, with the aim of enhancing their young viewers' understanding of the meanings of these words. *The Electric Company* was a programme aimed at children in their early school years, and used rather more dialogue, and as well as stressing single words, introduced novel words and some non-literal meanings. It also attempted to educate children in the use of certain grammatical forms. This programme was concerned with the enhancement of children's reading skills, and it used intensive forms of verbal presentation to achieve this objective.

Unlike the educational programmes, the more entertainment-oriented programmes exhibited little evidence of attempting to adjust their language codes to the level of young child viewers. These shows often tended to be relatively low in terms of complexity of dialogue (though in some instances contained many short verbal utterances), but scored higher in terms of action, pace of presentation, number of scene changes, use of special visual and sound effects, and varying camera shots. These production features were designed to attract and hold the attention of young viewers through perceptually salient features that constantly caused children to re-orient their attention to the screen.

Coders' perception and audiences' perception

Content analysis involves the use of trained coders who catalogue incidents, events and occurrences according to a prescriptive framework devised in advance by the researcher. In using content analysis as a starting point for a study of audience effects, the main problem is that the characteristics of content coded by trained coders may not necessarily represent the most salient or significant ingredients of that content for audiences.

A content analysis study of violence on television for example may quantify the frequency with which specified acts of violence occur in a programme, but whether or not the violence as coded actually represents a salient feature of that programme for viewers is another matter. An assumption of some content analysis researchers that the technique can identify 'messages' that are also recognized and encoded by audiences who assimilate them into their existing knowledge structures is not always borne out by audience research.

Content analyses, from which inferences about media effects are often made, may actually be poor indicators of audience responses to media (Ceulemans and Fauconnier, 1979; Perloff et al., 1982).

Although content analysis can produce reliable codings of specific kinds of incidents, these codings may have relevance only for the original coders and may lack any real meaning for the general viewing public untutored in this coding methodology.

Problems arise when generalizing from statements about or descriptions of television content and the symbolic messages carried by that content to how content is perceived and understood by the audience. It is necessary to establish the degree of equivalence between the meanings attributed to programmes by trained coders and the meanings attributed to them by ordinary viewers. To what extent do the images and messages defined by content analysis share the same universe of meanings as the perceptions of viewers? With incidents such as shootings or fights, it may be relatively easy to achieve correspondence between programme structures defined *a priori* by a system of content coding and audience perceptions of content. But it may be less easy to accurately infer meaningful messages concerning norms or relationships unless direct information is obtained from the viewers (Gunter, 1981, 1985a).

Research with audiences has shown that structures such as those monitored in content analysis are not always perceived by viewers as salient attributes of programmes. Violent scenes may not appear as important aspects of content, and viewers may fail to mention violence in discussions about films containing violent action, shortly after viewing, unless specifically asked about such content.

In a field study conducted by audience researchers at the British Broadcasting Corporation (Shaw and Newell, 1972), viewers were asked to fill out a questionnaire about specific programmes shortly after they had been broadcast, in which reactions to violence and other aspects of programme content were probed. Findings showed that perceptions of programmes as 'violent' did not depend on the actual number of violent incidents. Nor was there any strong relationship between perceiving a programme as violent and verbally reported emotional arousal. Assessment of violence as unjustified, however, was associated with negative evaluations of the programme. Most respondents also claimed that 'realism' was an essential element in their perceptions, with real life events depicted in news and documentaries perceived as more violent than similar violence in fictional programmes.

Research has indicated that adults and children alike are capable of highly refined judgements about television violence. Viewers have their own scales for deciding the seriousness of incidents, and their opinions do not always concur with researchers' categorizations of violence.

Gunter (1985a) reported 12 experimental studies in which groups of people were shown scenes taken from British crime series, American crime series, westerns, science fiction series and cartoons. Viewers were invited to make a variety of personal judgements about each scene along a set of qualitative rating scales. Scenes were shown singly or in pairs for comparative judgement. Variations in perceptions of the scenes were examined in relation to a number of things – the types of programmes the scenes came from, the types of weapons or instruments of violence that were used, the physical setting of the action, and the degree of observable harm the violence caused to victims in each scene. The results indicated that viewers may be significantly influenced in their personal opinions about television violence by many of these attributes of television portrayals.

Familiarity of surroundings is one of the most powerful factors influencing viewers' perceptions of television violence (Gunter, 1985a; Gunter and Furnham, 1984). The closer to home the violence is portrayed as being in terms of place and time, the more serious it is judged to be.

Some results exhibited even more complex patterns. One illustration of this was a set of paradoxical opinions about violence perpetrated by law enforcers and by criminals, or by men and by women, which varied with the type of programme from which they came. With extracts from British crime series, for instance, viewers were most concerned about violence inflicted by men upon women; while in scenes from American series, they were concerned more by women being violent to men (Gunter and Furnham, 1985). In an American context, violence performed by criminals was perceived in more serious terms than that used by law enforcers (usually the police); while in British settings, it was law enforcer violence that viewers were more troubled by (Gunter, 1985a).

Children can make distinctions between different forms of violence on television as well. While young viewers may not have the maturity of adults, they readily learn to distinguish broad programme genres and the conventions to which they adhere in the kinds of portrayals they contain.

Two American studies conducted as part of the US Surgeon General's research programme on television and social behaviour nearly 30 years ago represented early attempts to assess children's perceptions of television violence. In both cases, young viewers' reactions were obtained to brief extracts taped from prime-time entertainment programmes on the American networks. Groups of boys, aged 11 and 14 years, were individually shown six different scenes of which four were violent and two were not. In all, boys' reactions were obtained to eight different violent scenes. Each set of violent scenes contained an instance of violence against property, non-fatal violence against another person, a killing by gunfire, and a second killing by other means (Greenberg and Gordon, 1972b).

Each violent scene was evaluated in terms of amount of perceived violence, liking, realism, and acceptability of observed behaviour. The researchers focused more on differences in ratings between the various socio-economic and ethnic groups who were sampled than upon differences in ratings due to the nature of the violent content. Even so, they did present tables of results showing the average scores per rating scale obtained by each of the eight scenes. These scores indicated that scenes that featured the death of a victim by shooting were perceived as the most violent scenes by both 11-year-old and 14-year-old boys. For the older group the next most violent scene was one which depicted death by a fiery car crash, whereas for the younger group, it was a scene showing a killing by suffocation. For both groups, the least violent scenes depicted a stylised fist-fight or showed someone smashing up furniture.

Although objective cataloguing of incidents in programmes has the useful function of providing reliable counts of how often certain categories of items occur, the relevance or meaning of those items for the audience can be properly ascertained only through the perceptions of viewers themselves. There would be some merit in recommending a subjective approach rather than a purely objective one in the analysis at least of televised violence because this perspective enables one to identify the programme that viewers themselves take most seriously. A subjective audience input to a content analysis can therefore render a useful embellishment to an otherwise dry approach to analysing the appearance of violence on television.

Limits to quantitative content analysis

Quantitative content analyses tend to be purely descriptive accounts of the characteristics of media output and often make few inferences in advance about the potential significance of their findings in the context of what they reveal about production ideologies or impact of media content on audiences. To achieve meaningful insights into media processes and effects, the right decisions have to be made about the aspects of media content to be analysed and classified. The most informative content analyses are therefore likely to be achieved if the analyst chooses content categories within some theoretical framework concerning media operations or audience cognitive, emotional or behavioural reactions. In the context of analysing television violence, for example, purely descriptive accounts of programme contents may have little value unless they are reinforced with some idea about how audiences are likely to respond to different classes of violent portrayal. Violent behaviour may be defined by researchers in different ways from the definitions that might be applied by audiences. Attributes of violence are counted as discrete entities, when they may have different levels of significance to audiences' perceptual reactions to specific behavioural acts on screen. There is a certain reductionism of content meanings with quantitative forms of content analysis, with the application of common weights to portrayals. This may result in an interpretation of the meaning of media content that differs from what was intended by the producer and from what is apprehended by the audience (McQuail, 1994).

A further limitation of quantitative content analysis is that 'it is assumed that definite meanings can be assigned within the coding process' (Bentele, 1992: 170). This reflects a simplistic approach to the structure of media texts. In essence, 'the possibility to unambiguously identify certain perceivable signs as words, sentences, text fragments, images, action sequences, and technical characteristics such as panning, zoom, etc. is taken for granted' (Bentele, 1992: 170). Indeed, the aspect of reproducibility, so important to Krippendorf in terms of the validity of the results of an analysis, reflects this assumption that textual meaning is fixed and quantifiable. Yet some important aspects of media content which researchers have aimed to measure are clearly not fixed attributes, and the personal attitudes of analysts play a major role.

QUALITATIVE CONTENT ANALYSIS

There has been a growth in media research using interpretive and hermeneutic styles and methodologies. Methods used include observation, depth interviews and various forms of qualitative content analysis. Qualitative content analysis procedures were influenced by the writings of Weber (1907), Blumer (1933), and Lévi-Strauss (1963).

Methods of analysing media texts other than quantitative content analysis have emerged from different epistemological and theoretical perspectives. Analytical tools deriving from disciplines such as literary criticism, films studies, and linguistics have been applied to the investigation of text structures and the production of meaning. The growth of these approaches to media analysis was illustrated by Hijmans (1996), who found 280 published studies that had used qualitative content analysis methods during the 1980–95 period.

A fundamental distinction between qualitative and quantitative methodologies can be found in the location of meaning in media texts. Quantitative content analysis emphasizes a fixed meaning of media texts that can be repeatedly identified by different 'readers' using the same analytical framework. Qualitative content analysis procedures emphasize the capacity of texts to convey multiple meanings, depending upon the receiver.

Krippendorf (1980) distinguishes two key concepts of *framework* and *logic* in relation to content analysis. The framework of a content analysis involves a clear statement of the main research question, the kind of data, the context relative to the data, and the naming of inferences from data to certain aspects of their context or the target of the inferences. That is to say that, to accomplish these inferences, the researcher needs to have an operational theory of the data – context relationships. Logic deals with the procedures involved in the selection and production of data, the processing of data, methods of inference and analysis, including the assessment of validity and reliability.

Hijmans (1996) distinguishes several types of qualitative content analysis:

1. structuralist-semiotic analysis
2. discourse analysis
3. rhetorical analysis
4. narrative analysis
5. interpretative analysis.

Structuralist-semiotic analysis

This approach is concerned with the deeper meaning of the message. The method is concerned, not with manifest content, but with structural relationships of representation in texts since 'It's not "content" that determines meaning but "relations" in some kind of system' (Berger, 1993: 7). The referential nature and symbolic meaning of the message is explicitly taken to be the subject matter of the analysis. The production of meaning is grounded in conventions, codes and cultural agreement. Modern semiological analysis, as such, stems from the work of Swiss linguist Ferdinand de Saussure and the American philosopher Charles Saunders Pierce.

The communication process is regarded as signs organized in systems called codes. Codes are conventions or agreements that connect a sign with its meaning. There are all kinds of codes: cultural codes, ideological codes, representational codes, language codes and so on. Semiotic analysis is mainly descriptive. Sign systems, signification, representation and signifying practices are identified and subsequently interpreted, for example as ideological complexes.

De Saussure (1966 [1915]) divided the 'sign' into two components; the 'signifier' and 'signified'. The former is the sound image or visual image of the spoken or written word, while the latter is the object or concept it linguistically represents. Pierce distinguished three aspects of signs – iconic, indexical and symbolic. Iconic aspects comprised things that could be visibly seen. Indexical aspects comprised the recognition of relationships or causal connections between phenomena, such as links between symptoms and disease or between smoke and fire. Symbolic aspects of signs comprised learned meanings associated with linguistic forms (e.g. words). The relationship between the concept and sound-image of a sign is arbitrary (Berger, 1993).

In a media context, semiology is concerned with how meanings are generated in media texts, such as films or television programmes. Semiology examines signs and the relations between them. In doing so, it separates content from form and concentrates on the system of signs that make up the text. In determining the meanings conveyed by signs, de Saussure introduced another critical notion, and that is that relations among signs tend to be oppositional in nature. If something is described as 'hot', its real meaning can only be established by making comparisons with things deemed to be 'cold'. There can be no understanding of happiness unless there is also a concept of what it means to be sad.

In interpreting the meanings conveyed by media content, therefore, the semiologist identifies the signified and signifier aspects of signs and the relationships that exist between these two aspects within that particular text. Berger (1990: 136–7) illustrates how this form of analysis can be undertaken through a reference to the television science fiction series, *Star Trek*:

> Any one who has seen the program knows that it is a space adventure/science fiction series. We know this because we are 'told' so at the beginning of each episode. When the *Starship Enterprise* is sent on a mission in outer space – to explore new worlds and seek out new civilizations, to 'boldly go where no man has gone before', we can say that science fiction adventure is the general 'signified' and that numbers of signifiers are given to show this. For example, we find rocket ships, futuristic uniforms, ray guns, advanced computer technology, extraterrestrials with strange powers (such as Mr Spock, whose pointy ears signify that he is only partly human), and magic/science, among other things.

These are all associations we learn and use to interpret new texts with which we come into contact. Signifiers can change meaning, however. Over time, new associations and new meanings can become attached to signifiers. In a semiological analysis of media, the main concern is to establish how meaning is created and communicated through stories or narratives. Signs can be identified within media texts and, through the analysis of relationships between signs, meanings can emerge.

A further important distinction in semiological analysis is between the *synchronic* and the *diachronic*. A synchronic study of a media text looks at the relationships that exist among its various elements, while a diachronic study looks at the way the narrative evolves. A synchronic analysis examines patterns of paired oppositions within the text (or its paradigmatic structure), while a diachronic analysis focuses upon the chain of events (the syntagmatic structure) that forms the narrative.

A syntagm is a chain, and syntagmatic analysis looks at the text as a sequence of events that together form a narrative structure. Propp (1975 [1928]) analysed fairy tales for their major themes. Propp was concerned with analysing texts into their constituent 'functions'. Function in this sense represented an act of a character defined from the point of view of its significance for the course of the action. He identified 31 functions characteristic of fairy tales. Each involved a form of action on the part of a character in a story. Functions were believed to constitute fundamental components of a tale. These functions also always occur in the same sequence or order within a tale. Thus, all fairy tales are of one type in regard to their structure. Propp's ideas can be adapted to analyse media productions such as films and television programmes. A paradigmatic analysis involves searching for a hidden pattern of oppositions that are buried in it and generate meaning. The search for binary polar oppositions is important because meaning is based upon establishing relationships and the most important relationship in the production of meaning in language is that of opposition. There has been some debate about the meanings semiologists purportedly identify through the analysis of oppositions in texts. Critics argue that such oppositions are not really there, but are created by semiologists themselves. However, if meaning is fundamentally dependent upon oppositional relations, which on careful reflection is a notion that makes sense, oppositions must be present somewhere in the text otherwise it is difficult to conceive of how meaning could be apprehended at all.

Relationships between words and the concepts that lie beneath them must be learned. Meaning is constructed by linguistic or other sign systems, and the structural conventions or codes that determine the way meaning is constructed must be learned in each case. The media contain a number of codes relating to print media, television and film production, or the attributes that characterize specific genres of narrative story-telling. Knowledge of these codes is produced culturally and socially and, just as with the language a person speaks, the codes that make up these media sign systems are learned through experience (Bentele, 1992).

Semiotics acknowledges that individuals' knowledge of the codes of representation may differ, and also other codes of meaning (associated with a person's class, gender or ethnic group, for example) influence the understanding of media messages. Varying interpretations of the same media content can therefore occur across members of an audience. Hall (1980) identified three broad categories of reception: 'preferred', where receivers accept the interpretation of events offered in the content; 'negotiated', where receivers accept some of the preferred interpretations but reject others; and 'oppositional', where receivers fully reject the interpretation of events presented.

Although meaning is not seen as fixed in semiotics, with texts open to a range of interpretations, analysis of content can uncover a particular interpretation. Hall contends that content is structured in a way that produces a 'preferred reading' or the meaning the producers of the text intend the receiver to accept (Hall, 1980). Semiotic analysis of content can assess the *encoded* messages of the producers, which represent the latent ideological assumptions of the content. Semioticians examine the use of codes in the media, and news especially, since ideological positions are reflected in the kinds of representations that appear. The general belief of theorists such as Hall is that the professional codes of news media such as the choice of presentation occasions and formats, the selection of personnel, the choice of images and the staging of debates invariably contribute to the reproduction of a particular dominant ideology (Hall, 1980).

Structuralism is aimed at the myth underlying the narrative or story of the message. Myths are considered to be deep structures that represent the essence of human nature and society. Thus, attention is focused on the social functions of myth (Lévi-Strauss, 1963). Narrative analysis is often the initial phase of structural analysis because of the related concerns with chronological and logical structure and morphology of the narrative. The main difference consists of the subsequent decoding of symbolic systems in terms of characters, positions and oppositions relative to each other.

Research is generally aimed at contemporary cultural phenomena such as advertising, television drama or documentaries, and at revealing their hidden meaning. Goldman (1992) and Goldman and Papson (1994) aimed at decoding ideological complexes in advertisements. McLaughlin (1991) studied the image of prostitutes in television serials, and Parry-Giles (1994) analysed a documentary on the problem of Northern Ireland.

This type of content analysis is theoretically inspired and aims at the latent meanings of the media message. This analysis can have a layered character if the message is first analysed into narrative elements and subsequently searched for deeper meanings. Although concepts like myth and code are frequently used, it remains unclear what they imply in terms of the procedure; that is, the research accounts are poorly detailed in a methodological respect. Just as with any other form of qualitative research, the results of the analysis depend heavily on the qualities of the researcher as a competent member of a culture.

Structuralist analysis has been applied to advertising. Leymore (1975) reports one such analysis in which more than 250 television advertisements were sampled from American television over a four-year period. Six campaigns were chosen for competing products, with each product being a standardized, mass-produced, low-expenditure item. Transcripts of the advertisements were produced covering product categories such as packaged foods, beef curry, chop suey, chicken curry, and paella. The products resembled each other closely in terms of price, availability and convenience.

Structuralists make certain assumptions about the nature of the world and people's perception of it. There are three key aspects to this: (1) the perceived world can be structured into binary oppositions of the form A/not-A; (2) there are deep and universal rules that underlie individually-occurring incidents or events; and (3) these rules and relationships among elements can be studied as a closed whole. As we have seen, the binary assumption is based on an approach in linguistics associated with de Saussure (1966 [1915]) who believed that meaning in language is based on opposition. It was also held that there were deep and universal rules underpinning the use of language, regardless of variations in language usage associated with cultural or social contexts. In other words, all languages are underpinned by a common set of competences or capabilities that all humans possess (Chomsky, 1965). Language can therefore be analysed in terms of these deep-seated rules underpinning it as well as in relation to variations in its social usage.

Leymore's analysis began by describing each advertisement in terms of what was happening in it. In one case example concerning a pre-packaged meal product, the advertisement depicts two children being put to bed followed by their parents being shown settling down for a romantic dinner for two in which they use brand X. This dinner is then interrupted by the children waking up and demanding attention.

In applying a structuralist analysis of this advertisement, the researcher first identifies a number of binary opposites. Thus, brand X is associated with a romantic dinner for two, doing something special and the idea of creating an exotic atmosphere (the product was for a spicy foreign food product). In opposition to these associations, the concept of 'not brand X' can be linked to notions such as looking after the family, doing something routine and consuming something ordinary. Having identified these binary opposites, the researcher must then proceed on to the next stage of uncovering a common, underlying theme that underpins these implicit messages. In this case, the theme could be unusual versus usual. Thus, brand X is unusual, while consuming some other brand is more likely to be usual or nothing out of the ordinary. This kind of strategy can then be applied to other advertisements in a search for common themes running through advertising more generally. Leymore (1975) reported that this approach managed to identify common themes as such in the advertisements she sampled. Thus the strategy of structuralist interpretation is to begin with an initial observation of an advertisement, to create a hypothesis (unusual versus usual) about it, and then to test this hypothesis against other advertisements.

Discourse analysis

Discourse analysis, as well as being an aspect of semiotics, can be seen as a form of critical linguistics (Fowler, 1991). Discourse has been used to refer to written text, but it has also been used in connection with audio-visual media. Its application to the media grew out of semiotic studies attempting to assess the meaning of language in terms of its implicit ideological assumptions, and discourse analysis pays specific attention to the linguistic component of language use in the media.

Discourse analysis contends that 'news is a representation of the world in language ... it imposes a structure of values, social and economic in origin, on whatever is represented. News is a representation in the sense of construction; it is not a value-free reflection of "fruits" ... each particular form of linguistic expression in a text – wording, syntactic option, etc. – has its reason. There are always different ways of saying the same thing, and they are not random, accidental alternatives. Differences in expression carry ideological distinctions (and thus differences in representation)' (Fowler, 1991: 4).

The method asserts that underlying ideological positions, perceptions of power relations and producers' level of interest and authority, can therefore be determined from the textual structure of media content (van Dijk, 1983). According to one writer, the content of newspapers is not facts about the world, but in a very general sense 'ideas'. Thus, analyses of media discourses can assess 'the ideological practice of representation' through language (Fowler, 1991: 5).

Knight and Dean (1982) analysed and compared newspaper coverage of the same event in two newspapers. Jensen (1987) analysed news programmes on US network television and showed a particular ideological vision of the US economic system, referred to as a 'news ideology'. Wonsek (1992) focused on racism in the media, notably the portrayal of black basketball players on television. Harwood and Giles (1992) highlighted the role of agemarkers in the humorous context of the television series *The Golden Girls*. Griffin, Hacket and Zhao (1994) examined the portrayal of the peace movement in news editorials during the Gulf War.

Racism and the Press (van Dijk, 1991) serves as an example of this type of analysis. It consists of several parts in which news articles on ethnic themes are analysed. Van Dijk starts with an analysis of the semantic macrostructures, or the overall characteristics of meanings concerning ethnic minorities. This macrostructure consists of a conventional 'news scheme' or superstructure, as a hierarchical organization of news item categories. Ethnic minorities are depicted as problematic groups as van Dijk illustrates by means of descriptive categories. Subsequently, editorials were analysed to reconstruct their underlying ideological vision. Here the focus was on composition and structure: definition of the situation, the nature of the explanation and the moral of the story.

The procedure in most discourse analyses consists of a layered combination of several techniques. Specific linguistic analyses (e.g. choice of words such as 'riots' instead of 'disorders', or the search for textual patterns) and rhetorical strategies are followed by thematic analyses. This is a general form of content analysis to determine the main topics in a text. In most cases, but not all, it is followed by a macrostructure analysis, in which the interrelationship between topics in a text is represented in diagram form. Thus discourse analysis can be both general and detailed at the same time. The detailed analysis is rhetorical in nature. A problem with discourse analysis is that the critical stance of researchers using it may render its forms of analysis biased.

Rhetorical analysis

Central to rhetorical analysis is the question of how the message is presented visually or textually. It is broadly a kind of stylistic analysis – the organization as well as the presentation of a message and the choices the communicator has made are at the core of this type of analysis. It focuses on distinctive features such as composition, form, use of metaphors and structure of argumentation or reasoning.

The supply of information in news and current affairs programmes is a popular subject. Pitiela (1992) analysed news fragments from Finnish newspapers. Sorenson (1991) engaged in rhetorical techniques employed in the news coverage of the famine in the Horn of Africa. Potter and Wetherell (1994) and Potter et al. (1991) questioned the rhetorical use of quantification in an English documentary on cancer research. Kaplan (1992) and Durand (1987) detected visual metaphors in adverts.

Rhetorical analysis implies a reconstruction of the composition or organization of a directly observable and perceptible message by way of a detailed reading of fragments or larger units of text or visual matter. It involves unravelling formal external characteristics of the language and/or imagery used. Sometimes emphasis is laid on the construction and therefore syntactical properties of a text, sometimes the stress is put on pragmatic aspects of language use, and therefore on communicator choices, practices and strategies. Procedures in rhetorical analysis are primarily focused on qualities of the plain text.

This form of text analysis has been conducted on advertising messages. Through examining the rhetorical devices employed in advertisements, some researchers have argued that it is possible to dissect the contents of commercial messages to understand better how their persuasive purpose is operationalized. One such study identified five rules of interpretation of advertising. Under this framework of analysis, commercial messages were examined for their use of exhortations to buy or use a product or service and for their use of other devices often linked to human drives to persuade consumers to choose the advertised brand over others. In addition, guidelines were drawn up for reading the text of the advertisement, its subtle use of words, phrase and images (Andren et al., 1978).

In this study, the researchers sampled 300 advertisements from the largest circulating weekly and monthly magazines in the USA. They attempted to characterize the rhetorical devices used in these advertisements. The analysis itself was driven by a view that advertisements exhort people to buy products or services, and that they use special production techniques and linguistic devices to achieve that end.

Narrative analysis

This also focuses on formal structure, but from the perspective of narrative. The narrative distinguishes itself from other texts by a clearly marked beginning and ending. Narration itself involves the handling of characters and plot and of resulting patterns. In this type of analysis it is not so much the characteristics of the plain text as the characters themselves that are crucial as well as their acts, their difficulties, their choices and the general developments (see Propp, 1975 [1928]).

All kinds of media products and media contents, such as films, television series, documentaries and news accounts can be described from a narrative point of view. Newcomb (1981) analysed an entire evening (three hours) of prime-time television in America. Deming (1985) examined the innovative character of the well-known police series *Hill Street Blues*. Liebes and Livingstone (1994) examined the correspondence between the narrative structure and the structure of family ties or kinship structure, in English and American soap operas.

In narrative analysis, texts are considered as stories. The message is taken to be a presented or edited version of a sequence of events, of which elements are described and characterized as to their structure. The procedure focuses on the reconstruction and description of the narrative structure on the basis of acts, choices, difficulties and of events happening to characters. There are strict forms of analysis (Burke, 1969; Chatman, 1978), and other more impressionistic styles of narrative analysis.

Interpretative analysis

This form of qualitative content analysis is mainly of social scientific origin. This is shown in its design and procedural elements. Research methods are clearly spelled out. Coding rules are more explicitly explained. There are also often clear links between theory and method.

Research subjects are in no way different from those of the other methods. Liebes (1992) compared accounts of the Intifadah (on Israeli TV) with accounts of the Gulf War (on US TV). Dahlgren (1980) also examined TV news. White and White (1982) analysed the representation of Vietnamese boat refugees in the Australian press. Weber and Laux (1985) examined the use of the term 'stress' in the media. Alexander (1994) detected trends in the utilization of children in advertisements. Altheide (1992) examined the relation between news and media in general and extraordinary judicial sanctioning, such as public confession of guilt in the media. Altheide (1985, 1987) also examined several aspects of the production of news. Griffin et al. (1994) compared cultural stereotypes in adverts in India and the USA.

Researchers employing interpretative content analysis ask descriptive research questions aiming at the discovery and formation of theory. Analysis procedures are cumulative and comparative. This does not mean that the researchers enter the field without any theoretical notions nor that the illustration of theoretical concepts could not be the research objective. Both may be the case. Data serve to discover new findings, and therefore the procedure is such that in the end one knows more than at the beginning. The relation between data and concepts is fundamentally open; concepts serve to arrange data and to understand them in a substantially new way. Sampling is theoretically informed: researchers choose cases for strategic reasons because they represent the phenomena under study in a particular way. Cumulative analysis with open beginnings, sensitizing concepts that guide observation and analysis, testing of theoretical insights on empirical data, adjustments of concepts and working with temporary hypotheses are signals of interpretative content analysis. With the interpretative procedure, the methodology is always clearly spelled out.

CONCLUDING REMARKS

This chapter has examined methodologies concerned with analysing media output. As with media audience research, a broad distinction was made between quantitative and qualitative methodologies. In the former case, research attempts to produce descriptive accounts of media content in which discrete, predefined elements are counted and classified. The basic units of analysis may comprise the identification of themes, or the frequency of occurrence of specified categories of action or incident, or types of actor – whether an individual, group or institution. Further descriptive characteristics of these entities may also be catalogued. The end result is an analysis of how often particular entities occur, together with some additional information about their media location (e.g. position in a newspaper, type of programme, etc.).

Media content can also be analysed in a more qualitative fashion. In this case, a certain amount of counting may still be involved, but the depth to which media texts are assessed is the distinctive factor. The research may utilize analytical techniques that are designed to probe subtleties in the use of language, the construction of narratives and the types of information that are selected by media producers for presentation to an audience. In this form of analysis, however, the interest centres not just on the appearances that are made by certain themes, information sources, or categories of actor or incident, but with the way they are presented, the choices that are made (i.e. the selection of certain sources or actors, the omission of others), and the way themes, sources or actions are juxtaposed. Thus, a whole variety of subtle patterns of linguistic and production formats can be analysed to uncover meanings that may not immediately be apparent from a purely quantitative frequency count of content elements.

Since content analysis is often used to draw inferences about media effects or, in tandem with audience research, to understand audience reactions, it is essential to utilize a form of analysis that will be able to reveal the full range of potential meanings being conveyed by media content. Although it may be important to establish, through quantitative techniques, whether certain entities outnumber others or enjoy more prominent locations, since this information may indicate the probability with which certain types of messages will be apprehended by audiences, the identification of the messages themselves may require qualitative procedures.

CHAPTER 4

MEASURING MEDIA USAGE AND EXPOSURE

One of the fundamental questions asked about the media by researchers is to what extent are they used? How often or how much are audience members exposed to media? The question of media exposure is vital for a number of reasons. First of all, if the media are to have any impact, they must be experienced. A newspaper that is never read or a television programme that nobody views will have no impact. In connection with demonstrating or establishing media influences, therefore, there has to be some measurement of media exposure. Second, the media do not simply represent social phenomena with social and psychological influences of academic interest, they are also commercial entities. This means that they are unlikely to survive without patronage. Even publicly funded media services will have a significantly reduced probability of continuation if they attract no interest from their targeted consumers. Thus, for reasons of establishing their financial viability as well as their social, cultural and psychological impact, it is important to collect evidence about the size and shape of media audiences and their patterns of media usage.

There are various groups who have a vested interest in obtaining regular access to information about media usage and the size of their consumer markets and audiences. Producers of television programmes and films made for theatrical showing, broadcast schedulers, newspaper and magazine editors all need to know the extent to which their media products are being consumed. Audience data represent one form of performance assessment for these media professionals. Media owners require such information to guide future business strategies, to reach decisions about the competence of the people they employ, and to sell their organizations and services to business clients such as advertisers and sponsors. Buyers of advertising and sponsors of media outputs need to know whether their money has been well spent, by assessing whether particular media channels have delivered the market exposure they had expected.

Programme makers, broadcast schedulers and the editors of publications need to know how their media outlet is performing in terms of attracting audiences or readers, and maintaining market share in the face of competition from other media outlets. When a new publication, channel, station or programme is launched, media producers need to know how well it has performed. Programme scheduling, for instance, needs detailed information on the behaviour of viewers, including how often they switch between channels, the points at which they do so, whether they return to a programme every time it is broadcast, whether they view at regular times across the week, and so on.

Media owners operate in two distinct markets. The first market comprises the public consumers of their particular medium. The second market consists of advertisers to whom they hope to sell opportunities to communicate with purchasers or potential purchasers of the goods and services advertisers are offering. Media owners need to be able to convince potential advertisers that their particular medium will reach a given audience in terms of both size and composition, and that brand awareness will grow and product trial and purchase will increase as a result.

In buying opportunities to communicate with an audience, advertisers and sponsors need to decide which media or combination of media to use; which channel, station, or publication to use; how much to spend; what messages or content to convey; and when, where and how often to convey those messages. To select media or channels or publications, advertisers need information on audience or readership size and makeup. The latter measure involves an assessment of the demographic composition of audiences and readers (sex, age, socio-economic class, marital status, number of children, etc.), or possibly in terms of lifestyle, values and psychological classifiers. This information can then be related to advertising costs to determine the most cost-effective means of communicating with potential customers. Operating on behalf of the advertisers and sponsors are the advertising agencies, media consultants and other specialists, who depend on detailed information for all media so that they can advise clients on the effectiveness of different media in the context of achieving their objectives.

Key audience measures

The key concepts of media usage activity include such behaviours as attendance (cinema), watching (television), listening (radio) and reading (newspapers and magazines). Although common-sense notions of what each of these activities entails may seem to render them not worthy of detailed consideration, they do in fact represent complex concepts that can be defined in many different ways. Does 'watching' television comprise simply looking at the screen, or can one be 'watching' even when not visually attuned to the set? From a practical or operational definitional point of view, how long is it necessary to be pursuing that activity to be considered a 'viewer' or someone who has 'watched' a particular item, whether that item is a programme or an advertisement? How should one define a newspaper reader? Is this a person who reads a particular newspaper every day, or just occasionally? To be considered someone who has 'read' a newspaper, is it necessary to have read it through from beginning to end, or to have read only parts of it? If one has simply 'looked' at the paper, glancing at some of the photographs and headlines, can one still be considered to be a 'reader' of that publication? All these definitional issues present researchers with a complex array of questions to be addressed. One significant reason why they need to be resolved is that they have a crucial bearing on how media usage is actually measured.

For television audiences, 'watching' may mean simply being present in the room where a television set is switched on, or it may entail being in the room and indicating via a paper diary or electronic recording device that attention to the screen is taking place. Some systems of measurement may accept as evidence of watching a viewer's claim that a particular programme had been seen. Other systems require viewers to have watched television continuously for a minimum threshold of seconds or minutes. A listener to a radio programme may be anyone claiming in a face-to-face interview to have listened to more than half a programme or it may be somebody who has indicated *any* listening in a specified period. The possibilities of defining what counts as 'reading' a newspaper are equally varied.

DATA CAPTURE TECHNIQUES

Information about audiences or readers is the product of data collection and analysis. There are a number of instruments that are designed to capture data in a systematic manner. The resulting data may be qualitative, consisting of words, phrases, commentary, narrative or text, or they may be quantitative, arising as numbers that emerge from a process of measurement. Traditionally, in audience measurement on a large scale, three principal measurement instruments have been used:

1. questionnaires
2. diaries
3. electronic recording devices.

These measurement devices represent the techniques most frequently used by industry researchers whose business needs feed off the collection of reliable, quantitative data about audiences. Other research techniques have also been applied to analyse media audiences, including qualitative audience research techniques prized more by critical social scientists. Among the other techniques are:

4. experience sampling
5. observation
6. in-depth interviews.

A brief discussion of each of these techniques follows, before we turn to examine specific fields of application.

Questionnaires

This type of research instrument does two things. First, it lists all the questions a researcher wishes to address to each respondent, and second, it provides space or some mechanism for recording the responses. Questionnaires vary in the extent to which they are structured. An unstructured questionnaire may be just a checklist of open-ended questions with spaces for writing in the replies in the respondent's own words, producing qualitative, textual data. At the other extreme are fully structured questionnaires which list all the questions to be asked, put them in a logical sequence, specify the precise wording that is to be used, and provide predefined categories for recording replies.

The idea of such questionnaires is that all the questions are standardized and asked in the same way, so that responses from different individuals can be counted up and compared. In practice, questionnaires are often a mixture of structured, semi-structured, and unstructured elements so that only a few of the questions give rise to qualitative data. Semi-structured questions arise where respondents are asked to write in specific pieces of information which then need to be classified and coded later back in the office after the interviews have taken place.

Questionnaires, whatever the degree of structuring, are of two main kinds: (1) those that are completed by the respondent; and (2) those that are completed by an interviewer on behalf of the respondent. Self-completion questionnaires are usually posted to respondents. Interview-based questionnaires are usually administered face-to-face or via a telephone call.

Diaries

These instruments are distinguished by the fact that they capture data on consumer behaviour longitudinally, that is, on an individual-by-individual basis over time. Furthermore, they require the respondent to complete an entry every time that behaviour occurs over the time period to which the diary refers. Usually, diaries are self-completed. They may be placed personally with respondents by an interviewer or sent by post. They may then be collected personally or returned by post. Diaries are most closely associated with television and radio audience research, although time-use diaries may collect data on all kinds of activities, including reading behaviour.

Some media diaries are fully structured or pre-coded with a listing of all the channels, stations, or even programmes that may be received in a market area. Other types of diaries may be unstructured, leaving respondents to write in entries. Media diaries often tend to arrange entries by time segment on a daily basis. Time segments tend to be in 15-minute or 30-minute periods identified down the left-hand side of the page. The channels, stations or programmes will be listed across the top. The respondent is then asked to indicate all segments in which listening or viewing took place.

There are a number of sources of potential error in diary keeping. The diary keeper may forget to enter their listening or viewing in the diary.

This will often be because instead of making entries as they go along, many respondents will try to remember the details of their media-related behaviour perhaps a couple of days after it has occurred or may attempt to recollect their entire week's viewing or listening at the end of the week. Then mistakes occur through faulty memory or erroneous recording. The diary may be deliberately falsified either by omission of some media use, or by the inclusion of imaginary uses. Another source of inaccuracy will occur whenever the diary keeper is unaware of media use or activity by other members of the household.

Electronic recording devices

These methods of media usage measurement tend to be largely confined to television, although there have been attempts to use them with other media. Their use for radio, the print media and poster audience research is limited by the complexity of the environment in which media use activity occurs.

In its original form, electronic data collection methods in television audience research were restricted to measuring set usage only. The meter detected whether the television set was switched on and the channel to which it was tuned. It did not measure the behaviour of viewers, however. Viewers had to declare their presence in front of an active television set by completing a paper diary in which they marked the time periods or programmes they watched. Set data were stored in a meter attached to the television set. Tapes containing metered set data and diaries containing audience 'presence' data had to be collected each week and thus took much longer to process.

An enhancement of this methodology was introduced in the 1980s with the introduction of a television audience measurement device called a 'people meter'. The electronic set data collection component was retained, although the set meter was plugged into the telephone system. The paper diary was replaced for the collection of data from members of the audience by a handset through which viewers could register their presence in front of a television set by pressing a button. Thus, viewer data and set data were now both electronically stored in a set-top recording device linked to the home telephone system. Data could then be pulled off this storage device overnight for 'next day' estimation of audiences.

Experience sampling

This represents a methodology that was developed not exclusively to measure media use. Rather, it is a technique that can be used for measuring any behaviour that occupies a person's time across any given day. Within this context, however, the technique can also be used to detect when individuals are consuming mass media. The experience sampling method involves the collection of data through the self-reports of individuals that are made at random times during the waking hours of a normal week. The scheduling of these self-reports is controlled by a one-way radio communication. Each research subject carries a pocket-sized electronic paging device for a period of up to one week as well as a booklet of self-report forms. Radio signals are emitted according to a pre-determined random schedule. They may be able to operate over as much as a 50-mile radius from the transmitter. The radio signals cause the 'pager' to give off audible beeps that serve as the stimulus for subjects to complete a self-report form. The form asks a number of questions about the subject's behaviour at that particular point in time. In one study that used this methodology, signals were transmitted to subjects approximately every two hours (Kubey and Csikszentmihalyi, 1990).

Observational measures

In Chapter 2, observational measures were divided into participant and non-participant versions. In participant observation, the researchers record their observations about the behaviour of their subjects while physically present in the same environment and while interacting with those individuals. In non-participant observation, researchers may or may not be physically present in the observed situation, and do not interact with their subjects in any way. In some studies, observations are made remotely with the help of audio-visual recording equipment. Video recordings might be made of subjects' behaviour and the resulting tape-recordings are later analysed by the researcher.

Participant observation studies of television usage have entailed the placement of an observer in a sample of households. Often, the researcher becomes a temporary, part-time, live-in companion of the observed house-holders. In such situations, the researcher may eat with the occupants and will spend evenings with them while they watch television, observing how they watch and how they decide what to watch (e.g. Lull, 1978, 1980).

In non-participant observational studies of television viewing, several studies have been carried out using photographic or video equipment to capture what takes place in front of the television screen. Still cameras have been used to take time-lapse still photographs of householders as they watch television (Allen, 1965). This sort of visual evidence has fairly limited value, however, because it only provides an indication of who was physically present while the set was switched on, and how often the viewing room was left empty while the set was playing. Other researchers have used video cameras to capture time-lapse, semi-animated, visual records of viewers' behaviour in front of their television set (e.g. Anderson et al., 1985).

The best usage of video camera equipment derives from obtaining continuous video footage, including sound. In this way, it is possible not just to measure physical presence in front of the set, but also varying amounts of visual attention to programmes and comments that viewers make about what they are viewing (e.g. Bechtel et al., 1972; Collett and Lamb, 1986; Gunter et al., 1995).

In-depth interviews

This approach to data collection from media audiences has been promoted by media scholars who adhere to critical and interpretative forms of social scientific enquiry. Depth interviews have been carried out with family groups in their own homes in television viewing periods. For example, Morley (1986) interviewed 18 families in this way. Parents in the household were interviewed on their own, and then were later joined by their children in a wider discussion about television. Interviews lasted one to two hours and were tape-recorded and transcribed for full analysis. The study investigated what householders watched and how they reached decisions about viewing.

These, then, are the principal data collection methods that have been used in media audience research, where the focus has been placed upon measurement of audiences. The remainder of this chapter will examine different fields of application of audience measurement methodologies, under two headings – print media research and electronic media research – before finally turning to address the potential of more qualitative approaches to understanding audiences.

PRINT MEDIA RESEARCH

Research with magazines and newspapers was one of the first areas of mass media research. In the USA, for example, initial interest came from colleges and universities. In 1924 the *Journalism Bulletin* was first published by the Association of American Schools and Departments of Journalism. An article written by William Bleyer on 'Research problems and newspaper analysis' presented a list of possible research topics in journalism. Among them were the effects of form and typography on the ease and rapidity of newspaper reading, the effects of newspaper content on circulation, and the analysis of newspaper content (Bleyer, 1924).

In Britain, print media research began in the 1920s with the analysis of press circulations by the London Research Bureau (LRB) in 1928, followed by other circulation-related surveys by the LRB for the Institute of Incorporated Practitioners in Advertising (IIPA) in 1930, 1931 and 1932, a report on *Investigating Press Circulations* from Repfords in 1932, and *The Readership of Newspapers and Periodicals* survey produced by the Incorporated Society of British Advertisers (ISBA) in 1936. The earliest formal British research into individuals' readership was probably carried out by Gallup for J. Walter Thompson in 1932, followed by research from the London Press exchange in 1934 (Brown, 1994).

During the Second World War, newspaper reading was of equal interest to sociologists and to the coalition government of the day. That period saw the publication of *Newspaper Reading in the Third Year of the War* by Allen and Unwin; *Newspapers and the Public* from the Central Office of Information in 1943, and surveys by Mass Observation in 1941, 1942 and 1944. The year 1947 saw the publication of research from Attwood Statistics of another *Survey of Press Readership* by the IIPA and the first of the *Hulton Readership Surveys* from the Hulton Press. The Hulton series continued until 1954 when the IIPA took over responsibility for the design, commissioning and publication of regular surveys. From this research initiated by the IIPA just before the Second World War grew the present-day series of National Readership Surveys (NRS) in the UK. Over the years a great deal of methodological work was carried out on the NRS.

Much early print media research was qualitative. It focused on topics such as press law, history and ethics. Then, quantitative research began to emerge during the 1930s. This was often concerned with reader interest in newspaper or magazine content. The 1930s also saw the publication of many studies designed to assess the results of print media advertising. This led to studies in applied research, and several publications began sponsoring their own readership surveys. This research tended to be proprietary.

Wilbur Schramm (1957) published an article in *Public Opinion Quarterly* in which he reviewed 20 years of research published in *Journalism Quarterly*. He found that only 10 per cent of the 101 articles published between 1937 and 1941 concerned quantitative analyses. By 1952–56 nearly half of the 143 articles published were quantitative, a fivefold increase in just 15 years. The reasons identified for this growth were: (1) the growing availability of basic data; (2) the development of more sophisticated research tools; and (3) the increase in institutional support for research.

By 1960, newspapers and magazines were competing with television and radio for audience attention and advertiser investment. In the USA, this spurred the growth of private sector research. The Bureau of Advertising of the American Newspaper Publishers Association (now called the Newspaper Advertising Bureau) began conducting studies on all aspects of the press and its audience. In the 1970s, it founded the News Research Center, which reports the results of research to editors. The Magazine Publishers Association also began to sponsor survey research at this time.

In 1976, the Newspaper Readership Project was instituted to study the problem of declining circulation and sagging readership. One major part of the six-year, $5 million study was sponsoring research into newspaper reading habits. A news research centre was set up at Syracuse University to abstract and synthesize the results of more than 300 private and published studies. The Newspaper Advertising Bureau produced dozens of research reports and conducted extensive focus group studies. In addition, regional workshops were held across the country to explain to editors the uses and limitations of research. By the time the

Readership Project ended, most editors had accepted research as a necessary tool of the trade (Bogart, 1991). Research activity in the newspaper business grew rapidly during the 1970s. In 1977 the Newspaper Research Council (NRC), a subgroup of the Newspaper Advertising Bureau, was incorporated with 75 members. By 1992 this group had expanded its membership to more than 200 researchers. During the 1990s, the NRC has been involved with the American Society of Newspaper Editors in a circulation retention study with the International Newspaper Marketing Association on how to convert Sunday-only readers to daily readers.

Types of print media research

Two basic types of print media audience research will be distinguished: (1) readership research and (2) circulation research. Readership research is concerned with surveying readers to find out how they use newspapers or magazines. Circulation research examines the sales and distribution of media publications (see Brown, 1994).

Readership research

Many of the early readership studies were carried out in the USA before and during the Second World War. The George Gallup organization was a pioneer in the development of the methodology of these studies – a personal interview in which respondents were shown a copy of a newspaper and asked to identify the articles they had read. The most complete survey of newspaper readership was undertaken by the American Newspaper Publishers Association (ANPA), whose *Continuing Studies of Newspapers* involved more than 50,000 interviews with readers of 130 daily newspapers between 1939 and 1950 (Swanson, 1955).

Readership research became important to management during the 1960s and 1970s as circulation rates in metropolitan areas began to level off or decline. Concerned with holding the interests of their readers, editors and publishers began more than ever to depend on surveys for the detailed audience information they needed to shape the content of a publication. The weak economy of the early 1990s and increasing competition from other media have made readership research even more important today.

The oldest method that was American in origin was the *Through-the-Book* technique. This method is now only in limited use. It has been used to measure newspaper and magazine readership. Its history dates back to 1936 when the magazine *Life* discovered that several of its issues were selling out almost as fast as they reached the newstands. People who wanted to read them were therefore forced to obtain them from purchasers. It followed that circulation figures *per se* could not reflect the total readership of *Life*.

A method was developed which involved sampling the population, showing people a particular issue, taking them through it page by page and asking if they had read key articles. It was recognized that people might make false claims, confusing an issue shown them but previously unseen, with another, similar one they *had* read. A 'confusion control' correction was therefore introduced: pre-publication issues were shown to a sample of people and the proportion claiming to have read them (which was impossible) was applied to the TTB (Through-the-Book) scores for 'live' issues.

Confusion control demanded a costly research technique with difficult logistics, whilst corrections seldom amounted to more than one or two per cent of the TTB levels. It has been completely succeeded by the 'editorial interests' variant of the TTB approach. Here, people are taken through a specific issue, as before, and asked 'Does this look interesting?' in relation to each of a number of key items. This completed, the interviewer asks, almost as a throwaway 'Just for the record, are you sure you have (haven't) seen this issue before, or aren't you certain about it?' The levels of 'yes, sure' replies obtained when this approach was first introduced were very close to the original TTB claims, after confusion control correction.

There have been other changes to this research technique over the years. Researchers used to measure readership for one publication only. A later variant on the technique introduced the measurement of readership for more than one publication at a time. Skeleton issues were produced as prompts, rather than adopting the more cumbersome approach of using whole issues or numerous publications. These reduced issues nevertheless contained enough information about each issue to enable respondents to indicate how much they had read. Given the large number of publications available today, a further modification to the original approach is to use filter questions at the beginning of the interview to narrow down the list of publications about which more-detailed questions will be asked.

Another method is the *Recent-reading* survey, a technique developed in Britain in the 1950s. The recent reading method relies on the recall of having read any issue of a particular publication, rather than on the recognition of a specific issue as previously seen, as in the case of the through-the-book technique. In the recent-reading method, people are prompted on each of a number of newspapers and/or magazines, either in terms of just their titles or, more usually, by being shown their logos. Other prompts are also used, such as sets of typical or recent front covers. For each publication, a key question or series of questions then establishes when a person claims to have most recently read or looked at any issue of that publication. It does not matter whether the issue was a current one or not; the reading can have taken place anywhere and the issue seen may or may not have been the personal property of the reader. The recent-reading method then goes on to argue that an unbiased estimate of the number of people seeing the average issue is provided by the number reading any issue within a period of time immediately preceding the day of interview and equal in length to the interval between the appearance of successive issues – seven days in the case of a Sunday newspaper or weekly magazine – the 'issue period'.

There are two problems in particular with this technique. First, the accuracy of its measures depends on readers being able to report precisely when they last saw an issue of a particular publication. This is not easy to achieve when contact with a given newspaper or magazine is irregular or infrequent. Second, there is an in-built bias in the method. A person may read and re-read a single issue over an interval longer than the issue period. Issues of a weekly magazine may be retained and looked at over several weeks.

Another methodology called *First Reading Yesterday* (FRY) was devised to overcome problems inherent in the recent-reading technique. It focuses on newspapers and magazines a respondent saw 'yesterday' – the day before the interview - and, for each publication encountered on that day, the FRY method establishes whether the issue that was seen was ready yesterday for the first time. It is then argued that the number of 'first time readers yesterday' multiplied by the number of days in the issue period provides an estimate of average issue readership (although the calculation method employed in practice differs somewhat from this).

Using FRY, memory strain is minimized and recall accuracy maximized, by going no further back in time than 'yesterday', whilst the possibilities of both over- and underestimating readership are eliminated since, however many times a publication is picked up and over however long a period it is read, for one reader and one issue, there can be only one first reading occasion. In countries where FRY is developed – the Netherlands and Denmark – the use of FRY has become linked to Computer Assisted Telephone Interviewing (CATI) as the data collection method.

A more complex method of data collection and print media usage is the *readership diary*. Respondents are invited to maintain a day-to-day record of the publications they see. This record would normally be kept for one or two weeks, although some readership diary studies require respondents to keep a continuous record of their reading habits for much longer periods. The diary format and diary-keeping task can vary. The list of newspapers and magazines on which data are sought can be printed on each diary page or a look-up directory of publications can be provided to the diary keeper, with a code beside each title. This code has to be copied onto the appropriate space when a reading event takes place. Time periods – days or day-parts – may be pre-printed in the diary, or the respondent called on to record when reading took place, as well as what was read. Varying amounts of subsidiary information on each reading event may be called for, which might include the date or serial number of the issue read, whether it was a 'first reading' occasion or not, the source of the copy, or where the reading took place. The readership diary possesses two distinguishing characteristics. First, it provides a longitudinal record of a person's reading over a period of time, whereas recall methods tend to focus on single points in time. Second, a diary (in theory) captures reading events at or close to the time that they occur.

Strengths and weaknesses of methods

Each of the methodologies for measuring print media usage described above has its own distinctive advantages and weaknesses. The through-the-book technique represented a thorough method in its original form. Later variants in which filter questions were used in order to accommodate more economically surveys of reading of large numbers of publications, became more reliant on respondent memory and also restricted detailed questioning to just a few publications. There is another problem in the use of issues that are five or six weeks old for weeklies or 10 to 12 weeks old for monthlies as prompts. Readers who have only just begun to read a publication may exhibit no recollection of reading such prompt issues, if their publication date preceded the time of onset of their patronage of the publication in question.

The recent-reading technique gets over the weaknesses of the through-the-book technique. Even so, the number of people seeing any issue in a certain period is not an unbiased estimate of the number having contact with the average issue. 'Replicated' and 'parallel' reading can occur – biasing effects work in opposite directions – but are not always equal. Recent reading estimates critically depend on readers being able to state with precision when they last read or looked at any issue of a publication. In addition, evidence of 'telescoping' – reading events long ago are perceived as having occurred closer to the date of interview than was actually the case – can also have unequal effects on readership estimates.

The first-reading-yesterday approach should eliminate most problems arising from telescoping (because the recall period is so short) and all of 'model bias' (since first reading comprises a unique event in relation to one person and a particular issue). However, there are other problems associated with this technique. 'First reading' will not be as clear-cut an event for the respondent as it is for the researcher. It is quite a subtle concept and any erroneous categorization of reading events as between 'first' and 'not first' may have a critical effect on the readership estimates. Second, the sheer number of reading events taking place 'yesterday' across the FRY survey's sample will be small; the distribution of reading occasions will be particularly 'thin' for publications published at relatively long intervals and for those with relatively small circulations. Consequently, to give adequate precision, either data must be accumulated over some very considerable period or probabilities must be estimated by aggregating 'similar' titles within a publication group, which can only have the effect of erroneously smoothing out any real differences. Third, the estimation of average issue readership on the basis of a period shorter than the issue interval can introduce statistical problems and widen the error margins of the final estimates.

With the readership diary, there should be no problems with recall, provided the diary is kept continuously. With self-completion diaries, respondents may not always be that thorough. Not every title may be treated equally. Prompt lists may not be fully used. Diary-keeping will in reality often not occur concurrently with media usage. Further, out-of-home reading may not be as fully captured as in-home reading, and this may prejudice against some titles.

Reader profiles

A reader profile provides a demographic summary of the readers of a particular publication. This information can be used to focus the publication, prepare advertising promotions, and increase subscriptions. Such information is particularly helpful when launching a new publication. Because there may be significant differences in the nature and extent of newspaper reading among individuals who have the same demographic characteristics, researchers recently have turned to psychographic and lifestyle segmentation studies to construct reader profiles.

Item selection studies

This type of newspaper readership study is used to determine who reads specific parts of the paper. The readership of a particular item is usually measured by means of *aided recall*, whereby the interviewer shows a copy of the paper to the respondent to find out which stories the respondent remembers. In one variation on this technique the interviewer pre-selects items for which readership data are to be gathered and asks subjects about those items only.

A cheaper way of collecting these data is to conduct telephone surveys. Calls are made on the same day the issue of the paper is published. The interviewer asks the respondent to bring a copy of the paper to the telephone, and together they go over each page, with the respondent identifying the items he or she has read. Although this method saves money, it excludes from study readers who do not happen to have a copy of the paper to hand.

Another economical technique is to post respondents a self-administered readership survey. There are two variations on this theme. In the first case, the 'whole copy' method is used in which respondents receive an entire copy of the previous day's paper in the mail, along with a set of instructions and a questionnaire. The instructions direct the respondents to go through the newspaper and mark each item they read by drawing a line through it. A return envelope with postage pre-paid is provided. In the second case, a 'clipping' method is used. This procedure is identical to the first method except that respondents are mailed clippings of certain items rather than the whole paper. To save postage costs, the clippings are pasted up onto a page and photo-reduced by 25 per cent (Hvistendahl, 1977). A 67 per cent return rate has been found using this method.

Whole copy and clipping methods have been found to produce roughly equivalent results, though readership scores on some items tend to be slightly higher when clippings are used. Stamm et al. (1980) suggested a more detailed method of item-association analysis, which they called a tracking study. They supplied their respondents with a selection of coloured pencils and asked them to identify which parts of an article (headline, text, photo, cutline) they had read, using a different coloured pencil each time they began a new *reading episode* (defined as a stream of uninterrupted reading). The results showed a wide degree of variability in the readership of the elements that made up an item: for one story, 27 per cent of the subjects had read the headline; 32 per cent the text; and 36 per cent the cutline. There was also variation in the length and type of articles read per reading episode.

The unit of analysis in an item-selection study is a specific news article (such as a front page story dealing with a fire) or a specific content category (such as crime news, sports, etc.). The readership of items or categories is then related to certain audience demographic or psychographic characteristics. Using this technique, Larkin and Hecht (1979) found that readers of non-metropolitan daily papers read news about local events the most and news about national events the least. In another survey, Lynn and Bennett (1980) divided their samples according to residence in urban, rural or farming areas. Their survey found that there was little difference in the type of news content read by farm and rural dwellers, but that urban residents were more likely to read letters to the editor, society items, and local news. Griswold and Moore (1989) found that readers of a small daily newspaper most often read local news, obituaries, police news, state news, and weather forecasts.

A 1991 study found that, among a national sample of US adults, the general news and entertainment sections of the paper were read the most and the classified and 'Home' sections were read the least. Item-selection studies are often used to help newspapers reach certain groups of readers (Simmons Market Research Bureau, 1991).

Some item-selection studies have used comprehensive surveys that encompass many newspaper markets. For example, the Newspaper Research Council sponsored a national survey examining selection patterns for approximately 80,000 newspaper items. This study which occurred in 1984, found that item readership nationwide was characterized by a high degree of diversity. In a second study, Burgoon et al. (1983) surveyed approximately 6,500 adults in ten newspaper markets to identify clusters of items and topics that interested readers. Respondents were asked how often they typically read items dealing with about 30 topics normally found in the newspaper. Natural disasters or tragedies and stories about the national economy were the most read.

Reader – non-reader studies

The third type of newspaper readership research is called the *reader – non-reader study*. This type of study can be conducted via personal, telephone or mail surveys with minor modifications. It is difficult, however, to establish an operational definition for the term *non-reader*. In some studies, a non-reader is determined by a 'no' answer to the question: 'Do you generally read a newspaper?'. Others have used the more specific question, 'Have you read a newspaper yesterday or today?'. The rationale being used here is that respondents are more likely to admit they have not read a paper today or yesterday than that they never read one.

A third form of this question uses multiple-response categories. Respondents are asked, 'How often do you read a daily paper?' and they are given five choices of response: 'very often', 'often', 'sometimes', 'seldom' and 'never'. Non-readers are defined as those who check the 'never' response, or in some studies, 'seldom' or 'never'. Obviously, the form of the question has an impact on how many people are classified as non-readers. The largest percentage of non-readers generally occurs when researchers ask, 'Have you read a newspaper today or yesterday?' (Penrose et al., 1974); the smallest number is obtained by requiring a 'never' response to the multiple-response question (Sobal and Jackson-Beeck, 1981). Once non-readers have been identified, researchers typically attempt to describe them by means of traditional demographics.

Several non-reader studies have attempted to identify the reasons for not reading a newspaper. The data for these subjects have generally been collected by asking non-readers to tell the interviewer in their own words why they do not read. These responses are analysed and the most frequently given reasons are reported. Poindexter (1978) found that the three reasons named most often by non-readers were lack of time, preference for another news medium (especially television), and cost. Bogart (1991) identified four reasons: depressing news, cost, lack of interest, and inability to spend sufficient time at home. Lipschultz (1991) discovered that non-readers relied more on radio and television for news, found newspapers too costly, perceived papers as neither interesting nor useful, and thought that newspaper reading took up too much time.

Readership frequency

Once it was thought that establishing whether a person was a reader or non-reader of a publication was sufficient. As media markets developed, it became important to publishers and their advertisers to know whether people were regular readers or frequent readers. Information on reading frequency is important for a number of reasons.

First, an advertiser will usually be more often concerned with placing a series of adverts in a publication over time than only in a single issue. Over the period of a campaign, two figures will be of particular interest to the advertiser: how many people will have any chance of contact with the advertising ('coverage') and how often will the average reader have an opportunity of seeing an advertisement ('frequency'). The balance between these two figures is entirely determined by the regularity with which people see the title concerned. The larger the proportion of regular readers amongst its total readership, the lower the coverage, but the higher the frequency.

Second, regularity is highly correlated with other material features of the readership. For instance, people who purchase or subscribe to their own copy of a newspaper or magazine will usually be more regular readers than those to whom copies are passed on. Readers in the first group will also be prone to read the issues they see relatively more thoroughly and intensively. Third, it may be possible actually to estimate average issue readership size on the basis of people's claims about their frequency of reading.

As with readership itself, obtaining unbiased estimates of reading frequency is not easy. Four alternative approaches may be distinguished: (1) claims from the same group of people about their readership of just two different issues of a publication; (2) direct observation of behaviour over several issues; (3) asking a sample of respondents questions about their claimed regularity of reading, with answers taken at face value; and (4) posing questions about claimed readership and then employing an indirect method of turning answers into probability-of-reading estimates.

The through-the-book technique can be used here. Respondents are re-contacted at a second interview and questioned on their readership of different issues of the same publication as they were first shown. From their answers, it is possible to calculate audience 'turnover' – the proportions of the readership of issue one who did and did not read issue two. It is also possible to use a mathematical model to estimate readership build-up across successive issues.

Looking directly at reading behaviour over successive issues requires continuous measurement. A diary method may provide insights here, but it does not capture everything about reading. If completed thoroughly, a diary can provide indication of how many reading episodes the reader engaged in and which issues of newspapers or magazines were read on each occasion. Gaps or time lags in entries of issues read mean that diary data need to be treated with care.

Uses and gratifications studies

This approach is used to study all media content. In the newspaper area it is used to determine the motives that lead to newspaper reading and the personal and psychological rewards that result from it. The methodology of the uses and gratifications perspective is straightforward: respondents are given a list of possible uses and gratifications and are asked whether any of these are the motives behind their reading.

Several studies have taken this approach to explain readership. McCombs (1977) found three primary psychological motivations for reading newspapers: the need to keep up to date, the need for information, and the need for fun. Reading for information seems usually to be the strongest motivator. Weaver et al. (1979) found that the three motivations most common in explaining general media use are the need to keep tabs on what is going on around one, the need to entertained, and the need to kill time. These authors also noted differences among demographic groups regarding which of these needs were best met by the newspaper. For example, young males, young females, and middle-aged males were most likely to say they used a newspaper to satisfy their need to keep tabs on things, but they preferred other forms of media for entertainment and killing time.

Elliott and Rosenberg (1987) took advantage of the 1985 newspaper strike in Philadelphia to survey the gratifications of readers during and after the strike. They found that people deprived of a daily newspaper turned to other media to fill the surveillance/contact function, but the researchers found no evidence of compensatory media behaviour for the entertainment, 'killing time', and advertising functions associated with newspaper reading. Payne et al. (1988) studied uses and gratifications as indicators of magazine readership. They found three main classes of gratifications: surveillance, diversion and interaction. In addition, readers' scores on these three categories were consistent with the magazine they chose to read.

Editor – reader comparisons

In the final area of newspaper readership research, editor-reader comparisons, a group of editors is questioned about a certain topic, and their answers are compared with those of their readers to see whether there is any correspondence between the groups. Bogart (1989) presented two examples of such research. In one study, a group of several hundred editors was asked to rate 23 attributes of a high-quality newspaper. The editors ranked 'high ratio of staff-written copy to wire service copy' 1st; 'high amount of non-advertising content' 2nd; and 'high ratio of news interpretations... to spot news reports' 3rd. When a sample of readers ranked the same list, the editors' three top attributes were ranked 7th, 11th and 12th, respectively. The readers rated 'presence of an action line column' 1st; 'high ratio of sports and feature news to total news' 2nd; and 'presence of a news summary' and 'high number of letters to the editor per issues' in a tie for 3rd. In short, there was little congruence between the two groups in their perceptions of the attributes of a high-quality newspaper.

In a related study, Bogart (1991) gave readers an opportunity to design their own newspaper. Interviewers presented a sample of readers with 34 subjects and asked them how much space they would give to each in a paper tailor-made to their own interests. Major categories of news were omitted from the listings because they were topics over which editors have little control. When the results were tabulated, the contents of a sample of newspapers were analysed to see whether the space allocation made by editors matched the public's preferences. The resulting data indicated that readers wanted more of certain content than they were getting (consumer news; health, nutritional and medical advice; home maintenance; travel) and that they were getting more of some topics than they desired (sports news; human interest stories; school news; crossword puzzles; astrology).

Magazine readership research

Magazine readership surveys are fundamentally similar to those conducted for newspapers but tend to differ in the particulars. Some magazine research is done by personal interview; the respondent is shown a copy of the magazine under study and is asked to rate each article on a four-point scale ('read all', 'read most', 'read some' and 'didn't read'). The mail survey technique, also frequently used, involves sending a second copy of the magazine to a subscriber shortly after the regular copy has been mailed; instructions on how to mark the survey copy to show readership are included. For example, the respondents might be instructed to mark with a check the articles that they scanned, to draw an X through articles read in their entirety, and to underline titles of articles that were only partly read.

In the USA most consumer magazines use audience data compiled by the Simmons Market Research Bureau (SMRB) and Mediamark Research Inc (MRI). Both companies select a large random sample of households (about 19,000 homes) and interview readers. Company interviewers show respondents cards with magazine logos printed on them and ask if the respondents have read or looked through that particular magazine. If the response is 'yes', MRI asks more specific questions to pinpoint recent readership, whereas SMRB shows respondents a recent issue of the magazine and asks them to indicate what articles they have read. Since the two research companies use different techniques, their readership data do not always agree, and this discrepancy is a source of some concern to the magazine industry.

Many magazines maintain reader panels of 25–30 people who are selected to participate for a predetermined period. All feature articles appearing in each issue of the magazine are sent to these panel members, who rate each article on a number of scales, including interest, ease of readership, and usefulness. Over time, a set of guidelines for evaluating the success of an article is drawn up, and future articles can be measured against that standard. The primary advantage of this form of panel survey is that it can provide information about audience reactions at a modest cost.

Circulation research

The second major type of print media audience research is circulation research. The term *circulation research* is applied to two different forms of newspaper and magazine study. The first type of circulation research uses a particular group of readers as its unit of analysis. It attempts to measure circulation in term of the overall characteristics of a particular market – for example, to determine the proportion of households in a given market that are reached by a particular newspaper or the circulation pattern of a magazine among certain demographic groups.

Tillinghast (1981) analysed changes in newspaper circulation in four regions of the USA and found that the greatest decrease had occurred in the East and the South. He also reported that the degree of urbanization in a region was positively related to circulation. In a study of 69 Canadian daily newspaper markets, Alperstein (1980) discovered that newspaper circulation was positively related to the proportion of reading households within the newspaper's home city. In addition, daily newspaper circulation was found to be inversely related to weekly newspaper circulation. Lacy and Fico (1991) demonstrated that measures of the content quality of a newspaper were positively related to circulation figures. Lacy and Sohn (1990) found limited support for the hypothesis that the amount of space given to specific content sections in metropolitan newspapers will correlate with circulation in suburban areas. Earlier, Blankenburg (1981) analysed market structure variables and determined that county population and distance from the point of publication were strong predictors of circulation.

Another trend in circulation research has involved using computer models to predict circulation. *Playboy*, for example, collected data for 52 issues of its publication on number of copies sold, cover price, current unemployment statistics, dollars spent on promotion, number of days on sale, editors' estimates of the cover, number of full-page displays, and several other variables. These figures were subjected to a regression analysis to determine how each factor was related to total sales. Number of copies distributed, number of days an issue was on sale, and cover rating proved to be good predictors, but amount of money spent on promotion was found to have little impact on sales.

Blankenburg (1987) generated a regression equation to predict circulation after newspaper consolidation. Guthrie et al. (1988) also developed a regression equation and used theirs to predict metropolitan circulation in outlying counties. They found that the two most important predictor variables were an index of magazine circulation and an index of local newspaper competition for each county.

The second type of circulation research uses the individual reader as the unit of analysis to measure the effects of certain aspects of delivery and pricing systems on reader behaviour. For example, McCombs et al. (1974) studied why people cancel their subscriptions to newspapers. They found that the primary reasons had less to do with content than with circulation problems, such as irregular delivery and delivery in unreadable condition.

Magazine publishers often conduct this type of circulation research by drawing samples of subscribers in different states and checking on the delivery dates of their publication and its physical condition when received. Other publications contact subscribers who do not renew to determine what can be done to prevent cancellations. In recent years, several newspapers have researched the effects of price increases on their circulation. Studies have even been conducted to find out why some people do not pay their subscription bills promptly.

ELECTRONIC MEDIA USAGE

History

During the early years of broadcasting in the 1920s, there was little concern about audiences. Broadcasters (radio) were hobbyists and enthusiasts who were mostly interested in the technical side of the medium. The potential popularity of radio was unknown. During the 1930s, this situation changed. Radio became a popular mass medium for information and entertainment. As the audience for radio stations grew, so too did concerns about how radio would be financed. In the USA, it was decided that advertising was the most viable source of financing. In other countries, such as Britain, funding came via government. In commercial broadcasting regimes, advertising began to appear on radio. Advertisers were interested in knowing to what extent their commercial messages were reaching audiences, whom they were paying to reach (see Beville, 1985).

Advertisers and not broadcasters were therefore initiators of much early audience research in broadcasting. Once commercials were heard on air, advertisers wondered how many listeners were exposed to their messages and how effective those messages were. Broadcasters were thus compelled to provide empirical evidence of the size and characteristics of their audience. In addition to information about audience size, advertisers became interested in why people behave the way they do. This led to the development of the research area known as *psychographics*. Such data were not always precise enough, however. Other procedures were devised using *lifestyle* data and how they related to media usage. This information could be valuable to advertisers in designing advertising campaigns; if advertisers understand the lifestyle patterns of the people who purchase their products, they can design commercials to match these lifestyles.

Radio ratings research

When radio first became popular and advertisers began to see its potential for attracting customers, they were faced with the problem of documenting audience size. The print media were able to collect circulation figures, but broadcasters had no equivalent 'hard' information – merely estimates. The early attempts at audience measurement failed to provide adequate data. Volunteer mail from listeners was the first source of data, but it is a well-known axiom of research that volunteers do not represent the general audience. Advertisers and broadcasters realized that better data were needed.

From 1930 in the USA, when a group called the Cooperative Analysis of Broadcasting conducted one of the first audience surveys for radio, several individuals and companies have attempted to provide syndicated audience information. However, the bulk of syndicated information for radio and television stations and cable companies has been provided by two companies: A.C. Nielsen and Arbitron for local markets and network television and cable television, and Arbitron for local-market radio. The USA is divided into over 200 'markets' where no city is included in more than one market. A third local market radio ratings company, Birch Radio, entered radio research to compete with Arbitron, but went out of business on 31 December 1991.

Although Arbitron has provided ratings for both local-market radio and national networks, the company does not currently provide national network ratings information. Arbitron uses diaries to collect radio estimates and produces a variety of radio market reports. The only network radio ratings are gathered by Statistical Research Inc., which is hired by networks to produce a RADAR report (Radio's All-Dimension Audience Research).

Radio audience measurement

Radio is a broadcast medium that presents a number of different problems in the measurement of its audiences. Twyman (1994) listed the following problems with radio audience measurement: recall of radio listening tends to be more difficult than for other media; radio tends to be used as a companion rather than a medium to which primary attention is directed; listeners are often mobile, either listening while driving or moving around the house; unlike television, radio programming tends to flow continuously rather than being a series of unique broadcasts; radio is highly fragmented and there are many more radio stations than television stations to distinguish between; as a poorer medium than television, radio tends to invest less in audience research.

Many of these factors work together to affect recall of radio listening experiences. Listeners have to remember when they were listening by remembering where they were listening. If they were moving around at the time of listening, this may prove difficult. The large number of radio stations can also render memory for the particular station listened to at a certain time very difficult.

Research techniques

Research techniques vary according to a number of key dimensions:

- the criterion of 'listening' that they impose
- how far they reduce cooperation bias and sample the entire population
- their degree of reliance on unaided and unprompted memory
- the mode of data capture.

The first of these concerns refers to the question: 'How seriously do I have to have been listening to count?'. For example, some people may believe that their listening does not count when others choose the programme and are in control of the set. The issue of potential cooperation bias is an important one. There is a tendency in all media research for those most readily accessible to research to be more accessible to the media. People will have an inclination not to participate in research about something they do not do very much. It is therefore important to make sure that those who are not so committed to the medium also take part. When asking people about their listening, very different results will be achieved when they are given lists of programmes that have been or will be broadcast in their area compared with being simply asked to recall unaided what programmes they listened to. Prompted lists will produce much more reported listening, as will the thoroughness of attempts to help respondents to reconstruct their day (Twyman, 1994).

The mode of data capture is clearly of major importance in terms of what kind of radio listening is retrieved by the respondent. The major categories are:

- systematic recall
- diaries
- general habit questions
- coincidental interviewing
- recording devices.

Systematic recall

This involves asking people to reconstruct a previous period and report what listening occurred. This could be done for earlier periods on the day of interview or for several previous days. Usually, however, the method is day-after recall (DAR) and the respondent goes through the previous day and, it is hoped, identifies the occasions and content of radio listening that took place 'yesterday'. The interviewing can be conducted by telephone, but in the UK has usually been applied in face-to-face interviews.

Diaries

The respondent is asked to keep a diary of radio listening for a period of time. Thus a week or more of data can be derived from one interview.

Again, there is an immense variety of techniques available. Diaries may be personally placed and collected, or either or both of these operations may be conducted by post.

Diaries vary considerably in terms of layout. They may have time scales to be ticked or they may require entries to be made of times for starting and finishing listening sessions. Stations may be printed for the listener to tick, or he or she may have to write in the station listened to. In consequence, diary studies, like recall studies, are not equivalent.

Diaries have the advantage that they minimize reliance on memory – although much depends on when the respondent chooses to complete the diary. If it is not completed at the time of the measured behaviour, then entries will be reliant on memory accuracy. Diaries offer prompts to memory, however, by providing the names of stations or programmes possibly listened to.

General habits

Questions can be asked of respondents about when they usually listen and what they usually listen to. These can be expressed in terms of estimated frequency of listening to different stations at different times. Major problems are that much radio listening is not based on habit, certainly not to anything like the degree that television is, with its series or serials, nor like much of press readership. The task for the respondent is to summarize a whole range of casual events without being provided with the context or content cues to reconstruct even a single day. Thus, with this kind of analysis, there is a risk of underestimating radio listening where casual listening is a high proportion of the whole.

Coincidental interviewing

This involves interviewing people about their radio listening at the moment of interview. It is most appropriate to the measurement of in-home listening levels, but with a great deal of effort, samples of car-drivers (e.g. at traffic lights) have been asked about listening in North American studies. The coincidental approach is prohibitively expensive for any regular measurement.

Recording devices

Radio metering was, in fact, used long before its application to television. The first radio meter patent was filed in 1929 in the USA. The Nielsen Radio Index ran from 1936 to 1964 and combined metered measurement of the tuning of a sample of sets with diaries to measure listeners per set and the demographics of the audience. The demise of the Nielsen service was due in large part to the steady growth in car radios, the explosion in the number of portables, and the rise in multi-set ownership. Technologically, these problems could be overcome, but at great cost.

Comparisons of techniques

Research has been done to compare the effectiveness of these research techniques. The earliest study was by the All Radio Methodology Study (ARMS, 1967), carried out in 1965 for the Advertising Research Foundation. This compared five diary and three recall methods against a standard of in-home listening derived from a telephone coincidental interview (N = 28,000). Key conclusions were:

- day-after recall (DAR) techniques produce lower listening levels;
- covering other media at the same time depresses reported radio listening levels;
- weekly radio-only diaries with personal placement and collection give the nearest result to the standard.

Another North American study for the American Research Bureau/RKO General Broadcasting (1965) showed broadly similar results from comparing in-home listening from a multimedia diary, a radio-only diary, a telephone interview and a telephone coincidental, although it was the multimedia diary that checked out best with the coincidental standard.

Research in Germany, reported by Franz (1991), provides a special case where recall was conducted so thoroughly that it yielded listening levels similar to those for diaries. Here, respondents reconstructed their previous day in great detail, recalling all activities, including radio listening. This 'daily routines' approach was used with recall and with diaries, both yielding higher listening levels than conventional radio diaries. The study showed that if enough care is taken to reconstruct memory, then recall of listening to radio can match the levels obtained by the diary, which prompts people to take note of their behaviour.

From Canada the Bureau of Broadcast Measurement (1973, 1974–75) reported the results of a test comparing the existing two-media diary that combined radio and television with a revised version of this diary and a radio-only diary. Compared with the existing diary the modified two-media diary slightly reduced levels of in-home radio listening, while the radio-only diary increased them. A telephone coincidental check on radio listening levels revealed that the radio-only diary returners were heavier radio listeners than non-returners, and that the radio-only diary keepers were recording their levels of listening accurately.

Television ratings research

The measurement of viewing is fundamental to television research. Within the television industry, audience measurement is important to judge the performance of programmes, to guide decisions about programme scheduling, and for advertising planning and trading. The accurate measurement of television viewing also has importance in the context of more academically-oriented research concerned with the investigation of relationships between television viewing and public opinion or social behaviour.

In television audience measurement, four basic measurement approaches can be distinguished: (1) questionnaires and interviews; (2) electronic set-use recording with self-completion paper diaries; (3) people meter technology; and (4) passive observational or other behaviour-recording systems.

Questionnaires and interviews

These methods have already been introduced in an earlier part of this chapter. However, there are specific points worth making here about the use of techniques dependent upon viewers' self-reports about their use of television. When asked about their viewing, people give varying answers which depend upon the kind of question asked. The more precise the focus, the lower is the amount of estimated viewing. For example, asking people about how much television they watch in an 'average day' produces higher viewing estimates than does asking them about 'viewing yesterday'. One reason for this difference is that respondents do not factor-in their non-viewing days when judging their average amounts of viewing overall (Robinson, 1969). Probing for information about viewing by asking for reports about television watching at specific times of the day or in terms of which programmes were watched can lead to still lower estimates of amount of viewing.

Simple electronic meters

The earliest television audience research relied upon memory for viewing events either the next day or when a weekly diary was eventually filled in. Diary-based viewing estimates were generally provided in terms of viewing by quarter-hour time slots across any given day or by endorsing the watching of specific named programmes listed chronologically channel by channel.

Electronic meters were developed to measure the precise timing of switching between channels on the set, with individual viewing still being measured approximately by diary. As we will see in the next section, people meters added push button handsets so that viewers could record their viewing in real time, theoretically with the same precision that channel switching was measured (Twyman, 1994). For many years, industry measurement of television audiences depended upon combining data from two separate sources – an electronic set meter that recorded data only about set activity and paper diaries that collected data from viewers about their presence in front of the television set. The electronic meter in this system registered when a set was switched on and the channel to which it was tuned.

Even the electronic meter system evolved over time. An early version that was introduced in the United States by the Nielsen company comprised an instrument that recorded radio usage on a moving roll of paper. This 'audimeter' was introduced in 1936. The modern day version, called a storage instantaneous meter, is a much more complex device that records the time each set in a household is turned on or off, the broad-casting station to which a set is tuned, the length of time for which the set is switched on, and any channel switching that occurs. Data are retrieved from each household through an automatic telephone data retrieval system.

A second television audience measurement system is run in the USA by Arbitron. This system collects metered data via its television meter (TVM), a sensing device very similar to the Nielsen system. The TVM records the on/off condition of the set and the channel to which the set is tuned. However, no information is collected about the number of people watching, nor is there any demographic information about the viewers. Arbitron retrieves the household meter data nightly via a direct telephone line attached to the TVM.

For the second aspect of this form of data collection, subjects are asked to record in diaries the channels they watch or the stations they listen to, the time periods, and the number of people viewing or listening to each programme or daypart, a segment of the broadcast day such as 'prime time' (8.00pm to 11.00pm EST).

Another aspect of television audience measurement within the industry is the use of telephone surveys to check the accuracy of metered viewing data – also known as *telephone coincidental* surveys. This proce-dure measures the size of the medium's audience at a given time – the survey coincides with actual viewing. Basically, the method involves selecting a sample of households at random and calling these numbers during the viewing period of interest. Individuals are simply asked what they are watching at that moment. Respondents are asked to check that a particular television set was switched on at the time of the telephone call. For each set in the house that is on, respondents are then asked to indicate who is watching. This method avoids the necessity of trying to recall information from the previous day. Coincidentals are fairly inexpensive and are frequently used by station management to receive immediate feedback about the success of special programming.

People meters

The latest television industry method of ratings data collection, *people meters*, achieved widespread use from the mid-1980s as a standard method of measurement of television audiences in different parts of the world. They are in use across North America, Europe, the Far East, Australasia and even in South America. This methodology represents an attempt to achieve a higher frequency of ratings information and to have the ability to obtain 'single-source data', where research companies collect television ratings data, demographic data, and even household member purchasing behaviour at one time. Traditional set meters could tell only whether the television set was switched on or off, and the channel to which the set was tuned. There were no data about who is watching. Traditionally, such information was obtained by pooling simple electronic television meter data with information from households provided in self-completion diaries. People meters attempted to simplify this data collection task by requiring each person in the household, as well as all visitors, to push a specific button on a mechanical unit that records the viewing. Each person in the home is assigned a button on the meter. The meter instantaneously records information about how many people in the household are watching and about the identity of each viewer. In actual fact, the people meter does not record actual 'viewing', but the fact that a person is in the room when the TV set is switched on. The data from each night's viewing are collected by telephone.

In theory, people meters are quite simple. When a person begins or stops watching television, he or she pushes a button to document the behaviour. The button may be located on a handheld device or enclosed in a small box mounted on top of the television set. However, in practice, this system may work differently. The people meter methodology has been criticized with regard to its ability accurately to measure who is watching television in the household. Panel members whose homes are wired up with people meter technology have been found to exhibit a decline in compliance with the task of pushing buttons on their handsets to indicate their presence in the viewing situations when their TV set is switched on. This concern about people meters provided further motivation to examine ways of passive measuring of television watching which would not require viewers to actively press buttons all the time (Kirkham and Wilcox, 1994).

In the late 1980s, a survey funded by the American television networks, ABC, CBS and NBC, found that people meters 'turned off' participants, especially with children's programming on Saturday mornings. Additional criticisms came in 1991 specifically in reference to the lower television viewing numbers produced by the people meters. The criticisms have not subsided. In the UK, Kirkham and Wilcox (1994) described a picture-sampling technique which can be used to run validity checks on what people have been watching. The basic principle is that, in each home, samples are stored of pictures being displayed by each television, and back at the research centre similar samples are stored for all broadcast channels. They retrieve samples from the homes by the usual overnight telephone contact and then compare the samples from the home with those from each of the broadcast channels in turn until a match is found. This determines which channel is being watched at any given time. This information is compared with people meter information from the same home to find out if the latter information is telling what was actually going on.

A major concern about people meters is that participants will tire of pushing buttons to record when they watch television, and children cannot be depended upon to push the necessary buttons when they turn on the set. The possibility that respondents suffer from wear out and fail to use the system accurately is a cause of worry to broadcasters and advertisers. What evidence is there to shed light on whether it is reasonable to expect viewers at home to keep pressing buttons in a people meter system, to indicate their presence or non-presence in a room with a playing television set?

One review of the literature compared the results from eight validation studies with people meter systems. All of these studies used a similar methodology and criterion for testing the compliance of panellists. In each case, push-button, people meter panellists were telephoned and asked to report their viewing (and that of other household members) at the specific moment when the call was made. This reported viewing was then compared with the position of viewers' buttons as indicated by the down-loaded people meter data. This analysis was computed in a two-by-two table – telephone yes/no versus meter yes/no. The extent to which telephone 'yes' ('I am viewing') responses coincided with meter 'yes' (registered as viewing) responses was aggregated with numbers of agreements between telephone and meter 'no' responses, to give a score indicating the reliability of people meter data. A typical level of agreement was 90 per cent (Purdye and Harvey, 1994).

Even when panellists are diligent button pressers, do people meters provide accurate measures of television viewing? How do people meter measures of viewing compare with paper diaries, for example? A pilot study conducted in Britain by BARB (Broadcasters' Audience Research Board) on experimental panel data prior to full people meter adoption in 1985 found that people meters displayed more short and fewer long viewing sessions than did paper diaries with quarter hour time segments. According to a people meter measure 13 per cent of pilot panellists watched for 15 minutes during an eight-hour period of viewing measurement, while a paper diary method recorded 8 per cent of respondents viewing for that length of time. The people meter indicated that 11 per cent watched for more than four hours, compared with 15 per cent answering via a paper diary (Twyman, 1994).

Each of the audience estimates procedures is criticized. Simple electronic meters are panned because they do not provide specific audience information. Diaries are challenged because participants may fail to record viewing or listening as it happens and may rely on recall to complete the diary at the end of the week. In addition, many critics contend that diaries are used to 'vote' for or against specific shows, and actual viewing is not recorded. Critics of data collection by telephone say that the method favours responses by younger people who are more willing to talk on the phone; older respondents generally do not have the patience to answer the questions about their viewing or listening habits. Finally, people meters are condemned because of participant fatigue and a failure by many participants (especially children) to remember to push the required buttons when they watch television.

Television audience measurement in the USA

The research methodologies used by Arbitron and Nielsen are complex; each company publishes several texts describing its methods and procedures that should be consulted for specific information. The data for ratings surveys are currently gathered by two methods: diaries and electronic meters (commonly called people meters). Each method has specific advantages and disadvantages.

Nielsen's national samples are selected using national census data and involve multistage area probability sampling that ensures that the sample reflects actual population distributions. Thus, if Los Angeles accounts for 10 per cent of the television households in the country, Los Angeles households should compose 10 per cent of the sample as well.

Nielsen uses four stages in sampling: selection of counties in the country; selection of block groups within the counties; selection of certain blocks within the groups; and selection of individual households within the blocks. Nielsen claims that about two hundred households in the NTI-metered sample of approximately four thousand households are replaced each month (Nielsen, 1992). To obtain samples for producing broadcast listening and viewing estimates, Arbitron and Nielsen use recruitment by telephone, which includes calls to both listed telephone numbers and unlisted telephone numbers. Although all the ratings companies begin sample selection from telephone directories, each firm uses a statistical procedure to ensure the inclusion of unlisted telephone numbers, thus eliminating the bias that could be created if only persons or households listed in telephone directories were asked to participate in broadcast audience estimates.

Target sample sizes for local audience measurements vary from market to market. Each ratings service uses a formula to establish a minimum sample size required for a specific level of statistical efficiency, but there is no guarantee that this number of subjects will actually be produced. Although many people may agree to participate in an audience survey, there is no way to force them all to complete the diaries they are given or to accurately use electronic meters. Additionally, completed diaries are often rejected because they are illegible or obviously inaccurate. The companies are often lucky to get a 50 per cent response rate in their local market measurements.

In addition, since participation by minority groups in audience surveys is generally lower than for the remainder of the population, the companies make an extra effort to collect data from these groups by contacting households by telephone or in person to assist them in completing the diary.

Television audience measurement in Europe

The development of television in Europe was characterized for many years by the dominance or monopoly of government-run television channels. If commercial channels did operate, they were few in number. Therefore there was no demand for greater precision in measurement of audiences. It was important, however, to establish that television was important to the total population. The paucity of advertising-conveying channels meant that such channels tended to be sold out. Again, there was no significance attached to audience measurement among advertisers either.

The introduction of more commercial channels funded mainly by advertising revenue, created a need to know more about audiences and what and when they were watching. The UK was first in the 1950s, followed by other European countries though not until the 1960s. As more commercial channels appeared, so the demand grew for better data about audiences. Even in those countries which did not acquire commercial channels until fairly recently, a television audience measurement system nevertheless emerged modelled on those present in countries with commercial channels.

Meter systems were introduced throughout most European countries during the 1980s and 1990s. Until the mid-1980s, television audience measurement services in Europe were a mixture of incompatible meter systems and conventional diary and recall operations. Not only were the data collection methods and accuracy extremely variable, but the format and structure of the results were also incompatible, making comparisons on a country-by-country basis impossible.

In Britain, the earliest audience measurement surveys were conducted by the British Broadcasting Corporation using a day-after recall method. The first metered panel appeared in 1956, following the launch of commercial television. This meter panel was operated by TAM (Television Audience Measurement Ltd), a company jointly owned by AC Nielsen and Attwood Statistics Ltd. In 1968, the contract for the provision of this service switched to AGB (Audits of Great Britain). These two parallel systems operated until 1981 when the BBC joined with the commercial television network in using a meter panel for audience measurement. This audience measurement panel was run under the auspices of a new company called BARB (Broadcasters Audience Research Board), jointly owned by the BBC and Independent Television.

The early meter panel utilized two parallel strands of data collection. The set meter recorded when the set was switched on and the channel to which it was tuned. Data were stored in tape. In addition, viewers completed paper diaries, spanning a one-week period, containing quarter-hour grids throughout each day's transmission times. The meter tapes and diaries were returned to the audience measurement contractor at the end of each week. By the mid-1980s in Britain, and over the next few years in other European countries, people meter systems were launched.

The system introduced to Britain enabled set and viewer data to be more effectively collated, and it speeded up the data analysis process. Each television set in the panel households had a Meter Display Unit attached to it that recorded set-related data. A remote control handset was also supplied with each set-top device. In addition, there is a Central Data Storage Unit (CDSU) connected to a telephone socket. The MDU has a front panel with a 16-character display. This display can be used to show messages and information to panel members. It also stores information about whether the set is switched on or off, and which channel it is tuned to. It also stores viewer information entered by panel members through the remote control handsets. A button has to be depressed on the handset to signal physical presence in front of the set when it is switched on. The CDSU interrogates each MDU regularly throughout each day and pulls off set and viewer information for the entire household. The CDSU communicates with the MDU through the electric power circuits in the household. The data stored in the CDSU are extracted between 1am and 5am each night over the telephone system.

In people meter technology, there were two main pioneering companies. The AGB 4800 began in 1981, and the earliest installations of the equipment occurred in the UK and Italy (1984) and in Ireland (1985). Telecontrol, a Swiss technology company with links to the Swiss Broadcasting Corporation (SRG) installed systems in Switzerland and Germany (1985).

These systems had two significant technological developments in common. First, the retrieval of data from the homes in which the equipment was installed was by telephone. Previous meters had used a variety of storage and collection methods – paper tapes, compact cassettes and purpose-built modules. Under the new system the research company computer was loaded with the telephone number of the household and automatically dialled the household in the middle of the night to retrieve the meter data. Apart from being cost effective and enabling faster processing and reporting, this method also improved data quality by reducing the level of 'non-contacts' and also enabling the production of diagnostic information on the operation of the in-home system.

Second, the recording of the viewing behaviour of the members of the households was undertaken electronically. Each television set was fitted with a meter that included a set-top device comprising a station and channel selection monitor and display screen, plus a portable remote control handset. Panel members indicated their viewing by pressing a pre-designated button (identified by number or letter) on the handset. The signal – infrared or ultrasonic – was then received by the set-top unit, logged into the meter system, and the number/letter was displayed on the screen.

A television people meter audience measurement system can be very accurate, in the context of the type of market research it represents. It is very complex, and a number of factors have to be considered:

- establishing and tracking the characteristics of the television-viewing population (the universe)
- representing the population in the people meter panel through panel design and control

- deciding who are the viewers and what counts as 'viewing'
- recording the use of television sets and peripheral equipment
- capturing individual viewing behaviour
- taking raw data through editing, weighting and processing to make them ready for use
- reporting and allowing access to results.

The characteristics of the viewing population are established and monitored through *establishment surveys*. These are very large surveys undertaken across the population to obtain information about media equipment and demographics. Conducted by personal interview, it is also used as a means of recruiting new panel members.

Another important factor is the definition of what counts as 'viewing' and how much 'viewing' has to be done within a specified period for the individual to count as a 'viewer' within that measurement period. The definition of viewership varies from country to country. There are a number of levels at which viewing is judged to have taken place. The lowest level of eligibility – the respondent being present in the room when the set is switched on – does not impose any restriction on the respondent. Being in the same room as an operating set is sufficient. This definition does have its problems, however. Some rooms are open-plan or otherwise imprecise, and some 'viewing' may be done from doorways. A slightly tighter definition is 'in room and available to watch'. Although this definition is not entirely clear-cut, it does mean that the respondent has to be physically able to watch by virtue of location relative to the television set. At the highest level of stringency, 'watching' means that (in the respondent's own estimation) he or she is paying attention to the screen.

In respect of actual measurement of individuals viewing, all types of people meter work in a similar way. First, a particular button on a remote handset is allocated to each member of the household. When a button is pressed, a corresponding number is illuminated on the set-top display and the start of viewing by that individual is recorded at that point. A further press will extinguish the light, and the meter notes that viewing has terminated. This approach therefore measures viewing in real time; recall is eliminated from the measurement process, although 'claim' is not. The system still relies on individuals' activity, and hence people meter services are only really 'meters' in respect of the 'set' measurement.

Passive measurement of television audiences

At one time all metered television audience panels used paper diaries, either in the metered homes or in separate samples, to collect data on persons viewing television. From the mid-1980s, there was a move towards having panel members push individually-assigned buttons on small data-entry consoles (people meters) to indicate viewing status. There have also been suggestions that audience members carry individual electronic tags that would indicate their presence in a room where a television was in use. All of these methods require active cooperation on an ongoing basis by people in metered homes and thus suffer from potential cooperation biases.

To offset these panel biasing effects, television audience researchers have begun to explore alternative methodologies which remove some of the workload from panel members. A number of passive (from the viewer's perspective) methods for counting and identifying people using television have been explored. One of the earliest of these involved setting a camera near the television, periodically taking pictures of the viewers, and later having analysts look at the pictures to count the audience, to determine who was watching, and to make a judgement about the degree of attention being paid to a programme (Currey and Freeman, 1962). Allen's (1965) early published work in this area has been expanded by Bechtel et al. (1972) and Collett and Lamb (1986), who replaced Allen's photographic camera with a video camera. Although these methods required little active viewer participation, researchers' reports of peeking in on people's fighting and lovemaking demonstrate enough invasion of privacy to convince many prospective sample members to refuse to permit the equipment into their homes.

Automating the analyst out of the picture by having a computer to analyse the images of the room to see who was watching television has been mooted as one possible alternative. However, more advanced computer technology than is currently available will be needed to provide an acceptable solution for broadcasters and advertisers. A more modest goal, that of counting the audience without being able uniquely to identify individuals, has been examined. This sort of measurement system has been envisaged as an adjunct to a diary or people meter system.

Sonar

A sonar system can be configured to yield results analogous to what people are used to seeing on a weather radar display. In this case, the familiar blips can be generated by mechanically or electronically scanning one or more ultrasonic transducers across a fan-shaped sector of a room. The echoes received from objects in the room can be processed to yield a map that shows the audience members and other objects. Various signal-processing methods can then be used to get rid of echoes from walls, furniture, curtains and so on, leaving only the blips that represent the audience members.

Lu and Kiewit (1987) described a study with sonar which counted people viewing and mapped out each person's location. They did not test out the absolute accuracy of the system, but claimed that a small number of laboratory and in-home trials suggested about an 80 per cent correct hit rate.

There were several sources of error in measurement using this technique. First, if a viewer got up and left the room during scanning, he or she might or might not be counted, while the chair where they were sitting might be counted as a viewer. Second, if there were more than five or six people present, the scanner reported a smaller number. Third, ceiling fans raised the audience count. Fourth, unusually hard objects might set up echoes which might be counted as another person. Fifth, unusually soft objects might absorb echoes and reduce the viewer count.

Thermal infrared

All objects at ordinary temperatures radiate an amount of infrared energy that is a sensitive function of their temperature. Pyroelectric detectors, which respond to changes in the temperature of the scene they view, can detect a person in their field of view. By sweeping a pyroelectric detector in a fan-shaped arc, it is possible to detect all the people and other objects that are warmer than the ambient temperature of the room. The weakness of this technique lies primarily in the finding that infrared detectors sometimes count excess 'people' when aimed at a hot body such as an electric lamp or the warm spot left behind on a chair cushion when someone gets up and leaves the room.

QUALITATIVE APPROACHES TO AUDIENCES

In the past 20 years there has been an increasing emphasis placed on qualitative approaches to understanding media audiences and their involvement with the media. This methodological approach to the study of audiences has been underpinned, epistemologically, by critical and interpretive schools of social science. These use ethnographic methodologies to situate the use of media in the context of everyday life (Silverstone, 1990). This perspective utilizes observational techniques that are largely non-interventionist, often supplemented by depth interviews with members of the audience.

Whereas empirical social science approaches are based more significantly upon quantitative methodologies developed within psychology and sociology, ethnography derives from anthropology and, in its original form, was concerned with detailed accounts of the daily lives of particular cultures or social groups, primarily through the use of participant observation. This approach has been directed towards the study of media audiences. A growing body of work has emerged based on long-term participant observation of audience groups, particularly in the domestic context (Lull, 1988, 1990; Morley and Silverstone, 1990). One writer has argued that the attempt to understand how audiences read particular genres or media inevitably leads to a neglect of other cultural determinants. Yet any single leisure practice – such as watching television – inevitably intersects with other practices and with subjects' domestic and working lives (Radway, 1988). Thus, observational methodologies have been used to investigate the way that television is integrated physically into the home (Lindlof et al., 1988) and its role in relation to the way families organize their time (Byrne, 1978).

As we have seen already, observational research using video cameras has documented the wide range of activities that may take place while the set is switched on (Collett and Lamb, 1986; Gunter et al., 1995). This kind of approach has also been used to document the different forms of behaviour in front of the small screen enacted by children (Palmer, 1986).

Morley (1992) called for an ethnographic approach to understanding media audiences and their use of television, in particular. Television, it was argued, is a part of everyday life. To understand its significance to viewers, it is essential to study its position and use in the wider context of their domestic activities. Indeed, the domestic household is itself embedded in a wider social and cultural environment. This wider environment must also be analysed, through observation. To investigate communications-related activities occurring in people's natural environment requires a particular kind of methodology – mainly an ethnographic one.

In the home environment, television viewing is shaped by the presence of other established household practices which structure the day. These activities include sleeping and waking times, meal times, going to and returning from work times, and so on. Monitoring real-world behavioural phenomena in people's natural habitats is not easy, but can be worthwhile if tackled properly (Lindlof and Meyer, 1987).

Lull (1988) offers a warning that as ethnography has become increasingly fashionable, standards of data collection may have slipped. Data collection through such a qualitative perspective needs to be just as rigorous and systematic as with any form of quantitative research. Some writers have argued that the open-ended approach characterized by ethnography might be considered as a supplement to the standard media audience research approach (Ang, 1990). According to Ang : 'Rather than reducing a certain manifestation of "viewing behaviour" to an instance of a general category, we might consider it in its particularity, treat it in its concrete specificity, differentiate it from the other instances of the general category .... Only then can we go beyond statistical significance without much signification' (1990: 160).

Taken on their own, statistically based quantitative survey techniques for investigating television viewing are believed, by critical theorists, to be limited (Ang, 1990; Morley, 1992). Television watching is a very complex activity which is enmeshed with a range of other domestic practices and can only be properly understood within that context (Silverstone, 1990).

Quantitative empirical investigation has dominated audience research. Researchers in the positivist tradition have sought to isolate those factors in the communication process that can be seen to be effective, or to have effects on different groups of people, under different circumstances. According to Morley (1992: 174): 'the enormous research effort which has developed over the years has only, at best, a modest amount to offer on the basic question of influence. The constitution of the audience as amenable to a kind of clinical empiricism, which substantially involves processes of methodological isolation and abstraction, has led media research up too many blind alleys. It has consistently mistaken rigour for understanding'.

Ang (1990) has argued that television ratings describe viewers and the differences between them in terms of a few generalized and standardized viewing behaviour variables. Watching television, whatever this means to viewers, is reduced to the observable behaviour of having the set on, and is assumed to be a single act having the same meaning for everybody. What is needed is an improved methodology which does not simply measure what different types of viewers do, but also informs our understanding of why they do what they do, and with what outcome.

Quantitative research has to treat viewers as numbers – as units of equal value in a calculation of audience size. Morley has observed that: 'Thus "people-watching-television" are taken to be the basic units of audience measurement' (1992: 175). But it is even more basic than this. In television audience measurement systems, 'people present in front of the television set when it is switched on' is the unit of measurement. Whether they are actually 'watching' or not remains a debatable point.

The head counting tradition of industry audience measurement offers a one-dimensional view of television watching. It is not just that television ratings are based on an indication of a person's presence in front of a television set and not whether they are actually watching it, but that subtle meanings associated with the act of switching the set on to begin with are not detected by the industry audience ratings system. Television viewing may be a group decision, rather than an individual decision. Programmes watched may often be group choices. Thus, in order to predict future behaviour from past behaviour, it is important to have some understanding of how particular viewing behaviour decisions were reached. Furthermore, the same programme may be watched by different viewers for different reasons (Ang, 1990).

Television ratings need to be put into a broader context in order to understand the significance of television within an individual's life (Jensen, 1987). Head counting operates a binary code of watching versus not watching. If viewing actually comprises a variable behaviour, interwoven with other activities, however, this simple model fails properly to represent the true nature of watching television (Ang, 1990). Critical theorists have argued that qualitative distinctions need to be made between different types of viewing associated with different programmes, different times of day, varying social contexts of viewing, and so on. More emphasis is needed on context of viewing and on television as an aspect of a whole range of everyday practices (Scannell, 1988).

Ang (1990) has voiced concerns about the limitations of traditional empirical research to shed light on the reality of television viewing, given that the validity of any results depends on the degree of proximity of the researcher to those being observed. The real world can probably never be truly knowable, because there is always a degree of interpretation required in respect of any empirical data – whether quantitative or qualitative. Some writers have gone further than this and questioned the worth of undertaking empirical research at all (Feuer, 1986; Hartley, 1982). Ang too has noted that 'the empirical does not offer the answers as positivism would have it. Answers are to be constructed in the form of interpretations (1990: 106).

While qualitative approaches, driven by theoretical notions of critical interpretation of media have value, they have tended to suffer from a familiar tension between the 'micro' and the 'macro'. As Anderson (1987) has observed, there is often a sense of strain as researchers attempt to force detailed qualitative data into more general theoretical frameworks – for example, in the form of a taxonomy of media uses. Yet, there is a worry that such research may remain purely descriptive and provide no explanation of the phenomenon it seeks to study.

Examples of qualitative studies of media use

Ethnographic approaches to the study of media have been mostly concerned with how television and other electronic media are integrated into the infrastructure of daily family life. Some researchers have limited their focus to television-specific behaviours such as rules for using television, negotiating the meaning of televised content, or how to 'watch' television (Lull, 1982). Within this focus, ethnographers typically spent a limited amount of time with volunteer families. Little effort was made to get to know family members outside that context. While some studies have relied primarily or solely on in-depth interview data with family members (e.g. Morley, 1986), others have combined interviews with in-home observations (Lull, 1980, 1982; Silverstone et al., 1989).

Other researchers have spent extended periods of time with just one or a small number of families, getting to know the family members to the point where the researchers were accepted like other members of the family (Lindlof et al., 1988; Meyer and Meyer, 1994; Traudt and Lont, 1987). This approach enabled the researchers to witness in greater detail the role that television played in the daily lives of the families being observed. Such studies have also observed the use of the home video-recorder in addition to basic television viewing.

Such family ethnographies can reveal some of the underlying complexities of human behaviour that ordinarily escape researchers who rely only on traditional research from survey questionnaires, interviews or diaries. In-depth observations measured over extended periods of time can offer insights into how the use of television is negotiated among family members, the different meanings that are abstracted from television and the ways those meanings can change over time.

In a qualitative audience research study reliant entirely on open-ended, self-report evidence, Morley (1986) conducted in-depth interviews with the members of 18 families, all living in London. Each household comprised two parents living with two or more children. The aim of this exercise was to understand the role of television in the wider context of their general leisure activities. The families were interviewed in their own homes. Each interview had two parts. First, the parents were interviewed, and then later on, their children were invited to take part in the discussion. The interviews were unstructured and lasted between one and two hours. The interview asked about who controlled the use of the television, styles of viewing, planned and unplanned viewing, talking about television, use of video, viewing context (alone or as part of a group), programme preferences and opinions about television news. There was a special interest in the significance of gender in relation to television viewing.

Morley reported masculine dominance of the television set in these family households. Mothers and children complained that the father monopolized the remote control and therefore maintained direct physical control over set usage. There were gender differences in reported attitudes towards and perceived functionality of viewing. Men indicated that they liked to watch attentively in silence, while women regarded television as a more social activity with conversation occurring while watching. Often the conversation would be about television-related topics. Men claimed to undertake more advance planning of their viewing than women; the latter exhibited a more laissez-faire attitude towards viewing. Male control over viewing was also displayed through reported use of the video recorder. Women tended not to operate the VCR themselves, but relied upon their husbands or children to do it for them. Men and women reported different programme preferences. Women acknowledged enjoyment of soap operas, while men stated they much preferred factual programmes. Morley advises caution with these findings. They are based on a small and unrepresentative sample of households and the self-report evidence of family members who may not always have provided totally accurate accounts of their normal viewing.

In a subsequent British study, television usage was placed in the wider context of household use of domestic technologies (Silverstone et al., 1989). Sixteen families were studied, with detailed data being obtained from them through a variety of procedures including diaries, interviews, ethnographic observation and mapping of domestic space. Part of this exercise involved in-depth interviews with family members using a personal construct methodology (Kelly, 1955). This technique invited respondents to elicit key constructs or ideas (in the form of descriptive words or phrases) through which family members could express their understanding of domestic technologies (Livingstone, 1990). The typical personal construct approach requires respondents to take three items at a time and to indicate in what way two of them are alike and different from the third. In this study, respondents sorted domestic technologies in this way. Once again, special attention was paid to gender differences in the perception and reported use of domestic technologies, including television. One interesting finding concerned the concept of control. For both sexes control was a core aspect of domestic technologies, but the nature of control was perceived in different ways. For women, the control afforded by modern household technologies enabled them to keep order within the domestic sphere. For men, domestic technologies – especially items such as video, home computer and certain electrical implements – allowed the expression of expertise and enabled them to display control over things.

A series of observational studies was undertaken in the late 1970s and early 1980s by James Lull in which participant observers spent two to three days with each household, getting to know the families, eating with them, doing household chores and spending time with them in the evening while they watched television. In a naturalistic quasi-experiment, Lull (1978) found that fathers were regarded by other family members as most influential in family discussions that were conducted in order to select shows via a 'family vote' process. The findings also showed that fathers, mothers and older children were more likely than younger children to have their programme preferences selected for family viewing.

In a follow-up study, Lull (1980) classified the families under observation according to a model of family communication patterns developed earlier by Chaffee et al. (1973). They had distinguished between socio-oriented and concept-oriented family communication schemes. In a socio-oriented family setting, parents encourage their children to maintain a harmonious climate of personal relationships, to avoid arguments, anger and any form of controversial expression or behaviour. In a concept-oriented family, children are invited to express their ideas and feelings, even if they are controversial, and to challenge the beliefs of others. Lull (1980) reported that results of observations of families classified either as socio-oriented or concept-oriented on the basis of interview data, exhibited different patterns of television usage. Socio-oriented families watched more television and were more likely to use it to reach interpersonal objectives. Concept-oriented families did not regard television as a source of conversation to the same extent, but did use it to illustrate values and conduct, and exercised authority through control of the set.

A further study in this series indicated that the father tends to be the dominant influence in household television viewing (Lull, 1982). Fathers were observed to be less likely to ask others in the household about what they wanted to watch before changing channels. In this study, over 90 observers were placed in family households and instructed specifically to focus on how families turn on, change channels and turn off the main television set in their home. Trained monitors spent two days observing the families watch television and then returned on the third day to conduct interviews with each family member. The observers joined in other family activities so that the main purpose of the study was less obvious.

In all, 93 families were observed, of which 74 were two-parent families which formed the focus of the study. Fathers were named most often as the person or one of the people who controlled the selection of television programmes. Children and mothers were more likely to regard fathers as maintaining control over the main television set than were fathers themselves. Fathers believed that their partners were more responsible than any other single person for determining the choice of programmes. Overall, however, family members were just as likely to say that one of the children rather than the mother decided what was viewed on the main set. Children often perceived themselves, or one of their siblings as the primary controller of the set. Family consensus was another decision-making process mentioned by many of the families.

These perceptions were supported only in part by the observed instances of control of the main television set that were documented by the observers who spent time with the families. Observers noted who turned the set on, who changed the channel and who turned the set off. They also noted whether or not these actions were undertaken with any discussion of what would be viewed. The observations indicated that fathers controlled more programme decisions than any other single family member or combination of family members. They were more than twice as likely as their female partners to do so. Further, they acted alone in more than 90 per cent of these decisions. One of the children was next most likely to turn the set on, turn it off or change the channel. Children were responsible for 30 per cent of these actions (compared with 36 per cent for their fathers) and they were also extremely likely to do so without discussion (93 per cent of the time acting alone).

Mothers were observed to be far less involved in the actual manipulation of the set than were either their husbands (or live-in male partners) or children. They were the initiators of only 15 per cent of these actions. They were far less likely than either fathers or children to negotiate action alone. Three-quarters of all set alterations were made by one family member – mostly without observable negotiations.

A later series of investigations in the United States applied qualitative audience research methodologies to study family viewing, but placed more emphasis on the role of the video-recorder. Lindlof et al. (1988) reported a study of six families, all of whom possessed a VCR. A number of visits was made to each household, during which the families were interviewed to establish an inventory of media items and indications about media habits and rules governing media usage within the home. Further visits were undertaken to directly observe television-related family behaviour. Data were collected on non-verbal and verbal behaviours related to television viewing, including details about where family members positioned themselves in the television viewing room, the degree of movement in front of the set, and remarks that were made about things being watched. The researchers were allowed to move freely around the household and would even shadow particular family members as they moved around the house, as well as observing them closely during the acts of watching television or using the VCR.

Meyer (1995; Meyer and Meyer, 1994) conducted a longitudinal study of six families' use of television and video. The study was concerned with how television use had been affected by the introduction of the VCR and other home technology products such as video game players and the personal computer with CD-ROM and Internet connections. This research was able to track the dynamics of media use over time and point to patterns of use and meaning that elude one-shot quantitative empirical methodologies. Meyer's research, for example, purportedly shows that although families initially used the VCR for time-shifting, the practice eventually died away. Frustrations were caused by not always being able to find the time to watch recorded material, or sometimes errors occurred in the programming of a recording and the desired programme failed to be recorded. Further problems were caused by the inability of many family members to be able to effectively programme the VCR for time-shift recordings. Often it was the children who knew best how to operate it. Family arguments ensued about when and how the VCR should be used. Parents became concerned about excessive use of the VCR by their children. There was little evidence of popular compilation of home video libraries. Many users reached the opinion that there was not much worth saving from television in that way.

CONCLUDING REMARKS

The study of media usage has been closely tied with the needs of media industries to collect data, relevant to their business purposes, about their consumer markets and the performance of their publications and productions in attracting those markets. Hence, much research effort has been expended on the development of methodologies that are technically proficient at measuring audiences and their consumption of media, often on a large scale. During the course of this activity, there has always been a tension between the need to obtain sufficiently accurate and detailed data about media consumers and their media-related behaviour and the need to avoid imposing too much upon respondents lest they either fail to report effectively upon their normal media behaviours or cease to cooperate because the demands of researchers are deemed to be excessive. Much investment has therefore been made in the development of research methodologies that collect data about media consumers automatically or that require the minimum possible effort on their part. It is in this vein that developmental research has been conducted on passive registration of television-viewing behaviour.

Another need of media industries, however, is to obtain and process large quantities of data quickly and efficiently so that accurate measures of performance can be made available either the next day or within a week or so of behaviour being measured. This need has driven the evolution of electronic data-gathering methodologies in which, as far as possible, data about media consumption are registered automatically as it occurs. Even when collected 'by hand' (either through respondent self-report or interviewer data entry), technology is used whereby data are entered directly onto a computer data base ready immediately for further processing and analysis.

Within the academy, media researchers whose interest has centred on media use, have challenged industry audience research. This challenge has been made on two levels. At a technical level, doubts have been cast on the ability of industry audience research techniques to provide accurate measures of media-related behaviour. In the context of television audience research, for example, it is generally acknowledged that measures of 'television viewing' are in fact only measures of a viewer's presence in a room with an active television set. At a deeper level, however, industry audience research data are perceived to be of little value in enabling a broader understanding of the way people use media. The application of qualitative audience research methods is regarded by the critics of industry research as providing deeper insights into the meaning of television and other domestically consumed media in the lives of media consumers.

In the end, it is likely that both quantitative and qualitative audience research methodologies have something to offer. It is equally true of both, that, so far, they also have limitations that their respective users need to be aware of and to acknowledge. Certainly, large-scale quantitative assessments of media audiences have to adopt techniques that permit ease of management of large amounts of data collected from large numbers of people. The data have to provide a currency upon which business organizations can effectively trade. Yet, these data do only scratch the surface of media usage in terms of what it may mean for individual media users. At the same time, the mostly small-scale qualitative studies have so far investigated selective, non-representative samples of households and utilized methodologies reliant on self-report data that are as dubious as data collected in large-scale audience surveys, or ethnographic data requiring the physical presence of an observer in the household. The latter intervention may itself change the social environment to such a degree that the observed behaviour does not truly represent normal, unobserved behaviour.

CHAPTER 5

MEASURING AFFECTIVE RESPONSES TO MEDIA

As an adjunct to measuring media audiences and levels of media consumption, media researchers have also explored the different ways in which audiences react, psychologically, to media content. In the last chapter, the spotlight focused on measurement of audiences and their use of media. In the first instance, the discussion centred on the surface level measurement of audiences' exposure to media. We then saw that scholars who adopted more qualitative approaches, attempted to understand media consumption in a wider context of other domestic activities. This review showed that media researchers have applied a number of different methodologies to understand media exposure and how it takes place.

In the current chapter, the review of media research methods turns to the question of how media consumers evaluate the media and the content they carry. While the last chapter was concerned with audiences' mere exposure to media, this chapter focuses on how people respond to media in an emotional fashion. Human beings are capable of experiencing and expressing a range of different emotions. In relation to understanding the forces that control media exposure, research has already been reviewed that showed that media-related behaviour can be shaped by different motives and needs. Media exposure does not happen just by accident, but more usually by design. People choose to watch certain television programmes, listen to particular radio stations, or read specific publications because they expect to have certain needs satisfied by doing so. The media can create certain moods or feelings in their consumers, and the expectation of particular experiences through the consumption of certain types of media content is a fundamental aspect of the media usage phenomenon (Zillmann and Bryant, 1985).

In examining audiences' evaluative or affective reactions to media, the methodologies chosen by media researchers are often determined by their idiosyncratic agendas, information needs, or epistemological orientations. As with other types of media research, quantitative and qualitative methodologies have featured within media and affect research. Research can also be distinguished in terms of whether it uses off-line or on-line measures, takes place in natural or artificial surroundings and broadly in terms of whether it attempts to measure pleasurable or painful responses to media. Another important distinction is between research conducted for purely academic purposes and research conducted for more commercially oriented reasons. In some instances, these distinctions become blurred, and a study may combine more than one category of methodology and have theoretical and practical implications.

For the purposes of the current review, the following broad distinctions will be used to categorize the research in this sphere.

1. *Industry-driven affective research.* This is audience reaction research conducted primarily by media industry bodies for specific business (or regulatory) purposes. This work can be divided into ongoing data production in the context of routine measurement of audiences' appreciation of media content, and developmental research concerned with establishing new measurement systems or fine-tuning existing ones.
2. *Academic affective research.* This is media research carried out to understand how particular audience communities relate, emotionally, to different types of media content and respond during the act of consumption. Some of this research has been concerned specifically with examining the factors that determine children's emotional reactions to different types of media content.

INDUSTRY-DRIVEN AFFECTIVE RESEARCH

Much of the evaluative research conducted to measure audiences' affective response to media has been industry funded. In fact, most of the main methodological developments in evaluative research have occurred within the television broadcasting industry. This work has involved a mixture of off-line and on-line measurement. With off-line measurement, audience opinions are sought away from the media exposure situation, whereas with on-line measurement, audience reactions are measured on a continuous basis during media exposure and/or immediately after the exposure experience. Much of this research has been quantitative, although qualitative methodologies have also featured throughout the history of this branch of media analysis, especially during developmental phases of the major research techniques.

Evaluative broadcast ratings: history

An alternative way of addressing the issue of measurement of programme popularity to simply measuring how many people watch them, is to assess what people think about programmes, and whether the viewing experience was enjoyable or not. Not all programmes attract large audiences, but this does not necessarily indicate that they lack popularity. Instead, small audiences may reflect the time of day when the programme is broadcast. Some programmes are targeted at specific audience subgroups; they are not designed to appeal to everyone.

Research has been conducted over many years into audience appreciation of programmes. The concept of measuring audience appreciation for programmes as a distinct yardstick from audience size is not a new one. The first survey of audience appreciation measurement was introduced as long ago as 1941 by the British Broadcasting Corporation in order to monitor the listening experience of its radio audiences during the war-time years. Under the direction of Robert Silvey, its first head of audience research, the BBC set up a number of separate listener panels for different categories of programming (e.g. plays, music, features, talks and discussion, and light entertainment). There was also a women's panel which was used mainly for the evaluation of daytime programmes. Each panel had 500 members who were respondents to a radio broadcast appeal for volunteers (Silvey, 1974).

Panel members were sent a questionnaire every week which contained questions about three to six forthcoming radio broadcasts. The questions asked about different aspects of each listed programme. There was, however, one item common to all programmes; this was a request to award the programme marks out of ten. This item was designed to assess how much listeners had enjoyed the programme. A score of zero revealed that the listener could not like the programme any less. From these marks, an Appreciation Index was created by multiplying the raw programme score by ten, thus giving an Index score from 0 to 100. Comparisons of how well programmes performed on this basis were restricted to programmes of the same type; comparisons across genres were discouraged. It was found that appreciation scores tended to cluster in the top half of the 0 to 10 scale. This meant that Index scores tended for most programmes to be in the range of 65 to 85.

After the Second World War, the system was revamped and the marks out of ten method was abandoned in favour of a five-point alphabetical scale, A+, A, B, C, C–, with verbal explanations provided for each score as follows:

A+ 'I wouldn't have missed this programme for anything'; 'I can't remember when I enjoyed (liked) a programme so much'; 'One of the most interesting (amusing, moving, impressive) programmes I have ever heard'.

A 'I am very glad indeed that I didn't miss this'; 'I enjoyed (liked) it very much indeed'; 'Very interesting (amusing, moving, impressive) indeed'.

B 'I found this quite a pleasant (satisfactory) programme'; 'I quite enjoyed (liked) it'; 'A quite interesting (amusing) programme'; 'A rather moving (impressive) programme'.

C 'I felt listening to this was rather a waste of time'; 'I didn't care for this very much'; 'It was rather dull (boring, feeble)'.

C– 'I felt listening to this was a complete waste of time'; 'I disliked it very much'; 'It was very dull (boring, feeble)'.

For presentation purposes the BBC continued to express Appreciation Index scores along a 100-point scale, by awarding points to each position on the scale from four down to zero. Even with the new scaling method, however, scores for most programmes still tended to group around the 65 mark.

The advantage of the appreciation score was that it provided a different type of measurement from audience size. The degree of enjoyment obtained from a programme among its listeners could not be judged from the size of its audience. After the 1940s, television sets steadily spread throughout the UK, and the new audio-visual medium, whose growth had been arrested by the war, became increasingly popular. In order to track the public's use and experience of television, the BBC set up a Viewing Panel, again following a broadcast appeal, but this time the appeal was on television. The appreciation scale used to assess public reaction to radio programmes was applied also to television programmes. In order to underline the fact that there were two distinct services, the television programme scores were called Reaction Indices, while the radio scores continued to be known as Appreciation Indices (Silvey, 1974).

Later developments

Later research into audience appreciation measurement was undertaken by commercial television in the UK, beginning in the late 1960s. The Independent Television Authority, operating under its statutory obligation to carry out research into 'the state of public opinion concerning the programmes [on Independent Television]' and to ensure that the programmes were brought 'under constant and effective review', instigated a feasibility study into ways of systematically assessing the audience's attitudinal reactions to television programmes. Apart from enabling the regulatory body to fulfil its statutory duty, this research was conceived to have other important potential applications. It would provide a channel through which audience feedback could reach programme controllers, producers, writers, and others involved in the making of programmes, 'to allow them to assess their success in achieving their creative objectives' (Haldane, 1970: 63). Without such research the only judgements that could be made about programmes would almost invariably be subjective ones based on personal intuition. A second purpose of this research was to enable those in broadcasting, and perhaps especially professional practitioners of research, to understand the way audience preferences and attitudes work. It is not enough simply to establish that viewers like a programme. It is even more useful to know *why* they like it.

In setting up such a research project, however, there were, according to Haldane (1970), some essential principles to bear in mind. In understanding the nature of the relationship between audiences and the programmes they watch, any results 'must be based upon the *audience's own* language, concepts and ideas' rather than on those of producers, critics and administrators. Since the audience was the centre of concern, evaluations of programmes needed to be based upon terms which had meaning for viewers.

The second important principle was that, in classifying programmes, audience-generated attributes should be used rather than those found convenient by administrators or schedulers. And third, a system of programme assessment should not limit itself simply to the measurement of audience liking of or interest in programmes. It should attempt to measure all the different ways in which the audience thinks about or evaluates programmes.

Exploratory research was commissioned by the ITA during 1967 and 1968. Frost (1969) described five stages through which this feasibility study proceeded, culminating in the experimental operation of a panel of 300 viewers in the London area for a limited period. This work proceeded through five stages:

- Stage 1: The construction of a semantic differential scaling system which would be generally appropriate to all television programmes
- Stage 2: The use of this semantic differential scale to collect attitude ratings (programme profiles) of all television programmes
- Stage 3: The use of cluster analysis to group the obtained programme profiles into categories of 'similar' programmes
- Stage 4: The construction of specific semantic differentials – one for each programme type revealed by the cluster analysis
- Stage 5: The use of the specific semantic differential to obtain programme profiles.

It is worth looking at these stages in more detail. The first step was to create programme evaluative scales that used the language of the audience and reflected features which viewers perceived to be relevant to different types of programmes. A technique known as the Repertory Grid, derived from the work on personal constructs by Kelly (1955), was used which allowed viewers to make comparisons between triads of programmes stating the ways in which they felt two of these programmes were alike and different from the third. A list of 58 bipolar seven-point semantic differential scales was created from this exercise which were then used by a different sample of viewers to evaluate a set of 61 programmes currently being transmitted on UK Independent Television and the BBC at that time.

Next a statistical technique called Principal Components Analysis was used to reveal that viewers' assessment of these programmes on the scales provided could be reduced to nine general factors, given the names 'general evaluation', 'information', 'romance', 'violence', 'conventionality', 'scale of production', 'noise/activity', 'acceptability' and 'humour'. General evaluation, for instance, reflected how enjoyable, pleasing, absorbing and well presented the programme was perceived to be. Acceptability reflected a programme's perceived suitability for children or adult audiences.

With these factors identified, in Stage 2 the ratings of all 61 programmes were computed on each of the nine factors. This analysis enabled the researchers to find out to what extent each dimension discriminated among different programmes and programme types. Results showed that all nine scales provided effective discrimination between programmes.

Stage 3 turned the data around another way by examining the ratings profile for a single programme on all nine scale factors simultaneously. This provided a different sort of profile, with the focus being placed on the character of an individual programme in the audience's eyes. These programme profiles were then further combined through cluster analysis to produce a range of solutions in the shape of groupings of programmes. These different solutions yielded between two and twenty programme clusters. Frost (1969) presented the results of the 20-cluster solution with clusters containing a maximum of five programmes down to a minimum of only one programme. Most of the clusters were readily interpretable, although one or two threw out odd combinations of programmes. For example, wrestling was clustered with a well-known situation comedy of the day called 'Till Death Us Do Part'. Further compressed cluster solutions were explored and finally a six-cluster solution was accepted as one which was both manageable and sufficiently comprehensive.

At Stage 4 attention turned to the question of whether specific attitudinal frameworks were required for different programme types. This analysis revealed that different attitudinal factor structures emerged in respect of viewers' evaluations of programmes in each of the six programme clusters. Although there were a few attitudinal factors which emerged across more than one programme grouping, there were many differences among them as well.

The final stage of the pilot study consisted of a panel operation extending over five weekly reporting periods. Panellists were asked to rate the television programmes they watched on appropriate sets of semantic differential scales. These sets of scales were ones which earlier stages of the research had identified as being especially relevant to the programmes concerned.

Further exploratory procedures followed, and Haldane (1970) took up the story. Additional qualitative research was carried out to generate a battery of over 200 'constructs' which were converted into seven-point semantic differential scales. These scales were then divided into two sets, each comprising scales that appeared to measure the same dimensions. Around two hundred respondents for each battery then rated 130 current programmes on all scales. Factor analyses were computed on each set of data and their results combined to produce a final solution of eleven factors plus a General Evaluation factor. This set of scales was called the General Programme Rating Battery (GPRB).

The GPRB was then used in a series of theatre tests in which around 1,000 respondents rated all programmes currently being shown on BBC1, BBC2, and ITV. Cluster analysis was used to reduce all these data to produce a set of cluster solutions comprising groupings of programmes. As in an earlier stage of the research, solutions comprising between

2 and 20 groupings were generated, with the nine-cluster solution eventually chosen as offering the best option. Comparing the six-cluster solution obtained on this occasion with that produced earlier revealed a very similar programme taxonomy. This was especially promising given that both had been derived from two quite different sets of programmes.

This developmental work led to the setting up of a regular television programme appreciation survey during the 1970s by the ITA, which was subsequently continued by its successor organization, the Independent Broadcasting Authority. This service was called AUdience Reaction Assessment (AURA) and comprised a viewing diary that was sent out to representative regional samples and a London-based panel on alternate weeks. Each week aimed to achieve a return sample of several hundred usable diaries. The diaries themselves listed all programmes broadcast on UK television channels presented in their schedule order on a day-by-day basis. Each listed programme was presented with a six-point appreciation scale on which respondents were asked to provide an evaluation of how enjoyable and/or interesting they found the programme. Such judgements were to be made only once the individual had seen enough of a programme to have formed an opinion about it. Following data analysis, the appreciation reports presented ratings for each of the nine programme genres identified through earlier research (Frost, 1969), with programmes per category ranked by their appreciation scores.

By the early 1980s, an industry-wide audience measurement body called BARB (Broadcasters' Audience Research Board) was set up to provide a single set of audience size measurement data for the BBC and commercial television in the UK. BARB also provided a separate Audience Reaction Service, modelled on the IBA's system. This service consisted of a Television Opinion Panel which comprised two main elements. First, there was a national panel with an achieved (i.e. available for analysis) sample size of 3,000 respondents per week. Each panel member was expected to complete an AI (Appreciation Index) booklet every week. Second, regional panels in each commercial television area provided an overall achieved sample of 500 respondents in each case. Members of these regional booster panels were asked to complete a booklet every four weeks, with each region being contacted as part of a four-weekly cycle. The Appreciation Index score which ranged from 0 to 100 was calculated by giving a value of 100, 80, 60, 40, 20 or 0 to each of six points of the appreciation diary scale. (The scale was: extremely interesting and/or enjoyable = 100; very interesting and/or enjoyable = 80; fairly interesting and/or enjoyable = 60; neither one thing nor the other = 40; not very interesting and/or enjoyable = 20; not at all interesting and/or enjoyable = 0.)

Evaluative television ratings: off-line research

Debates about the quality of broadcasting led to consideration of methods for measuring audience reactions to television programmes as a separate exercise from measuring how many people watched them. For one thing, there was a growing realization, during the 1980s, that audience size did not always equate with quality of production because viewer availability and scheduling details could affect audience size much more powerfully than (perceived) 'quality', which could only really be judged after the audience, of whatever size, had assembled and had its viewing experience. A number of developmental studies were conducted into measurement methodologies and some new, experimental qualitative television ratings services were launched in the field at this time.

Enjoyment and quality

In the early 1990s in Britain, television audience researchers began to turn their attention to the potential value and informativeness of qualitatively distinct audience reaction responses to programmes. A number of experimental studies were conducted in which trials were run with different types of evaluative scale. One particular point of interest was whether viewers could make a distinct rating of a programme, in terms of its perceived 'quality', which was different in kind from a rating of the programme's 'enjoyment' value.

Wober (1990) asked 3,000 viewing panel members to rate a selection of 72 programmes in terms of their quality and enjoyment value. Ratings were obtained through weekly viewing diaries in which a standard appreciation measure was taken of programmes as a matter of routine. For the subsample of programmes identified in this study, an additional 'quality' rating was obtained along a five-point scale ('very high' to 'very low quality'). Quality ratings were found to be generally lower than enjoyment ratings, and in some cases, viewers enjoyed programmes even though they were perceived to be of poor quality.

Johnson (1992) reported another experiment with evaluative ratings of television programmes in which around 450 people completed viewing diaries over a two-week period, giving appreciation scores for the programmes they viewed. Half the sample responded to verbal scales and half responded to numerical scales. There were two sets of verbal scales tested that assessed perceived *liking* (version 1: 6-point scale from 'I enjoyed it very much' to 'I didn't enjoy it at all'; version 2: 7-point scale from 'It was a very good quality programme' to 'It was a very poor quality programme'); perceived *quality* (version 1: 7-point scale from 'It was a very good programme' to 'It was a very bad programme'; version 2: 7-point scale from 'It was a very good quality programme' to 'It was a very poor quality programme'); and perceived *missability* (version 1: 5-point scale from 'I was "glued" to it – I didn't miss a thing' to 'I hardly paid any attention to it at all'; version 2: 5-point scale from 'I'm very glad I watched it' to 'I wish I had missed it'). Following initial tests, no differences emerged between the ratings given to the two versions, and version 2 was eventually used in the full-scale trial. In the numerical diary, scales were out of 10 in responses to: 'How much or little you enjoyed it'; 'Thinking of the quality of the programme'; and 'How much attention did you pay'. Comparisons were made between the ratings given by viewers, using these various evaluative scales, to 18 programmes representing 12 major programme genres. The results showed that scales such as enjoyment, quality and missability discriminated among programmes in a similar fashion; there was no strong indication that they represented qualitatively-different types of audience reaction.

In another more sophisticated study, Gunter et al. (1992) examined the way viewers used evaluative scales such as 'quality', 'enjoyment' and 'memorability' in relation to individual programmes they had watched. A sample of nearly 1,400 respondents, recruited across Britain, completed viewing diaries or self-completion questionnaires and were interviewed by telephone. The diaries covered one day, five days or seven days of television output. In the diaries, each listed programme that had been viewed was rated for enjoyment, quality and memorability along 10-point scales. Quality ratings were obtained globally for each channel, globally for listed programme genres, and for individual programmes that had been watched. When rating programme genres, respondents were asked to base their scores either on programmes they had watched in the past week or past four weeks.

Global measures of quality (i.e. rating an entire channel) produced lower ratings than did channel ratings produced by averaging over the specific ratings provided by respondents for individual programmes seen on each channel in their viewing diaries. Despite this, channels that scored highest on one version of the quality measure also scored highest on the other version. In general, ratings of quality were lower than ratings of enjoyment, whether ratings were provided for individual programmes, programme genres or globally for entire channels.

The Canadian enjoyment index

The Canadian Broadcasting Corporation carried out enjoyment measurement and associated subjective measures, routinely. This audience reaction measurement service began in 1965 and was modelled on the service developed by the BBC to assess audience reaction to programmes in Britain. The principal measure in the Canadian system was the Enjoyment Index (EI) – a measure of audience appreciation of individual programmes, obtained from a weekly panel. There was a national sample of around 1,100 people aged 12 and over. One quarter of the panel was replaced each week. The 'enjoyment diary' differed from that used in Britain in several ways. In the Canadian version, while the left hand part carried the routine enjoyment scale, the right hand part had specially tailored questions for individual programmes.

The British system's aim was to list every programme, while the Canadian procedure was to list only 20 items shown that day, not even mentioning time and channel. There were two routine questions for each item listed – first, did the respondent watch part only, or all of the programme (i.e. if they saw it at all) and then, on a five-point scale, how much they enjoyed it. News and documentaries were included, so enjoyment could be severely influenced by content rather than by production values.

The EI or Enjoyment Index was calculated using non-equal weights, thus 100 = very much, 60 = quite a bit, 40 = all right/not bad, 20 = not too much, and 0 = enjoyed not at all. This index could be calculated for every item listed. For selected items additional questions enabled two other indices to be calculated. These were the RDI (Relaxing-Demanding Index, defined as the average per cent of viewers agreeing with each of the statements 'it was a programme you could relax with', 'it was good company' and 'you could just sit and watch without thinking about it' *minus* the average per cent agreeing with each of the statements 'you had to concentrate on it', 'it made you think' and 'it kept you in touch with what's going on'). The RDI could theoretically take any value from +100 to –100. There was also an XC (Exciting Index) for selected episodes defined as the per cent of viewers agreeing 'it was very exciting'. Early studies indicated that demanding programmes tended to get smaller (and older) audiences but, after controlling for audience size, demanding programmes had higher enjoyment than did relaxing programmes. Within each main programme type, higher enjoyment tended to go to programmes with larger audiences.

Savage (1992) reported a special study in which the panel was split so that half were provided with diaries that asked them to judge programmes using the EI question ('How much did you enjoy today's program? I enjoyed it: 1, very much; 2, quite a bit; 3, alright/not bad; 4, not too much; 5, not at all'), while the other half received diaries with the word 'quality' embedded in the appreciation question ('How would you rate the quality of the following program? 1, very good; 2, good; 3, alright/not bad; 4, poor; 5, very poor'). Responses to the 'quality' question (QIs) were calculated as indices on a 100-point scale, as were EIs.

Of the 29 programmes evaluated in this manner, no statistically significant differences between EI and QI were found in the case of 15. In all cases, for which QIs were different from EIs, QIs were higher. This result contradicted earlier research in Britain by Wober (1990), who found quality ratings of programmes to be generally lower than enjoyment ratings. This discrepancy was explained in terms of the use, in these two studies, of different question wordings and response scales.

The TVQ service

This was a national postal survey which was used to provide measures of national awareness of all current commercial television programming and viewers' overall programme valuations along a five-point scale. This system was tested as a measure of audience reaction using a pool of

Public Television (PTV) households in the USA. In each of two survey waves, 1,200 PTV viewers were drawn from this pool and asked to indicate whether they were 'familiar with' a sample of approximately 100 PTV programmes. If familiar, they were then asked to rate each programme's appeal along a five-point scale ranging from 'one of my favourites' to 'poor'. Two basic scores were derived: a familiarity score (percentage of respondents indicating familiarity with a programme) and a PTVQ score (percentage of respondents familiar with a programme who claim it is one of their favourites).

For the same PTV viewer samples, comparable scores were available through coincident TVQ survey waves for virtually all commercial PTV programmes. Additionally, for the two special PTVQ waves, Black and Hispanic respondents were over-sampled, in order to permit analysis of the programme preferences of these audiences.

The principal purpose of these PTVQ studies was to assess the feasibility of collecting an overall qualitative programme rating for PTV programmes, similar to those (appreciation index) ratings collected by British broadcasters. The two survey waves were successful explorations, in terms of identifying effective PTV viewer sampling procedures, obtaining a range of apparently discriminating viewer programme evaluations and uncovering provocative demographic variations in audience response.

Some of the most interesting research questions studied with these data were whether PTV viewers appeared satisfied by available offerings, and whether they appreciated PTV programmes more than commercial offerings. Average qualitative evaluations indicated that PTV viewers were no more appreciative of public television programmes than they were of commercial television programmes, although certain public television programmes far exceeded average qualitative evaluations.

These results underscored the importance of using special evaluation practices for targeted programmes. Programme 'familiarity' scores varied widely across programmes, with some types clearly a great deal more familiar to audiences than others. The implications of this research were that programmes intended for a minority or special interest audience may not fare well with the total viewing audience, yet will apparently satisfy special needs and interests among their smaller viewership. With these data, such differential audience reactions can be measured for more informed decisions about the effectiveness of targeted programming.

Television qualitative ratings (TQR)

The TQR Service provided a profile of television programmes along 14 factors derived from an extensive analysis of viewer programme perceptions. In a pilot study, conducted by an agency called Marketing Evaluations Inc. for the Corporation of Public Broadcasting in the United States, 258 descriptions of television programmes (as identified in preliminary focus group discussions and analyses of the television criticism literature) were used to profile 96 commercial and public television programmes. Judgements as to whether each descriptor did or did not apply to all 96 programmes were collected from a total national sample of 3,000 respondents. Data reduction yielded the 14 factors in viewer programme evaluations. As a syndicated service, TQR aimed to provide ongoing measurement of current programming along these 14 factors, and along the complete set of descriptors from which the factors emerged:

What the programme does for the viewers
Factor 1 – provides *knowledge and enrichment*
Factor 2 – provides *diversion and escape*
How the programme affects the viewer
Factor 3 – gives *fun and amusement*
Factor 4 – builds *tension and excitement*
How the viewer feels about the programme
Factor 5 – *positive evaluation* – wants to watch
Factor 6 – *negative evaluation* – not interested
The programme's type of appeal
Factor 7 – acceptable for *kid/family viewing*
Factor 8 – primarily for *adult entertainment*
The contents of the programme
Factor 9 – subject/people are *familiar and realistic*
Factor 10 – subject/people are *unfamiliar or unusual*
The viewer relationship to the programme
Factor 11 – viewer becomes *emotionally involved*
Factor 12 – viewer is *interested observer*
Sensory emphasis of the programme
Factor 13 – visual stress on *beauty and glamour*
Factor 14 – aural stress on *wit and clever lines.*

The TQR was envisaged as an instrument which could provide diagnostic information about the sources of viewer (dis)satisfaction with a given television programme. Analyses of the data from this system were tested in regard to identifying gaps in available programming that were not being addressed by commercial or public sources.

Television audience assessment

TAA conducted experimental studies with an audience reaction system in the USA in the early 1980s. Prototype instruments were tested in which respondents supplied evaluative ratings of programmes they had watched, using two different scales. The first scale required respondents to indicate how much a programme appealed to them along a 10-point scale, and also to respond to two additional scales ('this programme touched my feelings' and 'I learned something from this programme') which were combined to give an 'impact' score. This research was conducted with samples of 3,000 people recruited from cable television markets in the USA. Programmes were listed on sheets of paper and each programme viewed was rated on the scales described above. A researcher placement and postal return survey was supplemented by a series of tele-phone surveys, with data eventually collected on hundreds of broadcasts and cable-delivered programmes and on the respondents' backgrounds and media-related habits.

The research found that although most people seemed to enjoy most of what they watched on television for most of the time, opinions could vary dramatically from programme to programme. Not all programmes were liked equally well. Some programmes scored in the 80s or even 90+, while others scored below 50. Programme Appeal could vary from one type of programme to the next and from one programme episode to the next within the same series. Viewers could also vary widely in their ratings of the same programme. Thus, a programme might have been liked a lot by younger viewers, but not liked at all by older viewers.

The review of audience reaction research methods so far has indicated that industry-based television audience researchers have tested a variety of evaluative scales in the context of measuring programme appreciation. However, the basic procedure has been largely the same throughout. Viewers are supplied with a paper diary or questionnaire on which pro-grammes are listed. A 5–10-point scale is then presented alongside each listed programme. Viewers then provide ratings for those programmes they have watched. Ratings are as likely to be provided at some time after the programme being rated was viewed as they are to be completed at the time of viewing. For this reason, such measures can broadly be regarded as 'off-line' measures and therefore susceptible to memory-related errors on the part of respondents. In the next part of this chapter, we turn our attention to 'on-line' measures in which audience response to media con-tent is measured at the time of exposure.

On-line measures

On-line measures are taken at the time of media exposure. In the context of measuring audiences' affective responses to media content, this means that evaluative or emotional reactions are assessed while the individual is read-ing a newspaper or magazine, listening to a radio broadcast or watching a television programme. Most on-line, media affective response research has been conducted with television content. On-line studies in this context can be differentiated in terms of whether the measures taken involve the conscious reactions of respondents to content via paper and pencil or elec-tronic reaction instruments or involve autonomic, physiological responses to content of which individuals may not be consciously aware.

Continuous response measurement

Media researchers have become more sensitive to the fact that the psychological states of individuals change continuously as they attend to, understand, and react to messages. Continuous response measurement (CRM) systems allow subjects to report continuously on their changing mental states, evaluations and opinions while observing and processing media content. The present generation of audience response systems tend to comprise a set of electronic components designed to measure momentary shifts in self-report during message processing.

This kind of system has been used to evaluate reactions to advertising (Hughes, 1992; Thorson and Reeves, 1986; Zabor et al., 1991); film, television programming and educational video (Beville, 1985; Biocca et al., 1992; Philport, 1980; Rust, 1985; Sneed, 1991); political communications (Biocca, 1991a, 1991b; Katz, 1988; West and Biocca, 1992); and health communications (Baggaley, 1986, 1988).

The present generation of audience response systems comprise a set of electronic components designed to measure momentary shifts in self-report during message processing. Computerized measurement systems are built around the use of a simple continuous signalling device. The essential components are the input devices, the central processing unit, and data storage devices. The input device, often a dial or a keypad, allows the audience member to continuously signal changes in the same mental state using an interval scale; these reports are collected and recorded by the computer. Some systems are connected to video-recorders and video overlay systems which allow the researcher visually to display the data as the message is in progress.

The computer gathers the audience's reactions, computes summary statistics, and displays the results in numeric and graphic form. The video overlay box takes the image from the input VCR and the image of the data from the computer to create a composite of the two images, one overlaid on the other, and this image is then recorded at the output VCR or displayed on a television monitor, allowing the researcher to visually display the data as the message (e.g. film or programme) is in progress. CRM systems collect in real time discrete or continuous introspective self-reports, evaluations, or opinions in response to any stimulus for any duration along any discrete or continuous scale. The present CRM systems are the latest models of research technology that can be traced back to the 'program analyzer' patented in 1945 by Paul Lazarsfeld, the director of the Bureau of Applied Social Research, and Frank Stanton, a media researcher and later president of CBS (Levy, 1982; Millard, 1992; Upton, 1969).

The concept of continuous response measurement emerged in 1932 when Lazarsfeld, then a junior researcher at the Psychological Institute of the University of Vienna proposed a way to examine affective responses to broadcast music (Levy, 1982; Millard, 1989). The original machine was built into a wooden box. Inside the box was a constant speed motor which pulled a six-inch wide roll of white recording paper at the rate of approximately one-fifth of an inch per second. Mounted in contact with the recording paper was a row of ten black 'Inko-graph' pens. A further pen situated a small distance away from the others marked off elapsed time in seconds. Each of the ten pens was held in place by a metal fitting, which secured the pen close to, but not in contact with, an electromagnet. Trailing from the box were ten electrical cords, one for each pen. Each electrical cord was approximately six feet long and was connected to an 'on – off' button. When the button was depressed, it was locked into the 'on' position and activated an electromagnet. The electromagnet attracted the metal fitting around each pen, jerking the Inko-graph pen a quarter of an inch off the recording paper and holding it there until the button was released by a second push. Each subject held one 'on – off' control and was told to push the button whenever he or she 'liked' the experimental stimulus, which was either recorded music or an acetate 'transcription' of a radio broadcast. The subject's response was recorded by the Inko-graph pens onto the recording paper.

The research assumed that measurement of like – dislike could serve as meaningful indicators of the entire nature of subjective reactions to the stimulus. Another assumption was that judgements of liking – disliking were made more or less constantly throughout exposure. There was also an issue about whether subjects evaluated 'parts' of the stimulus, rather than reading holistic judgements about it. A further question is whether the setting of exposure is as important as the stimulus itself in conditioning audience responses. There are factors linked to the way subjects provided continuous ratings that need to be addressed. It was found early on that some subjects turned their 'like' buttons on and simply forgot to release them; others complained that while they 'disliked' the stimulus, there was no means to indicate that reaction. Later models of the Lazarsfeld – Stanton Program Analyzer gave subjects two controls – a button to indicate 'like' and a second button to show 'dislike'. The original 'on – off' buttons which locked into place when depressed were replaced with new, non-locking controls which required constant pressure to trigger the recording pens.

Stanton significantly improved the system by developing an electronic push-button version which was first used by CBS. This early technology, used by CBS into the 1980s, consisted of two buttons, one green and one red, to signal 'like', 'dislike' or (if no button was pressed) 'indifference'. The data were collected on rolls of graph paper, and analysis was difficult. Under the control of CBS, the measure was used primarily as a ratings system and for similar commercial research applications (Hallonquist and Peatman, 1947; Handel, 1950). The measure was used for war-time research (Hovland et al., 1949) and for the analysis of educational programming (Hallonquist and Peatman, 1947). The Hollywood film industry (Handel, 1950; Millard, 1992), the NBC television network and advertising agencies such as McCann-Erikson and Young and Rubicam used it to test programmes, films and advertisements (Millard, 1989, 1992).

Early attempts to explore the measure and define its psychological properties (Hallonquist and Suchman, 1979; Hallonquist and Peatman, 1947) were later abandoned, probably due to the high cost of the measure – and lack of theory of moment-to-moment psychological responses. Some theoretical development did occur, however. Merton and his colleagues explored the use of the technique in the context of their work with focus group methodology. Recorded on-line responses were played back to focus groups to serve as prompts to stimulate and guide the ensuing discussion (Merton et al., 1956).

Developments in technology and in the theory of information processing led to a reconsideration of the measure in terms of what is known about the fine-grain processing of meaningful stimuli, in particular television content (Biocca, 1991a,b; Biocca et al., 1987; Reeves et al., 1983; Thorson and Reeves, 1986). Newer versions of the progamme analyzer emerged in the 1980s. The Ontario Educational Communication Authority and the Children's Television Workshop developed what was called PEAC (Program Evaluation Analysis Computer), a relatively portable, 16-variable, microcomputer-based response device for use in formative research. Used in a group setting, PEAC has buttons whose labels can be changed to introduce new, content-specific evaluation variables.

The R.D. Percy Company of Seattle designed a qualitative on-line measurement system known as VOXBOX for use in the field. A panel was recruited of 200 television households in which a VOXBOX had been wired to the main television set. Panellists agreed to record their spontaneous evaluations of whatever television programme they chose to watch, using eight specially labelled qualitative response buttons on the VOXBOX. Channel selections and qualitative responses were fed continuously into the system's main computer via special telephone lines. Data were collected 24 hours a day, seven days a week.

This system was tested as a measure of an early audience reaction to a new television programme. Its advantages over usual, centralized, focus group discussion techniques were that it enabled larger and more representative samples of viewers to offer opinions. Furthermore, these individuals used a standardized vocabulary (i.e. button labels on the VOXBOX) and made judgements in the privacy and normal surroundings of home viewing.

What can continuous response measurements measure? In general, CRMs are used to obtain a person's self-report on some changing psychological state or judgement. They are useful because they provide a continuous track of psychological responses to media content, even though that media content may be constantly changing. For example with sequential and dynamic content such as a film, video or television programme, the CRM technique can monitor the extent to which a particular evaluative reaction remains at a constant level or shifts around significantly from one part of the production to another. In general, CRMs are used to measure audiences' affective responses or evaluative judgements about media content. It is, however, possible to use this technique to measure more cognitive-level judgements about media content, such as its meaningfulness.

CRM scales

It is possible to use a number of different types of measurement scale in continuous response measurement. These might include nominal or categorical scales, interval scales, single-scale or multiple-scale measurements. CRM methodologies have deployed nominal scale measures through which viewers can judge the content they are watching as belonging to one category or another. For example, a television programme may be judged 'boring' or 'interesting', 'difficult to understand' or 'easy to understand'. Most CRM systems have been used to determine audience enjoyment of films, programmes or advertisements. Hence, they usually display a linear like – dislike scale. These continuous audience response systems lend themselves to the potential use of a wide range of semantic differential scales such as enjoyable – unenjoyable, simple – complex and so on.

Single-scale studies may not adequately measure concepts of interest. Instead, it can be better to use multiple scales. There is evidence that viewers' evaluation of television programmes has a multidimensional structure (Philport, 1980). Multiple scale procedures can also provide a more effective measurement paradigm for probing mental models of the semantic processing and framing of television (Biocca, 1991a). One problem with multiple scale procedures is a logistical one for respondents. The application of several different scales in quick succession during a continuous response session may prove a difficult task which taxes respondents' concentration beyond a point where they can effectively provide meaningful responses. It may be necessary therefore to repeat the rated material (e.g. a film or programme) more than once when obtaining ratings along a number of distinct linear scales.

The programme analyzer – a contemporary case study

A continuous response measurement system has been used to explore the antecedents of programme quality and enjoyment in which measures of quality programming were derived from viewers' reactions while watching. In this particular case study, two genres were examined – quiz and game shows and soap operas (Gunter, 1995, 1997a). In both cases, the research comprised two stages. In the first stage, a programme analyzer system was used in the context of focus groups to elicit from viewers key attributes which underpinned a programme's popularity. In the second stage, evaluative scales were produced from the work completed in stage one and administered to a nation-wide viewing panel who used them to rate quiz shows and soap operas they had watched at home.

In the initial stage, episodes of well-known television quiz shows or soap operas were rated continuously by small groups of respondents using an electronic Group Response System. Each respondent received a handset that comprised a push button key pad and a dial. The buttons could be used by respondents to enter categorical data about themselves such as their gender, age, social class and so on. The dial was used to provide a continuous scalar evaluation of the television programme while viewing it. Ratings were made along a 100-point enjoyment scale. Respondents turned their dial to the left as their enjoyment decreased and to the right as their enjoyment increased. Each respondent's handset recorded their ratings on a second-by-second basis with the data being entered electronically into a PC to which each handheld device was connected. While their responses were invisible to them at the time they were made, they were visibly displayed as a moving line graph on a screen being monitored by a hidden operator who controlled the equipment.

After viewing the episode, a group discussion ensued, led by a moderator, which focused on what respondents liked and disliked about the programme they had just viewed. Segments of the programme were played back to respondents with their continuous evaluative ratings superimposed on screen over the programme. Points at which there were marked shifts in level of enjoyment were used to probe for factors within the programme which may have led to shifting opinions about it. This technique enabled respondents to identify specific features which had the effect of either increasing or decreasing their enjoyment of the programme. Across a series of focus groups in which a number of different soap operas or quiz shows were examined in this way, a consistent set of attributes emerged which seemed to represent core dimensions of each genre. These dimensions represented aspects of the production which were expected to be in place in respect of a particular genre, and which held the key to whether a particular programme would be seen by viewers as attaining a high quality for programmes of its type.

In the study of television quiz and game shows, seven genre – attribute dimensions emerged: *unpredictability, tension, contestants, presenter, reward, involvement* and *plot* (Gunter, 1995). *Unpredictability* evolved from fluctuations in fortunes of contestants; the suspense generated by anticipating whether or not the star prize will be won at the end of the show and by whom; the spontaneity and naturalness of delivery of both contestants' and presenter's comments; and the anticipation of whether an answer to a question is correct. *Tension* could evolve from: the pace of the show, especially the way in which the format and flow are unbroken and the game builds a smooth rhythm; the end game, especially the climax involving a large prize, and the way the contestants are eliminated during the course of the game; willing-on contestants when they are faced with a time limit to answer questions or complete a task, and identifying with their dilemmas when they have to choose between different options or between a guaranteed smaller prize or a less certain larger prize.

The *presenter* was a key factor and was expected by viewers to be at ease, natural and witty. Presenters who were spontaneous, rather than hiding behind obviously scripted jokes and remarks were better liked. It was also important that presenters had the ability to bring the best out of the contestants, and should generally have a personality which was in harmony with the show. Key elements about the *contestants* were that they should be allowed the opportunity to display distinctive personalities, including a sense of humour; they should display appropriate skill in the game; and they should invite viewer identification.

The key attributes of the *reward* dimension were that the game should be fair in the way prizes are allocated, the winner or winners should deserve their rewards, and the prizes should be suitable or appropriate for the stage of the game being played. *Involvement* of the viewer was important and was underpinned by the ability of the show's questions to engage viewers and encourage them to participate; by identification of viewers with contestants; and by the speed with which answers were revealed as the game was played (the more instantaneous the answers were given, the greater the enjoyment). Finally, the game's *plot* was important and referred to the structure of the game, the attractiveness of the regular features and sets, and the way the game itself progressed through logical stages, increasing rewards and penalties and filtering down contestants.

In the soap opera study, eight dimensions of viewer enjoyment emerged following a study of focus group reactions to episodes from eight different drama serials. These dimensions were labelled *verisimilitude, established characters, tension and drama, entertainment/involvement, coherence/cohesion, technical professionalism, contrast/balance* and *plot/setting* (Gunter, 1997a).

Verisimilitude embraced the opinion that a good soap should have a believable story-line, with plausible characters and the use of language which might normally be found in everyday conversations. The setting and scenery needed to create an authentic atmosphere, so that viewers felt that the drama was shot in a real location in real time. There was a general opinion that all good soap operas must include a core set of characters who are *established* over a period of time. Among these characters there must be someone for everyone to identify with. The characters should be capable of evoking a range of emotional responses among viewers.

Tension and elements of *drama* or unpredictability were also important. Anticipation of a likely conflict or clash seemed to prompt high enjoyment or involvement levels. Tension was also achieved via the depiction of impending or unfolding tragedy. Sudden or unexpected acts seemed to be another factor contributing to the tension during an episode. *Viewer involvement* represented a factor that was largely a by-product of the successful inclusion of certain other factors. Essentially, it was dependent upon the extent to which viewers were involved with both the characters and the plot. Better soap opera episodes seemed always to prompt viewers into wanting to know what happens next.

The *coherence or cohesion* of a soap opera included a number of component attributes. The first of these concerned the continuity of characters, which allowed viewers to build up identification with and knowledge of established characters. Continuity of plot was another identified feature. Here, viewers wanted to see a story being developed along a number of episodes. However, even within a single episode there should be coherent and self-contained plot elements.

The attribute of *technical professionalism* had four principal components. The acting was enjoyable if it was perceived to be both reasonably natural and dynamic. Wooden acting, devoid of emotion or depth was disliked. The camera work was cited as important, especially when evoking the atmosphere of an event by using a suitable mix of long and close-up shots. The scenery and props also needed to be as realistic and detailed as possible in order to suggest authenticity. Finally, the editing was important. Viewers felt that it should allow for a smooth transition from scene to scene.

The factor labelled *contrast and balance* essentially concerned the ability of a soap opera to incorporate a balanced range of elements so that one element functions as a foil to or contrast with another element. Such a balance was found to be achieved via certain specific devices. One involved the use of one predominant story which was tempered by one or two minor subplots. Indeed, when this balance is not achieved, enjoyment levels remained fairly low. Contrast was also found to be attained by balancing confrontation or mystery with reconciliation or resolution. Another feature enjoyed by viewers was any contrast between everyday discourse among characters and heightened drama in the form of some unusual event or a highly charged emotional scene. A further point of contrast was between dominating characters and at least one passive or weak character. This contrast in characterizations often created situations in which tension was generated, particularly where viewers hoped that for once the tables might be turned, with the weaker character showing some assertiveness.

The last major factor was *plot and setting*. The plot was found to work best when in 'rolling form'. In its ideal form, one story-line is in its embryonic stage, one is in mid-stage, and one is being resolved. Viewers liked plots that stimulated anticipation. This was generally achieved through the establishment of mystery so that the viewer becomes keen to discover what happens next.

The foregoing research has illustrated the power of using combinations of quantitative and qualitative techniques in audience research. It also demonstrates the value of bringing the audience into direct contact with the media content being assessed. Viewers can display complex patterns of evaluative responses to television programmes that are mediated by their expectations of specific genres. Research techniques such as the programme analyzer enable the media researcher to explore subtle features within programmes that viewers may ordinarily be unaware of responding to. When such features are drawn to their attention through a combination of on-line evaluation while viewing and follow-up group discussion, it becomes clear that programmes are perceived to be characterized by genre-specific attributes that viewers expect to find and which affect their personal ratings of how good or bad a programme is considered to be.

ACADEMIC RESEARCH

Academic research into audiences' evaluative reactions to media content has embraced a range of on-line and off-line quantitative and qualitative methodologies. Much of this work has been concerned with the measurement of various psychological reactions to different media content attributes. In relation to television, for example, research has investigated the ways audiences react to specific areas of programme content.

In particular, concerns about the tastefulness of media content and the sources of offence to audiences that derive from violent, sexual or profane subject matter, have led to the development of methodologies that enable members of the audience to respond directly to media materials. In some studies, researchers have conducted individual or group interviews with respondents to assess their reactions to programmes or to the coverage of specific issues or events, divorced from any direct and immediate exposure to media content. In other studies, methodologies have been used that have tested viewers' direct responses to programme content. In some instances, viewers have been shown and reacted to programme excerpts, while in other cases they have watched full length programmes and offered their opinions. Another important distinction is between research carried out with adult viewers and studies conducted amongst children.

Viewers' reactions to TV clips

In ascertaining how viewers respond to specific content features, one approach has been to obtain opinions about extracts of media content in which those features have been isolated. In this context, for instance, media researchers have explored viewers' perceptions of televised violence or the emotional reactions of children to frightening media content.

The immediate reactions of viewers to programme excerpts have been measured in the context of identifying the attributes taken into account by individuals when judging the seriousness of televised violence. In an experiment reported by Greenberg and Gordon (1972a) young boys were presented with a series of violent scenes, taken from movies and programmes, which differed in terms of various attributes such as the use of weapons, and degree of harm caused to victims. After each scene, respondents provided a series of evaluative ratings of it. Scenes in which weapons were featured or in which actors harmed themselves or another person were rated as more violent and less acceptable than scenes in which weapons were not featured or where harm, though intended, did not occur. Scenes depicting damage to another person were rated in more serious terms than scenes depicting property damage.

In another series of experiments in Britain, a similar approach was used to assess viewers' evaluative ratings of violence-containing clips from UK and US crime-dramas, westerns, science series, and cartoons. After each clip, which lasted for up to two minutes, viewers gave their ratings along a series of seven-point adjective scales. Scenes were shown singly or in pairs for comparative judgements. The programme clips had been selected to isolate specific features such as genre, dramatic context, physical setting, use of weapons, degree of harm to victims, and gender of perpetrators and victims. Results showed that the perceived serious-ness of violence was strongly associated with the realism of the setting, the degree of observable harm caused to victims, the use of certain types of weapon (sharp instruments), and the gender of the attacker and victim (Gunter, 1985a).

Research with children, using laboratory-based experimental method-ologies, has explored their emotional reactions to different types of tele-vision content. Many of these studies used a combination of continuous physiological measures and immediate post-viewing psychological reac-tions. Physiological measures have included facial expressions, heart rate and electrical conductivity of the skin (galvanic skin response or GSR). The latter measures are all known to provide reliable indicators of emo-tional responding. Psychological measures generally comprised verbal responses, describing their feelings or how much they liked the material shown to them.

Some studies have investigated the mediating effect of the realism of television portrayals upon children's emotional responding and enjoy-ment. Osborn and Endsley (1971) obtained continuous measures of GSR from four- and five-year-old children while they watched either a cartoon or non-cartoon programme excerpt that was either violent or non-violent. A post-viewing interview was then conducted with the children to find out which clip(s) they found to be 'scariest'. The programme featuring 'human' characters with violence was selected as the scariest of the four clips and also produced the highest GSRs.

A Swedish study used the analysis of children's facial reactions while viewing to measure how emotionally aroused they were by different scenes of violence (Lagerspetz et al., 1978). Pre-teenage children were shown five-minute extracts from television programmes that depicted physical violence, verbal violence, cartoon violence and non-violent behaviour. The children's facial expressions were videotaped while they were watching and then subsequently judged by coders trained to iden-tify the emotional meaning of such expressions. The children viewed in pairs and were unaware that they were being observed for their reac-tions. Facial expressions were classified according to nine evaluative scales: joyful – serious; afraid – not-afraid; worried – not-worried; angry – indifferent; understands – incomprehension; concentrated – distracted; tense – calm; active – immobile; and withdrawal – no-withdrawal. The children were interviewed afterwards to nominate their most liked film clip. The strongest emotional reactions occurred to the clips depicting the most realistic violence. Such scenes invoked the greatest expressions of fear and worry, tenseness and anger. Cartoon violence elicited joy and understanding, and along with more formulaic physical violence generated the greatest concentration.

Heart rate was used to measure degree of emotional responding to televised violence in a study with pre-teenage children, aged 8 to 11 years (Surbeck and Endsley, 1979). In this investigation, the children were each shown two three-minute duration video clips depicting exactly the same series of violent acts. In one case, however, the clip involved human actors, while in the other case it involved puppets. The children were tested in an experimental room designed to resemble a living room in someone's home. They were wired up to heart-beat apparatus for pre-testing several days before the experimental session proper and then again while being shown the two television clips. After viewing had finished, they were taken to a separate room for further testing. Here they were shown some photographs from each clip and asked to say 'how scary it was' and which clip they liked best. Neither version was overwhelmingly preferred, but the more realistic version was seen as more scary. Heart rates were observed to drop during the violent incidents in each clip, reflecting greater attentiveness at those points.

Other laboratory investigations have shown that children display higher emotional arousal when viewing television scenes in which a character displays expressions of fear than for scenes that focus upon the frightening stimulus that causes those fear expressions, as evidenced through immediate post-viewing verbal response of young viewers and continuous physiological measures such as galvanic skin response and skin temperature change (Wilson and Cantor, 1985).

Sometimes, watching a scary film or programme with someone else present can moderate children's emotional responses. In one experiment, pre-school children watched one of two versions of a suspenseful movie clip, either alone or with an older brother or sister. In one version the scene was portrayed as a dream sequence with a prologue and epilogue to provide cues to the fact that the depicted events were part of a dream (Wilson and Weiss, 1993).

In the scene taken from a television movie, *Invaders from Mars*, a boy follows a woman into a cave. He proceeds down a long dark tunnel until he reaches a cavern in which a spaceship is found occupied by a number of giant creatures. The boy hides behind a wall and watches the woman and the creatures. At this point a commercial break occurs. After the break, the scene continues. The woman notices the boy and threatens to get him. He runs out of the tunnel and escapes into the forest outside.

After watching the scene, the children were asked how scared they felt while watching it and how much they liked it. The children's facial expressions were also continuously monitored and video-recorded while they were viewing, and later categorized by coders.

The pre-schoolers who viewed with an older sibling were no better than those who watched alone in identifying the dream sequence version, but were generally less emotionally aroused by this suspenseful scene when watching with someone else. As a result of this, they also liked the film better. Many of the very young children in this experiment were unable to understand and identify the cues that indicated when the sequence was portrayed as a dream.

Reactions to full-length programmes

Research with full-length programmes has explored how viewers respond to variations in the nature of programme content. The use of full-length programmes has certain distinct advantages over evaluative ratings obtained to programme excerpts. First, the viewing experience is closer to a real life one. Second, viewers may be kept unaware of the changes in programme content that are being manipulated. In some such studies, programmes have been edited into different versions by the researchers, while in others they have been presented in their original form only. In the latter case, the main interest rests upon discovering whether certain features are most salient to viewers when they talk about the programme immediately afterwards.

Researchers at the British Broadcasting Corporation questioned viewers about their enjoyment of programmes immediately after their transmission. Questioning probed for viewers' opinions about different aspects of a programme to find out how salient its violent content had been. Post-viewing interviews revealed that few viewers mentioned the violence in the programme spontaneously; it was apparently not a significant aspect of the drama. It was found that perceptions of programmes as 'violent' did not depend on the actual number of violent incidents. Nor was there any relationship between perceiving a programme as violent and verbally reported emotional arousal (Shaw and Newell, 1972).

In experimental research into the significance of violence to liking of a programme, Diener and De Four (1978) presented 100 male and female college students with two versions of an episode of the US police drama *Police Woman*. One version was uncut, while the other consisted of the same episode minus almost all violent scenes. The uncut version was 47 minutes long and scored 40 when coded for violence; the cut version was 44 minutes long and scored only 9 for violent content.

It was found that the violent version was perceived as being more violent than the non-violent version, and that it was liked more too, although the difference in liking was non-significant. Among the students who saw the violent version, those who perceived it as more violent liked it less. Diener and De Four (1978) took this evidence as an indication that violent content may have little impact on the liking of a programme.

In a later report, three experimental investigations were presented that had been carried out with college students and families to determine relationships between content perceptions for full-length programmes and how much they were liked (Diener and Woody, 1981).

In the first study, 58 one-hour episodes of adventure shows on mainstream US television were video-recorded and each violent scene in the programme was rated by five male and five female judges for the seriousness of its violence, and its realism, excitement and action. The programme as a whole was also scored on scales of liking, violence, humour, romance, novelty, predictability, character development, plot, emotional conflict and action. From this poll of programmes, eight were chosen on the basis of whether they represented high- or low-violence and high- or low-conflict programmes. High- and low-conflict programmes that were selected were matched on the violence dimension, while selected high- and low-violence programmes were matched on the conflict dimension.

Experimental subjects then watched two programmes (high- and low-conflict or high- and low-violence). Subjects were 54 college students. After each programme, they evaluated it on ten-point scales in terms of violence, realism, action, excitement, humour, romance, novelty, emotional conflict, and suspense. High-conflict programmes were liked better than low-conflict programmes. However, low-violence programmes were enjoyed slightly more than high-violence programmes.

In a second study, programmes were selected from the same pool on the basis of three dimensions: violence, realism and action. Selected programmes scored either high or low on a particular dimension, while being controlled as far as possible for differences between them on the other two dimensions. A sample of 159 college students were allocated to conditions in which they watched either a high- and low-violence programme pair (controlled for realism and action), or a high- and low-realism pair (controlled for violence and action), or a high and low-action pair (controlled for violence and realism). After viewing each programme, it was evaluated along a series of ten-point scales as in the first study. While all three dimensions produced differences in programme perceptions, only violence level and action were associated with liking. Low-violence and low-action programmes achieved higher liking scores than did high-violence and high-action episodes.

In a third study, 62 families (161 individuals) were interviewed in their own homes, in which full-length programmes from situation comedy and crime-detective series were rated on dimensions such as action, realism, violence and liking. Each family saw two shows and rated each one in turn immediately after it had ended. Each programme pair comprised one high-violence and one low-violence episode. Diener and Woody found that high-violence programmes were generally liked significantly less than low-level violence programmes, but only by light viewers. There was no difference in liking of violent and non-violent programmes among heavy viewers.

Research has been conducted among children, whose reactions to full-length programmes were gauged under controlled viewing conditions. Van der Voort (1986) measured children's perceptions of televised violence at three schools in Holland. In all, 314 children, aged 9 to 11 years, were shown full-length episodes from eight television series. These series included realistic crime drama (*Starksy and Hutch, Charlies' Angels*), adventure series (*Dick Turpin, The Incredible Hulk*), and fantasy cartoons (*Scooby Doo, Tom and Jerry, Popeye, Pink Panther*).

Immediately after showing each programme, a post-exposure questionnaire was filled in by children measuring ten perception variables: (1) readiness to see violence; (2) approval of violent actions seen in the programme; (3) enjoyment of the violence seen; (4) evaluation of the programme; (5) emotional responsiveness; (6) absorption in the programme; (7) detachment while watching; (8) identification with the programme's chief characters; (9) perceived reality of the programme; and (10) comprehension and retention of programme content. Van der Voort investigated whether programmes perceived to be realistic were also more absorbing for children who would thereby respond to them with more emotion and less detachment than they showed toward programmes perceived to be more fantastic.

Results showed that law enforcement programmes were rated as the most realistic of those programmes presented to the children in this study. Thus, *Starsky and Hutch* and *Charlie's Angels* were perceived to be realistic, while *The Incredible Hulk, Dick Turpin* and cartoons were seen as fantastic. Realistic programmes were watched with more involvement, more emotion and less detachment. The two crime-drama series were also regarded as containing the most violence.

Viewers as editors

In the above studies, full-length programmes were, in some cases, edited by researchers to vary the nature of their content. A different approach that has been developed more recently is to put viewers themselves in the position of being editors. Viewers are invited to watch a programme and then re-edit the material as 'they would like to see it'. Respondents might approve the programme in its current form or require certain editorial changes to be made to it (Morrison et al., 1994). Morrison et al. reported a study in which this methodology was applied to programmes which contained violence. Five discrete areas were identified for investigation in this study: '(1) actual violence: fly-on-the-wall style – real violence captured by a film crew working with the police; (2) victims of violence: local news of interview with victim, close-up pictures of injury and description of violence; (3) perpetrators of violence: interview with serial killer; (4) reconstruction of violence: dramatic reconstruction of violent attacks on people; (5) actual violence: documentary and news violence, including untransmitted violence of same news items that had been broadcast' (1994: 365).

In the actual method itself, respondents are arranged in focus group format to begin with. They are then shown a programme or extracts from a programme, which they subsequently are given the option to re-edit. To assist with re-editing, respondents receive a transcript of the programme material which describes the visual form as well as narrative content. They may also receive still photographs from the programme. A video-tape editor is on hand to carry out the editing process to respondents' instructions. The final result could then be played back to respondents for further comment. Throughout, respondents could give reasons for the changes they wished to make. Thus, the technique brought viewers into direct contact with programme materials, caused them to think about these materials, and to explain their concerns, if any, with the original production.

The method could enable researchers to pinpoint the forms of violence which viewers were most concerned about and to understand the sources of their concern. It could assist broadcasters by specifying the kinds of treatment of particular types of subject matter that are likely to work best for audiences, or which kinds are likely to be found unacceptable. It is also sensitive to differences of opinion about programmes or specific portrayals related to the demographic composition of the audience.

CONCLUDING REMARKS

This chapter has examined research methodologies connected with the assessment of audiences' evaluative or affective responses to media. Most of this research has been conducted with television. The literature was divided, in this case, broadly by whether research was conducted by industry or the academy.

The measurement of audience reactions within the television industry has been regarded as an important supplement to the measurement of audience size and composition. Audiences for programmes can vary with scheduling factors and with the seasons. The size of a programme's audience is also determined by the channel on which it appears and by the nature of the intended audience (e.g. whether it is designed for a mass or niche audience). Whether the audience is small or large, the success of a programme is critically dependent on whether those individuals who do watch it, also like it. The measurement of audience reactions has therefore tended to focus on the measurement of audience appreciation of programmes. Much of this research has taken the form of 'off-line' measurement in which viewers' responses are captured after viewing has ended. 'On-line' measures of audience liking have been used to tease out more detailed evidence concerning specific production features of programmes that may underpin audience appreciation.

Within the academy, audience reaction research has more often tended to take the form of 'on-line' measurement, usually implemented in an experimental or focus group framework. This research activity has examined a variety of emotional reactions displayed by adult and child viewers to specific areas of content, such as violence. Thus, the concern in this research context extends beyond the establishment of levels of audience liking for programmes. There is an interest instead in whether certain types of material within programmes can cause adverse or upsetting affective reactions. Some of this academic audience reaction research has been sponsored by industry and may have regulatory or policy implications.

CHAPTER 6

MEASURING COGNITIVE RESPONSES TO MEDIA: ATTENTION AND COMPREHENSION

A great deal of thought has been invested in creating research techniques to measure media audiences and their exposure to media content. Much of this work has been quantitative in nature, deriving primarily from the positivist empirical school of media analysis. Research into media usage has been largely motivated by the needs of media industries and media advertisers to measure the size and composition of audiences that are exposed to media outputs. Data on audience measurement in this context serve as a commercial trading currency that determines the cost of advertising and the survival of publications and broadcasts. The notion of the audience as conceived within this commercially oriented approach to the measurement of media usage has been challenged by some writers as providing an excessively narrow definition of the 'audience' and of audiences' involvement with the media (e.g. Ang, 1990). Criticisms of quantitative audience research have queried the validity of the measuring techniques applied to quantify and classify audiences and their media-related behaviours. A call has been made for the use of qualitative approaches to get beneath the skin of the media – audience relationship.

In exploring media research methods, however, there are other levels of audience involvement with media that need to be examined other than simply whether and to what extent media are used by audiences, and the extent to which audiences are exposed to media. Exposure to the mass media, in the sense of reading a newspaper or magazine, listening to the radio or watching television, has so far been considered only in terms of a behavioural relationship. Watching television, for example, has often been defined for commercial purposes as a viewer simply being present in a room with the television set switched on. Another concept of 'watching' though, is whether the individual actually looks at the screen and pays attention to what is going on in the programme being broadcast at that time. Individuals may be exposed to television in so far as they engage in the behaviour of switching the set on and remaining in the room while it is operating. But to what extent do they pay attention to what is happening? This is an important question in the context of understanding how the media impact upon their consumers. Unless media users pay psychological attention to the media content they appear to be reading, viewing or listening to, it may have little if any direct influence upon them.

In this chapter, the topic of attention to the media is examined. When an individual is exposed to a mass medium, how do we know whether he or she is really paying attention to its content? While we can infer from a diary or people meter system that a particular television programme was tuned into via a respondent's television set, we do not know to what extent that individual paid continuous and focused attention to the materials that appeared on the screen. To assess the nature of media exposure in terms of whether there was a degree of cognitive effort invested in processing the content being consumed, a number of specialized research techniques have been devised, some of which are quantitative and some of which are qualitative. Some of these techniques can be used in natural viewing conditions, while others require more artificial conditions to operate effectively.

In an academic context, measurement of attention to the media is significant in relation to the debate about whether media audiences are 'active' or 'passive'. This debate has been especially pronounced in regard to discussions about the nature of television viewing. The notion of television viewing as active or passive has operationally defined the level of activity at cognitive and behavioural levels. Cognitive activity refers to the degree of mental activation invoked in paying attention to a medium. A number of research techniques have been developed to assess the degree of cognitive attention to a medium, including measures of physiological responses to media content and measures of information-processing capacity. Behavioural measures of activity include overt channel switching behaviour and observational evidence of television viewing in which viewers are heard to make verbal responses about programmes while watching.

There has been much discussion of television viewing as active or reactive (passive) in relation to the way viewers process information from television programmes. Alternative schools of thought posit either that viewers' attention to programmes is controlled by the formal features of the medium, such as scene changes, physical events on screen, background music, sound effects and so on (reactive) or that viewers learn to control their attention for themselves in relation to deeper-level factors such as anticipating what might come next in a story (active). In the latter case, attention to the screen is actively and strategically guided by attempts to understand and follow the programme.

OFF-LINE MEASUREMENTS

Off-line measures include the kinds of quantitative measures that are taken in survey interviews and laboratory experiments, and, more qualitatively, in focus groups. In a survey context, respondents may be asked questions about the degree of attention they pay to the screen when viewing television or to the page when reading newspapers. In an experimental setting, subjects may be asked to indicate how much mental effort they invested in a programme shortly after watching it in a controlled environment. In focus groups, participants may be asked to provide impressions, in a more open-ended form, about how attentive they are when watching television, listening to the radio or reading a newspaper or magazine.

Survey interview measures

One off-line measure that is commonly used in studies which attempt to quantify relationships between media attention and specific kinds of post-consumption media impact is to ask respondents how many hours a week they watch television, listen to radio or read a newspaper, or how regularly would they consume that medium. For example, in relation to television viewing, two questions are often used in partnership. The first one asks: 'During an average week, on how many days do you personally watch television? 7 days, 6 days, 5 days, 3 or 4 days, 1 or 2 days, less often, hardly ever/never?'. This would then be followed by: 'On a day when you personally watch television, for about how many hours do you view on average? Less than one hour, more than one hour but less than two hours, more than two hours but less than three hours, more than three hours?'.

Another off-line approach is to obtain from individuals an indication of the degree of attention they pay to a medium. Sometimes, researchers measure the self-professed orientations of media consumers towards particular media. For instance, viewers can be asked about their motives for watching television or tuning in to a particular programme. The measurement methodologies used in this context tend to be either structured questionnaires or focus groups in which questions tend to be open-ended. Levy (1978) used a combination of focus group discussions and personal interviews to question people about their reasons for watching television news interview programmes. Respondents gave such reasons as: 'interview programmes give me food for thought'; 'I learn new things about public issues from interview programmes'; and 'I like it when the reporters ask tough questions'. While this approach can provide some interesting insights into why individuals orient themselves towards certain television programmes, they do not really reveal accurate or precise indications of the degree of attention being paid to these programmes during the act of watching.

Another form of questioning used in a survey interview format is one that tries to establish whether the consumption of a particular mass medium normally engages all or only part of a person's attention. Survey research has indicated, for example, that individuals report engaging in other activities at the same time as watching television. From this evidence, albeit based on the testimony of those interviewed, it appears that watching television does not invariably command the viewer's entire attention.

In his study of the audience's experience with television news, Levy (1978) asked his respondents: 'Do you sometimes do something else, like eat dinner, work, read, or things like that [while watching television news]?'. Respondents were permitted more than one answer, and their multiple responses were coded to provide a list of viewer activities while watching television news. One in four respondents reported no other activity while they were watching the news, while another one in four mentioned one other behaviour, notably 'eating dinner'. Of course, not all of these alternative or concurrent behaviours are likely to be equally distracting. One could still give fairly complete attention to the news while eating, because the two activities would not demand the same degree or kind of mental processing. On the other hand, an activity such as reading, could occupy some of the information-processing systems needed for encoding the news from television, and might therefore cause much more interference.

Levy also asked a question about the proportion of a television newscast his respondents would normally watch. When sitting down to watch the news, would they typically sit through the entire broadcast from beginning to end, or watch only parts of it? The great majority of those individuals he questioned (70 per cent) claimed ordinarily to watch the entire newscast. However, it is not altogether clear what this response really meant. Indeed, it could be interpreted in a number of ways. A viewer might leave the set switched on throughout the newscast, but leave and re-enter the viewing room at least once during the transmission. Alternatively, the viewer might remain in the viewing room for the entire duration of the newscast, but also read the paper or take a telephone call at the same time. His or her attention would therefore not be totally devoted to the newscast, even though they had sat in front of the screen for the entire programme. In using such off-line measures to determine the degree of attention people devote to media, there is a strong reliance on what they can accurately remember and effectively articulate about the normal behaviour.

Many surveys of television viewing have taken a fairly global view of what 'watching television' really means. Some surveys have asked respondents to estimate their viewing in terms of periods of time devoted to the medium. Others have questioned respondents about the amount of attention they pay to a programme. Other approaches have focused on the extent to which respondents reportedly pay attention to a part of a programme (Chaffee and Schleuder, 1986). A number of studies have found that correlations between reported exposure levels and how much people remember from programmes tend to be small (Patterson and McClure, 1976). Therefore, it may be important to distinguish between asking people about 'exposure' and asking instead about 'attention' (Chaffee and Schleuder, 1986).

Attention measurement in an experimental framework

Another off-line measurement technique has been used to measure attention to a mass medium in an experimental framework. In this case, the experiment was designed to measure learning from television programmes by children. One of the factors investigated as a potentially significant predictor of learning was level of attention invested in the viewing experience. In this case, children's level of attention was measured by asking them to report how much mental effort they believed they expended in processing television (Salomon, 1983; Salomon and Leigh, 1984).

In this research, Salomon developed a concept called AIME, or the Amount of Invested Mental Effort during learning from a particular medium. AIME was assessed with a short series of questions such as 'How much did you concentrate or pay attention to the show?'. Children responded to these questions along a five-point scale. Salomon found that children generally perceive watching television as requiring less effort than reading – although there were some cross-national differences in this respect, with Israeli children he interviewed reportedly finding television a more demanding medium than American children. Salomon hypothesized that because children think that television is an easy medium to learn from, they therefore do not try as hard when watching an educational programme as when reading a textbook. However, this difference can be offset by giving children instructions to concentrate harder while viewing because they will be tested afterwards on a programme's content. Measures of increased, self-reported mental effort while watching television have been linked to better actual recall and comprehension test performance on a programme later on (Salomon and Leigh, 1984).

Focus group measures

Research into attention to media content has been conducted in a focus group format. This has not been a commonly used methodology in this context, but it is worth mentioning in view of the growing confidence certain media scholars have expressed in this methodology over the past twenty years. In a study of attention to television news, Robinson and Sahin (1984) conducted seven focus group interviews in two parts of Britain to examine how people actually process news from televised bulletins. One aspect of this research was to establish how much attention people normally paid to television news while it was being broadcast.

Groups of between six and ten people took part in three-hour sessions in which they were shown a news programme and were then invited to discuss the features of televised news coverage in Britain that they liked and disliked. At 9 o'clock, during the course of these evening sessions, they watched that evening's main news programme on the BBC. While the newscast was being shown the researchers developed questions about the news items in the programme to measure the groups' recollection and understanding of them. The researchers had already gathered some earlier information from the programme's producers about the probable content of the bulletin. These questions were then put to respondents in a subsequent discussion about the programme.

In order to gain some notion of how much attention respondents had paid to the newscast, the researchers switched off the television set three or four times during the programme and asked respondents what they were thinking about at the exact moment the set was turned off. Even though this was a group watching situation dealing with the news they were about to discuss, fewer than half the respondents reported attention to the news item that was on the screen at the time. This reaction was more likely to occur during news items about topics such as politics, economics or foreign affairs than among items about human interest matters. Here we have an example of a methodology that is partially on-line in its technique of attention measurement in that, besides questions about the programme after it had finished, the researchers attempted to measure attention, albeit on a self-report basis, while the programme was being shown. Its limitation is that it merely indicated whether a respondent was paying attention or not, and did not measure the degree of attention. It was also dependent on a respondent's honesty in admitting, in a potentially embarrassing context, that they were not paying attention to the programme.

ON-LINE MEASUREMENT

As we have seen, attention to the media has been assessed through off-line or part off-line/part on-line measurement techniques. Off-line methodologies, whether quantitative or qualitative in nature, used in this context, have serious shortcomings, however. On-line methodologies have the distinct advantage of providing direct evidence of what happens when a person is actually consuming media content. Many on-line techniques measure non-verbal rather than simply verbal behaviour. In other words, they do not necessarily require the media consumer to say anything about their media experiences.

In the examination of on-line media research techniques that follows, a broad distinction will be made between research methods used in the field and research methods used in a laboratory setting. Field research in this context generally comprises *observational research*. Laboratory research comprises a variety of physiological and psychological tests and measurements that are taken while an individual is consuming predetermined media content.

Observational research

Observational research was introduced in Chapter 2 where the fundamental characteristics of this research technique were outlined. Observational research has been used primarily to investigate the way people use specific mass media and has also featured as a technique deployed in the context of examining media influences. It represents a form of qualitative research generally deployed by researchers who adhere to a critical social science school of thought. In the context of media use, observational research has featured most often in studies of television viewing. Here, two distinct versions can be distinguished:

1. participant observation, where an observer joins a household and monitors household members' behaviour, especially anything that occurs in front of the television set
2. photographic, film or video observation in which researchers set up equipment within the household either next to or inside the television set to provide time-lapse or continuous recordings of activity in front of the screen.

Such methodologies can yield insights into the use of television by different kinds of household, which are, by and large, difficult to obtain or unattainable by more traditional methods.

Participant observation

The application of observational methodologies to the study of media use and attention has been sporadic. In a small study conducted among five- and six-year-old boys from poor families in Washington DC, Murray (1972) collected observational data across two sessions which lasted no more than one hour on each occasion. He reported that the amount and style of viewing varied widely across the children he observed, and that their visual attention to the television screen averaged 52 per cent.

Observational research conducted by Lull (1978, 1980, 1982) has already been reviewed in Chapter 4. This research provided a good illustration of the insights that can be gained through ethnographic methodologies about viewing behaviour under natural, domestic conditions. Lull's research is also relevant to any consideration of the nature of attention to the screen during television viewing. In this series of studies, the researcher or his assistants entered the homes of families and interacted with family members as well as observing them during the act of viewing. Conversations about television were audio-taped for later analysis, while other data collection exercises were also utilized to enhance understanding about the way families use television.

Much of the research effort in this project was directed towards understanding how viewing decisions are made and the nature of any negotiation processes that occur among family members concerning what they will watch. One exercise used by Lull presented families with fabricated programme menus from which they were invited to choose a number of viewing options (Lull, 1978). Data on attention to the television derived primarily from the observations of the researchers and the notes they made at the end of each day about the nature of the viewing behaviour they had witnessed.

The observers' procedures for data gathering were standardized as far as possible from family to family. Each observer maintained a pre-printed log on which the ongoing viewing behaviour of families was documented throughout the day. Since the observers were known to the families only as students, the observers took most of their notes in the guise of 'homework' chores which they conducted while they sat in the living rooms or television viewing areas of the homes. In this way, observers were able to take many notes on the premises and record the details of family television viewing practices as they occurred.

The television set was observed to occupy a pivotal role in many family households. Behaviour was organized around it and it was in the background for much activity. Moreover, family routines were often structured in time around the established television viewing routines (Lull, 1978, 1980, 1982).

Photographic, film and video observations

Observational evidence is not always collected by researchers or their assistants being physically present in the environment in which behaviour patterns are being monitored. An alternative approach has been to place photographic, film or video cameras in the natural environment and capture visual evidence in film or tape which can be replayed and studied at leisure. A small number of studies have used this method to obtain insights into the nature of television viewing in home viewing environments.

The first major investigation of this sort was conducted by Allen (1965) who installed time-lapse film cameras in 95 homes in Oklahoma for two weeks, during 1961, 1962 and 1963. Allen noted that inattention and activities concurrent with television viewing were common. He found that no one was in the viewing room more than 19 per cent of the time the television was switched on and that the least-attentive viewers were pre-school children.

In this investigation, the cameras photographed the area in front of the television set and the set itself at a rate of four frames per minute. Allen provided little methodological detail or quantitative description of his findings, apparently because the data were obtained for proprietary commercial purposes. According to this researcher, differences between observational and self-reported diary accounts of viewing were substantial for some families and only small for others.

A few years later, a study by Bechtel et al. (1972) installed real-time video equipment in 20 homes in Kansas for six-day periods during 1970. Video cameras were installed alongside television sets, with a camera recording events in the viewing room that took place in front of the set and another camera recording what was being viewed. The video equipment was wired up to a control console operated from a vehicle parked outside the home.

The researchers found that viewers frequently engaged in activities in parallel to watching the television, which affected the degree of visual attention paid to the screen. Age differences in attention levels were also noted. Children aged 1 to 10 years paid visual attention to the screen for about 52 per cent of the time they were watching, while those aged 11 to 19 years averaged 69 per cent, and adults averaged nearly 64 per cent. Respondents who completed family viewing diaries were found to overestimate the amount of time they spent viewing by about 25 per cent in their diary returns as compared with video evidence.

In the same study, participants also filled out a variety of questionnaires designed to estimate viewing behaviour. These consisted of a diary comprising 15-minute time intervals for each day of the five-day observation period. Respondents had to mark off the intervals during which they had watched television; another questionnaire asked respondents to specify programmes watched the previous day and to fill out one sheet for each programme, estimating the amount of time each programme was actually watched; and finally another questionnaire, administered following the sixth day, asked for an estimate of family viewing during the five days for which viewing was filmed.

A number of important findings emerged from the comparisons between self-reports of television viewing and behavioural measures. With respect to diary estimates, for example, cases of underreporting amount of viewing were infrequent (5.5 per cent of the total time), whereas over-reporting was more generally the case (24.8 per cent). This means that for roughly every four hours watching reported, only three hours were actually spent watching. Comparisons of previous-day reporting and behavioural observations produced even less agreement. The average agreement between these two measures was only 45.5 per cent. This meant that for over half the time respondents reported watching television, they were not actually doing so. Finally, the comparison between five-day questionnaire estimates of amount of television viewing and observational behaviour measures produced even less agreement. With this particular self-report measure, respondents were required to estimate the number of hours viewed per day during the five-day period, both for themselves and for each member of their family. Comparisons with observational measures indicated that nearly all respondents over-reported the amount of television watching both for themselves and for others. Average agreement was about 44 per cent.

A third American study conducted a few years later provided a more detailed analysis of viewing and visual attention data. This study, however, focused on children's viewing. Anderson et al. (1985) compared parent diaries of five-year-old children's time spent with television with concurrent automated time-lapse video observations. They also ran a number of control groups to assess the effects of observational equipment in the home.

The observed sample comprised 334 mostly white middle-class families, of whom 106 had video observational equipment installed. The project was conducted in four phases over two months. The sample was split into four groups. Group C–NE (Control, No Equipment mentioned) was a control group of 102 families that was recruited with no mention of in-home observational equipment. These families went through the four-phase procedure and did not have observational equipment installed in their homes.

Group C–EP (Control – Equipment Possible) was a control group of 42 families that was recruited with mention of in-home equipment and who agreed to have such equipment installed in their homes should this have been requested. These families, however, did *not* have equipment installed in their homes, and went through the same four-phase procedure as Group C–NE.

Group E–E (Experimental – Equipment Installed) was recruited with mention of in-home equipment and was the only group to actually have observational equipment installed in their homes. This group of 106 families otherwise went through the same four-phase procedure as the other groups.

Group C–ER (Control – Equipment Refused) was originally recruited to be part of Group E–E. These 85 families, however, later withdrew their agreement to have observational equipment installed in their homes. They remained in the study and went through the same four-phase procedure as the other control groups.

The four phases of the procedure were (1) an initial visit by a parent and the focus child to the research centre. During this visit the child was observed viewing television and was given a number of tests of cognitive status. The parent filled out an extensive questionnaire concerning family demographics and television viewing activities. (2) After the first phase visit, the family maintained a 10-day television viewing diary. (3) One month after completion of the viewing diary, a second 10-day viewing diary was filled out. Group E–E had observational equipment installed in their homes concurrent with this second diary-filling period. (4) Following the completion of the third phase, the parent and focus child returned to the research centre for additional testing and to fill out a debriefing questionnaire.

The home observational equipment comprised two cameras. One had a zoom lens and recorded programmes on the family's television, while a second camera filmed the room area from which individuals were most likely to watch the television. Control circuitry activated a time-lapse video-recording deck only when the television set was switched on. This recorded one video frame every 1.2 seconds. The time and date were continuously superimposed on the tape. All families kept viewing diaries for two 10-day periods.

Two British studies got underway in the 1980s. In one study, Collett and Lamb (1986) examined relationships between actual presence in the room while the television set was on and actual looking at the screen, and subjective ratings of enjoyment and impact of the programmes being viewed. Respondents were six professional and six non-professional class families (24 viewers altogether) with whom special observational equipment was installed for a period of seven days. This equipment consisted of a cabinet which contained a television set, video camera and two video-recorders. One VCR took a picture and sound feed from the television, while the other took feeds from the camera. The camera was activated when the television set was switched on and filmed whatever happened in front of the set.

The researchers measured 'presence' and 'looking'. Presence was calculated as a percentage of the actual amount of time the programme had been on the set (i.e. not its actual broadcast time) for which a viewer was physically present in the viewing room. Looking was calculated as a percentage of the actual amount of time someone had spent gazing at the screen over the amount of time they had spent in the room.

In each home, the husband and wife filled in a viewing diary which listed all programmes broadcast on the four main channels (BBC1, BBC2, ITV, Channel 4) between 6pm and closedown each day. Against each listed programme, respondents were required to supply five separate pieces of information. Three of these dealt with viewing estimates: presence in front of the screen during a programme, looking at the screen while a programme was on, and attentive viewing of programmes. The other two measures were indicators of audience reaction. Respondents were asked to rate each programme they had watched or looked at, for enjoyment and impact, using scales from 0 to 100.

Collett and Lamb examined the relationship between actual presence, actual looking and ratings of enjoyment and impact. Programmes were excluded where it was not possible to determine how long the programme had been on television and in all those cases when someone denied being in the room during the programme. 'Presence' was then re-calculated as a percentage of the actual amount of time the programme had been on the set. 'Looking' was re-calculated as a percentage of the actual amount of time someone had spent gazing at the screen over the amount of time they had spent in the room. Presence and looking were significantly, though weakly, correlated at $r = 0.21$, and enjoyment was correlated with impact at $r = 0.51$. Presence was related to enjoyment at $r = 0.22$ and to impact at $r = 0.14$. Looking had slightly higher correlations with enjoyment ($r = 0.32$) and impact ($r = 0.27$).

A crucial question is whether these findings provide any support for the idea that people are likely to stay in the room or to look at the television more if they are enjoying a programme or if it is having an impact on them. The answer to this question is that there is a positive and significant relationship between the objective measures of presence and looking on the one hand and the subjective measures of enjoyment and impact on the other, but it may be worth noting that the amount of variance explained by the relationship between these objective and subjective measures is not particularly large. For example, in the case of looking and enjoyment, which has the highest correlation of 0.32, enjoyment is only accounting for something in the region of 10 per cent of the variance of looking. In the other cases, the percentage of variance explained is even lower.

A second British study used similar equipment to that of the first study. On this occasion, a specially designed television cabinet was placed in the main television viewing room of six family households and was operated in the same way as a standard television set. Whenever the set was switched on, a video camera and recording equipment were activated, making a continuous recording of all activity in camera shot in front of the set. The equipment was placed in each household for between two and four days (Gunter et al., 1995).

Observational data of viewers watching television were coded in 30-second units. A record was made of who was present in front of the screen, degree of visual attention to the screen, performance of other activities and use of the remote control device. These observations were cross-referenced with data on types of programmes being shown at the time and the channel on which they were being played.

Time was recorded at the start of the recorded viewing session, which was initiated by the television set being switched on and terminated at the time of the television set being switched off. Further punctuation points in viewing were signalled by a change of channel or a change of television material (i.e. start of a new programme, ad-break, etc.).

Observational data noted who was viewing and the kind of behaviour in which they engaged. Behavioural measures were divided into presence in the room, television watching, activities, conversation, and posture. Presence was divided into three levels: Full, Partial and Not at all. Full presence, within a 30-second interval, was determined by the viewer's being in the room for 99–100 per cent of that period. Partial presence represented 10–98 per cent of the time spent in the room. Calculating this measurement was made easier by an electronic auditory beep which broke down the observation time into 10-second intervals. The 'Not at all' category was allocated when a viewer was present for less than 10 per cent of each 30-second time interval. There were occasions when the viewer was out of camera shot, but was known still to be in the room since they had not been seen exiting it. In this instance, the viewer was coded as out of view.

Watching signified looking at the television screen. This indicated that the viewer appeared to be looking at the screen, which is to be distinguished from actually paying full attention to it. As with Presence, Watching was divided into Full, Partial and Not at all. There was also a fourth 'out of view' category.

Results showed that family members were absent for substantial proportions of the time the television set was in operation, and even when present, viewers did not always pay full attention to the screen for more than a minority part of the time. Families and family members varied significantly in respect of certain patterns of television watching. The evidence indicated that viewers pay far from unbroken attention to the television after switching it on. In the current study, there was no one even present in the viewing room for over half the observed time. Even when family members were present with the set switched on, they did not look at the screen all the time.

The distribution of set switched-on time, presence in front of the set, and looking at the screen varied with the type of programme. The programme types occupying the greatest proportions of time spent looking at the screen were thriller drama, quiz shows, children's programmes and the news. The level of visual attention was greatest for factual programmes such as news, documentaries and religious programmes. Sport and crime drama also emerged as being among the programmes most likely to attract visual attention to the screen. Even among these programmes, however, looking behaviour was far from continuous and viewers were looking away from the screen for substantial proportions of the time such programmes were being watched.

OTHER ON-LINE APPROACHES

A number of laboratory-situated techniques have been developed for assessing the degree of attention viewers pay to the screen when watching television. Broadly, these techniques can be divided into those grounded in (1) behavioural measures, (2) physiological measures, and (3) information-processing tasks.

Behavioural measures

These measures utilize continuous monitoring of viewers' behavioural reactions while watching the screen to determine the degree of attention that is being invested in viewing by the individual. One such technique includes measurement of visual attention behaviour as defined by the degree to which the viewer's eyes are fixated on the screen. Another behavioural measure again involves monitoring visual attention to the target medium, but in a context where other behavioural distractors are present.

Eyes on screen

Eyes on screen or EOS is an index of 'how much' an individual looks at the television screen (Thorson, 1994). It is a continuous, over-time index of attention. The usual way of obtaining EOS data is either to observe in person or to videotape individuals while they are watching. Often the camera is located behind and slightly above the television on the other side of a one-way mirror. These tapes are then analysed to determine when viewers' eyes are oriented toward the screen, the duration of each EOS event, and the number of such events.

EOS is frequently coded in terms of looking, not looking or undetermined looking for each consecutive time interval of some arbitrarily chosen duration. This duration is usually short (e.g. 2–5 seconds) so that changes in response to rapidly varying television content can be tracked, but not so short that coders would not be able to determine the placement of the eyes without specialized equipment. Whether observing 'live' or via video-recorded footage, the observer's main task is to judge when a viewer is actually looking at the screen. Thus, the data are observational in nature and operationalized by requiring the observer to press a button when the viewer looks towards the screen and away from it again. The button is part of an electronic data-recording device linked to a computer.

If the observer has synchronized the computer program with the beginning of the television programme being watched by the individuals being observed, then a continuous record of the onset and offset of 'looks' at the screen can be obtained that is directly linked to events happening in the programme. It is then possible to establish the significance of certain on-screen events to the motivation or maintenance of visual attention on the part of the viewer.

To ensure that good quality data are collected it is obviously important to situate the viewer so that the observer can see their eyes and detect in which direction their gaze is focused. It is recommended that the television monitor is placed at an angle to the viewers so that they are required physically to turn their heads to a small degree to watch the screen. This helps the observer to identify onset or offset of 'looks'. In research with children, who have a tendency to fidget and move around, it is important to ensure that they remain within the observer's field of view.

What EOS cannot do is measure all kinds of attention. It is possible for someone to be paying attention to the television, auditorily, while looking away from it. The EOS method would not normally sense this kind of attention.

Research using visual orientation has been used to address a number of questions about viewers' involvement with television other than simply how much visual attention they pay to the screen. There has been a debate about whether children are active or passive viewers (Gunter and McAleer, 1997). One school of thought has posited that children view in a 'passive' way, with their viewing controlled by the dynamic nature of television (Singer, 1980). An alternative view is that children are cognitively active viewers. Their attention to television is believed to be directed by their knowledge and expectations about programmes or the storylines within programmes (Anderson and Lorch, 1983; Huston and Wright, 1983; Salomon, 1983).

Research with children's programmes

Early research with EOS methodology was concerned with identifying which programme attributes caused children to attend visually to the television rather than to competing stimuli. The amount of visual attention children direct at television is also known to be influenced by the informativeness of visual and auditory formal features of programmes. Children's attention to the screen tends to be greater in the presence of such features as children's voices, peculiar voices, sound effects, auditory changes, animation, rapid movement and some visual special effects, and relatively low in the presence of adult male voices and character inactivity (Calvert et al., 1982; Campbell et al., 1987).

Research with television advertising

At about the same time as these studies with children were being set in motion, EOS measures were developed to investigate how people attend to television advertising (Webb and Ray, 1979). With time, this branch of visual attention research established increasingly-sophisticated methodologies. In a typical study, the researchers would create a simulated living room environment in the research centre and film small groups of individuals as they watched television. These individuals were free to talk to each other, walk around, leave the room and return to it at will, just as they would behave at home. They watched 90 minutes of material, comprising different genres of programming (news, comedy, action-drama, etc.), with commercial breaks embedded within the programming. EOS was used to measure degree of visual attention to the commercials as distinct from the programmes. Some findings indicated that the more attention viewers paid to the commercials, the more they were subsequently able to remember these advertising messages (Thorson and Zhao, 1988, 1989).

Research with environmental distractors

In addition to experiment-based studies in which children or adult viewers were observed while watching television and had their looks at screen quantified, another variation on the eyes-on-screen methodology has been to measure the degree of attention paid to a television screen by viewers in the face of competing distractions for their attention in the viewing environment. In typical studies of this sort, episodes of educationally oriented television series such as *Sesame Street* or *The Electric Company* served as stimulus materials and attention was defined exclusively in terms of watching the screen as opposed to doing something else (e.g. playing with toys in the same room) (Alwitt et al., 1980; Anderson and Levin, 1976).

A system of analysing programme complexity was developed by Krull (1983) in which production variables were linked to measures of viewer appeal. Work with children showed that such formal features were also linked to young viewers' level of attention to the screen. The methodology in which these relationships were explored included environmental distractions. Children were tested in a room that allowed them to pay attention either to the television set or to some alternative form of stimulation. The alternatives or distractions included a slide projector, toys, other children or some combination of these things. Coders hidden behind a one-way mirror observed the children in front of the television set and measured the amount of visual attention they paid to the screen. It was reported that the coders could tell with high reliability if the children were looking at the screen.

Ratings of attention to the screen were conducted on a continuous basis using push buttons connected to mechanical recording devices. Either the onset or offset of attention or the average attention during a specified time interval were noted (Krull and Husson, 1979). Often these data were aggregated over programme segments or over a number of children (Anderson and Levin, 1976). The resulting data represented an average response to programmes rather than point estimates for individuals.

In another study, Watt and Welch (1983) analysed the dynamic complexity of two education programmes. They then conducted an experiment with four- to six-year-old children who were randomly allocated to view an episode of the pre-school educational programme, *Mister Rogers' Neighborhood* or edited extracts from editions of *Sesame Street*. The experimental procedures were identical for both programmes. Subjects viewed a videotape alone in a room with a variety of toys and other activities provided as alternatives to viewing, while the experimenter observed and recorded the subject's attention to the screen through a one-way mirror. Immediately after the programme had finished, the experimenter administered a learning test that required the subject to recall and recognize material from the programme.

Second-by-second measurement was used to examine relationships between the complexities of the two programmes and children's visual attention to the screen. *Mister Rogers' Neighborhood* differed from *Sesame Street* in having a less complex audio track and having a more complex visual track. Audio static complexity was strongly associated with visual attention in *Mister Rogers' Neighborhood*, but was not linked to level of visual attention devoted to *Sesame Street* clips. Audio dynamic complexity showed a positive relationship with attention in respect of both programmes. Changes in the audio track over time produced higher levels of visual attention. Visual static complexity exhibited a consistent relationship with visual attention in both programmes. Visual dynamic complexity was positively related to visual attention as well, with greater amounts of visual change on the screen giving rise to higher levels of visual attention on the part of young viewers.

One interesting study using this method was reported by Mielke (1983). This research represented part of a formative exercise associated with the development of a children's science programme called *3-2-1 Contact*. A behavioural measure of attention, called the Distractor Method, had been developed and used successfully with two other children's education programmes – *Sesame Street* and *The Electric Company* (Palmer, 1974; Palmer et al., 1968). This method involved an observer continuously recording whether attention was being paid to the television screen by a single child. A 'distractor' placed near the television set consisted of a rear-screen projector with slides that changed every few seconds. By summing levels of actual attention across subjects and plotting this across time, the resulting attention profile was diagnostically useful in making recommendations to production staff.

When the distractor method was tried on the *3-2-1 Contact* audience, it did not work. These older children were able to figure out what was going on, and devised clever strategies to view the distraction and the test programme. One methodological answer to the 'divided attention' problem was a procedure reported by Wakshlag, Day and Zillmann (1981). Here, a test programme and one or more 'distractor' programmes could be fed simultaneously via cassettes to a single television monitor, where actual channel selection behaviour could be recorded electronically and observed directly. Mielke and his colleagues devised and experimented with a research apparatus called the Programme Selector which allowed group administration as well as behavioural measures of viewer choice. Three monitors displayed different programmes simultaneously, fed by three video cassette players. The audio was fed through individual earphones to test audience members. Through push buttons, they selected the one audio channel of choice, and the audio selection patterns were recorded as an index of viewing choice. The device was cumbersome, however, and not easily portable to schools, where most of the test audiences were recruited. Because the prototype device had other mechanical problems, such as having the audio-selection buttons visible to others in the group, thus introducing a potential group influence on individual responses, and because time was not available during production to revise and thoroughly test the apparatus, developmental work on the Programme Selector was stopped.

Physiological measures

These measures entail wiring up respondents in a laboratory situation so that various physiological responses can be continuously monitored while they watch a television programme. This approach has also been used to measure audience responses to advertisements. Techniques have included changes in heart rate, brain wave patterns and in the electrical conductivity of the skin during viewing.

Heart rate measures

Measurement of the beating of the heart can provide an indication of how much attention a person is paying to something. Two kinds of attention can be considered in this context: (1) long-term or tonic attention and (2) short-term or phasic attention (Lang, 1994).

Phasic attention refers to brief changes in attention that are related to sudden changes in the environment. These changes involve an orienting response (OR) that is a short-term reaction brought about by something new or interesting that happens in the environment. A new stimulus in a person's immediate surroundings may make them sit up and take notice of it. The OR is associated with certain physiological changes in the body. Upon orienting towards something, the heart rate decreases. Such short-term changes in heart rate can be measured to discover the direction and intensity of an individual's attention to something.

Tonic or longer-term changes in attention are interesting too. This involves the degree of vigilance or concentration an individual invests in any activity. How much a person is focused upon something is also reflected in their heart rate. When people are concentrating on mental work, the heart beats faster. Completing numerical or linguistic tasks can have the same effect. The increase in heart rate generally lasts as long as the task continues.

There are two ways to measure heart beats. One is to measure the electrical impulses that run the heart as they occur. This type of recording is called an electrocardiogram (ECG). The time between beats, called the interbeat interval, is measured and then converted into heart rate. The other way to measure heartbeats is to measure the wave of blood or pulse wave that results from the second pump of the heartbeat. This wave can be easily measured using an optical device that passes light through the skin tissue and translates the amount of light transmitted through the skin into a measurement of the amount of blood present in the tissue. Thus, the wave of blood from the heartbeat can be detected in, for example, the finger. It is a relatively simple matter to measure the duration between pulse waves (the interbeat interval) and convert it into a measure of heart rate.

With tonic heart rate measurement, analysis involves a measure of heart rate over the duration of an activity, enabling a calculation to be made of the average heart rate or interbeat interval during that time. Second, an examination can be made of changes in heart rate variability. This entails measuring the standard deviation of the heart rate over a period of time. Third, an analysis can be made of the tonic level data through a time series analysis. Here, heart activity comprises several cyclical trends, and data can be analysed in terms of changes in these trends.

With phasic heart activity, the researcher can construct a cardiac response curve (CRC) or an evolved response curve (ERC).

A CRC can be created in heart time by averaging Ss' interbeat intervals – starting with a specified beat over some number of beats. In real time, the CRC is constructed by averaging heart rate over successive seconds beginning at a predetermined point in time. When this is done, changes in heart activity that are specific to individuals average out. What is left are only those changes in heart activity common to all subjects. Thus, if the stimulus does not evoke a cardiac response, the CRC should be a flat line. If, on the other hand, a consistent cardiac response is elicited, you should see a curve representing the pattern of that change. (Lang, 1994: 109)

An evoked response curve (ERC) is created by subtracting the pre-stimulus level from each post-stimulus score for each subject and then averaging and plotting these change scores. Again, only those changes common to all subjects should be evident.

Brain wave measures

One other form of on-line measurement of audience reaction to media content is the use of brain waves. An instrument called an electro-encephalogram (EEG) is used to monitor brain activity during occasions when it is involved in processing information. The potential of the EEG in the context of media research has been explored in relation to the measurement of individuals' responses to television commercials (Olson and Ray, 1983; Rust et al., 1985). A series of further studies have examined attention and mental effort invested in media consumption, by using brain wave patterns (Alwitt, 1985; Reeves et al., 1985; Reeves et al., 1989; Rothschild et al., 1986).

The use of the EEG has been linked with attempts to establish hemispheric lateralization of information processing. Most brain wave research in the media context has focused on measurement of electrical brain activity in the so-called alpha frequency. Alpha waves are associated with increased relaxation and even drowsiness. When a person displays increased attention to an external stimulus, alpha activity decreases.

Clinicians working with brain damaged patients during the Second World War noted that people who had suffered damage to the left hemisphere of the brain exhibited abnormalities in their verbal, audio and analytical skills. Meanwhile, patients who had suffered severe trauma to the right hemisphere experienced difficulties in their non-verbal, visual and spatial skills (Galen and Ornstein, 1972; Walker, 1980). These findings were interpreted to mean that the left hemisphere specializes in non-verbal and visual skills (Corballis, 1980).

Among normal people, without physical damage to the brain, evidence has emerged that although there does appear to be some hemispheric specialization in types of information-processing skills, each side of the brain is also capable, to some degree, of performing the skills of the other side (Kinsbourne, 1982). The dominant theory of laterality is that both hemispheres of a normal person's brain process stimuli in parallel, but one side may be dominant depending on the nature of the task.

Rothschild et al. (1988) showed that audio events (onsets of voices or music) in television commercials were associated with alpha wave suppression in the parietal cortex (where audio information is processed) and that visual counts were associated with alpha suppression in the occipital cortex (where visual information is generally processed). This study also showed differences in alpha patterns in the two hemispheres. These patterns were consistent with the notion that the right hemisphere processes spatial information and the left hemisphere processes verbal information.

In another study, Alwitt (1985) defined a number of categories of variables in commercial structures and showed that many of them were correlated with alpha (associated with drowsiness) and beta (associated with arousal and alertness) brain wave patterns. Alwitt's variables included camera movements, music presence, brand name and product attribute mentions, visual shots of brand in use, superimposed text, and voice-overs. She also included depictions of human reactions, including a measure of when two or more people were engaged in a relationship, touching, looked like real people, or experienced an emotional or humorous moment. The findings showed that visuals of the brand in use were most consistently related to brain wave activity. Alwitt concluded that commercial impact on brain wave responses was primarily due to brand-message events.

Brain waves can be used to indicate level of attention to commercials and are linked in turn to recall and recognition of advertising messages. Rothschild and his colleagues used the alpha frequency of the brain wave pattern to index locations in commercials where added attentional demands are present. These studies have shown that commercials in which there is added attention paid (i.e. which show suppression of the alpha frequency) are better recalled and recognized (Rothschild et al., 1986). In this methodology, electrodes are placed on the scalp of experimental subjects, who might be male or female. The subjects are normally given a period to get used to the electrodes and participate in test runs with neutral materials to provide the researcher with base-line brain wave activity data before the experimental stimulus materials (i.e. television advertisements) are presented. Brain wave patterns are then recorded continuously during exposure to these materials. Afterwards, subjects may be tested for their recall or recognition of the advertisements they were shown. Usually, these advertisements are shown within a programme, and no prior warning is given to subjects that the purpose of the study is to test their ability to remember advertising. Instead, they are told that they will be asked for their opinions about the programme or programmes surrounding the advertising.

Using this methodology, Rothschild and his colleagues have shown that easily identifiable variables in commercials (words in the audio-track, superimposed words on the screen, package appearance, actor movement in camera shot, camera edits, scene changes, dissolves and zooms and pans) are associated with hemispheric differences in brain wave patterns. These changes in brain waves signal changes in levels of attention (Rothschild et al., 1988).

Electrodermal measurement

Electrodermal measurement became established in the latter part of the 19th century and is a technique that is sensitive to involuntary physical reactions that occur in the skin when people are exposed to stimuli that have a specific meaning for them (Hopkins and Fletcher, 1994). Electrical processes within animals were discovered in the late 1700s by Luigi Galvani. He developed an instrument called a galvanometer that could measure levels of electrical voltage and resistance in the skin. Electrodermal responses, as measured by this instrument, also became known as the galvanic skin response (GSR). The GSR is measured by placing two electrodes in contact with the skin and measuring changing levels of body voltage between them. One electrode must have direct contact with the skin's living tissue layer below the epidermis. Often this contact is made by scraping the outer layer of the skin back at a less sensitive area of the body's surface, such as an earlobe. This method is used to measure what is known as 'skin potential levels'. It is not used much today because of concerns about the spread of HIV/AIDs.

Skin resistance level is another measure that is used instead. In this case, a small electrical charge is applied by the experimenter between two electrodes attached to the skin, and the experimenter subtracts from the initial applied voltage the voltage detected at the second electrode. With skin resistance response, a change is detected over a period of a few seconds after a stimulus has been presented. Electrodes are placed on a subject's hand, often the hairless side of the fingers or palm. Electrodermal responses vary across individuals. They may also vary for the same person depending on how tired they are, or whether they are on drugs.

Electrodermal responses have been taken as indicators of emotions (Veraguth, 1907). A number of writers have agreed with this assessment (Abel, 1930; Chant and Salter, 1937). However, electrodermal responses may indicate some kind of general activation or arousal in response to an external stimulus. There may be a cognitive component as well as an emotional component to this response (Neuchterlain et al., 1989). Within an information-processing framework, there is an assumption about interpretation of meaning in a stimulus. Emotional reactions to external stimuli may vary in their depth and complexity from simple reflex reactions to quite sophisticated expressions of emotion (Lang et al., 1992).

Electrodermal responses have been used to indicate on-line reactions to media content that may signal the degree of audience involvement with the material being presented (Fletcher and Shimell, 1989). Electrodermal measures may also indicate levels of attention to media measures (Dawson et al., 1989). Electrodermal measurement has been used to indicate attention to television commercials at different points within the commercial message. Patterns of change in electrical resistance in the skin during exposure to television commercials have been linked to subsequently verbalized brand purchase intentions. There is some indication from this work that an advertisement must grab a viewer's attention within the first few seconds to increase the likelihood that he or she will continue to pay attention to it (Wesley, 1978).

Information-processing measures

Measures of attention to the media have been used in which the capacity of individuals to process information from media content is used as an indicator of the amount of attention invested in that content during exposure to it. On-line methods have usually involved the assessment of how effectively individuals can respond to a task that also requires their attention when watching a television programme. The less accurate or the slower their responses are to this parallel task, the more attention they are inferred to be paying to the programme they are watching at that time.

Secondary reaction time

The secondary reaction-time task procedure provides a method of assessing attentional engagement during exposure to a mass medium. The technique is based on the assumption that mental processing takes time and that central processing capacity is limited (e.g. Kahneman, 1973; Posner, 1982). The reasoning is that the more central processing capacity is invested in some continuous primary task, such as watching a television programme, the less there will be for a secondary task (e.g. pressing a button in response to an occasional tone or probe). Therefore, slower reaction times to secondary tasks are assumed to reflect greater mental capacity directed to the primary task.

This technique asks people to perform an additional task while processing media content. People may be asked to press a button at specific points while watching, listening to or reading a particular message. According to this perspective, watching, listening to or reading the message is the primary task and pushing the button is the secondary task. Performance on these secondary tasks is believed to provide insight into remaining cognitive resources. Indirectly, this should provide information on the effort being invested in processing the media message. Performance on the secondary task provides clues about how much capacity is being used by the message. The more attention that is being paid, for example, to a television programme or a newspaper story, the slower will be the reaction time of the individual in relation to a parallel secondary task.

The earliest research in this area proposed that the attention mechanism worked as a filter (Broadbent, 1958; Cherry, 1953). People select one channel at the expense of others. Researchers have noticed that people generally miss information in the non-attended channel. However, the extent to which information in the non-attended channel is missed may depend upon the meaning and significance it has for the individual. In a modified theory of selective attention, it was posited that people primarily select information in one channel and alternate information in the other (Treisman, 1969).

Another theory developed since the 1970s proposes that attention is a process of sampling incoming material. This sampling takes place at specific intervals (Meadowcroft and Watt, 1989). As a task demands additional resources, people 'sample' the incoming information less frequently.

To measure secondary reactions, a person is asked to perform an ongoing primary task. The person is instructed to perform a secondary task at the same time. The secondary task may require solving a problem or responding to a tone or a flash of light. The fundamental assumption is that as more effort is dedicated to the primary task, fewer resources remain for the secondary task (Kahneman, 1973). As resources available to the secondary task diminish, so more errors in it occur.

Meadowcroft and Reeves (1989) showed edited 'He-Man' cartoons to five- and eight-year-old children. When the children who were relatively familiar with the structure of these stories watched a conventionally structured 'He-Man' episode, they responded more slowly to probes occurring during the scenes judged central to understanding the story than during scenes incidental to the plot. This study indicated that young children's attention is engaged not only by relatively comprehensible content but more especially by content that is recognized as central to understanding the story as a whole.

In another study with young children, Lorch and Castle (1994) tested the ability of five-year-olds to respond to a buzzer by pressing a key pad while watching an episode of *Sesame Street*. The buzzer occurred at irregular intervals during the programme. The children had been told to watch the programme as they normally would and to enjoy it as much they could. The programme itself had been especially edited and changed so that some sections were presented as normal, while others were presented backwards or in a foreign language. Reaction times to the secondary task of pressing the key pad in response to a buzzer were slower while the children were watching the normal segments than when watching the segments which had relatively little meaning because of the way they were presented.

Research with the media has investigated the impact of competing channels of communication upon viewers' or listeners' effective processing of media content. For example, resource limitations have been examined to affect viewers' memory for televised news. The addition of visuals to news stories can interfere with processing of information from the news narrative (Davies et al., 1985; Drew and Grimes, 1987; Edwardson et al., 1976; Edwardson et al., 1992; Hoffner et al., 1988). Another area of research investigated whether the presence of background television interferes with a variety of tasks that require concurrent intellectual performance (Armstrong and Greenberg, 1990). Using a continuous, on-line reactivity measure, Thorson et al. (1985) found that secondary reaction times were slower as the nature of the television material they showed as a primary monitoring task increased in its informational complexity.

Memory response latencies

The length of time that a person takes to remember something is a measure of memory response latency. This measure of elapsed time can be used to shed light on what has been stored in memory. Memory response latency is a measure in milliseconds of the time that has passed between onset of presentation of test items and initiation of a subject's response. Longer memory response latency times can be used to indicate the degree of attention invested in a stimulus.

Shoemaker and Reese (1991) suggested that the time has come for different levels of mass communication research to relate more closely to each other. Memory response latency can play a key role in linking one level of research to another. Response latency data can be used to test or constrain assumptions made at another level of analysis about how an audience processes media messages. For instance, a societal level theory such as the cultivation theory makes the fundamental claim that media exposure changes people's mental sets about the world. If so, some of these changes may be discernible in the extent and organization of memory traces for media-related information, such as the nature of memory for acts of violence. Response latency data could assess the relative extent of memory networks for heavy and light television viewers by measuring the time required to search memory. In this way, a position taken at the macro-level of analysis about cultivation effects can be examined at a micro-level of analysis involving memory processing.

Geiger and Reeves (1991) conducted a study of political advertising that successfully demonstrated the use of response latency to illuminate how visual structure and content factors affect memory processing. Specifically, response latency was used to assess whether the structural features of political advertisements (number of cuts, edits, scene changes, zooms, etc.) and the type of advertisement (issue versus image) affect memory for visual and audio information in the adverts. Structurally simple advertisements were recognized faster than structurally dynamic ones. This effect on processing time supported the prediction that dynamic structure interferes with memory processing for political adverts, leading to longer processing times.

There are two basic varieties of latency measures that are associated with different levels of theoretical sophistication in cognitive psychology. First, simple response latency is a relatively pure measure of the processing efficiency of a person on a task. This measure is informative about detection and decoding processes or the total time needed to complete a task, and need not be linked to memory models that involve additional assumptions. Simple response latency is useful in studying effects of individual differences (e.g. age differences in processing speed) and task variables on processing efficiency (e.g. stimulus intensity, task complexity).

Recognition response latency, the second basic variety of latency measure, is perhaps more relevant to mass communication studies. Recognition response latency is used to understand stages of processing subsequent to detection (e.g. recognition, classification and response selection) and is intimately tied to formal memory models like spreading activation (Anderson, 1983, 1985). The additional assumptions for choice response latency are determined by the memory model or models being tested. Specifically, memory response latency is a measure in milliseconds of the time elapsed between onset of presentation of a memory test item and initiation of a subject's response. In a typical memory response latency experiment, the subject is shown a video recording of a television news sequence, for example, including some stories with captions and some without. Later, the subject's memory for the news is tested by showing him or her brief (1/30th second) snippets of television news from the test material as well as snippets from other broadcasts. The subject has to indicate, as quickly as possible, whether the snippet was in the newscast just seen.

Signal detection measures

These involve individuals giving true – false responses to statements as judged against media content recently seen. Recognition memory tests as such involve two phases: a study phase and a test phase. The tests have two types of items: old items contain information the subject was exposed to previously; and new items contain information that was not presented earlier. New items are called distractors.

Measures of recognition memory have been used in a variety of communication studies: television information processing (Thorson et al., 1985, 1986); journalism (Shapiro et al., 1987); advertising (Childers et al., 1986). The task is usually to discriminate material seen earlier from similar material not seen earlier. True – false questions are typical of recognition memory questions. Researchers then record the number or percentage correct.

An assumption made here is that memory is either available or not available. This may be a poor assumption. Often a person is not sure if he or she remembers something. Memory psychologists have long recognized that judgements and motivation in memory vary between individuals and between situations (Zechmeister and Nyberg, 1982). For example, when asked if a particular sentence is true based on a newspaper article read 30 minutes ago, a person must query memory and then decide whether the meaning seems familiar enough to say 'true' or if unfamiliar enough to say 'false'. Signal detection theory can be used to examine such judgement effects in memory. Signal detection provides a good summary statistic for the subjects' ability to discriminate between old and new items, and it also provides another statistic that allows an investigation to look at judgement effects (Shapiro, 1994).

When asked whether a stimulus item has been seen before, there are four possible outcomes to a decision – two possible correct decisions and two possible incorrect decisions. Calling true correctly represents a *hit*. Calling false, when true is correct represents a *miss*. Calling false when false is correct represents a *correct rejection*. Calling true when false is correct represents a *false alarm*. Signal detection theory takes all these response possibilities into account when measuring a subject's performance over a series of recognition trials. Recognition decisions can vary with the perceived familiarity of test items (Zechmeister and Nyberg, 1982). Individuals also set criteria for judging whether a stimulus is correct or not. Depending on the judgement of rewards for hits or penalties for misses, the individual will set a particular criterion.

CONCLUDING REMARKS

This chapter has examined research methodologies that have been deployed to investigate the degree of involvement people exhibit in media, at the point of consumption. In that regard, the research reviewed here must be distinguished from that discussed in Chapter 4, which was concerned with general levels or rates of consumption of media. In the context of television viewing, for example, the measurement of television audiences can indicate how many people were watching or even how often they watch, but not how much attention they paid to what they were watching.

Much of the research on attention to media has been carried out with television. As this chapter has revealed, the degree of involvement of audiences with television programmes or advertisements can be assessed through qualitative and quantitative methodologies. Quantitative approaches have dominated the literature, however. The reason for this is because verbal self-reports of respondents may lack the sensitivity to indicate the degree of mental effort being invested in television viewing. Viewers may not always be consciously aware of how much attention they are paying to the set, since viewing behaviour can often be automatic and occurs without a second thought. Ethnographic approaches in which attention is assessed by a participant observer, sitting in the viewing situation with a viewer, are dependent on the ability of that observer to judge how much attention the subject is actually paying to whatever is being shown on screen. While observational measures based on the visual orientation of the viewer towards the screen may be reasonably accurate, attention to a programme does not require that the viewer actually look at the screen.

Hence, experimental methodologies have been predominant in this sphere of media research. Researchers can create controlled environments in which subjects are presented with specified materials and their involvement measured not just through reactions of which the viewers are consciously aware, but also through those of which they may not be aware. In so far as autonomic, physiological reactions can be demonstrated as valid and reliable indicators of psychological responses, such measures represent a useful set of tools in the quest for a better understanding of the way individuals attend to and get involved with media content.

CHAPTER 7

MEASURING COGNITIVE IMPACT OF MEDIA

The foregoing chapters have examined research methodologies used to study the way people use, get involved with and evaluate the mass media. Those aspects of media research have held as much interest for the media industry as for academics making a more theoretical study of the media. Media producers and distributors need to know, in the first instance, how their products are performing. This means how big is their market share, how loyal are their consumers, and do their consumers like what they get. As we have seen, though, questions about how to measure media audiences, the amount of attention different media or types of media content are able to attract, and how not only to describe but also to explain what turns an audience on to specific media outputs, have also represented significant areas of enquiry for media researchers in the academy.

In the current chapter, this book takes a new turn. Moving on from how researchers have analysed media audiences in relation to their use of the media and direct reactions to media content, we now shift our attention to whether the media have effects upon their audiences. Are viewers, listeners and readers changed by their exposure to audio-visual, audio and print media? If they are changed through their media experiences, what forms do these effects take among audiences? Across the history of media research, media effects have been identified to occur at a number of political, economic, social and psychological levels. Perhaps the most critical concern has focused upon the capability of media to shape the way people behave. This is regarded as an especially significant area of enquiry in relation to concerns about the possible role of the media in promoting antisocial behaviours, especially among young and potentially more malleable members of the public. There are types of behavioural influence with which the media have been identified which may be regarded as equally important. For example, the media convey messages about commodities and services, with which certain attractive lifestyles or attributes are associated. In this context, they might play a significant role in shaping people's consumer habits and even in encouraging people to consume when there really is no need to. The media also have an important part to play during political elections when they represent sources of information about political candidates and their policies. As such they may influence voting behaviour.

Media effects are not restricted to behavioural-level reactions of audiences, however. The media represent sources of information that are relevant to people's knowledge and understanding of events and issues, and to the beliefs and opinions they hold on a wide range of topics. Thus, media effects can be 'cognitive' as well as 'behavioural'. The study of the behavioural effects of the media is the subject matter of Chapter 8.

This chapter begins our analysis of media research methods in the context of media effects measurement by looking at the way media researchers have studied cognitive-level effects. In this discussion, cognitive-level effects will include the measurement of media influences on public awareness, knowledge and understanding of topics, issues, events, groups, organizations and institutions. It will also include an examination of research into media effects upon public beliefs, attitudes, perceptions and opinions. In sum, it will set out the key approaches adopted by researchers to establish whether people learn factual information from the media and the ways in which public opinion is shaped through such learning.

As with all other areas of media research, any review of methodologies is assisted by establishing a typology that distinguishes effectively and comprehensively among major forms of research. In broad methodological terms, research into media effects has been conducted using quantitative and qualitative techniques. Research in this domain has also taken measurements among audiences as well as of media output. Data concerned with media effects at a cognitive level have been obtained from surveys, experiments (laboratory and field-based), focus groups or individual depth interviews and observational analysis. Media output analyses, using quantitative content analysis and the more qualitative forms of linguistic analysis, semiology and discourse analysis, have been applied within cognitive effects studies. Indeed, the latter analytical techniques have been applied to media texts and to the discourses produced by audiences in response to media texts.

We have already seen that one important methodological distinction in media research is between research that measures audience responses at the time of media exposure ('on-line' research) and research that measures audience responses not at the time of media exposure ('off-line' research). While the measurement of media effects almost inevitably means waiting until media exposure has taken place before establishing whether members of the audience have been changed subsequently as a result of the experience, research into cognitive-level effects of media content has varied in terms of whether impact measures occur in close proximity to the critical media exposure or following a lengthier delay. Taking the latter distinction a stage further, a category of research into the cognitive impact of the media can be distinguished in which media effects are inferred even though no measurements were taken of audience exposure to media.

For the purposes of this chapter, our analysis of media methods will be broadly differentiated under three headings: (1) the media and agenda-setting; (2) the media and cultivation of beliefs and opinion; and

(3) factual learning from media. These are distinctions of convenience and should not be taken to imply that these three types of media impact represent mutually exclusive, unconnected forms of cognitive-level audience response to media content. Opinion formation, for example, often depends upon factual learning or implies that learning has taken place. Under each of these broad headings, further subdivisions can be made of the major strands of research, as follows:

- *agenda-setting:*
    1. parallel analyses of media coverage and public awareness of specified topics
    2. parallel analyses of media coverage and public awareness of specific topics using survey data in which audience exposure to media is also measured
    3. experimental studies measuring the impact on issue awareness of controlled exposure to pre-selected media materials

- *cultivation of beliefs and opinion:*
    1. correlational surveys of self-reported media exposure and opinions about topics, combined with parallel content analyses of media output
    2. controlled experiments measuring changes in perceptions as a function of exposure to pre-selected media content

- *factual learning:*
    1. correlational surveys of media exposure and topic-related knowledge
    2. field surveys testing audience retention of media content from specific outputs
    3. controlled experimental studies of memory for specific, natural media outputs
    4. controlled experimental studies of memory for artificially produced media outputs
    5. controlled experimental studies comparing information retention from different media
    6. qualitative reception studies of learning from media using focus groups, depth interviews and discourse analysis.

In the sections that follow, each of these types of research approach to the analysis of audience learning, topic awareness and opinion formation are reviewed in turn.

AGENDA-SETTING RESEARCH

Agenda-setting research represents a methodology that was developed to facilitate the study of processes of influence in society. It is concerned with establishing the interplay between the agendas that exist within the media, the public and sources of social policy making. An *agenda* in this context comprises a collection of issues or events that, at any one point in time, are ranked in a hierarchy of importance.

Research by communication scholars and political scientists has typically conceptualized either the mass media agenda, the public agenda, or the policy agenda as a dependent variable in order to explain how it is influenced by other factors. Some scholars have identified the mass media as omnipotent communication systems that link the public to policy makers. Public electorates, for example, are linked predominantly to political parties via the media, creating what some writers have described as a 'media dependency' (Linsky, 1986). In understanding the role that the media play in this context, a methodology has been created, under the general heading of *agenda research*, that is concerned with exploring relationships between mass media, public and policy agendas.

Rogers and Dearing (1988: 556) identified two main research traditions in agenda research:

> (1) *agenda-setting*, a process through which the mass media communicate the relative importance of various issues and events to the public (an approach mainly pursued by mass communication scholars) and (2) *agenda-building*, a process through which the policy agendas of political elites are influenced by a variety of factors, including media agendas and public agendas. The agenda-setting tradition is concerned with how the media agenda influences the public agenda, while the agenda-building tradition studies how the public agenda and other factors, and occasionally the media agenda, influence the policy agenda.

The question of who sets the media agenda, and the implications of that influence for society, were initially explored by Lazarsfeld and Merton (1948). They conceived of the media issue agenda as a result of the influence that powerful groups, notably organized business exerted as a subtle form of social control. 'Big business finances the production and distribution of mass media. And, all intent aside, he who pays the piper calls the tune' (Lazarsfeld and Merton, 1948). The media support the dominant, institutional status quo, rather than upset the apple cart. Given that commercial and public media systems are controlled by the establishment in business and politics, they cannot ultimately be expected to challenge strongly and persistently the values of that established order (Qualter, 1985).

Understanding how the content of the mass media influences the public's perception of which issues are important has been a topic of investigation by media scholars since the early part of the 20th century (Frazier and Gaziano, 1979). Early empirical results cast doubt on the power of the media to exert profound or direct influences upon the public agenda. Following research conducted on the impact of early radio broadcasts, it was concluded that media effects acted indirectly rather than directly upon public opinion, and were usually mediated by interpersonal sources of influence (Klapper, 1960).

Turning to the policy agenda of society, scholars have been interested in finding out about the relationship between public opinion and policy decisions taken by ruling elites. An explanatory mechanism of a policy maker to public transfer was suggested by Katz and Lazarsfeld (1955) in their hypothesis about the 'two-step flow' of communication. According to this view, opinions in a society are first circulated by the media and then passed on via opinion leaders by interpersonal communication.

In tracking the chronology of agenda-setting research, Rogers and Dearing (1988) found that more than 150 publications could be identified, dating back to 1922. These works could be organized by two research traditions of (1) public agenda-setting by the mass media and (2) policy agenda-setting. In compiling this review, Rogers and Dearing selected studies that qualified on methodological grounds, and not because they referred overtly to agenda-setting. Thus, qualifying studies included analysis of the *media agenda*, usually measured by a content analysis of the mass media; the *public agenda*, usually measured by an audience survey, and the *policy agenda* as indexed by interviews with public officials, from legislative records or political documents.

For many years, the basic conception of agenda-setting was a theoretical idea without much empirical research basis. This position changed with a study by McCombs and Shaw (1972) of the media's role in the 1968 US presidential campaign. These researchers interviewed a sample of 100 undecided voters during a three-week period in September – October 1968. These voters' public agenda of campaign issues was measured by aggregating their responses to the survey question : 'What are you *most* concerned about these days? That is, regardless of what politicians say, what are the two or three *main* things that you think the government *should* concentrate on doing something about?' (p. 178). The number of mentions of each of five main campaign issues was utilized to index the public agenda.

McCombs and Shaw concluded from their analyses that the mass media set the campaign agenda for the public. The media agenda influenced the public agenda. Was their study really so new and different? In terms of methodology it was not. Content analysis of mass media messages and surveys of public opinion about an issue had been used before in media research. Nor was their linking of these two methodologies to test the degree of agenda-setting a totally new departure (Chaffee, 1987). In the early 1950s, Davis (1952) had combined content analysis and survey research in testing the public agenda-setting hypothesis. McCombs and Shaw, however, clearly explicated the hypothesis and referred to the process as 'agenda-setting'.

Another important distinction in agenda-setting research is between *events* and *issues*. Events were defined as discrete happenings that are limited in space and time. Issues were defined as involving cumulative news coverage of a series of related events that fit together in a broad category (Shaw, 1977). Events, however, can be considered specific components of issues (Rogers and Dearing, 1988).

To date, insufficient effort has been given to classifying the issues and events that are studied in agenda-setting research.

> Certainly, a rapid-onset news event like the 1986 US bombing of Libya is markedly different from a slow-onset natural disaster issue like the 1984 Ethiopian drought. A high-salience, short-duration issue like the 1985 TWA hijacking is different from such low-salience issues as the ups and downs of US unemployment or from such long-duration issues as Japanese – US trade conflict in that an agenda item (such as in the case of an election issue) may influence the agenda-setting process. (Rogers and Dearing, 1988: 566–7)

While research on agenda-setting can be traced back over 70 years, it is really only in the past 25 years that considerable attention has been paid to this media-related phenomenon. Even so, some scholars have concluded that despite the proliferation of research on agenda-setting, it has not advanced far, either theoretically or methodologically (Iyengar and Kinder, 1987).

Why agenda-setting research?

One of the main reasons for interest in agenda-setting research is that it appeared to offer an alternative to the scholarly search for direct media effects on attitude change and overt behaviour change. Earlier mass communication research had found limited effects, which seemed counter-intuitive to many researchers, especially to those who had previous mass media experience. According to McCombs (1981: 220): 'Its [agenda-setting's] initial empirical exploration was fortuitously timed. It was at that time in the history of mass communication research when disenchantment both with attitudes and opinions as dependent variables, and with the limited-effects model as an adequate intellectual summary, was leading scholars to look elsewhere'.

For much of the 20th century, media research, particularly in the USA, concentrated on the measurement of media effects. Much of the focus of research attention was placed upon attitude change or persuasion. Decades of research into persuasive effects on attitudes and behaviours had left many scholars frustrated. Attitudes were not clearly connected to behaviour, and media were not clearly and consistently connected to either. Agenda-setting rejected persuasion as the central 'effect' of concern. Rather than having their attitude reshaped as a consequence of exposure to media, the alternative assumption was that people acquired information about the salient events and issues of the day from media.

Agenda-setting offered a new topic for media scholars wanting to break free of the limited-effects paradigm established by earlier research (Klapper, 1960). On the surface, agenda-setting is a rejection of persuasion for an alternative framework that asks whether the media simply tell people what to think *about*, rather than what to think (Cohen, 1963).

Edelstein (1993: 85) observed: 'Although agenda-setting research grew out of the metaphor that "the mass media do not tell people 'what to think' but 'what to think about,'" researchers have yet to define conceptually what is meant by "thinking about," and to operationalise it in cognitive terms as a criterion variable'.

Most agenda-setting research has conceptualized the term 'thinking about' as a decision about the *salience* of an event or issue. In other words, how much importance is accorded to an event or issue by the media and members of the public? A causal relationship is presumed to exist between the amount of coverage the media give to an event, and how prominent it is in the public consciousness. The act of judging the salience of an issue is deemed to be equivalent to, or an operationalization of, the concept of 'thinking about' something. For McCombs and Shaw (1972), agenda-setting embraces psychological processes of 'attention' and 'learning'. People not only learn about an issue through the media, they also judge how much importance to attach to the issue on the basis of the amount of coverage it has recently been given by the media.

Types of methodology

Agenda-setting research has involved the use of a number of methodologies and research designs. The principal concern has been to demonstrate that the agenda set by the media impacts upon the public's agenda and shapes it. Conceptually, media scholars have recognized that, in addition to the media agenda and public agenda, there is also a policy agenda, and that the three types of agenda may be interdependent. Establishing the direction of causality among these agendas has been a problem yet to be effectively resolved in the research conducted to date. Indeed, some of the research designs employed by agenda-setting researchers are unable to demonstrate causal relationships.

Many early studies of agenda-setting relied upon one-shot data collection exercises and cross-sectional analysis of data. This type of research design is, in fact, not well-suited to the analysis of agenda-setting. In determining whether a media agenda influences a public agenda, for example, it is necessary to collect or to analyse data collected at more than one point in time.

As agenda-setting research has evolved, three methodological approaches have emerged that satisfy this 'over-time' condition:

1. the collection of data on the media agenda and the public agenda at two points in time, which are then analysed using cross-lagged correlational techniques
2. the tracking of media and public agendas longitudinally over a number of weeks, months or years
3. the controlled manipulation of the media agenda in advance of its exposure to media audiences.

Media agendas

Usually some form of content analysis is used to establish the nature of the media agenda. At a simple level, researchers measure the amount of time (in broadcast media) or space (in print media) devoted to particular topics. Some content analyses focus on topic coverage in a single mass medium, while others may attempt to assess coverage across a number of media. Studies also vary in terms of the length of time over which they assess the media agenda. Television news broadcasts and newspapers may be monitored for just a few days (Williams and Semlak, 1978a) or over several weeks (McLeod et al., 1974). Some analyses have looked back at media coverage of specified topics over many years (Funkhouser, 1973). Analysis of newspaper coverage may concentrate on front pages only or measure coverage of specific topics throughout entire editions. With television coverage, the agenda-setting impact of visual material can be analysed as well as the spoken narrative (Williams and Semlak, 1978b). Visual format features can draw differential attention to news items in television bulletins and affect their memorability (Gunter, 1987b). This aspect of cognitive impact of media will be examined more closely in the last section of this chapter.

Public agendas

A number of different forms of questioning have been used to measure the public agenda. Survey respondents can be asked to produce their personal choices of most important issues of the day. Respondents can also be presented with a list of options and choose the one they perceive as being the most important current issue. They may also be given a list of options and asked to rank order them. A further technique is to present a pool of issues and invite respondents to compare each issue with each other issue in a pair-wise fashion. This procedure is carried out exhaustively until every item has been compared with every other item in the pool. Each item receives a score when it is deemed the more important of the two. When all possible comparisons have been made, the issues can be rank ordered from most to least important on the basis of these scores.

When measuring the public agenda, the researcher has to decide on the duration over which to measure people's perceptions, the length of time for which media coverage should be measured, and the amount of time that should elapse between measuring media coverage and taking soundings from among the public. Researchers have investigated the public agenda on a single day, over several weeks, or even over several years. The time lag between assessment of media coverage and surveying public perceptions can also vary from a few days to many months. Indeed, some researchers have shown that different time lags are appropriate in respect of different issues. General issues about such topics as science or the environment may require a lag of a year or more before the media agenda is detected in the public agenda. With political campaigns, the lag should be only three or four weeks, while with major disasters such as Chernobyl, a lag of a few days will yield signs of apparent media influence (Brosius and Kepplinger, 1990).

Difficulties of long-term agenda analyses

One of the methodological difficulties faced by researchers adopting longitudinal approaches stems from the absence of trend data on public perceptions of issues or events of significance ascertained through polls that regularly ask some version of the question: 'What do you think is the most important problem facing the country/society today?'. Behr and Iyengar (1985) reported an exceptional case study in which public opinion poll data were obtained from three national surveys in the USA that had carried a similarly worded open-ended question as such. Using these data, they counted the percentage of 'responses', rather than 'respondents' citing each of a number of issues. Through this analysis they were able to produce a measure of problem importance for every two-month period between 1974 and 1980, except for three missing data points. They were then able to set these data alongside content analysis data measuring the number of stories in total and number of lead stories connected with the same issues broadcast on a major network's news broadcasts over the same period. The issues were energy, inflation and unemployment. Their trend analysis explored the correlation between the prominence of broadcast news coverage of these issues and salience of each issue among the general public. They also included a further analysis of real-world indicators of level of public concern with each of these problems. They argued that the public salience of certain issues, such as unemployment, might be affected by direct public experience of this problem in their own everyday experience. Hence the public agenda can be influenced by real-life events as well as by exposure to a media agenda. In relation to two areas, energy and inflation, the public agenda was driven by television coverage of these issues. In the case of unemployment, however, no evidence emerged to support the view that the public agenda was set by television. Instead, public concern was directed by ambient economic conditions affecting their own lives. Indeed, this study revealed that media agenda-setting may entail reciprocal effects, with media coverage and public concern feeding on each other.

Methodological issues

Agenda-setting studies are concerned both with media content and audience perception. It is a media effects model that explicitly prescribes a particular way of dealing with media content. Put simply, the amount of space or time devoted to a particular issue should be measured. This measurement should relate either to the amount of attention people pay to the issue or to their judgement of the issue's importance.

Agenda-setting research has generally tried to demonstrate a positive association between the amount of mass media content devoted to an item and the development of a place on the public agenda for that item. The basic principle is that as the amount of media coverage given to an item increases, so too does the salience of that item for the public. The next step in this analytical framework is to establish a causal relationship between the media agenda and the public agenda and seek evidence for the expected time-order. Thus, if an item achieves prominence among the public before it achieves prominence in the media, the media could hardly be invoked as a causal agent.

Rogers and Dearing (1988) pointed out that agenda-setting research suffers from serious methodological limitations. These mostly concern the validity of the inference that media agendas determine audience agendas. The reverse possibility cannot be ruled out. The diffusion of econometric and other simultaneous equation techniques across the behaviour sciences has enabled agenda-setting researchers to test more effectively for precise direction of the causal flow (Iyengar, 1987). Public agenda-setting, for instance, is not a straightforward concept to measure. In addressing this problem, researchers have formulated many different measures of agenda-setting as a dependent variable.

One aim of agenda-setting is to rank order issues from most to least covered and most to least important. It is also characterized by proposing cause – effect linkages between specific media content or changes in that content and specific public perceptions of issue significance, rather than generalized effects of media exposure *per se*.

Kosicki (1993) identified several measurement issues as being of special significance in assessing the value of agenda-setting research: (1) micro versus macro measurement; (2) direct measurement versus conditional measurement; (3) attitudinal measurement versus behavioural measurement; (4) alteration measurement versus stabilization; and (5) long-term versus short-term measurement.

The original idea of agenda-setting linked the overall amount of media coverage accorded an event to its public salience (McCombs and Shaw, 1972). Initially, this media 'effect' was measured in terms of aggregated levels of awareness among large groups or samples of survey respondents. In due course, researchers recognized agenda-setting could be considered at more than one level. Distinctions could be made between agenda-setting measured at group level or at the individual level and between agenda-setting for a single issue or set of issues (McCombs, 1981).

Media effects do not occur in the same way or with equal probability for everyone. Sometimes media may exert direct effects on their audiences, while on other occasions effects are conditional upon other factors. The extent to which particular media are consumed, perceptions of source credibility, and personal interest in an issue can all mediate media agenda-setting effects (Iyengar and Kinder, 1985; Weaver, 1977).

Agenda-setting has been concerned primarily with an information processing approach to explaining media effects. It represents a movement away from attitudinal research, but has not usually included behavioural measures as dependent variables either. A few exceptions to this rule have been published, however (Kepplinger and Roth, 1979; Roberts, 1992). Agenda-setting proposes a causal hypothesis that posits that media treatment of issues produces changes in public response. Methodological concerns here stem from studies using cross-sectional analyses that amount to little more than 'agenda-matching' exercises. Analyses of media agendas and public agendas must take place over time to enable a proper investigation of the potential causality in the link between them. However, even if this condition is satisfied, survey-based studies of the public agenda are largely inadequate for demonstrating causality. Experimental approaches are much better equipped to do so (Iyengar and Kinder, 1987).

One-shot or even two-shot studies, in which media content coverage and public perceptions are measured at one or two points in time only, may lack the sensitivity needed to establish an agenda-setting relationship. Stronger evidence is likely to emerge from studies that collect larger numbers of measures over time. For example, Salwen (1986) content analysed three Michigan newspapers for 33 weeks as to their coverage of seven environmental issues, such as disposal of wastes, quality of water, and noise pollution. The public agenda was measured by about three hundred telephone interviews in three waves. The week-by-week media agenda had its first effect on the public agenda after the accumulation of five to seven weeks of media coverage of an environmental issue; the peak relationship of the media agenda to the public agenda occurred after eight to ten weeks of media coverage; thereafter, the correlations declined with the passage of time.

Another methodological problem facing agenda-setting research concerns disentangling the effects of news coverage from the effects of direct experience. The media constitute one of several potential determinants of the public's agenda. Real-world indicators concerning the seriousness of an issue can affect its public salience (Behr and Iyengar, 1985). Several issues, most notably those in the economic realm, can be felt directly. The unemployed worker may not need news coverage of unemployment to convince him or her that unemployment is a significant national problem. Analogously, one whose home has been burgled may regard crime as a significant problem quite independently of the level of crime news. Personal experience may make individuals more or less receptive to the media agenda. Rogers and Dearing (1988) recommended that agenda-setting research would be enhanced theoretically and empirically if real-world indicators were included. Such research could be methodologically strengthened by using designs that control for extraneous variables when trying to demonstrate the specific agenda-setting influences of the media.

Experimental research

In a few agenda-setting studies the independent variable of the media agenda has been controlled when measuring the extent of its impact upon the public agenda. In a series of studies by Iyengar and his colleagues during the 1980s, an experimental methodology was applied to control media content and exposure to it. These studies have comprised a mixture of laboratory-based and field experiments.

In one early study in this series, Iyengar et al. (1982) reported a field experiment in which they paid families to watch only special television news programmes created by the investigators. When national defence was stressed in the television news programmes constructed by the researchers, this issue became more salient to the families who were regularly exposed to it. A similar agenda-setting 'effect' was achieved for the topic of pollution in a second field experiment, and for inflation in a third experiment.

In two further experiments, Iyengar et al. (1984) exposed samples of college students to specially edited television newscasts, based on old news materials obtained from a television news archive. In these studies, they manipulated the number of stories contained within a single 40-minute bulletin about a particular issue. In one experiment, for example, there were three conditions: in one version of the specially edited news programme, six stories were presented about energy issues; in another version, three stories were presented; while in a further version no energy stories were presented. Central to the study were students' perceptions of President Carter's performance on energy matters as well as measures of his general performance. Stories that emphasized energy problems reflected badly on the president's perceived performance, and the more that experimental subjects were exposed to such stories, the more critical their judgements about the president became.

Iyengar (1991) examined the impact of television news on the way individuals framed issues in their own minds. In particular, the study examined how television influenced viewers' attributions of responsibility for political issues and the specific effects of the way issues were presented in the news upon public opinion formation. Iyengar used multiple methods, drawing evidence from content analysis, field experiments and correlational analyses of national survey data. Content analysis was used to identify the degree of thematic or episodic framing in television news coverage of public issues. Field experiments provided a rigorous test of the impact of particular news frames on attributions of responsibility. National surveys provided generalizable evidence concerning the effect of attributions of responsibility on political opinions and attitudes.

This research examined attributions of responsibility with respect to two major categories of issues and a specific governmental decision. The two categories were public security (law and order) issues, and issues of social or economic welfare. The law and order category consisted of crime and terrorism. The social welfare categories consisted of the specific issues of poverty, unemployment and racial inequality.

The content analysis was conducted on verbal summaries or 'abstracts' of daily network newscasts on the ABC, CBS and NBC networks as maintained by a university Television News Archive. These abstracts were highly condensed summaries of news story transcripts. Relevant issues were retrieved using key word searches. Stories which fell into the five thematic categories were further classified into those that offered episodic or thematic framing perspectives. Episodic stories depicted issues mainly as concrete instances or events, while thematic stories depicted issues more generally in terms of collective outcomes, public policy debates or historical trends. Limited visual analyses of stories broadcast by CBS were undertaken to validate the story classifications applied on the basis of the verbal summaries.

Field experiments were designed to manipulate how political issues are framed in television newscasts. In one experiment on the presentation of stories about poverty, for instance, one group of experimental participants watched thematic framing while another group watched episodic framing. Nine such media framing experiments were conducted among the residents of a community who were recruited through newspaper and other advertisements and paid a small sum as a financial incentive to participate in 'television research'. Participants visited the experimental laboratory where they were shown a randomly selected compilation of news stories that had been broadcast in the past year. They were then invited to complete a questionnaire to give their reactions to what they had seen. They were shown a 20-minute videotape with seven news stories. The fourth story represented the experimental manipulation. This story framed one of six target issues in accordance with the experimental design. With the exception of this story, the videotapes were identical. After viewing the taped news stories, participants completed lengthy post-test questionnaires, individually, in separate rooms. Questions probed their attributions of causal and treatment responsibility for the target issue as well as their perceptions of other matters, including the president's performance, and the competence and integrity of other public figures, groups and institutions.

Attributions of causal and treatment responsibility were elicited with open-ended survey questions. Specifically, individuals were asked, 'In your opinion, what are the most important causes of [...]?'. They were then asked, 'If you were asked to suggest ways to reduce [...], what would you suggest?'. Each individual was allowed to answer freely without further prompting. Up to four separate responses were coded for each question. Two coders read each questionnaire and classified each response. Correlational analysis was used to explore the connection between attributions and opinions. These investigations were carried out using the data obtained from the experiments and various national opinion polls. The opinions examined in the survey analyses fell into two categories: *general evaluations of government* included questions concerning the president's overall performance in office, his competence and his integrity; *issue-specific opinions* included evaluations of the president's performance in specific issue areas (e.g. reducing unemployment), respondents' specific policy preferences, and respondents' feelings about a number of groups or individuals involved in different issues.

Agenda-setting research represented a movement away from the notion of limited effects. It embraced and promoted the idea that the media can exert notable effects upon mass publics of certain kinds. The level at which media effects can be potent is in influencing public perceptions of which events and issues are currently the most important. The media draw attention to specific stories or topics and encourage people to talk about them. For some media scholars, the effects of the media go further than this. At a cognitive level, the media do not simply influence topics of conversation, but also shape the way that people think about them. In depicting a certain view of the world, the media can cultivate perceptions and beliefs about social reality.

CULTIVATION OF BELIEFS AND OPINIONS

Another form of cognitive-level impact of media concerns the potential of media exposure to shape public beliefs and perceptions concerning external reality. Cultivation theory was introduced to provide a model of analysis for demonstrating long-term media effects, operating principally at the level of social perception.

Gerbner (1972) hypothesized that television, amongst modern media, has acquired such a central place in people's everyday lives that it dominates our 'symbolic environment'. Its messages about social reality may displace or override personal experience or other sources of information about the world. However, the 'social reality' projected by television, especially in its fictional drama programming, does not always accurately reflect social 'actuality'. Persistent exposure to the world of television therefore may lead to an eventual adoption of its view of social reality over and above any other view of society.

Gerbner argued that television is a powerful cultural force of considerable depth and penetration. It is an arm of the established social industrial order that serves to maintain, stabilize and reinforce, rather than to change, threaten or weaken conventional systems of belief, values and behaviour. The main effect of television is one of enculturation; that is, it cultivates stability and acceptance of the status quo. Television, however, does not minimize change in isolation but in concert with other major cultural institutions (Gerbner and Gross, 1976).

According to Gerbner, television has effectively taken the place of tribal elders, of religion and even of formal education in its role of myth-telling. Common rituals and mythologies are crucial for a society because they function as 'agencies of symbolic socialisation and control,' and as such, 'demonstrate how society works by dramatising its norms and values' (Gerbner and Gross, 1976: 173).

The cultivation approach departed from other analytical frameworks in its emphasis on the victims rather than the protagonists of violence. In the complex world of television drama, for instance, lessons may be taught not only about how to behave violently, but also about which social groups are most likely to suffer at the hands of an attacker. Recurring patterns of victimization constitute symbolic demonstrations of the power structure of the television world. These patterns may be learned by viewers and affect their impressions about the real world. The effects of continually experiencing a symbolic world largely ruled by violence, where certain groups of individuals are considerably under-represented and harshly treated are conceived by Gerbner to be much more far-reaching than mere tuition in occasional violent behaviour.

Gerbner et al. (1979) argued that it was necessary to examine the 'total phenomenon of television' (p. 179) rather than isolated segments of it. They devised an analytical framework they called Cultural Indicators. This model begins with the premise that information is learned from dramatic television material and incorporated into the individual's conceptions of social reality. Through analysis of relationships between individuals' reported television-viewing habits, particularly the amount of time they spend watching, and their perceptions of their social and cultural environment, it is possible to reveal television's contribution to the attitudes, beliefs and values people hold with respect to the world in which they live.

Conceptually, the cultural-indicators project involves two broad assumptions about the nature of television content, the audience, and the functional relations between them. First, television's images, regardless of whether these are offered as fact, fiction or 'reality' programming, are assumed to cultivate stereotyped notions about the social environment. Through its use of violence, for example, the major function of television is to teach the audience about the characteristics and status of different types of people and about the distribution of power in society.

A second assumption concerns the non-selective or ritualized nature of television viewing for the mass of the public. According to Gerbner et al. (1979: 180) 'television audiences (unlike those for other media) view largely non-selectively and by the clock rather than by the program. Television viewing is a ritual, almost like a religion, except that it is attended to more regularly'. Consequently, the more time individuals spend watching television, the more they are assumed to be affected in their socio-cultural beliefs by its dramatic content. For people who spend large amounts of time viewing, television predominates over all other sources of information about the world. This phenomenon is embodied in the notion of the *heavy viewer*, defined for convenience as one who views for over four hours a day, thus 'living' in a world of television (Gerbner and Gross, 1976). In general, heavy viewers have been found to give different answers compared with lighter viewers, to informational or opinion questions, biased in terms of the way people and events are portrayed on television. This has been interpreted as a function of the greater amount of television they watch.

Methodologically, the cultural-indicators project consists of empirical analysis at two levels, designed to investigate, first, the message structure of the symbolic world of television drama, and second, the impact it may have on the way individuals perceive the world around them.

The traditional cultural-indicators research began with an assessment of the content of television drama. A coding technique called *message system analysis* was developed by Gerbner to monitor the world of television drama in order to identify the symbolic messages conveyed by television portrayals. Such an analysis indicated significant and in some cases massive discrepancies between the proportions of people and events shown on television and their actual occurrence in real life. For example, women, ethnic minorities and older people tend to be under-represented in television drama programmes relative to their respective proportions in the real world and yet at the same time are greatly over-represented as the victims of violent acts in television stories. Other social groups, such as law enforcers, criminals and various professional or business institutions (e.g. doctors, lawyers, reporters, etc.) tend to be over-represented and glamorized).

Television's fictional world also emphasizes certain personal attributes of individuals. Thus, women tend to be shown as young and attractive, and preoccupied by personal, romantic, and family activities, but are much less often caught up in professional occupational problems. Men, on the other hand, predominate in the professional sector, and also show more competence and assertiveness generally than do women (see Gunter, 1997b; Tuchman, 1978).

Observations of the portrayal of old people indicate that aging is generally not depicted as an attractive process; the elderly are usually shown as highly dependent, and physically and intellectually inept. Examination of patterns of victimization (e.g. being on the receiving end of a violent physical attack) indicate generalized tendencies for women and old people to be victims proportionately a great deal more often than young males (Gerbner et al., 1977, 1978, 1979).

Through its stereotyped portrayals of various groups and institutions, television presents a dramatic world with a clearly definable power structure in which the strong and the just dominate, while the weak and the strong but corrupt are suppressed or eliminated. An important question following on from this stage of analysis is, to what extent are television's images assimilated by viewers into their conceptions of social reality.

To investigate the consequences of viewing television drama's ongoing and pervasive system of cultural messages, Gerbner and his associates developed a second stage of assessment, based on measurement of audience reactions, called *cultivation analysis*. Essentially, this technique set out to provide a quantitative measure of 'television biases' in public beliefs and attitudes among people who watch a great deal of television. The aim of this form of analysis was to ascertain whether viewers' social conceptions bore a closer resemblance to the world of television drama than to the real world or some other perspective.

Controlling for demographic factors such as sex, age, social class, and educational attainment, responses of light viewers (i.e. people who watched television for less than two hours a day) were compared with those of heavy viewers (i.e. people who watched television for more than four hours a day). The differences in the percentages of heavy over light viewers giving 'television answers' provided the *cultivation differential*, indicating the extent to which misconceptions about social reality were attributable to television's influence. It was generally reported by Gerbner and his colleagues that even when taking into account the effects on social perceptions of demographic factors, heavy viewing, both among adults and adolescents, was associated with a television-biased view of the world (Gerbner et al., 1977, 1978, 1979).

The content analysis component

The cultural-indicators project represents the most extensive across-time analysis of television drama output in the published research literature. Research began in 1967–68 with a study for the National Commission on the Causes and Prevention of Violence. It continued under the sponsorship of the Surgeon General's Scientific Advisory Committee on Television and Social Behavior, and subsequently for the National Institute of Mental Health, American Medical Association, the National Science Foundation, and other agencies.

The content analysis component of this project involved the monitoring of samples of prime-time and weekend daytime television output on all the major networks each year. Analysis was limited to dramatic content, which meant that news, documentaries, variety and quiz shows, and sports programmes were excluded from coding. A simple normative definition of violence was employed: 'The overt expression of physical force against self or other, compelling action against one's will on pain of being hurt or killed, or actually hurting or killing' (Gerbner, 1972). This definition was used by trained coders to record the frequency and nature of violent acts, the perpetrators and victims of violence, and the temporal and spatial settings in which the acts occurred. From a certain combination of these measures was derived the 'Violence Profile' which purported to represent an objective and meaningful indicator of the amount of violence portrayed in television drama programmes.

The Violence Profile itself consisted of two sets of indicators: the Violence Index and the Risk Ratio that were described in detail in Chapters 3 to 6. The Profile combined a number of measures including occurrences of qualifying behaviour, characters involved as aggressors or victims and consequences of violence.

Gerbner et al. (1978) reported that while 30 per cent of all characters and over 60 per cent of *leading* characters monitored in prime-time programming over a ten-year span were involved in violence as perpetrators, victims, or both, United States census figures during this period indicated that in actuality only one third of one per cent of individuals in the general population tended to get involved in violence. The Gerbner group argued that viewers learned these content patterns, drew inferences from them and then generalized this information to their perceptions of the real world.

Questions have been raised about Gerbner's measurement system and especially about the aggregation of several distinct measures to produce a composite violence index. Doubts have been cast on which of the measures that have been combined in this case really belong together (Blank, 1977a, 1977b; Coffin and Tuchman, 1972). One critic challenged the Violence Index as an invalid measure of the amount of violence on television because its constituent elements comprised non-violent as well as violent components. For example, one ingredient was the number of leading characters involved in violence on screen. This meant that the number of violent scenes on television could decrease, but the Violence Index could still increase if the numbers of characters involved in violence increased (Blank, 1977a). Gerbner and Gross (1976) argued that indices by definition are arbitrary correlations and that their Violence Index served as a heuristic device leading to the analysis of the shifts in components behind the trend in index scores. This argument, however, failed to address the criticism that changes in apparent levels of violence on television, as indicated by their index, could be caused by changes in the character of violence rather than by any shifts in the frequency with which it occurred.

Cultivation analysis

Through their research technique called cultivation analysis, Gerbner and his colleagues found that people who watched a great deal of television, especially of dramatic, violence-containing, action-adventure programmes, tended to endorse different beliefs about the world in which they lived from individuals who experienced a relatively light diet of television (Gerbner and Gross, 1976; Gerbner et al., 1978, 1979). Thus, heavy television viewers tended to exhibit a measurable 'television bias' in their perceptions of the frequency with which violence occurs in reality. They also produced greater overestimates than did light viewers of the numbers of people working in law enforcement, the likelihood of personal involvement in violent crime, and exhibited greater fear of crime.

There are a number of methodological issues connected with cultivation analysis that need to be examined closely in order to determine if the original research findings can be taken at face value. The key issues concern the operational definitions that have been used of television viewing and social reality perceptions, and the ways in which other potentially important factors that may relate to both these measures, have been controlled. Most cultivation effects research has involved the use of survey data. Some studies, however, have used experimental methodologies and manipulated the television content to which viewers have been exposed before measuring their social reality perceptions.

Measuring television viewing

A central tenet in cultivation analysis is that people who are 'heavy viewers' differ from people who are 'light viewers' in their perceptions of social reality. In order to establish the existence of such differences and measure, quantitatively, how significant they are, it is necessary to define what constitutes a 'heavy' or 'light' viewer. Before this question can be answered, the research has to decide the method for measuring television viewing. Gerbner classified viewers into heavy, medium or light on the basis of a global measure of self-estimated television viewing in terms of hours of viewing per day.

Hirsch (1980) challenged this division of viewers on the basis of their claimed viewing behaviour. He pointed out that different definitions of light and heavy viewers were used by the Gerbner group in different studies. For example, in a survey with a New Jersey school sample, a child was classified as a light viewer if reportedly watching three hours or less per day (Gerbner et al., 1979). In studies with adult samples, two hours a day or less was the definition used for light viewing.

In a comprehensive re-analysis of the original survey data used by Gerbner and his colleagues, Hirsch included two new categories: non-viewers (zero hours viewing) and extreme viewers (eight or more hours). Although a principal assertion of the Gerbner group in their late 1970s papers had been that heavier viewers, in response to the lessons they learned from television, were likely to have higher scores on items tapping fear of victimization, and social mistrust, Hirsch found that on many of these items *non-viewers* had higher scores than did light, medium, heavy or extreme viewers.

Turning next to the other end of the viewing spectrum, Hirsch compared the responses of 'heavy' (four to seven hours viewing daily) and 'extreme' viewers (eight or more hours daily) on a series of survey items also used by Gerbner. Hirsch found that the demographic composition of these heavy viewing divisions was different. Markedly higher proportions of 'extreme' viewers than 'heavy' viewers were women, housewives, retired workers or black, lower-class and less well educated.

The cultivation hypothesis proposes that people who watch the most television will provide 'television answers' to survey items more often than those who watch for fewer hours per day. By dividing the Gerbner group's 'heavy viewers' into two subgroups of heavy and extreme viewers, Hirsch was able to test this hypothesis and also the logic of collapsing both of these types into a single category. Hirsch found that extreme viewers provided 'television answers' less often than did heavy viewers on 11 of 18 survey items used by Gerbner.

The use of a single measure of television viewing based on self-reported hours of viewing does not take into account the variations that might occur in viewing diets among viewers in a television environment that offers a varied mix of programme genres to choose from. Thus, two heavy viewers may consume widely varying viewing diets in terms of the actual types of programme they watch. One heavy viewer may indeed watch a great deal of violence-containing serious drama. Another heavy viewer may watch much less of such programming and instead fill much more of his or her viewing time with light entertainment that is virtually violence free.

Another approach has been to measure viewing behaviour in terms of the programmes individuals claim to watch. British research that attempted to replicate Gerbner's American findings in a different national environment used diary measures of viewing behaviours. Survey respondents received a seven-day viewing diary that listed all the programmes broadcast by the main television channels. Respondents registered an appreciation score against each programme they had watched sufficiently to form an opinion about. Their amount of viewing was then measured in terms of the numbers of programmes they had watched. However, in addition to differentiating among viewers in terms of whether they were light, medium or heavy consumers of television, the data enabled the researchers to distinguish among viewers who were light, medium and heavy consumers of specific categories of programme (e.g. drama). It was also possible to calculate the proportion of total viewing that was devoted to particular categories of programming. Thus, a light viewer might watch mainly action-drama, while a heavy viewer might watch the same amount of such programming, but it would represent a far smaller percentage of his/her overall viewing diet (Gunter, 1987a; Gunter and Wober, 1983; Wober and Gunter, 1982, 1988).

This approach indicated that while overall amount of television viewing *per se* did not invariably predict social reality perceptions, the amount of viewing of specific genres was sometimes a more significant predictor of perceptions of risk from crime or violence in different types of environment (Gunter, 1987a).

Measuring perceptions of social reality

Measures of social reality perceptions have included perceptions of the frequency with which certain events (e.g. crime) occur in reality, the prevalence in society of particular groups or institutions (e.g. medical practitioners, police officers, lawyers, etc.), perceptions of likelihood of personal involvement in certain activities (e.g. victim of violent attack), perceptions of others' likelihood of involvement in such incidents, and more generalized anxieties (e.g. fear of crime) or opinions (e.g. mistrust of others or of institutions).

Gerbner et al. (1977) compared the answers of heavy and light viewers to questions about the occurrence of criminal violence and law enforcement agencies in society, for which two response alternatives were derived either from the quantitative programme measures generated by content analysis, in the case of 'television answers', or from official statistical sources in the case of 'real world answers'. The four questions posed in this study asked about personal chances of being involved in some kind of violence (TV answer – 'about one in ten'; real-world answer – 'about one in a hundred'); about the proportion of all men, who have jobs, who work in law enforcement and crime detection (TV answer – 'five per cent'; real-world answer – 'one per cent'); about the percentage of all crimes that are violent, such as murders, rape, robbery and aggravated assault (TV answer – '25 per cent'; real-world answer – '15 per cent'); and about whether most fatal violence occurs between strangers (TV answer) or between relatives or acquaintances (real-world answer).

These four questions were presented to two samples of adults and two samples of adolescents and, in every case, responses indicated a significant tendency for heavy viewers to overestimate the incidence of violence in society by endorsing 'television answers', compared with light viewers. This association between amount of television viewing and perception of violence remained even after the major demographic variables of sex, age, education and, in the case of one sample of adolescents, IQ had been individually controlled.

The cultivation effects hypothesis proposed that it is not only perceptions of the occurrence of crime and violence in the social environment which can be distorted by regular exposure to television's fictional world, but also the extent to which people fear being victims of crime themselves. Conceptions of social reality are believed to generalize into the realm of affect to produce corresponding emotional reactions to perceived environmental dangers. To demonstrate this affective response, in addition to obtaining responses to questions relating to the occurrence of crime and violence, criminals and law enforcement officers in society, Gerbner and his colleagues examined data from large samples of adults and adolescents on their hopes and fears with respect to the way things are or are likely to be. Gerbner argued that if exposure to television could give rise to an exaggerated perception of the prevalence of certain criminal behaviours, it might also produce an accompanying heightened fear of violent crime and the personal dangers it holds.

In order to investigate this question further, Gerbner et al. (1978) computed statistical relationships between television viewing claims and fear of walking alone in the city or in their own neighbourhood at night among a sample of New Jersey schoolchildren and individuals sampled in the 1976 American National Election study and the 1977 National

Opinion Research Center's General Social Survey. Comparisons were made between the responses of those individuals who claimed to watch television for four or more hours a day and those who said they watched for less than two hours a day. Throughout these samples there was a greater tendency of heavy viewers to be more fearful than light viewers.

Controls for mediating factors

Two challenges to Gerbner's work came from scholars within the USA who questioned the extent to which appropriate controls had been deployed for extraneous variables that might independently affect amounts of television viewing or social perceptions. Although Gerbner and his colleagues had employed statistical controls for the effects of respondent sex, age, class and education, these had been partialled out one at a time. Furthermore, there was also the accusation that Gerbner had been selective in his choice of third-variable controls. There were other demographic factors for which controls could have been introduced, that appeared to have been selectively omitted from consideration.

Hughes (1980) conducted further analyses of the survey data used by Gerbner but introduced controls for new demographic variables and used simultaneous controls for groups of demographic factors. Amongst the control variables used by Hughes were age, sex, race, income, education, hours worked (per week), church attendance and size of home town. Some of these variables were significantly related to amount of television watching even in the presence of statistical controls for the others, while some were not. For example, an initially strong relationship between sex of viewer and television viewing disappeared when controls were employed for hours worked per week. This indicated that women watch more television than men perhaps because they are likely to work fewer hours outside the home.

On relating five social perceptions examined by Gerbner and his colleagues with amount of television watching whilst controlling simultaneously for a range of demographic factors, Hughes (1980) found that only one of the five relationships claimed by Gerbner et al. (1978) still held up. Fear of walking alone at night was found to reverse the direction of its relationship with amount of viewing, indicating that those individuals who claimed to watch television were *less* likely to be afraid of walking alone at night in the neighbourhood.

Hughes discovered a number of items included in the NORC's General Social Survey not reported by Gerbner et al. which provided response patterns counter to the cultivation hypothesis. With one such item ('Are there any situations you can imagine in which you would approve of a man punching an adult male stranger?'), Hughes found that, when controlling for sex, age and education, there was not one instance, overall or within each demographic division, when 'heavy' viewers were more favourable towards physical violence than 'medium' or 'light' viewers.

Within many demographic groups, the proportion of 'heavy' viewers who expressed a distaste for violence was significantly higher than among lighter viewers. In Hughes' own words, such findings raise 'the possibility that in failing to ensure cross-sample comparability, introduce multiple controls, and report items where the data do not support tne argument for television's "cultivation" of beliefs and attitudes, the Gerbner group has itself contributed to distorting scientific reality' (1980: 288).

Experimental research

One purpose of cultivation analysis has been to provide indications, through analysis of survey data, of influences of television operating at the level of viewers' social perceptions, beliefs and attitudes. The computation of correlations between self-reported television viewing data and subjective perceptions of societal groups or events, however, cannot prove cause – effect relationships. Causation is best explored through experimental methodologies in which the amount and nature of media exposure is systematically controlled by the research and specific (content-related) effects are measured as a direct reaction to the content to which respondents have been exposed.

Experimental research has been carried out within a cultivation effects framework. Bryant et al. (1981) presented groups of respondents with a controlled television viewing diet for a six-week period. At the outset of the experiment, respondents were divided into low- and high-anxiety types on the basis of responses given to items from Taylor's Manifest Anxiety Inventory. Low-anxiety and high-anxiety individuals were randomly assigned to one of three viewing conditions: (1) light justice-depicting, (2) heavy justice-depicting and (3) heavy injustice-depicting action-adventure programming. Justice-depicting programmes concluded with a clear triumph of justice or good over evil, while in injustice-depicting programmes, order was never truly restored. The viewing diet was controlled inside the laboratory, but outside, at home, respondents were free to watch whatever and whenever they pleased.

After six weeks of controlled laboratory viewing, anxiety, fearfulness and other social belief measures were also taken. Respondents were also told that tapes of six action-adventure series were held in stock and they were invited to view these programmes further as part of a study on television formats. The number of these programmes viewed during this subsequent stage provided a measure of voluntary selective exposure to action drama.

Results showed that both amount and type of viewing affected viewers' anxiety levels. Light viewing and heavy-justice viewing produced a slight increase in anxiety levels among low-anxiety individuals – but resulted in a reduction in anxiety in individuals already highly anxious. For heavy viewers of programmes in which injustice was habitually depicted, both low- and high-anxiety individuals exhibited significant increases in anxiety, with the greatest increment occurring for those who were already highly anxious. Individuals high in anxiety at the outset also held stronger beliefs that they would at some time be victimized than did those initially low in anxiety. For both groups, however, a heavy diet of action-adventure material, with or without justice, resulted in increased perceptions of victimization. As for *fear* of victimization, as distinct from its *perceived likelihood*, Bryant et al., found that viewing television injustice produced significantly greater increase in fearfulness than did television justice. Heavy viewers of action-adventure programmes who saw repeated incidents of restoration of justice also rated their chance of vindication in the event of personal victimization greater than did injustice viewers.

In another experimental investigation, Wakshlag et al. (1983) manipulated individuals' initial apprehension levels before giving them the opportunity to select films to be viewed from a list. Participants in this study were shown either a documentary about crime or an innocuous documentary about the Himalayas. A series of items designed to measure degree of apprehension about crime or fear of victimization were given after viewing and indicated that the crime documentary did produce significantly stronger apprehension reactions. Participants were then shown a list of titles of films with accompanying synopses which, according to earlier independent evaluations, varied in the degree to which they featured victimization and restoration of justice. Individuals who saw the crime documentary chose fewer victimization and more justice restoration films than did their counterparts who saw the nature films.

Strong sex differences also emerged. Violence in drama appealed to males much more than to females. Regardless of these sex differences, however, the appeal of violence in television drama dropped significantly for individuals who were apprehensive about the possibility of being victimized themselves. This finding indicates that violence *per se* is not an attractive element of entertainment for people who are fearful of victimization. For such individuals, violence is a turn-off.

Looking at the effect of restoration of justice, it emerged that this held more appeal to females than to males. Crime-apprehensive individuals established great sensitivity to the theme of justice restoration. The appeal of drama featuring this theme grew significantly with such apprehensions. Hence, people who are worried about crime may seek comfort in programmes in which justice is restored or prevails.

Explaining cultivation effects

A large number of studies have been published that offer support for Gerbner's cultivation model. Even those researchers who have called for a more sophisticated analysis of television viewing patterns have observed links between exposure to specific types of television content and semantically related real-world perceptions. Such findings may be especially likely to occur in respect of those instances where television depicts aspects of social reality about which few alternative information sources are available to viewers (Gunter, 1987a; Wober and Gunter, 1988).

Another issue about cultivation effects that has been debated increasingly, concerns their external and internal validity. The external validity of cultivation effects has been regarded as supported by the widespread replication of results across different audience communities and content domains (Hawkins and Pingree, 1990). The demonstration of internal validity, however, is dependent on a satisfactory explanatory model that can account for the psychological processes underlying cultivation effects. One model that has been proposed is based on the notion of construct accessibility. This model hypothesizes that heavy viewers give higher real-world estimates than do light viewers for events frequently portrayed on television, because such events are rendered more accessible in memory for heavy viewers (Shrum and O'Guinn, 1993).

To test this hypothesis, Shrum (1996) conducted an experiment in which respondents were presented with cultivation questions about the real-world prevalence of crimes, marital discord and various occupations. The dependent variable comprised not simply whether respondents chose a higher estimate over a lower estimate of prevalence in each case, but also how long it took (in seconds) for any estimate to be given. This 'response latency' measure indicated how accessible each such construct was in the respondent's memory. Quicker response times indicated greater construct accessibility.

The cultivation questions were based on themes prominent in three leading television soap operas. In each case, a number of episodes of each serial were analysed to establish how these dramas represented specific themes, and from which cultivation questions could be framed. Experimental subjects were all college students who, through prescreening, were divided into heavy and light soap opera viewers.

During the construct accessibility test, cultivation questions were presented on a computer screen. These included questions such as: 'What percentage of women are raped in their lifetime?', 'What percentage of police draw their guns in the average day?', 'What percentage of the US workforce are lawyers?', 'What percentage of Americans have extramarital affairs?'. Responses were given by pressing keys along a scale from 0 to 9. Each key corresponded to an intuitive percentage range. Thus, a response of 3 corresponded to 30 per cent to 39 per cent; 4 corresponded to 40 per cent to 49 per cent, and so on. The crucial measures included the choice of key and the elapsed time between presentation of the cultivation question and a key response being given.

Results showed that soap viewing was linked significantly to frequency estimates of crimes, marital discord and occupations, even after statistical controls had been implemented for respondent's education, income and other television viewing-related factors. Results for perceptions of crime prevalence and occupations prevalence indicated that soap viewing also exerted an indirect effect on judgements through its effect on construct accessibility. The claimed level of soap opera viewing was related to the speed of key-pressing responses for these perceptions. Heavy soap opera viewers responded more quickly than light soap opera viewers in every case. The value of this research, and the new methodological element of response latency, is that it represents a movement towards a better understanding of why cultivation effects may occur.

FACTUAL LEARNING FROM THE MEDIA

The study of factual learning from the mass media has traditionally been grounded in quantitative methodologies normally associated with sociology and psychology. In sum, much of this research has comprised field surveys and field or laboratory experiments. Much of the factual learning research has concerned an audience learning from factual broadcasts on television and radio, with news programming being the most commonly studied stimulus material. In addition to this work, studies have been conducted with educational media materials, usually specially produced for children and aimed at improving localized knowledge or more general cognitive (i.e. numerical and language) abilities.

General correlations between media exposure and knowledge

Much of the early research on learning from the media depended upon survey information in which public knowledge was tested in regard to a specific topic or event in the news. The main divisions that can be made within this category of research are between surveys that correlate self-report evidence from respondents on their use of different media news sources and their knowledge of topics, issues or events and studies that are concerned with demonstrating differential rates of diffusion of information from the media among different subgroups of the population. Correlational surveys can also be differentiated between those that focus on the role of the media in imparting information about major events such as political elections, the role of the media in enhancing general public affairs awareness, and the role the media can play in enhancing children's political awareness.

The media and political campaigns

Research under this heading has investigated the political functions of the media, especially in connection with the impact that the media might have on voter turn-out or the choice of candidate. While these effects are behavioural in nature, they represent the end of a chain of influence that begins with the hypothesis that the mass media represent sources of information about politics. During political campaigns, the public are generally more attuned to political messages, and the media are a key source of information about election issues and events, and about candidates themselves.

Methodologically, further distinctions can be made between campaign surveys in terms of the major categories of survey design. Studies of media impact on electorates during political campaigns have comprised cross-sectional surveys conducted at one point in time, though more often comprise repeat surveys either with different samples or with the same panel of respondents at key points during the campaign period.

Gunter et al. (1986) reported a three-wave national survey of political knowledge and opinions in Britain that explored the role of the media during the 1983 General Election campaign. Different national samples were contacted at the beginning of the campaign, and then again shortly before and just after polling day. Interviews were conducted face-to-face in respondents' homes. Comparisons were made of the effectiveness of the media in informing respondents about election issues and of voters' perceptions of the usefulness of different media in that context.

Some studies have combined surveys of the public with content analyses of media news output. This combination of methods enables the researchers to explore parallel developments in media coverage and public awareness or opinion. In a study of television's effects during the 1972 US presidential election campaign, McClure and Patterson (1973) examined the content of major newspapers and weeknight network newscasts and conducted a three-wave panel survey over a two-month period. They found that while the emphasis television placed on campaign issues did not result in heavier viewers becoming better informed, greater emphasis on certain issues within newspapers did result in more avid consumers of the press becoming better informed.

General media exposure effects

This methodological approach comprises either cross-sectional or longitudinal surveys of samples of respondents in which self-report data are obtained about media exposure habits over a designated period of time and awareness, knowledge and understanding of a topic. Correlational analyses are computed on these data to indicate whether significant degrees of association exist between claimed media exposure and topic-related knowledge. Statistical controls might also be applied for various demographic factors, such as gender, age, social class and education, that might also contribute to differences in knowledge levels. Such studies hoped to find significant correlations between reported media news exposure and topic knowledge, even when the effects of demographics had been multiply controlled.

Some studies have attempted to demonstrate a general role of media in the development of current affairs awareness. Often this type of research has been conducted within the political context. Work with children has explored the role of different media in political knowledge levels of children and adolescents. Cross-sectional studies have asked children to nominate the media from which they get most of their information about political issues (Dominick, 1972). Other surveys have asked children to report their media exposure habits and to answer questions about their political and civic affairs knowledge (Conway et al., 1975).

One-off surveys reveal degrees of association between reported media use and topic-related knowledge or opinions, but do not demonstrate the extent to which the news media might contribute to the growth of knowledge over time. Longitudinal research with children has enabled researchers to track statistical relationships between media usage and current affairs knowledge over time. Atkin and Gantz (1978) conducted two waves of questionnaire-based surveys with children to measure their political knowledge and patterns of media exposure across a one-year interval. The children were asked whether they watch main evening television newscasts, special news slots for their own age group on Saturday mornings, and about their levels of interest in news issues. A test of political knowledge was also run. Evidence emerged that children who watched more television news had better political knowledge, both at one point in time and over time. Early television news viewing was linked to later political knowledge development.

Differential rates of news diffusion

In a different approach, assumptions have been made by researchers that differences in knowledge levels already exist among population subgroups, often associated with the educational level people have attained. Thus, better-educated people also tended to be better informed about current affairs. Not only that, but the better-educated learned at a faster rate from news media than did less well-educated people, meaning that the gap in their respective knowledge levels would grow wider as a function of news media exposure. Research conducted to investigate this knowledge-gap hypothesis tended to measure public knowledge and understanding of specific topics or events that received extensive media coverage over a given period. Knowledge levels were measured for people pre-classified as well-educated and less well-educated across the period of target topic coverage. Comparisons were then made of knowledge change among these population subgroups over time. Findings have usually shown that better-educated people do appear to assimilate more information about events or issues than less well-educated people (Robinson, 1967; Tichenor et al., 1970).

Awareness of recent news events

Another approach has been to measure self-reports of media usage and how these reports relate to knowledge of recent news events. Gunter

(1985b) reported a telephone interview survey with over five hundred residents in London. Respondents were asked a series of questions about eight political figures and three stories prominent in the news during the previous week. This was a knowledge test on which respondents were scored for correct answers. Information was also obtained about usual exposure to television and radio news and current affairs broadcasts and about newspaper readership. These data were correlated, with statistical controls introduced for the effects of demographic factors such as gender, age, social class and educational level. Claimed television news exposure was positively correlated with awareness of political personalities, while type of newspaper readership was positively related to better knowledge of news stories.

A more qualitative approach was used by Graber (1984) to study the impact of news exposure on learning. She interviewed a small panel of 21 people individually ten times during a single year. Respondents provided information about the sources to which they turned for news and the information they had absorbed from the news stories they had experienced. Eighteen panellists also kept diaries of the news stories to which they had been exposed. These panellists noted more than ten thousand news stories and were considered through depth-interviews to have acquired reasonable knowledge about over fifteen hundred of them. Newspapers emerged as more important sources of information than television.

Studies of audience retention from specific media outputs

Some researchers have tested learning from specific media outputs by asking respondents to recall informational content shortly after exposure to it. These investigations have generally been of one of two types. The first are field surveys in which respondents are contacted in their own homes either in face-to-face or telephone interviews, with or without prior warning of being tested. They are then asked questions about stories reported in a specific news broadcast that has occurred within the past 24 hours. The second type are studies in which participants are invited to watch either a live or specially prepared television news programme in a central viewing location or, occasionally, at home, and are tested for retention of its content shortly afterwards in the presence of the researcher.

Field studies

Stern (1971) reported a study that comprised a series of telephone surveys with people in the San Francisco area. Every evening the researchers monitored the main television newscasts on all three major networks and listed the stories carried in each newscast as well as factual details from it. Respondents were telephoned shortly after these programmes had finished and asked if they had watched any of them. If so, they were then asked to recall as many stories as possible from the programme before being given more detailed content-specific questions on factual points. In another study, respondents were interviewed face to face shortly after televised news broadcasts and required to recall without prompting as many stories as they could from the programme they had seen, before being given brief descriptive labels from each story to provide triggers to further recall (Robinson et al., 1980).

In some telephone surveys, respondents are forewarned beforehand that they will be tested for their memory of a news broadcast's story content. Stauffer et al. (1983) reported such a study in which respondents were telephoned within three hours of a television news broadcast and asked to provide brief descriptive recall accounts of stories from the programme and then to reply to more detailed questions about these stories. Those people who had been forewarned remembered nearly 60% more than those who had been given no advance notice.

Theatre tests

Although field surveys have the advantage of testing memory and comprehension of media news content under normal exposure conditions, the researcher has little or no control over the viewing situation. There is no guarantee that all respondents paid the same degree of attention to particular news broadcasts while viewing them at home. Some researchers have therefore tested news recall under more controlled exposure conditions, where all respondents participate in exactly the same media exposure environment.

Research in Britain in the early 1970s recruited people to view a live edition of an evening newscast in a theatre condition (ORC, 1972). Tests of knowledge about topical issues were conducted before and after the transmission was viewed. Pre-viewing questions established baseline knowledge of topics to be covered in the television bulletin. Post-viewing tests measured knowledge improvements contingent upon exposure to relevant television news coverage. Programme-related knowledge was tested via questionnaires shortly after the programme had finished.

Controlled experimental studies of retention from edited media outputs

The research reported up to this point has investigated the ability of media consumers to remember factual content from media outputs in which those outputs were presented in their original, unaltered form. This approach reveals nothing about the reasons why certain informational content is remembered and other content cannot be accurately retrieved. In particular, what evidence exists that the take-up of information from factual media is affected by the way that information is presented? To answer this sort of question, it is necessary to control the way in which mass-media information is presented to isolate specific presentation features whose effects upon learning and memory can then be measured. A considerable body of research has accumulated in which controlled experimental procedures have been used to measure the effects of specific content and format attributes upon audience retention of media news. Much of this work has been conducted on broadcast news.

Such studies have investigated the effects on audience news retention of factors such as the packaging of news stories in broadcasts, the construction of story narratives, and the visual presentation of news. In each case, research has primarily been conducted on the cognitive impact of televised news. Controlled laboratory experiments have been conducted with specially edited broadcast materials designed to manipulate specific production attributes of broadcast news. Most designs have comprised experiments with pre-tests and post-tests or post-tests only. Experimental subjects are brought to the laboratory, shown specially-prepared broadcast material, and then tested for their retention of its informational content. Retention is tested using unprompted or free recall, prompted or cued recall, or recognition of content. In some cases, subjects write recall accounts in their own words, while in other cases, they respond to multiple-choice answers. Some researchers have provided subjects with a transcript of the news narrative with certain key words or phrases missing, which they have to fill in (Baggaley, 1980). Correct answers are scored numerically.

Packaging effects

News packaging effects are concerned with identifying and explaining the effects upon story retention of the position a story occupies in the running order of the programme and the effects of being grouped with other stories about similar topics. In a typical experiment concerned with the impact of story position within the bulletin, subjects are presented with a specially edited sequence of 10–15 news items, video-recorded from a radio or television bulletin. The researcher cuts each story so that all stories in the sequence are similar in length and selects or edits items so that they are similar in terms of visual presentation format. In other words, the experimenter controls as far as possible for the effects of other variables that may prejudice item recall. The items are presented once to viewers who are run either individually or in small groups. Immediately or shortly afterwards, they are prompted to recall as many items as they can in their own words. Subsequently, topic-specific prompts or more detailed questions about items may be presented. The typical result is that items that occur at the beginning and end of the sequence are best recalled, while those in the middle are worst recalled (Tannenbaum, 1954; Gunter, 1979, 1980). In a variation on this design, the visual format of items can be varied as well as their position. Thus, the items in a sequence may comprise talking head format only, a talking head with still photograph, or a film report. The use of visuals as such can offset the disadvantage of an item being presented in the middle or a new sequence (Gunter, 1979).

The effects of grouping together stories about similar topics have been examined by setting up sequences of televised news items so that they occur in quick succession with similar other items or with dissimilar items. In a series of experiments reported by Gunter and his colleagues, subjects were presented with televised news materials and tested immediately afterwards over a series of four test trials. In each trial, a sequence of three brief news items or a single longer item would be presented, and a test for content retention administered immediately after the news sequence had ended. After the test, a further news sequence was presented and again tested. This procedure was repeated over four trials. If the news materials on each of the four trials comprised stories about similar topics (e.g. political news, news about the economy), content retention deteriorated progressively across trials. While 70–80% of content might be correctly recalled on trial one, by trial four this performance might have dropped to 30%. If, however, on trial four, the nature of the news material was changed to a different topic, performance immediately improved almost to trial one levels (Gunter et al., 1980; Gunter et al., 1981).

In a follow-up study, Berry and Clifford (1985) found that such topic-related interference would occur across a group of news stories presented in a more natural television bulletin format, and could be modestly alleviated by switching between topics. In this case, subjects received a sequence of four news stories either about similar topics throughout, or topically-related across the first three items, with a topic switch occurring at item four. Subjects were then tested once following the completion of the entire sequence.

Narrative construction

Much of the research on retention of broadcast news has assumed that viewers and listeners remember story content as isolated groups of facts. A different view that has emerged is that people learn from texts at a macro-level as well as at a micro-level. Isolated factual propositions from stories can be remembered more effectively when individuals process each of those factual items as parts of an integrated whole. A story has a structure. There are rules concerning the way stories are told or unfold. Stories have a grammatical structure and this represents an aspect of a story that has to be learned in addition to its individual factual constituents.

The ordering of elements within a story such as its theme, setting, plot and resolution can affect how easily it can be learned (Thorndyke, 1977). In processing information from a text, the received messages are assembled by establishing coherences between the different story elements. In sum, there are different ways of telling a story, with some story structures enabling information retention to occur more readily than others.

A typical experiment was reported by Berry et al. (1993). News material originally recorded from a television newscast was re-recorded as a sound-only broadcast by a professional news presenter. Two versions of each story were audio-recorded. The first version was the original transmission version. The second version involved a rewrite of the original story according to story grammar principles established through earlier research (e.g. Thorndyke, 1977). In the revised presentation, the story structure was changed so that setting and theme information were presented first and the remainder of the narrative adopted a coherent sequence of plots and outcomes. Two groups of subjects were randomly assigned to listen to one or the other of these two versions and then tested afterwards for their retention of story content. Text restructuring was found to improve learning.

Visual format

Tests of the impact of visual format have been run with televised news. In the simplest designs, groups of experimental subjects are presented with a sequence of news items of varying visual formats. In some cases, the items are presented by a studio-based newsreader speaking to camera. In other cases, the item is also illustrated with static visual material such as maps, graphics or photographs, or presented as an outside broadcast film report. Comparisons are made between levels of unprompted recall of the items to find out if items with visual material are better remembered (Gunter, 1979).

In more sophisticated designs, researchers have attempted to find out more about the importance of the nature of the relationship between spoken text and visual illustrations for audience recall of news content. Some studies have simply explored the effects upon news narrative recall of the physical presence of film footage running alongside the spoken text. Others have explored the effects of the way the visual material is coordinated with the spoken text. Yet further studies have examined the degree of informational similarity between text and visuals.

In one type of experiment interested in the impact of the physical presence of different kinds of visual material, the same news stories are presented in two versions. This comparison has generally been achieved in one of two ways. The same news stories are presented in the audio-visual modality with picture accompaniment or in sound only (Furnham and Gunter, 1985; Gunter, 1980). Alternatively, different audio-visual versions of the same news stories are produced in which format varies between talking-head presentation and talking head plus visual illustrations (Edwardson et al., 1976; Edwardson et al., 1981; Edwardson et al., 1992; Gunter, 1980).

Edwardson et al. (1976) showed subjects eight different news items that consisted of actual stories written with some alteration of names and facts so that subjects would not remember the information from previous newscasts or newspaper reports. A male newscaster was recorded on videotape reading the news stories in two versions. In one treatment, four of the stories were also accompanied by film footage, while the others had no film added to them. In the second treatment, the four stories that initially had no film now had film added to them. Meanwhile the film stories from the first condition were presented on this occasion minus any film footage. Retention of details from each item was tested by a series of multiple-choice questions. A pre-test of a separate sample of subjects who saw the film from each item without audio and were then tested for knowledge acquisition indicated that none of the film clips conveyed any of the information contained in the news items. In the experiment proper, no substantial differences emerged between the number of correct responses to questions concerning news materials given with or without film.

In a later experiment, Edwardson et al. (1992) compared retention from television news stories presented either as talking heads or as voice-overs with video footage, a soundbite to camera by a person other than the main news presenter, and a graphic. Experimental subjects were allocated to these conditions and then tested afterwards for identification of material spoken by the newscaster. The graphic comprising a bar chart packed with information was found to distract viewers' attention from what the newscaster was saying.

In addition to the effects of visual material on the degree of attention paid to the spoken narrative, there is also a question about the informational relevance of visual footage to spoken footage in news stories. Swedish researchers systematically investigated the impact of visuals that were specially manufactured to illustrate specific aspects of television news stories. Either the visual illustrated points about the persons involved in the news or the locations of events, or about the causes and consequences of the events. Specially constructed news stories were produced in which visual illustrations such as maps, graphics and photographs were created to illustrate one or other of these aspects of each news story. Different versions of these stories were then presented to experimental subjects who were tested afterwards for story content recall. Results showed that illustrating the persons and locations featured in stories enhanced recall of those features only. Illustrating causes and consequences of information, however, enhanced recall of the entire story (Findahl and Hoijer, 1976).

Further systematic tests of the significance of informational redundancy between the pictorial and narrative elements of television news to its recall and recognition by audiences have been conducted throughout the 1990s, using a variety of experimental designs (Crigler, Just and Neuman, 1994; Grimes, 1990; David, 1998). Informational redundancy within the news aids audience recall of news content. Such redundancy is more likely to be achieved when the verbal narrative uses concrete rather than abstract language (David, 1998).

Modality effects

There have been numerous experimental studies since the 1930s that have examined learning from informational media as a function of the presentation modality. These studies have been concerned with the relative effectiveness of audio-visual, audio-only and written media in instructional or educational contexts and have been designed to find out which is the best channel through which to impart information. As well as research with educational materials, comparisons have been made of different media of presentation of news information.

Barrow and Westley (1959) conducted an experiment to compare the effectiveness of equivalent radio and television versions of 'exploring the News', a series of background-of-the-news programmes for young children. Each version of the programme was shown to randomly allocated classroom groups of 11- to 12-year-olds. Results indicated a superiority of television over radio.

Williams et al. (1957) compared television, radio, print and live presentations of a lecture. A sample of over one hundred college undergraduates was divided into four groups and received the lecture at the same time in different rooms under one or other of these presentation conditions. A test of knowledge acquisition was given to all groups immediately after the lecture and again eight months later. Once again, it was found that learning was best for the television group, followed by radio, reading and finally the live studio lecture group.

Canadian research reported in the mid-1970s showed large losses from all media during immediate, unaided recall of simulated news presentations, and losses were greater from broadcast media than from print. Wilson (1974) constructed two fictitious but plausible news stories in standard inverted pyramid news styles. That is, the first sentence or two delivered the central point of the story, and successive sentences elaborated on that with further details. An independent panel of judges was employed to categorize the information contained in each story as *essential* (central to the meaning of the story) or *contributory* (elaborative detail). Short, medium and long versions of each story were then prepared in audio-visual, audio-only, and written form. Over four hundred college students were allocated to one or other of these presentation conditions. Afterwards they were given a free recall test of everything they could remember from each story, which they produced in written accounts.

Points of information judged essential to the stories received two points if recalled fully and accurately, one point if recalled in general, and no points if omitted. Points of information judged contributory were scored one point if recalled fully and accurately, and received no points if recalled otherwise or omitted. The greatest information loss was from radio, second from television, and least from print. There was also less loss from short stories than from medium-length stories, and most loss from long stories.

Stauffer et al. (1980) examined recall from television, radio and print news among Kenyan and American college students. In both countries, the experiment consisted of showing an actual television newscast with sound to one group (viewers), presenting the soundtrack only to another group (listeners), and the printed transcript of the narrative to another group (readers). Those reading the transcript were allowed to read through the material once at their own pace.

Immediately after news presentation, respondents were asked to make a list of all the stories they could recall by providing a brief description of each item. Following this unaided recall test, respondents completed a four-option multiple-choice test based on the narrative content of the news stories. Both US and Kenyan newscasts contained 14 stories and were about 16 minutes long. Among the American and Kenyan samples, recall from television and print was similar and significantly better than from an audio source.

Gunter and his colleagues ran 128 male and female sixth-form college students aged 16 to 18 years. To test the robustness and reliability of this experiment, Furnham and Gunter (1985) replicated it with a new and slightly older sample of 68 university undergraduates. Subjects were randomly allocated to television, radio and print conditions in each experiment. The news materials were originally taken from television and presented either in their original form, in sound-track only, or as printed transcripts of the news narrative. In both studies, recall of news from print was best of all, but findings were inconsistent regarding the relative efficacy of audio-visual or audio-only presentation modes.

Research with children has indicated a superiority of television presentation over print. Dutch researchers randomly allocated 10- to 12-year-old children to either watch five news stories from a children's television news programme or to read the same stories in a newspaper format. This research also distinguished between children who were good and poor readers and utilized conditions in which children were forewarned or not of a memory test to follow news presentation. Cued recall questions tested for children's memory of story details. Television presentation produced the better recall results regardless of forewarning or reading proficiency of the children (Walma van der Molen and van der Voort, 1997).

Qualitative reception studies

Research into the cognitive impact of the media has been conducted largely from a positivist empiricist orientation. As Chapters 1 and 2 indicated, however, this paradigm has been challenged by scholars who follow the critical or interpretivist schools of social science on the grounds that understanding the impact of the media requires methodological approaches that are sensitive to the meanings audiences take from media texts.

In critical media studies and cultural studies, the 'critical' tradition, whose beginnings can be located in the work of the Frankfurt School, has generally derived its philosophical and political inspiration from European schools of thought such as Marxism and post-structuralism. Critical media researchers have mainly been concerned with the analysis of the ideological and economic role of the media in capitalist society. For some writers, however, the distrust of positivist empiricism on the part of 'critical' theorists does not necessarily imply an inherent incompatibility between 'critical' and empirical research (Ang, 1990). Indeed, as we will see in the remainder of this section, many of the principles and concepts of media impact invoked by media research following a critical analytical perspective have counterparts in empirical models and methodologies.

Growing out of the critical studies tradition of media analysis, a number of published investigations have emerged during the 1980s and 1990s in which qualitative methodologies have been applied to examine the cognitive impact of media. The methodological arm of this branch of critical social science is reception analysis. It posits that audiences' reception of media content is governed by the interpretive communities to which audience members belong. Such communities can be defined in terms of social, economic or other demographic criteria, but also in relation to lifestyles, value systems and interest domains (Lindlof, 1995).

Following this school of thought, a view has achieved prominence that there are many individual- and group-level differences in the interpretation of media texts. Research into learning from factual television programmes, using focus group or depth-interview techniques of data collection, has illustrated the significance of community contexts in relation to the way audiences absorb meanings from media texts (Hoijer, 1989, 1990; Jensen, 1986; Morley, 1980).

In a study regarded within the critical media literature as a 'classic', Morley (1980) reported a study of the audience for a British news magazine programme broadcast on weekday early evenings by the BBC, called *Nationwide*. This study involved the collective viewing and discussion of the programme by groups of viewers over a period of months to establish its recurrent themes and presentational formats, supplemented by a detailed analysis of one particular edition of the programme. The aim of this study was to find out about the ways viewers interpreted the content presented in this programme.

According to the researcher:

> the project attempted to relate the analysis of practices of 'decoding' of media material to the theoretical problematic centring on the concept of hegemony. In brief, the concept of hegemony enables us to understand the process of meaning construction as occurring, within any society, in the context of a set of power relations, in which different groups are in competition for the 'power to define' events and values.... Our concern in the *Nationwide* research project was to

connect the theoretical question of the maintenance of hegemony with the empirical question of how a particular programme acts to 'prefer' one set of meanings or definitions of events. (Morley, 1992: 91)

Given the significance of this study in the literature, it is worth looking at the audience analysis methodology it deploys in some detail. One *Nationwide* programme was shown to 18 viewer focus groups drawn from different social, cultural, and educational levels in two regions – central England and London. Participants were schoolchildren and students in further and higher education. A second edition of the news magazine was shown to 11 groups. Some groups again comprised students, while others obtained participants from trade union and management training centres, who worked in the banking and printing industries. Most of these individuals were recruited in London.

The recruitment procedure adopted a strategy of selecting respondents who already knew one another as a group in the belief that this would facilitate a conversation among participants after the programme had been seen. Each group comprised between five and ten people who discussed the programme for up to 30 minutes after it had been watched. In relation to this fieldwork, three levels of analysis were deployed to determine the meanings apprehended by respondents from the programme seen. Morley (1992: 93) described these as:

(a) where the audience interprets the message in terms of the same code employed by the transmitter, e.g. where both 'inhabit' the dominant ideology; (b) where the audience employs a 'negotiated' version of the code employed by the transmitter, e.g. receiver employs a negotiated version of the dominant ideology used by the transmitter to encode the message; (c) where the audience employs an 'oppositional' code to interpret the message and therefore interprets its meaning through a different code from that employed by the transmitter.

The data were analysed to identify the prominent messages or meanings obtained by viewers from the programme. Comparisons were made between respondents from different socio-economic and educational levels. The methodology used an analysis of the language displayed by respondents to discuss programme-related topics and compared this with the language used by the broadcasters when discussing the same topics within the programme.

A deliberate choice was made to use group rather than individual interviews because this was judged to be closer to the usual way people interpret media content, namely by talking about it to other people. According to Morley (1992: 97): 'the aim was to discover how interpretations were collectively constructed through talk and the interchange between respondents in the group situation – rather than to treat individuals as the autonomous repositories of a fixed set of individual "opinions" isolated from their social context'.

The data were the textual transcripts of the focus group discussions. Analysis of these transcripts proceeded at three levels. The first mode of analysis 'attempted to establish the visible particularities in the lexical repertoires of the different groups – where particular terms and patterns of phrase mark off discourse of the different groups one from another' (Morley, 1992: 98). The second level examined how different topics within the programme were identified by group members and what sense they made of them. The third level involved a propositional analysis of respondents' comments to examine the deeper levels of understanding or meaning apprehended from the content by viewers. The ways audiences 'decoded' or understood and made sense of programme content were compared across audience subgroups defined in terms of social and demographic factors and cultural charactersitics (e.g. trades unionists versus students). The analysis was also concerned with the degree of relevance different topics had for viewers. Some topics may have had greater significance because of viewers' own experience. Other topics may have been seen as abstract and distant from their everyday concerns. Blumler et al. (1985) saw Morley's work as an important step in the right direction by critical researchers. But positivist researchers themselves have begun to adopt concepts such as 'text' and 'reader', as semiological perspectives have informed empirical research. At the same time, a methodological concession has been noted among critical researchers, who have begun to drop some of their ideological suspicions about empirical research.

Another study, from Denmark, progressed further in an exploration of the range of expectations among viewers that enter into the reception of televised news. According to Jensen (1988) the interpretation of news reports is guided by: (1) general expectations concerning the news genre and (2) particular kinds of background knowledge (the relevance of which needs to be understood in relation to specific stories and audience groups). In sum, there are two vital considerations in connection with understanding how audiences interpret news: their understanding and expectations of news as a genre, and the community context upon which they draw when interpreting the informational content of the news.

In a qualitative empirical investigation of these concepts, Jensen conducted in-depth interviews with 33 individuals who viewed and then answered questions about a 30-minute television news programme. The respondents were recruited from different parts of Denmark to represent different age, gender and socio-economic groups. On the evening of the particular news broadcast, an interview guide about the content of the individual news stories in this programme was formulated immediately after the programme ended. All respondents had agreed beforehand to watch this news broadcast. Interviews then took place in the homes of respondents on the following day. A semi-structured interview guide was used. Respondents were asked to recount the subject matter of each news story, which was identified via a cue word. Then, specific details were probed from individual stories. Respondents were also asked to evaluate each story in terms of its relevance to them and its presentation format. The interviews were taped and transcribed. Verbatim transcripts were prepared of the news stories and interviews and a linguistic discourse analysis of all the transcripts was then conducted.

This methodology aimed to establish to what extent the language and grammar used by viewers to talk about news stories resembled the linguistic styles used by broadcasters to report news events. This form of analysis departed from the more structured day-after recall approaches that would be used by positivist empirical researchers in that it allowed viewers the opportunity to discuss news events at length in their own terms. The features of this viewer-generated discourse could then be compared with the features of professional news discourse. This parallel analysis of discourses was conducted at three levels: (1) identification of major categories of linguistic discourses; (2) the structure of individual stories in the news programme; and (3) viewers' reconstructions of specimen stories.

It is worth elaborating on these different levels of analysis. The categories of discourse analysis assessed the basic elements of news and the links between them as part of an overall linguistic structure which might reappear in the discourses produced by viewers when discussing news stories. Three principal categories of news texts were identified in this regard: actors, coherences and themes.

An analysis of the central actors in the news meant identifying who were the main participants in news stories, e.g. politicians, voters, experts. Were the actors individuals, groups, organizations or entire nations? Other lexical references to actors were also established such as the adjectives used to describe particular perpetrators of events, e.g. the distinction between 'terrorists' and 'freedom fighters'.

News stories were analysed in terms of their coherence, a concept that has been defined as 'a semantic property of discourses, based on the interpretation of each individual sentence relative to the interpretation of other sentences' (van Dijk, 1977: 93). It is well known that a particular form of the news text, including repetitions and the supportive use of visuals, may improve audience comprehension (Findahl and Hoijer, 1976, 1984). Explicit references to the relations between causes and consequences, generalizations and exemplifications, can be provided at various points of the news story, whether in the commentary or the visuals. Indeed, the visual side of television news may be thought of as a discourse in its own right. It may support the spoken text or present striking information of its own which on occasion can become the dominant element of the story.

A coherence analysis explores the extent to which coherence exists between what viewers have to say about a news story and what was actually said or shown in the narrative. This coherence might occur locally in reference to some specific element in a news story or globally in reference to the story as whole. The third analytical category is themes of news. It is by reference to certain unitary themes that the global coherence of the news text may be established, even in cases where the local coherence is more difficult to ascertain. In practice, a theme may be defined as a proposition entailed by a set of propositions summing up a news story or another text. Jensen (1988) refers to a story with an East – West theme which on one level had implications concerning international relations and, on the other, possible ramifications for the individual member of the audience if world peace was threatened.

An analysis of audience responses to news stories revealed a considerable degree of personal reconstruction and reformulation of stories by viewers – apparently in accordance with themes of significance to them. Thus, viewers might begin to recount a story from a particular perspective and this would affect the particular details recalled and the order in which they were discussed. Recall accounts would often focus on specific story ingredients, especially when they were illustrated by film footage. Some respondents would nevertheless place the story in a wider context of implications.

Jensen (1988) identified what he called 'super-themes'. These were defined as 'interpretive procedures which are employed by the audience for the reconstruction of meaning in the news genre' (p. 293). Sometimes super-themes might take precedence over those journalistic pegs or angles that point to a particular agenda or policy in day-to-day political life. Jensen further explained: 'In terms of communication theory, the super-themes can be said to constitute a meaning potential of the news genre which is activated, for example, in further talk about the stories, and it is in this form that they become accessible for analysis' (1988: 294). In recalling news stories, viewers would often depend upon these super-themes in shaping their overall interpretations of the stories. Major themes included war, environment, unemployment, government and class. According to this study, the reception of news is a complex process. Super-themes cut across the news themes as defined by journalistic convention and produce new and sometimes unexpected patterns of meaning.

Empirical or critical: points of commonality

The qualitative approaches preferred by critical social scientists are conceived to yield a greater sensitivity to the way audiences extract meanings from media content. The disadvantage of more quantitative approaches stems not just from their methodological limitations but also from their customary theoretical underpinning that requires the transformation of everyday experiences into numerical measurements. However, there are areas of conceptual commonality between the positivist and critical social science perspectives.

The idea that audiences are active interpreters of media content is not the preserve of critical social science. The notions that reception of news content, for instance, is shaped by the expectations audiences hold about the genre and by the social, cultural and political environments in which relevant knowledge, belief and value systems have been conditioned have been as prominent in positivist theories as in critical theories. In research into the audience memory and comprehension of broadcast news since the 1950s, it has been established through methodologies grounded primarily in experimental psychology, that comprehension of news narratives is related to a range of psychological and social characteristics of news consumers as well as to structural features of programmes (Belson, 1967; Findahl and Hoijer, 1976, 1982, 1985; Trenaman, 1967). Moreover, the uses and gratifications tradition within empirical media research had repeatedly stressed the different needs and orientations of audiences as a function of their social and psychological characteristics (Jensen and Rosengren, 1990).

While this 'active' notion of the audience has been discussed in various forms for many years, approaches such as reception analysis have supported it because its methodology can provide in-depth descriptions of the ways audiences interpret media content. It can compare textual data from the audience with the original textual form of media messages to see which meanings have been extracted (Hoijer, 1992a, 1992b). It also enables the researcher to make comparisons between individuals in their content interpretations. The more simplistic verbal responses solicited by telephone survey interviews or laboratory experiments may have placed too many constraints on the mode of response of audience members to reveal the full richness of the knowledge and meanings they extract from televised news.

In another illustration of the convergence of paradigms, Rhee (1997) reported a study that was conducted within an experimental framework, but utilized a qualitative form of analysis on textual data. A social cognitive model was used to examine how news frames political campaign coverage and the way in which a news frame in turn influences the processing of news information by the audience. Using van Dijk and Kintsch's discourse comprehension model (Kintsch, 1974; van Dijk and Kintsch, 1983), Rhee conceptualized framing processes as an interaction between textual features of the news narrative and the audience member's social knowledge. Two news frames were distinguished for campaign coverage: strategy coverage and issue coverage. The former focuses on candidates' strategies for fighting a campaign and the win or lose aspects of the campaign itself, and the latter focuses on who is advocating which policies and what those polices stand for.

Strategy and issue formats were produced in respect of campaign-related news stories in a Philadelphia mayoral campaign for print and broadcast presentation. A professional reporter was used to rewrite original stories in accordance with the requirements and emphases of these experimental news frames. Experimental subjects were allocated to conditions in which they read or viewed newspaper-style or news broadcast-style news presentation containing either strategy-frame or issue-frame versions of campaign-related stories. They read or watched these stories at home over a period of five days. Prior to this treatment, they were asked to write a letter to a friend about an earlier presidential election. After five-day exposure to the experimental material, they were asked to write another letter about the Philadelphia election. The texts of these letters were used as primary data sources.

Both the news narratives and letter discourses were analysed for their propositional contents. Sentence structure was assessed and clauses were identified concerning certain events, issues or relationships between actors and between actors and issues, in order to find out whether the news frame adopted by news stories about the election campaign affected the recall and comprehension of story details by experimental subjects in the letters they wrote about the election. Thus, did respondents who received strategy-framed campaign coverage use more strategy-oriented clauses in describing the campaign? Likewise, did respondents who received issue-framed coverage use more issue-oriented clauses in their letters? Results showed that the news frame did appear to exert some influence upon respondents' own letter discourses, but only in the case of print news, and not with broadcast news. Such presentational effects also interacted with the social knowledge structures of respondents. If respondents already exhibited a strategy frame or an issue frame in terms of their pre-existing knowledge, they were more sensitive to a similar frame being used in print news stories. The significance of this study goes beyond its results. It shows that narrative data can be generated within an experimental research methodology and provide evidence of the dynamic cognitive processes involved in assimilating news information. It also demonstrates the added value of using an experimental paradigm rather than, say, a depth interview or focus group approach, in that differences between media in terms of the effectiveness of news frames could be systematically demonstrated.

Reception analysis has been represented as a 'reorientation of audience research' in which the definition of 'the audience' itself has been refined (Jensen, 1988). There are two principal aspects to this evolution of audience analysis. One is an implicit claim in much of the scholarly writing within this tradition that the methodologies that are being deployed, primarily in-depth individual interviews or focus group discussions, have a greater sensitivity to the subtleties of audience interpretation of media content, and therefore have greater ecological validity than other approaches largely derivative from the empirical, positivistic social sciences. The second is a more sophisticated recognition of audience heterogeneity and measurement of the origins and significance of often widely varying audience interpretations of media content. Both these points need to be addressed head on.

The concept of 'interpretive communities' has potential value in respect of understanding how audiences process broadcast news, by drawing attention to a wider array of different audience groupings than positivist empirical research would normally identify. In particular, demographic audience groupings can provide a useful descriptive taxonomy, but are less useful in explaining differential reactions to media content than groupings based on values, beliefs and media content loyalty (e.g. readers of a particular newspaper, viewers of a particular news bulletin). Such cultural, social and media-centric audience grouping factors may offer greater scope for explaining the different interpretations audiences place on news issues, and the different weights they attach to broadcast news in terms of its balance, credibility, impartiality, objectivity and even enjoyment. These judgements may, in turn, mediate news recall. Renewed interest that is being shown in the importance to news retention of factors such as audience appreciation of televised news therefore represents a promising direction of enquiry (Heuvelman et al., 1998). The notion of 'appreciation', however, will need to be conceptualized in a more sophisticated manner than traditional operational definitions of this measure (Gunter and Wober, 1992).

It is debatable whether reception analysis represents a significant theoretical or methodological advance in the context of research into media news comprehension. It has provided the useful service of underlining the need to move beyond simplistic verbal tests that characterized much early experimental psychological research in this area. The latter research attempted valiantly to force the study of learning from complex narratives into conceptual models and empirical methodologies that were not equipped to explain or properly investigate the nature of the information processing that transpired among audiences exposed to broadcast news. However, by the late 1970s and through the 1980s, even cognitive psychologists recognized the need for more sophisticated modelling of human cognitive processes and the emergence of schema theory and associated methodologies designed to operationally define the way people process narrative content reflected significant advances in thinking and research (e.g. van Dijk, 1988; van Dijk and Kintsch, 1983; Thorndyke, 1979). There has been growing support for the view that a cognitive perspective is needed to provide a complete explanation of information processing from the media (Cappella and Street, 1989; Livingstone, 1989). However, what is meant exactly by a 'cognitive perspective' still needs some further thought both in terms of theory and methodology.

A promising line of empirical development has been the combining of text analysis to assess television narratives and qualitative depth interviews and associated analysis of self-generated discourses about those programmes among viewers, but with a cognitive analytic twist. The analysis of professional journalistic discourses and discourses produced by audiences during post-exposure discussions of broadcast news is embellished through close reference to cognitive schema theory (Hoijer, 1992a, 1992b). A schema has been defined as 'an active organisation of past reactions, or of past experiences....Determination by schemas is the most fundamental of all the ways in which we can be influenced by reactions and experiences which occurred some time in the past' (Bartlett, 1967: 201). This approach has begun to produce interesting insights into the way individuals process factual narrative content on television.

In one Swedish study of audience interpretation of programme episodes from different television genres, viewers were interviewed about the content of a soap opera, a serious drama and a news programme. Some respondents watched the programmes alone and others in small groups. All were interviewed individually after viewing. During the first part of each interview, respondents were initially asked to recount the programme in general and were subsequently asked to describe their reactions to specific scenes. In the second part of the interview, each scene or sequence was reviewed again, and on this occasion the respondent was primed to consider class and gender-related issues in connection with the programme's content. In the final part of the interview, individual scenes and sequences were reviewed one more time with respondents being asked if they had any first-hand experience or knowledge of what was being depicted.

This analytical framework revealed the extent to which themes identified in television texts emerge in the open-ended recall protocols of viewers, and the extent to which particular cognitive schemata or interpretive frames of reference are applied by different viewers. This qualitative approach indicated that viewers use multiple cognitive schemas when interpreting television programmes. In order to make sense of a programme, viewers must find connections between the media text and their own inner world. One characteristic of this inner world is that it is cognitively organized in terms of schemas that represent social experiences, cultural knowledge and specific personal experiences. When interpreting a television programme, viewers spontaneously use a whole set of cognitive schemas to serve as interpretative frames of reference (Hoijer, 1992a).

While differences in news comprehension have been observed between viewers in relation to their socio-economic class, or gender, these differences do not offer explanation as to why news comprehension levels vary across these audience subgroups. Are these social factors associated with distinct ways of mentally representing news story content? Morley (1985) stated:

> It is simply inadequate to present demographic and sociological factors such as age, sex, race or class position as objective correlates or determinants of different decoding positions without any attempt to specify *how* they intervene in the process of communication. The relative autonomy of signifying practices means that sociological factors cannot be 'read in' directly as affecting the communication process. These factors can only have effects through the (possibly contradictory) action of the discourses in which they are articulated.

This argument for a more sophisticated classification of audiences than the traditional marketing distinctions used in commercial audience research is to be welcomed. However, the notion of 'interpretive communities' must not be used loosely. Certainly there are many different ways in which individuals develop commonalities. The idea, however, that viewers of a particular television programme are members of the community of watchers of that programme is likely to beg more questions than it answers. An almost infinite array of 'communities' could be generated in this way. Many of these communities will have a transient rather than a lasting membership and therefore may not always prove to be a useful basis on which to develop a better understanding of audiences' involvement with television.

CHAPTER 8

MEASURING BEHAVIOURAL IMPACT OF MEDIA: FROM ASSOCIATION TO CAUSATION

In this chapter, we turn our attention to research into the behavioural effects of the mass media. This has been one of the primary concerns about the media from the very earliest days of social scientific research into the impact of film, radio and the press. Most research into behavioural effects of media has focused on social behaviour. More precisely, most media effects research has been concerned with the influences the media have on the development and manifestation of *anti*social behaviour. The media have been accused of engendering violence at the individual and group level, encouraging already aggressive individuals to become more so, demonstrating different forms or techniques of aggression, and promulgating civil unrest. Behavioural effects of mass media can, however, take on other forms. Some media researchers have explored the capacity of certain media content to promote *pro*social behaviour – enhancing the likelihood that people will behave altruistically, kindly and cooperatively towards one another. In addition to social behavioural effects, research has been undertaken to investigate the role of the media in affecting voting behaviour during elections, consumer behaviour, and health-related behaviour. The media are extensively used as advertising vehicles carrying promotional messages for commodities and services. The media have also been used to convey health campaign messages designed to change dietary habits, alcohol consumption, smoking, exercise, and drug abuse.

Behavioural effects do not necessarily occur on their own or follow on directly from exposure to a mass medium. Often behavioural effects occur along with cognitive-level effects, such as those examined in the previous chapter. Information imparted by a mass medium has to be assimilated and processed by members of the audience first before it can be acted upon. Portrayals of violence have to be perceived as relevant to an individual's own behavioural repertoire before being absorbed into it. Commercial messages have to be remembered to affect brand awareness and then retrieved at points of purchase to influence consumer behaviour. Health messages have to be understood for the relevance to an individual's own situation before behaviour change will follow.

In conducting research into behavioural effects of media, the principal methodologies have comprised surveys and experiments. One-off surveys have explored degrees of association between reported patterns of media use and reported patterns of social, consumer or other forms of behaviour. Longitudinal studies employing repeat surveys have explored trend relationships between media-related behaviour and other behaviour with separate groups of respondents, or developmental relationships between media exposure and other behaviours among the same groups of individuals over time. Inferences or even conclusions have been reached about behavioural effects of the media from these studies on the basis of correlational data only. In consequence, there must remain doubts about the veracity of such evidence in demonstrating causal links between media exposure and audience behaviour.

Exploration of causality has been tackled more directly through experimental methodologies. In this framework, researchers are able systematically to manipulate media exposure before it occurs. One limitation of survey research is that the researcher has no control over a respondent's media exposure and indeed only limited confidence that the measures of media consumption that are customarily obtained reflect actual media exposure patterns. Such off-line measurement of media exposure means that there is also some doubt about which content members of an audience were actually exposed to. In an experiment, the researcher knows precisely which content particular subjects witnessed or consumed and for what period of time exposure occurred. Although laboratory experiments lack ecological validity, experiments conducted in the field have enabled researchers to measure media exposure and subject behaviour in more realistic surroundings, while still retaining a degree of control over media-related events and experiences.

In the past twenty years, all empirical approaches to the study of media effects have come under criticism from media scholars who have argued that the social science paradigm from which they derive fails to take into account, either theoretically or methodologically, the richness of media content and the range and complexity of meanings audiences process from media output (see Gountlett, 1995). An alternative analytical approach has been offered that places emphasis upon in-depth processing of meanings from media, whose interpretations can vary widely among media consumers and are mediated by the kinds of communities to which they belong or with which they identify. Quantitative methodologies are eschewed and qualitative methodologies are embraced instead as more sensitive and more appropriate frameworks within which to understand audiences' involvement with different media and media outputs (Ang, 1990; Morley, 1992). Yet, in the context of measuring the possible behavioural effects of the media, methodologies are needed that can clearly establish media exposure, measure media consumers' behaviour in a realistic fashion, and establish convincingly where there is a link between the two.

Media effects research has evolved conceptually and methodologically in the past twenty years. Even among empiricist-oriented social scientists, there has been a growing recognition that behavioural effects, if they occur, are not knee-jerk responses to media messages. Instead, audiences process media content in a cognitively active way and place their own interpretations on the meanings that content may convey. Behavioural effects flow from an interpretative process in which individuals evaluate the implications of media content for their own lives and their own actions.

TESTING FOR ASSOCIATIONS: SURVEY RESEARCH

Survey research has been firmly established as an activity used by many business sectors to obtain information about their actual or potential markets. Surveys have been a prominent feature of media research. Media organizations use surveys to measure their audiences or readership levels and to track the responses of their consumers to their productions or publications. The results of surveys are also regularly reported by the media, usually in connection with elections or the performance of government and politicians. Survey research has also been a key methodology in academic social science research and commercially oriented market research concerned with measuring the impact of the mass media.

Academic social scientists have been interested in measuring impact of the media from a number of perspectives. The mass media have been hypothesized and found to have effects upon public knowledge, awareness and understanding of topics; on public opinion, beliefs and attitudes regarding issues, objects, institutions and groups; and on public behaviour. Behavioural effects concerns have focused primarily on social behaviour, political behaviour, consumer behaviour and health-related behaviour. In some instances, the effects are intended in that the media deliberately set out to influence, shape or change the way people behave. This is frequently true in relation to consumer behaviour and health-related behaviour, and on certain occasions, in relation to political behaviour. In other cases, concerns have settled on incidental side-effects of media, which usually refer to the unintended effects believed to derive from exposure to media content which was not produced with the aim of producing any such reactions among members of the audience. The latter effects tend to occur within the realm of social behaviour, and are invariably focused upon hypothesized antisocial behavioural influences of media content. Thus, the media, especially television programmes, are frequently accused of engendering violent and criminal conduct through their regular depiction of such behaviour.

History of survey research

The modern survey can be traced back to ancient forms of census (Converse, 1987; Moser and Kalton, 1971). A census is a compilation of the characteristics of an entire population in a territory. It is based on what they tell officials or what officials observe. For example, the *Domesday*

Book was a famous census of England conducted in 1085–86 by William the Conqueror. Early censuses assessed the property available for taxation or the young men available for military service. With the development of representative democracy, the use of the census expanded to assigning a number of elected representatives based on the population in a district.

While a census attempts to obtain data from everyone in a population, a survey uses sampling techniques to recruit a subset of the population from whom to collect data. Social theorist Max Weber used survey research methods in his work on the Protestant ethic. In addition to his comparative, historical examination of economic development, he also studied Protestant and Catholic factory workers to provide data on individuals (Lazarsfeld and Obershall, 1965).

Surveys were used in the USA and UK to document the extensive urban poverty that followed industrialization in the late nineteenth century. In the nineteenth century, such surveys began to be used in conjunction with town planning and various government activities. Methods of data collection included observation, interviews and questionnaires, though scientific sampling and statistical analysis were limited. Sampling was often based on purposive or snowballing techniques, with people selected on a convenience or availability basis, rather than according to probability or random recruitment procedures.

In the USA, survey research developed through the efforts of the US Census Bureau, major polling agencies, and survey research centres in universities. Throughout the middle decades of the 20th century, all three entities experimented with sampling methods, question wording, data collection and analysis techniques.

Booth's (1889–1902) survey of *Labour and Life of the People of London* and Rowntree's (1906) examination of *Poverty: A Study of Town Life* represent two early examples from Britain. Rowntree set out to obtain information directly from householders using interviewers. During the early part of the 20th century, further surveys, of living conditions, particularly of the working classes, were conducted by Bowley and Barrett-Hurst (1915), Bowley and Hogg (1925), Ford (1934) and Smith (1930–35). In Britain, the Second World War period witnessed the setting up of the Government Social Survey which has played a significant part in raising the standard of survey methods and in persuading policy makers in Government to pay attention to survey results.

During the first half of the 20th century, survey research benefited from advances in scientific sampling techniques, the design of scales to measure attitudes and subjective perceptions, and the emergence of market research as a distinct field. There was a particular interest in understanding more about consumer behaviour. Professional agencies developed to undertake such research on behalf of clients, who were primarily manufacturers of leading consumer goods with short shelf lives and rapid repeat sales – food, soaps and detergents, toiletries and certain household appliances.

Survey research also came to be used by the media during the latter part of this period. Journalists used surveys to measure public opinion on issues that were prominent in the news. Newspaper publishers and broadcasters recognized the value of surveys to measure market shares, readership or audience sizes, and in due course, public opinion about their products. However, surveys were not only used to assess media markets. The Second World War years saw a growing interest in the study of the power of the media to exert certain influences over the public. This interest centred on the role of the media in shaping public opinion and, during the war years, public morale. Academic researchers began to cooperate and collaborate with commercial polling agencies as part of the war effort. This partnership resulted in important methodological developments that improved survey research techniques during those and subsequent years. Over the next three or four decades, the volume of survey research grew steadily.

Within the academy, two figures stand out – Samuel Stouffer and Paul Lazarsfeld. Stouffer conducted pioneering work into social patterns during the depression years with white and black Americans. In the Second World War, he conducted social research for the US Army and subsequently in the 1950s studied public opinion towards the effects of anticommunist investigations by McCarthy.

Lazarsfeld went to America from Austria in the 1930s. Although known for his work with Stanton and Merton on the programme analyzer and focus groups, he was also responsible for important early work that produced enhanced survey techniques. In particular, he introduced the idea of panel studies in which the same individuals are re-interviewed over a period of time. This approach has proven important in research on the effects of media on a wide range of behavioural phenomena.

Types of survey research

Surveys can be distinguished according to a number of criteria. These include the type of sample, the ways they are administered, the regularity with which they are conducted and the length of time over which they are carried out. All surveying in the media effects context involves the correlation of variables. In general, data are obtained from people about their self-reported use of the media and about some other aspect of their character, background, daily lives, values, beliefs, opinions or behaviour. One important distinction is between cross-sectional and longitudinal surveys (Babbie, 1990). In some cases, links are made between claimed media use and other social or psychological attributes or activities of individuals at one point in time, and in others, the interest resides in establishing links between such variables over long periods of time.

Cross-sectional surveys obtain self-report data from samples of respondents about their patterns of media exposure and attitudes or behaviour at one point in time. They can reveal degrees of association between claimed media usage and other attitudinal or behavioural measures on individuals, but cannot prove cause – effect relationships. Longitudinal studies conducted with the same group of individuals over time, with two or more survey waves obtaining information about reported media use and other personal characteristics of respondents, are regarded as a more powerful methodology for testing causal hypotheses regarding the media (Wimmer and Dominick, 1994). This approach enables researchers to explore developing relationships between media use and media consumers' attitudes or behaviour that may take many weeks, months or even years to emerge. Such research assumes the possibility of cumulative effects of media as well as those that may occur immediately upon exposure to specific kinds of media content. In the context of the debate about the effects of media violence, several major longitudinal studies have been carried out with children that have attempted to uncover long-term relationships between television viewing habits in early childhood and the development of aggressive tendencies in later life.

Cross-sectional surveys

A cross-sectional survey may be used to determine the status of public behaviour on an issue at the time the survey is conducted. For instance, a sample of television viewers could be questioned about their current viewing patterns. A cross-sectional survey could be used in an election campaign to establish whom respondents intend to vote for. Usually, the question is phrased as if polling day were 'today' or 'tomorrow' to give the decision a sense of immediacy, even though in reality voting may not be due to take place for several more weeks. Cross-sectional surveys have also been employed to try to uncover associational links between patterns of media exposure and self-reported behaviour.

The basic approach in cross-sectional survey research is to obtain a measure of media exposure and then to relate this to a measure of media user behaviour, feelings, perceptions or knowledge. The ultimate goal of any media influence research is to demonstrate a causal connection; the first step is to find that some relation exists. One of the prime areas of media research in which correlational surveys have been used is the study of the effects of media violence.

In the context of violence on television, for instance, respondents are asked to identify or recall details about their television viewing. They may be given lists of programme titles, asked to report the programmes they like watching best of all, or complete viewing diaries to provide the researcher with some indication not just of how much television they watch, but also of the kinds of programmes they watch. Throughout this approach to measuring television exposure, assumptions are made about the contents of named television programmes, but rarely are these assumptions tested by actually analysing the programmes themselves. Thus, it is assumed that programmes from the action-adventure or crime-drama genres contain violence. Hence if a respondent nominates such a programme among his or her favourites, that is taken as evidence of exposure to televised violence. In such research there is a tendency to treat any such programmes equally in terms of the violence they contain, when in actuality they may contain different amounts and types of violent portrayal.

Respondents' personal aggressive tendencies are also assessed through self-report measures and sometimes also through the reports of other people to whom the respondent is known (e.g. parents, teachers, friends or peers). Correlational surveys do not measure actual behaviour; instead conclusions about behaviour are drawn from self-reports or other-reports.

A survey approach by McLeod et al. (1972) employed a questionnaire that contained measures of exposure to televised violence, personal aggression, and family environment. Television viewing was measured by giving respondents a list of 65 prime-time television programme titles with a scale indicating how often each title was usually viewed. An index of overall television violence viewing was obtained by using independent ratings of the violence level of each programme and multiplying it by the reported frequency of viewing. Aggression was measured by seven scales. One measured respondents' approval of manifest physical aggression (e.g. 'Whoever insults me or my family is looking for a fight'). Another examined approval of aggression (e.g. 'It's all right to hurt an enemy if you are mad at him'). Respondents indicated their degree of agreement with each of the items composing the separate scales. Family environment was measured by asking about parental control over television, parental emphasis on non-aggression punishment (such as withdrawal of privileges), and other variables. The researchers found a moderate positive relationship between the respondents' level of reported viewing of violence-containing programmes and their self-reports of aggression. Family environment showed no consistent association with either of the two variables.

In another survey in the same series, Robinson and Bachman (1972) obtained self-reports of 1,500 tenth-, eleventh- and twelfth-grade boys. No correlations were presented. Instead, subjects were divided into four groups on the basis of the amount of violence in their four favourite television programmes, and these groups were compared. Those with the most violent favourite programmes tended to be involved in more aggressive behaviour than those in the two intermediate groups, who were in turn involved in more aggression than the group whose favourite programmes were judged to be least violent.

McCarthy et al. (1975) collected information on television viewing and various measures of deviant behaviour as part of a much larger study of mental health in an urban area. None of the measures of aggression (fighting, delinquency, conflict with parents) was significantly correlated with a simple measure of viewing television violence. These measures were correlated with both total amount of reported television viewing and weighted violence viewing (a measure that took into account total viewing time). No correlation of aggression and viewing of television violence occurred, when total television viewing was partialled out.

Hartnagel et al. (1975) obtained self-reports on respondents' four favourite television programmes and their own violent behaviour. The correlation between the violence of the favourite programmes and self-rated violent behaviour was low, but statistically significant. In a more extensive report, McIntyre et al. (1972) noted that with 2,299 high school subjects, the correlation of the rated violence of subjects' favourite four television programmes with personal aggressiveness was 0.109; with more serious aggressive deviancy the correlation was 0.158. Using only the violence of a single-favourite television programme reduced the correlations to just above zero, indicating the importance of getting a reasonably representative measure of television viewing.

Greenberg (1975) interviewed 726 boys on their television viewing habits and their attitudes toward aggressiveness. There was a correlation of 0.15 between watching violent television programmes and the perceived effectiveness of violence and a correlation of 0.17 with expressed willingness to use violence. When the total amount of television viewing was partialled out, the remaining correlations were both 0.12.

Longitudinal research

Longitudinal surveys can be either descriptive or explanatory. They represent an effective procedure for identifying long-term relationships between variables because they are designed to permit the collection of data over time. Carefully designed longitudinal methodology enables researchers to examine the plausibility of two different types of causal hypotheses. First, researchers can begin to untangle the potential bidirectional causal relationships that may exist between the media and audience attitudes or behaviour. In other words, exposure to media violence may increase the likelihood of aggressive behaviour in individual viewers, but an aggressive predisposition might also cause individuals to favour watching programmes with violence. In addition, research using this methodology can determine whether exposure to the media is associated with long-term developments in social attitudes and behaviour.

Three main types of longitudinal survey can be distinguished: (1) trend studies; (2) cohort studies; and (3) panel studies.

Trend studies

A given population may be sampled and studied at different points in time. Different respondents are studied in each survey, but each sample is drawn from the same population. Public opinion polls conducted at different points during an election campaign are one example.

Cohort studies

Trend studies are based on descriptions of a general population over time – although the members of that population will change. The people alive and represented in the first study, for instance, might be dead at the time of the second. A cohort study focuses on the same specific population each time data are collected, although the samples studied may be different. For example, a study might survey all children aged five to six years in a community before the introduction of television. Then two years later, after television transmission has begun, another survey may be conducted with all five- and six-year-old children available on that second occasion. Five years later, a further study could be carried out with the same age group in the community to examine television usage among such children (see Williams, 1986).

Another example would be to draw a sample repeatedly from the same generational group. Thus, one might survey a sample of ten-year-olds in 1980, and a sample of 20-year-olds in 1990, and a sample of 30-year-olds in 2000. In each case, respondents would be chosen from a group of people born in 1970.

Rentz et al. (1983) conducted a cohort analysis of consumers born in four time periods: 1931–40, 1941–50, 1951–60, and 1961–70. Soft drink consumption was measured throughout all samples, and a range of potential predictors of such behaviour were assessed. The results indicated a large cohort effect suggesting that soft drink consumption will not decrease as successive cohorts age. Rosengren and Windahl (1989) used cohort analysis as part of their in-depth longitudinal study of television usage by Swedish youngsters. Among other things, they found a slight cohort effect but noted that age seemed the prime determinant of habitual television viewing.

Panel studies

Trend and cohort studies permit the analysis of process and change over time, which is not easily possible in a cross-sectional survey. A limitation of these two types of longitudinal study is that on each occasion different people are surveyed. This means it is not possible to track changes in attitudes or behaviour over time for specific individuals.

Panel studies involve the collection of data over time from the same sample of respondents. The sample for such a study is called a 'panel'. For example, in a study to test for the effects of televised violence on viewers' aggression, repeated surveys might be carried out with the same individuals at intervals ranging from one to ten years in order to assess whether an earlier diet of violent programmes is not only associated with aggressiveness at that time, but also linked to the emergence of aggressive tendencies in later life.

Panel studies need to be conducted as part of an original data collection exercise, whereas trend or cohort studies can be conducted through secondary analysis of previously collected data. A problem faced by panel studies is loss of panel members over time. People interviewed in the first survey wave of a panel investigation may be unavailable for or unwilling to participate in the second or third survey waves. There are also cases where people move home and become untraceable. Consequently, it is quite commonplace in panel studies that such panel attrition causes the panel gradually to diminish in size as the study progresses.

Examples of panel studies   Singer et al. (1984) employed a longitudinal panel design to examine potential long-term effects of television violence on behaviour and on beliefs about the world. The researchers examined the influence of a variety of family variables and children's television viewing habits on (1) children's beliefs about the world (whether they perceived the world to be a 'scary' place), (2) children's display of direct aggression, (3) their school adjustment, and (4) their patience (self-restraint and ability to wait). Family qualities of particular interest to Singer et al. were parents' use of power and punishment in the disciplining of their children, mother's imaginativeness, and family television viewing habits.

This study was begun in 1977 and involved 63 children. The average age of the children was four when the study began and nine when the last measures were collected in 1982. All the data on family variables were collected through interviews with parents and children. The only data not involving parental reports were IQ scores and children's 'Scary World Test' scores.

When the researchers controlled for the previous aggression level of each child, they found later aggressiveness in children strongly related to heavier viewing of television violence, pre-school viewing of violence, and the parents' emphasis on physical punishment. In addition, the most powerful predictor of children's scores on the Scary World Test was the extent of the children's television viewing habits. In particular, children who viewed the most violent adult-oriented programmes scored high on the Scary World Test.

Catch-up panel design   A catch-up panel involves the selection of a cross-sectional study done in the past and location of all possible original participants for observation or interview in the present. The catch-up panel is particularly attractive if the researcher has a rich source of baseline data on these individuals. Lefkowitz et al. (1972) used a catch-up technique in their study of television viewing and child aggression. After a lapse of ten years, the investigators tracked down 735 of 875 original respondents for further interview. By this second stage the respondents were aged 18 years, having originally been interviewed at the age of eight. Huesmann and his colleagues (1986) caught up with this same panel of respondents one more time when they were 30 years old. After re-interviewing 409 of the original panel members, the authors concluded that this 22-year panel study demonstrated that viewing television violence as a child can have lasting consequences into adulthood.

This study reported evidence that the level of exposure to television violence at age eight is associated with increased rates of aggressive behaviour when viewers achieve early adulthood (Eron et al., 1972; Huesmann et al., 1984; Lefkowitz et al., 1977).

A variety of measures relating to aggression and television viewing were included in the study during each wave of data collection. Aggression was measured through peer nomination techniques at both age 8 and 18–19. Additionally, measures of parent-rated aggression were obtained at age 8, whereas self-report measures, criminal records, and scales from a personality inventory were used at age 18–19. For peer ratings, each child at age eight had to name all the other study-related children he or she knew who demonstrated aggressive behaviours such as 'Starting a fight over nothing'. Ten of these specific questions were interspersed with other questionnaire items. Other peer ratings measured aggression anxiety – those classmates who avoided aggressive encounters and never responded aggressively when picked on. A child's aggression rating was determined by adding the number of times he or she was peer named on the aggressive items and dividing by the number of questions in total.

Violent television watching was gauged by asking subjects to report their favourite television shows at both ages, along with their total hours of television watching. Of course, self-reported television viewing does not guarantee actual attention to violent programmes. All television programmes were later categorized as violent or non-violent by two independent raters.

Several different types of analytic approaches have been applied to these data. For example, multiple regression analyses were performed in order to identify the contributions of the demographic variables, television watching, and previous aggression on levels of aggression at age 18–19. Correlational relationships between television viewing and aggressive behaviour were computed not only at these two points in time, but also across time. The researchers reported that claimed viewing of programmes independently rated as containing violence was significantly correlated with aggressiveness at age eight and over time at age 18. Furthermore, while earlier viewing of television violence was linked to later aggressiveness, there was no indication that early aggressiveness predicted later preferences for violence viewing. Results provided what the researchers called unequivocal evidence that a preference for violent television programmes in young boys was related to concurrent and subsequent aggression. This relationship was consistent across several measures of aggressive behaviour. In contrast, the violent-programme preference among the girls was not significantly related to their level of aggression.

The actual correlations over time, however, were weak and only found among boys. A more significant problem is the rather simplistic measure of exposure to television violence that was based on nominations of the respondent's three or four favourite programmes. While at age 18, respondents made their own nominations, at age eight, these programmes were selected by parents. The measure of aggressiveness was also problematic and relied at age 18 on peer recall of how respondents had allegedly behaved a year earlier. These flaws seriously undermine the validity of the results.

When the same respondents were later followed up at age 30. Nearly all those who had been reinterviewed at 18 were located again. The study reported that those who had been more aggressive as children and teenagers continued to be among the more aggressive as adults. Although seeking evidence to support their earlier conclusions about the role of television in the development of personal aggressiveness, this later analysis revealed that there were other factors which underpin an individual's aggressiveness quite independently of how much television they watch.

Cross-cultural research   The Eron – Huesmann study was extended internationally with further surveys being launched in Finland (Lagerspetz et al., 1986), Poland (Fraczek, 1986), Israel (Bachrach, 1986), Australia (Sheehan, 1986) and The Netherlands (Wiegmann et al., 1992). Little data emerged from Australia to support the American findings. In Israel, the American results were replicated among urban, but not among rural children. Weak links between television viewing and aggression emerged among children in Poland, while in Finland the American findings were most strongly supported.

The Dutch study moved off in a different direction when its researchers decided to develop their own measures of television viewing and aggression rather than adopt what were seen as inferior measures from the original American study. The Dutch results failed to support the view that television violence is a likely long-term factor of any significance in the development of personal aggressiveness.

The NBC study   A much larger-scale panel study was undertaken by researchers working for the National Broadcasting Company (NBC). NBC commissioned a large-scale longitudinal study to examine the potential effects of television violence on the aggressive behaviour of more than three thousand youths aged 7 to 19 (Milavsky et al., 1982). The aim of the research was to find out if there were links, either at any one point in time or over time, between the character of television viewing and the propensity to aggressive tendencies among the children and teenagers under study. Among the primary school children, evidence about verbal and physical acts of aggression was obtained from school friends, while teenagers reported on themselves. Television viewing was measured by giving respondents check-lists of programmes available on the major networks which had been pre-classified for their violent content. Thus, not only did the researchers obtain some indication about general viewing patterns but also more specific information about levels of exposure among these young viewers to violent programmes.

During the analysis phase, the researchers assessed linkages between aggressive behaviour and levels of claimed viewing of different types of programming among different subgroups of children as well as among children as a whole. Only small statistical associations were found in any of these cases. Further analyses showed that, compared with the influence of family background, social environment and school performance, the significance of television viewing as an indicator of aggressiveness was very weak. This led the authors to conclude that television viewing was not a factor in the development of aggressive behaviours among the children and teenagers in their sample.

Milavsky et al. (1982) provided important evidence about the effects of television on aggressive behaviour. Their conclusions, however, are quite different from most other researchers who have examined effects of media violence using longitudinal designs. Some important design and analysis features of the research may be responsible for the differences in this study's findings (Kenny and Judd, 1984).

The project itself comprised two separate studies to examine their hypotheses. The first study involved approximately 2,400 boys and girls aged 7 to 12 years. These children's television viewing and aggression were measured six times over a three-year period (May 1970, November 1970, February 1971, May 1971, May 1972 and May 1973). A second study involved more than 600 teenage boys who were measured in four waves. In both studies, television viewing was based on a carefully designed self-report measure. Aggression was measured by a peer nomination procedure in which children were to name other individuals in their class who pushed, shoved, kicked or otherwise hurt other students. The potential effects of television on aggression were examined by statistically controlling for children's earlier level of aggression. The statistical control was achieved by computing a partial coefficient in which television viewing at one time interval was correlated with aggression at a second time interval, after the time one aggression was partialled out of the time aggression measure.

In the first study with younger children, the six waves of observations collected on each child were analysed in 15 pairs of waves (i.e. wave 1 with 2, wave 1 with 3, through wave 5 with 6). In some of the analyses, the researchers separated the sample into boys and girls. The researchers obtained relatively few significant findings that predicted change in aggression from earlier violence viewing for the younger children. For the teenage boys, the researchers also obtained few significant findings. Altogether, the researchers performed hundreds of tests of significance. They reasoned that the small number of significant findings could easily be explained as due to chance given the number of significant tests performed.

A problem that did occur in this study was that the attrition rate was high, which changed the composition of the sample from beginning to end. An important aspect to this study was that the authors controlled for the fact that children may not produce valid results in terms of the television programmes they said they watched. They gave fictional titles to the participants and took out the children who claimed to have seen non-existent programmes. They found that the correlation they had recorded originally, decreased when the invalid responses were taken out (Cumberbatch and Howitt, 1989).

Retrospective studies

This is a type of longitudinal study that actually obtains data from respondents at one point in time, but invites them to report on their past history. There are two versions of this research approach: the *retrospective panel* and the *follow back panel*.

Retrospective panel The retrospective panel design was outlined by Schudsinger et al. (1981). With this method, respondents are asked to recall facts or attitudes about events, situations and experiences from their past. These recalled factors are then compared with a later measure from the same sample. By recalling facts about media usage and behaviour at two points in their lives – one current and the other historical – a panel simulation can be established through which changes in behaviour over time are assessed and linked to media use.

In the UK, Belson (1978) used a variation of this approach in his survey of adolescent boys in which he obtained a great deal of information about their viewing habits and aggressive behaviour. The study used a simulated panel design. Respondents were not actually studied across separate points in time, but were questioned retrospectively at a single point about their viewing and social behavioural habits over the previous ten years. The degree of association between television viewing and aggressiveness was assessed by dividing the sample into those high and low on one aggression factor and obtaining a mean viewing score for the two groups on a second factor.

Detailed and lengthy interviews with these teenage boys revealed a relationship between certain aspects of their claimed viewing behaviour and self-reported attitudes and dispositions towards the use of violence in their lives. It was reported that boys who watched in greater quantities particular types of dramatic programmes classified by Belson as containing violence tended to commit more violence than did those who watched smaller amounts of such programming on television. However, it is difficult to separate watching violent television from simply the amount of television that is watched, which is also related to aggressive behaviour.

Belson's study had four measures of aggression: total number of acts of violence; total number of acts of violence weighted by degree of severity of the act; total number of violent acts, excluding relatively minor ones; and total number of more serious acts of violence. On the first three measures, the effect of viewing television violence on aggression is less significant than the opposite effect. Thus, within the logic of the analysis, there is no evidence that viewing television violence affects aggression rather than the reverse being true. On the fourth measure (serious acts of violence), the forward effect is more significant than the reverse, and Belson considered this as evidence that television viewing causes serious acts of violence rather than the reverse.

There are a number of problems with this technique. Belson's results have not been universally accepted and critics have questioned the validity of the biographical information obtained from his young respondents about not only their current viewing habits and behaviour, but also those they tried to recall from ten years earlier (e.g. Freedman, 1984). Many people will have faulty memories, some will deliberately misrepresent the past, others will try to give a socially desirable response. The results may have been affected by recall bias where the respondents recalled programmes not representative of their overall viewing, or may have forgotten the kinds of programmes they used to watch. Belson indicated that the recall accounts had been tested for reliability. But just because programmes had been recalled consistently did not prove that they represented accurate recollections. Instead, respondents could have been making consistent mistakes about their past viewing.

A few studies have examined the extent to which retrospective panel data might be misleading. Powers et al. (1978) re-analysed data from a 1964 study of adult men. In 1974 all the original respondents who could be located were re-contacted and asked about their answers to the 1964 survey. In most instances, the recall responses presented respondents in a more favourable light than did their original answers.

Surveys have been one of the most widely used methodologies in media research. They have been especially prominent in research into the behavioural effects of media. Despite their prevalence, survey methodologies are limited in how much they can reveal or demonstrate about causal relationships between media and behaviour. The evidence offered by surveys statistically is based on correlational analyses, whether between variables measured at one point in time or at two or more points over time. Further, the data on which such analyses are computed derive largely from verbal self-reports about past or recent media behaviour and social behaviour, and not on measures of actual behaviour. Although surveys can indicate where cause – effect relationships might exist, through their demonstration of associative links between variables, the further demonstration of actual causal connections is much more difficult to prove through surveys alone. Tests for causality require a different methodological approach in which the researcher is able to manipulate sets of circumstances involving media exposure and systematically measure behavioural responses under controlled conditions. This type of research usually takes place in artificial, laboratory conditions, although sometimes opportunities arise for such research to be conducted in naturalistic environments.

TESTING FOR CAUSATION: EXPERIMENTAL RESEARCH

A great deal of academic social science research surrounding the mass media has been concerned primarily with the measurement of media effects. The media have long been presumed to exert influences upon their audiences at a number of psychological, social, cultural and political levels. The media have been identified as having effects upon people's awareness, knowledge and understanding of issues and events, they have been investigated in relation to public attitudes, beliefs and opinions, and they have been thought to affect the way people behave. Although the media can have many positive and beneficial effects in society by enhancing public understanding, stimulating debate, and motivating people to act on important matters, much more attention has been devoted to establishing and demonstrating the adverse and negative influences of the media.

The media have been blamed for contributing to society's ills through their depictions of criminal and violent behaviour. They have been accused of creating a greedy, avaricious society driven by consumption for its own sake through the depiction of attractive lifestyles most people will never achieve. The media, especially television, have also been criticized for poor cognitive development and educational performance among children. Throughout all these debates about different kinds of outcomes of media use by individuals, young and old, there is an underlying assumption that the media are causal agents. People use the media and as a result are changed by them. Reading newspapers and magazines, listening to radio, going to the cinema, playing with video games, and watching television are activities that are invested with the ability to change people or to motivate them to behave in specific ways. The debate about media effects, however, is full of contradictory arguments. The media are believed to have the power to increase people's knowledge, but also in some cases, to decrease their ability to learn (Gunter and McAleer, 1997). The media are regarded as having the ability to warn people of the dangers of drug abuse, promiscuous sexual behaviour, smoking and alcohol abuse, though not necessarily to change these behaviours, but also to contribute directly towards the growth in crime, by offering encouragement to the have-nots in society to take for themselves using violent means if necessary. It is possible, of course, that the media may have all and any of these effects, and even more that have not been mentioned here. But how does media research establish the existence, nature and strength of such effects?

The remainder of this chapter will examine the approaches adopted by media researchers to study media effects and influences. Depending on their theoretical background and the paradigm that dominates their approach to research, media researchers have used both quantitative and qualitative techniques to measure media effects. Sometimes, quantitative and qualitative methods are used in combination. The predominant quantitative methodologies are experiments and surveys, while the qualitative approaches to the study of media effects have depended on open-ended interviews (e.g. focus groups) or observation. Another key distinguishing characteristic of media effects research has been whether or not it is conducted under artificial conditions over which the research has a great deal of control or in natural conditions where the researcher has much less control or no control at all over sequences of events.

Qualitative measures of media effects have usually focused on media effects that occur at a cognitive level. Dependent variables have tended to comprise measures of comprehension and the reception of meanings, ideas, values, beliefs and opinions. At a behavioural level, media effects methodologies have been drawn from the positivist social science paradigm. As such, research into the behavioural effects of the mass media has almost invariably used quantitative measurement of behaviour.

Within the positivist empiricist school of social science, carrying out media effects research is designed principally to quantify causation. The media are regarded as agents of causality. This means that they are endowed with the power to cause changes in members of their audiences. These changes may take place at a number of levels: behavioural, cognitive ability, knowledge and understanding, or even personality. Hypothesizing that the media have such effects is one thing, proving it is another. Of all the research methodologies at the disposal of media researchers, one is believed to stand out from the rest in relation to the effective demonstration of cause – effect relationships – experiments. Experiments derive largely from a psychological perspective (Comstock, 1998). Much experimental research on media has used techniques adapted from psychological research. It has been argued that experiments provide evidence on the question of whether the media *can* produce certain effects, though do not necessarily demonstrate that such effects *do* actually occur in reality (MacBeth, 1996). This distinction is very important. It is possible for experimenters to create the conditions in which a whole range of effects can be measured following exposure to media stimuli, presented in a controlled environment. The problem for this kind of research is that if the environment in which such media 'effects' are measured is quite different from the everyday reality in which individuals consume and enjoy media, those effects may be specific to that artificial environment and occur in no other environment.

In the general overview of media audience research methodologies presented in Chapter 2, we saw that experimental research has taken on a variety of methodological forms. The key distinguishing features are: (1) whether or not researchers run pre-tests and post-tests or post-tests only; (2) whether they run just one group or two or more groups in parallel; (3) whether they examine one independent variable (causal variable) or two or more independent variables; and (4) whether they take measurements over a limited or extended period of time. As mentioned earlier, the other major distinguishing feature is whether experiments are conducted in an artificial laboratory setting or in a natural setting in the field.

Laboratory experiments

Most experimental research has been carried out in laboratory settings. This means that the subjects under study are brought to a central location, usually within an academic institution, and placed in an artificial situation in which they are shown media materials (the stimulus materials of the experiment) and then are tested subsequently for their behavioural reactions. Behaviour can be measured by experimental apparatus (e.g. the delivery of an electric shock to another person) or by observing behaviour in a more natural environment once the subject has left the laboratory (e.g. stealing money from a charity box, play behaviour in a room full of toys). In some experimental designs, behaviour is measured before and after the subjects are shown media content (e.g. a film clip, a picture of a weapon), while in other designs it is measured only after exposure to the stimulus material.

The range of experimental designs, including classic, pre-experimental, quasi-experimental and special designs, was described in broad terms in Chapter 2. The application of some of these designs in the context of investigating media effects is examined further here, with reference to some specific examples.

Classic pre-test/post-test design

The classic design involves the measurement of experimental subjects' behaviour both before and after they are shown media stimulus materials. In this way, their pre-exposure behaviour represents a benchmark against which later behavioural responses can be compared. This design was used by Potts et al. (1994) to examine the effects of television on children's physical risk-taking tendencies. Children aged six to nine years of age were pre-tested and post-tested on self-reports of likelihood of taking risks across a range of different scenarios. Ten pictorial representations of common situations associated with injury were shown to the children and for each one they indicated how much risk they personally would take in that setting. In one example, a tall tree was depicted and the children were asked how high in the tree they would climb to retrieve a kite that was stuck in the tree. In another case, a swimming pool was shown in cross-section to reveal five levels of increasing depth; children were asked to indicate at what depth they would swim. Other scenarios depicted retrieving a ball in the street while a car approaches (when would you wait before getting the ball?), approaching a vicious dog to retrieve a toy (how close to the dog would you go?), jumping off porch steps (how high would you jump?), approaching exploding fireworks (how close would you go?) and so on.

After responding to these items for the first time, the children were randomly allocated to watch either an animated or non-animated programme, or were put in a control group that saw no programme at all. The two programmes were, in turn, edited to emphasize or omit risk-taking behaviour among the central characters. After watching the programmes, all children were tested on another series of risk-taking scenarios and their pre-viewing and post-viewing scores were compared. Results showed that children who were shown a television programme that depicted leading characters taking risks, increased their reported risk-taking likelihood after the programme more significantly than did children who watched the programmes with most risk-taking behaviour taken out or who watched no programme at all.

Post-test only – two groups

With this design, the researcher again tests for media effects on one occasion only, after subjects have been shown a media stimulus, but more than one media condition is examined. However, this design does not also include a control group who receive no media material. This design has been used in studies of cognitive-level effects of media more often than in demonstrations of behavioural effects. For example, a number of studies have been carried out to demonstrate the role of television in priming viewers' subsequent impressions of different aspects of social reality (Hansen, 1989; Hansen and Hansen, 1988; Hansen and Krygowski, 1994). It is presumed that the media provide audiences with stereotyped images of social groups and situations and condition 'scripts' that represent fixed event sequences that typify different settings, governing the way individuals are expected to behave.

Hansen and Hansen (1988) examined whether viewing stereotypical depictions of males and females would prime sex role stereotypical schemas, which, in turn, might colour viewers' interpretations of subsequently observed male and female interactions. In the first part of the experiment, participants viewed either neutral music videos or stereotypical music videos in which females were portrayed as pawns and sexual objects. All participants then viewed videotaped interactions of a male and female interviewing for positions as video jockeys. In the videotape, the male made sexual advances to the female, who either reciprocated or did not. After viewing this interaction, participants rated the characters on several dimensions. Results indicated that the music video was effective as a prime. When sex role stereotypical schemas were primed by the stereotypical music video, the female was judged according to whether she adhered to or did not adhere to the standard gender role script; this occurred significantly less in response to the neutral music video.

Post-test only, with control group

Among the classic experimental studies are those associated with research into the effects of media depictions of violence. A series of studies conducted by Bandura and his colleagues in the early 1960s employed a methodology that used observational measures within an experimental framework (Bandura et al., 1963a, 1963b). These studies addressed the issue of whether children will imitate behaviour they see modelled by actors on screen. In the context of violence, for example, Bandura believed that by watching favourite television or movie characters behave violently, youngsters might identify with these role models and copy their actions.

A demonstration of this hypothesized influence was provided through an experimental methodology in which children first observed, without acting out, a number of novel and unusual aggressive behaviours performed by an adult model. This model was shown on film performing a range of physical attacks on a large inflated clown doll (called a 'bobo doll'). The actor pummelled the doll with his fists and also vocalized a number of aggressive remarks. Shortly after witnessing this footage, the children were frustrated by being told that they could not play with some attractive toys even though they had earlier been told that they would be allowed to. The children were then placed in the same setting as that in which they had earlier seen the clown doll attacked. The typical finding of several studies was that children who had previously seen the aggressive model emitted more of the observed acts than did children, in a control condition, who had not observed the aggressive model.

Subsequent studies using this same basic design find that the level of modelled aggressive behaviour can vary with a number of mediating factors such as whether the aggressive model is accompanied by another person who also behaves the same way (Leyens et al., 1982; O'Carroll et al., 1977; O'Neal et al., 1979) or whether the model is punished for his aggressive behaviour (Bandura, 1965).

Factorial designs

In the laboratory experimental designs presented up to this point, only one key independent variable or experimental manipulation has been employed per study. In much experimental research, however, there is an assumption that the dependent variable under scrutiny can be influenced by more than one causal agent. Indeed, causal agents may often act together in an interactive or mutually dependent fashion. In a factorial design, therefore, the researcher examines the effects of more than one independent variable within a single study. This design has been frequently used in research on the behavioural effects of media violence. While the modelling hypothesis explains the effects of media violence in terms of observational learning and imitation associated with viewing specific acts of violence, there is an alternative hypothesis about how depictions of media violence can influence aggressive behaviour among members of the audience. According to this view, media violence can prime thoughts about aggression that increase the likelihood of a viewer's behaving violently in a much more general fashion, rather than one tied specifically to the imitation of media portrayals (Berkowitz, 1984).

During the 1960s and 1970s, Berkowitz and various colleagues devised an experimental design in which such media influences were studied in the laboratory. In the basic design, subjects were randomly allocated to conditions in which they either watched a violent or non-violent film clip or no clip, after which they were given an opportunity to display aggressive behaviour towards another person (usually an assistant of the experimenter). Aggression was operationalized using a special device called a Buss Aggression Machine. This device enabled subjects to deliver electric shocks to the other person. In addition to the type of viewing condition to which subjects were allocated, there was another important manipulation used in this design. Prior to viewing the film clip, subjects were allocated, again at random, to two further conditions in which they interacted with the experimenter's accomplice who either annoyed them or was friendly towards them. This disposition of the accomplice was either established by having him be insulting towards the subject, or deliver electric shocks to the subject.

In this basic design therefore there were two factors manipulated: (1) prior annoyance of the subject and (2) viewing of violent/non-violent film clip. This yielded four distinct sets of conditions: prior annoyance plus violence viewing; prior annoyance plus non-violence viewing; no prior annoyance plus violence viewing; no prior annoyance plus no violence viewing (Berkowitz and LePage, 1967; Leyens and Parke, 1975; Turner and Goldsmith, 1976).

In a slightly modified version of this design, Geen and O'Neal (1969) gave subjects an opportunity to deliver electric shocks to another person after viewing either a film clip of a prizefight or a non-violent clip. While giving the shock, some subjects were stimulated with a noise of moderate intensity. The remainder of the subjects received no such noise. Subjects who were aroused by the noise were more aggressive after seeing the violent movie clip than after seeing the non-violent movie film. No such difference was found among non-noise aroused subjects.

In an early study using this experimental design, Feshbach (1961) investigated whether media depictions of violence could have a cathartic effect upon aggressive impulses. Male subjects who had initially been annoyed by another person making insulting remarks to them in the laboratory setting subsequently watched a film of a prize-fight before being given an opportunity to turn the tables on their annoyer. Subjects who had been provoked and then watched a violent film clip were subsequently *less* hostile in their retaliatory remarks as compared with subjects who had been shown a non-violent film. This difference in reaction, apparently as a function of the type of film, did not appear among subjects who had not been insulted at the outset. Feshbach concluded that the violent film clip had produced a symbolic draining off or catharsis of hostility in previously provoked subjects.

Experiments beyond the laboratory

Media research using experimental design has been conducted beyond laboratory settings. Such studies attempt to get close to the media exposure circumstances that typify people's real lives. As such, the research trades off the measurement precision and control over events that characterize laboratory research for greater ecological validity.

Experiments beyond the laboratory can be divided broadly into two categories: field experiments and natural experiments. Field experiments involve studies that take place in non-laboratory environments over which the researcher nevertheless still retains a degree of control over media exposure. Naturalistic experiments comprise studies that take advantage of naturally occurring events, involving the mass media, in order to attempt to assess their impact upon individuals or more usually entire communities. In these cases, the research has no control over events and must devise a research design which fits around events that have occurred, are occurring or will occur anyway.

Field experiments

These are studies in which subjects, in relatively natural surroundings, are randomly assigned to conditions, are exposed to varying kinds of media stimulus materials, and then have their perceptions, attitudes or behaviours measured. Field experiments usually involve the study of intact or pre-existing groups, but whereas in the former case the groups vary naturally, in the latter case the researchers assign each group to some particular condition. These kinds of experiments have often been conducted in residential schools, although other environments have been used. The effects are almost always assessed over a period of time, at the least over a few hours, but more often over several days or weeks.

Most major field experiments have involved an analysis of the impact of television. Usually, two or more groups are assigned by the researchers to a particular television diet for some period, and their behaviour is compared with that of an untreated control group that has no television diet (other than, in some studies, regular home viewing). Or, one group may be exposed to a particular type of television diet (e.g. aggressive content), whereas another group is exposed to a different type of television diet (e.g. television segments of equal length with no aggressive content or with prosocial content). Thus the word 'untreated' does not necessarily mean zero exposure; rather it means no exposure to the content of special interest. Behaviour assessed during a pre-test period is used to demonstrate the equivalence of the groups on the behaviour(s) of interest.

Most field experiments have used the classic pre-test/post-test with control group design. One alternative and convenient way of classifying field experiments is in terms of the settings in which the research is conducted. Much of this kind of research has been conducted among very young children in nursery school settings or among older children and adolescents in residential or institutional settings. A small number of studies have been carried out among adults in home settings over which the researcher has been able to gain control.

Pre-school studies

One early field experiment was conducted by Steuer, Applefield and Smith (1971) on effects of televised aggression. They studied five girls and five boys aged 41–60 months (mean = 51 months). They were ranked on the basis of a questionnaire about their amount of television viewing that their parents completed several weeks before the experiment, and for each successive pair of ranks (1 and 2, 3 and 4) one child was assigned to an experimental group (which saw aggressive videotapes) and one to a control group (which saw non-aggressive tapes). The groups played concurrently in different rooms for one ten-minute session per day, with the first ten sessions/days providing a baseline comparison. For the next eleven sessions/days, each group viewed a videotaped Saturday morning children's television programme for ten minutes immediately prior to free play. The aggressive videotapes had been scored according to the same interpersonal aggression behaviours that were observed for the children and contained 15 to 32 (mean: 22) such behaviours.

The non-aggressive tapes were edited to contain no such aggression. During each session, each child was observed for two minutes: one minute in the first half of the session and one minute in the second half. Observers were systematically alternated between the groups. They were told (wrongly so that they did not know which children had seen aggressive films on a given occasion) that children in both groups saw a random sequence of aggressive and non-aggressive programmes. The analyses were conducted for each matched pair of experimental and control children. The focus was on the difference in mean interpersonal aggression scores between baseline and viewing sessions.

In another field experiment conducted in a summer nursery school, Friedrich and Stein (1973) observed the free-play behaviour of boys and girls in classroom settings over a nine-week period. In a pre-test/post-test design, behaviour was observed for an initial three-week baseline period, a four-week experimental period, and a further two weeks. Measures of physical, verbal, object and fantasy aggression were taken. During the experimental period, the children were randomly allocated to groups that watched either prosocial, educationally oriented programmes (*Mister Rogers' Neighborhood*), aggressive cartoons (*Batman* and *Superman*), or neutral children's films that had little or no prosocial or aggressive content.

There were two morning and two afternoon classes of 25 children each that met for two and a half hours three times a week. In each classroom, the children were divided between one of the experimental conditions and the neutral condition, with experimental treatments assigned to classes by the toss of a coin. One morning and one afternoon class had 15 children in the aggressive condition and 10 in the neutral one, and one morning and one afternoon class had 15 in the prosocial condition and 10 in the neutral one.

Gender, age and socio-economic status (SES) were balanced in assigning individual children to classrooms; however, to include lower SES families (which were more difficult to recruit), it was necessary to give them their preferred (mostly morning) session. This provides a good illustration of the difficulties involved in establishing initially-equivalent groups in quasi-experimental studies.

Procedurally, the television programmes and films were shown in small, windowless rooms. Each classroom was divided into two shifts (A and B), each comprising children in both experimental and neutral conditions (7–10 children per shift). Children alternated between being in the first and second shifts, that is, whether they viewed earlier or later within their nursery school session on a particular day. In the aggressive condition, each cartoon consisted of two stories lasting slightly more than 20 minutes, with six *Batman* and six *Superman* cartoons shown on alternate days. The prosocial condition consisted of 12 *Mister Rogers'* programmes of about 28 minutes each. Two neutral films of 10 to 15 minutes each were shown per neutral session. There was almost no aggressive content in these films. Some prosocial content inevitably was included, but only if it was not emphasized and did not form the central theme. Observations of the children's aggressive and prosocial behaviour, as well as of self-regulation in free play, were made throughout the entire nursery school session, with a total of 64 discrete categories of behaviour observed.

Field experiments in institutions

Some quasi-experiments involving television have been conducted in institutional settings. Such settings have the advantage that the residents' media diet can be more precisely controlled over a longer period than is possible for participants living at home and attending a group setting on a part-time basis. The disadvantage, of course, is that external validity is limited to the types of individuals residing in those settings. The best-known examples all have focused on adolescent males.

In the USA, Feshbach and Singer (1971) studied adolescent males residing in seven residential schools and institutions (five in California and two in the greater New York area). Three were private schools and four were residential homes for youths from working-class families who were having difficulties at home. Both pre-test and post-test assessments were obtained for 395 adolescents. In some cases, the individuals were randomly assigned to watch television with non-aggressive or aggressive content, whereas in other cases, they were randomly assigned by living group. In two residences, all were required to participate, whereas in the others, participation was voluntary. They were required to watch a minimum of six hours of television a week for six weeks, but could watch as much as they wished provided that they watched only programmes on the designated list (of non-aggressive or aggressive content). During the six-week viewing period, and in most cases the week preceding as well as tne week following that period, a houseparent, supervisor, teacher, or proctor most familiar with each youth's daily activities completed a rating sheet five days a week covering aggressive acts toward peers and authority figures.

The variations in the ways in which the treatment was implemented in each location provide a good illustration of the difficulties involved in doing research with intact groups. At first glance the decision to include two different types of institutions, private schools and residential homes for youths with difficulties, might not seem unusual. It did increase the range of social backgrounds from which subjects were drawn and, thus, potentially increased the external validity. As it turned out, the differences between adolescent males who saw the aggressive versus non-aggressive content were greater for those in the youth homes, who also were rated higher in initial aggression. Differences for the private schools tended to be non-significant. Thus, the inclusion of both types of institutions enabled the researchers to address the potential threat to external validity of the interaction of selection with treatment.

This study has been criticized on a number of grounds. In several schools the television programme *Batman* was allowed in the non-violent condition after complaints by the subjects, and this may have been interpreted as a sign of weakness by the authorities that encouraged aggressive behaviour. Another criticism is that the effect was significant in only three schools, all for delinquent boys. This is so but it must be remembered that the subjects were randomly assigned within the school, thus producing in essence seven totally independent experiments. A score of six out of seven in the same direction, with three significant and one almost significant is reasonably consistent. Finally, it is argued that because the violent programmes were somewhat more popular than the non-violent ones, subjects in the non-violent condition were frustrated and less happy, and this made them more aggressive. This is a reasonable criticism that suggests a plausible alternative explanation of the findings that cannot be rejected with the available data.

Another illustration of the use of a pre-test/post-test design within a field experiment context was provided by three studies of the possible impact of television violence on adolescent male aggression in institutionalized settings. One study was conducted in Belgium (Leyens et al., 1975) and the other two in the USA (Parke, Berkowitz, Leyens, West and Sebastian, 1977). The design of all three studies was very similar.

In the Belgian study four cottages at an institutional secondary school for boys were randomly assigned to conditions. Two cottages saw a violent film every evening for one week; two cottages saw a non-violent film every evening for a week. All subjects were observed before the study, during the study and for one week after. The boys were observed each day from noon to bedtime and coded a number of categories of physically and verbally aggressive behaviour.

There were pre-existing differences in aggressive behaviour among the groups. One of the cottages in the aggressive film condition and one in the neutral or non-violent film condition had higher average levels of aggression than did the other cottages in each condition. The data were therefore analysed by cottage, noting which ones were initially high or low in aggression. The most likely explanation of the pre-existing differences in aggression according to the researchers was the strict control exerted by some counsellors especially in one of the cottages in the aggressive movie condition.

Another problem with the Belgian study was that the boys in each cottage were highly dependent on each other. Thus, aggression by one boy would involve others in the same cottage. While the researchers tried to control for this factor statistically, the results that emerged were nevertheless mixed. One of the violent-film cottages showed a general increase in aggressiveness; the other violent-film cottage showed an increase only in physical aggression. One of the neutral-film cottages showed a decrease in overall aggressiveness; the other showed no change.

By noon of the day after the films were shown, the only appreciable increase in aggression was in interpersonal verbal aggression for one violent-film cottage (no effect on four other measures of aggression or on overall aggression). By the week after the experimental week, the only remaining effect was on a combined measure of interpersonal and non-interpersonal aggression, which was higher for that same cottage but not for the other.

In a minimum-security penal institution for juvenile offenders in the USA, Parke et al. (1977) conducted two field experiments. In the first study, adolescent males, ranging in age from 14 to 18 (68 per cent Euro-American, 26 per cent African-American, 6 per cent other), were randomly assigned by the institution to cottages (30 each). During a three-week baseline period, trained observers recorded the behaviour of youths in two cottages about two hours per day for three consecutive days each week. Then, during a five-day experimental period, the residents of one cottage saw a violent movie each evening, whereas the other cottage saw a neutral, non-violent film. Behaviour was observed before, during and after the movies on Wednesday, Thursday and Friday.

The youths rated each movie on aggressiveness and interest scales after seeing the movie and again at the week's end. Unfortunately, it turned out that the aggressive films were rated as more interesting and exciting, thus confounding interest and content. On the day after the final film, all youths participated in a laboratory test of aggression that involved shock to a confederate under either an angered or a non-angered condition. During the final three-week follow-up phase, behavioural observations were made as in the baseline phase of three consecutive evenings. The boys were rated on 14 categories of aggressive behaviour, covering a variety of physical, verbal and interpersonal interactions.

Subjects who saw the violent movies were more aggressive during the movie week than were those who saw the non-violent movies. There was also some indication that the effect was stronger for initially low-aggressive subjects than for high-aggressive subjects. By the week after the films were shown, the level of aggressiveness for all groups was back to normal except for the high-aggressive, violent-film boys, who scored somewhat higher on the general aggression measure.

This study provides a good illustration of the importance of having a pre-test, because the youths in the cottage assigned to watch aggressive movies turned out to be more aggressive during the baseline phase than did those in the cottage who subsequently saw the non-violent films. This was dealt with by sub-classifying them into high and low groups on the basis of their baseline aggression scores.

One potentially serious problem with this study is that the boys rated the neutral movies less exciting, less likeable, more boring, and more silly than the violent films. Having discovered some limitations in the design of their first field experiment, Parke et al. (1977) conducted a second one in the same institution. This study included two conditions. The first was a seven-week replication of the first field experiment, with two changes. Behavioural observations were made on five days rather than just three days during the pre- and post-movie weeks, and more interesting neutral films were shown. The youths in this second field experiment rated them as being as interesting and exciting as the aggressive films, thus eliminating the confounding of interest and content that occurred in the first one. The second condition of this second experiment was a two-week assessment of the impact of a single film shown on Friday at the end of the first week of observations. This provided a shortened version of the full-scale study to permit a direct comparison of single-exposure and repeated-exposure effects. All participants in this second field experiment took a verbal aggression laboratory test rather than the shock test used in the first field experiment.

Again, the subjects in the violent-film condition were more aggressive before the films were shown. It was reported that with five films, those who were shown the violent films were significantly more aggressive than were those who saw the non-violent films on general aggressiveness, whereas on two other measures of aggression this effect was marginally significant. With one film, none of the main effects was significant, but there was a significant interaction on the measure of physical aggression, indicating that boys who were high in aggression initially, displayed more aggression after seeing the violent film than after seeing the non-violent film, with no difference found for those initially low in aggression.

Field experiment methodology has been used to test the effectiveness of advertising campaigns. Robertson et al. (1974) reported a study of a campaign designed to increase the use of car seat belts. Six public service announcements were shown to households on one-half of a dual cable system; households on the other half of the system served as a control group and were shown no messages.

The researchers used traffic flow maps to select 14 observation sites likely to maximize the possibility of observing vehicles from the neighbourhoods that received the message and those who did not receive the message. Traffic was observed at different times of the day. The observers were strategically placed to allow them to observe the drivers of the cars that passed their position. As a car approached, the driver's sex, apparent ethnic background, estimated age and use of seat belt were noted. The car licence number was recorded as the car drove away. With the cooperation of the state department of motor vehicles, the licence plate numbers were matched with owners' names and addresses. These were then checked to see whether the person was or was not a subscriber to one of the dual cable systems. This process ultimately led to four different groups for analysis: Cable A households in which messages were shown; Cable B households, the control group for which no messages were shown; non-cable households in the same county; and out-of-county households. Observations were made *before* the seat belt campaign aired and for several months *afterwards*. The advertisements were scheduled so that an average television viewer would see two or three messages per week.

The results of the observations revealed that the campaign had no measurable effect on seatbelt use. Drivers in the half of the cable system that carried the messages were no more likely to use seat belts than were motorists in the control group. The limitations of this otherwise clever study include the fact that the researchers had no way of testing whether the public service announcements had been seen by drivers, and no way of telling if drivers who lived outside the cable market where the announcements were shown had seen them at friends' homes.

Randomized experiments conducted in the field

Random assignment of individuals to groups is a defining characteristic of laboratory experiments but is not usually employed in field experiments, because of the logistical difficulties associated with doing so. However, random assignment has been used even in field studies.

Josephson (1987) described a field experiment with 66 groups of boys, with six boys per group. These groups were randomly selected from the eligible boys in Grades 2 and 3 at each of 13 schools. The 66 groups were randomly assigned to six different conditions of the experiment. All of the boys watched either a violent or a non-violent 14-minute excerpt from a commercial television programme. The non-violent excerpt was about off-duty members of a state highway patrol coaching a boys' motocross bike-riding team. It contained no violence but was rated as being exciting and as well liked as the violent excerpt by other boys the same age as those in the study.

The violent excerpt was from a police action drama that included snipers and a SWAT team whose aggression was portrayed as justified revenge and was both successful and socially rewarded, features thought to make viewers more likely subsequently to behave aggressively (e.g. Bandura, 1983; Berkowitz, 1984). The violent excerpt also included a violence-related cue, which was the use of walkie-talkies by the snipers when the SWAT unit's attack began. Pilot testing revealed that 95 per cent of boys who saw this excerpt remembered the walkie-talkie (Josephson, 1987). The experiment also involved a frustration procedure. The boys were told that they would see some really neat cartoons, but when the videotape started it quickly became static and then 'snow'. Half of the boys were frustrated before they saw the television programme (violent or non-violent) and half after they saw it.

Procedurally, the boys were taken to a 'TV room', were frustrated by the cartoon, and then saw the violent or non-violent programme (or vice versa). Then they were taken to the gymnasium for what they had been told was the second study. A male referee and two observers (one man and one woman) who did not know the boys' frustration order and television programme type participated in this part of the experiment. The experimenter gave the referee a card with the six boys' team and number assignments (randomly determined) and left. The referee gave each boy his jersey and a hockey stick, explaining that the boys would play a short hockey game and take turns playing each position. He also explained that observers would be doing a 'play-by-play' of the game 'like they do on the radio', and so he needed to know who the players were. The referee then did a pre-game interview with each boy (name, class, and favourite position in hockey), and, following the instructions on the (randomly assigned) card, used either a tape recorder or a walkie-talkie for the interview. It was assumed that the tape recorder and microphone would be neutral to all boys and that the walkie-talkie would be neutral for those who saw the non-violent television excerpt. But it would be violence-related for those boys who had seen the violent excerpt.

The six boys then played floor hockey for three periods of three minutes each, rotating between periods so that each boy played centre, wing, and goal. The observers watched the boys from the moment they put on their jerseys and dictated into a tape recorder every instance of aggressive action, identifying both the aggressor and target player by jersey colour and number. Both physical and verbal aggression were recorded. If either rater was sure that an action was accidental, or if both thought that it might be, it was not included in the aggression score. Body checking was not included unless it involved pushing or elbowing.

Post-test only with control

Some field experiments have departed from the classic pre-test/post-test with control group design. Some field experiments have used a post-test only, with or without a control group. A series of studies conducted in the early 1970s by Milgram and Shotland (1973) investigated whether someone viewing an actor commit a particular antisocial act on television would be more likely subsequently to commit the same or a similar action themselves. All the studies in this series followed the same basic design.

In the first experiment the researchers recruited subjects either through advertisements placed in local newspapers or by handing out business reply cards to pedestrians. In each case, volunteers were invited to spend one hour watching a television show in return for which they would receive a free transistor radio. Subjects were asked to report to a special television theatre to view the programme. Upon arrival, each person was randomly assigned to one of four groups and each group was shown a different programme.

Three different versions of an episode from a television series called *Medical Center* were constructed. One version depicted antisocial behaviour that was punished by a jail sentence; another portrayed antisocial behaviour that went unpunished, and the third contained prosocial behaviour. The antisocial behaviour consisted of scenes of a distraught young man smashing a plastic charity collection box and pocketing the money. A fourth control group saw no programme.

After viewing the programme and completing a short questionnaire, subjects were instructed to go to an office in another building to receive their free radio. The office was monitored by hidden cameras. When subjects arrived at the office, a notice was posted to the effect that the radios were no longer available. There was a charity collection box in the office with money clearly visible in it and a dollar bill hanging from the box. The key measure was simply whether the subject took the money and/or broke into the box. The same design was used with some variations over eight studies across which almost six hundred subjects were studied. None of the studies found a significant effect of televised antisocial behaviour on the behaviour of subjects.

In another field experiment using a post-test only design, Loye et al. (1977) asked a number of married couples to participate in a study of the effects of viewing television. Each husband was assigned to watch one of five diets of programmes: programmes high in prosocial content; programmes high in violent content; programmes high in both types of content (mixed); programmes that were strong neither in prosocial nor antisocial content; or programmes that they would normally watch when free to choose for themselves. In each couple, the husband was the subject and was required to watch the assigned programmes from Monday to Sunday. Meanwhile each wife was supposed to observe her husband, rate him on various scales, and make notes of his behaviour. The major measure was the change in the ratings of the husbands' moods from Monday evening to Sunday.

The wives' reports of their husbands' behaviour showed that the highest level of hurtful behaviour was manifested by those who had chosen their own programmes. Those who had been constrained to watch only violence were no more hurtful than those who had watched only prosocial programmes. Although the idea of enlisting the aid of people in their natural living condition to study the effects of television is clever, there are many problems with this particular study.

Although the provision of programmes, by type, was controlled by the researchers, there was no control over how much television the husbands actually watched during the observation period. There was therefore no control across groups for viewing patterns. The wives used in this study were not trained observers, and there are question-marks over whether they all used the rating scales in the same way. What was classified as 'hurtful' behaviour by one spouse may not have been judged in the same way by another. It is also unclear as to whether the wives were blind to the particular experimental condition into which their husbands had been placed. If they were not ignorant of this, as they should have been, their ratings could have been biased by expectations about the effects of a particular programme diet.

Natural experiments

Natural experiments involve the study of intact or pre-existing groups that vary naturally rather than through researcher assignment. They entail researchers investigating naturally-occurring social or media events, the effects of which are measured through the analysis of historical data or the collection of new data from small or large samples at several different points before and after those events have occurred. What types of natural experiment assessing the effects of television on behaviour have been conducted? Five main categories can be identified: (1) the pre-test/post-test design with controls, (2) the pre-test/post-test design with only one group; (3) the post-test only design with one group; (4) the post-test only design with more than one group; and (5) the time series design.

Pre-test/post-test with control

This type of design has been used in a small number of studies of the impact of television on communities in which broadcasts were introduced for the first time and where the researchers were able to obtain pre-test baseline data on subjects before television transmissions began. This experimental design provides a potentially powerful method for testing cause – effect relationships involving television and audience behaviour, but is dependent upon effective measures being taken before and after the introduction of the new medium.

The earliest example of a natural experiment of this kind involved television, but focused more on use of the medium than on its effects. This research was conducted in Japan by Furu (1962, 1971). In 1957, he surveyed a group of children in Shizuoka whose families had television. At that time, it was rare in Japan to have a television set at home, although a 'street corner TV system' with sets in shrine compounds and plazas in front of railway stations had been popular since 1953. These children with television sets in their homes were compared with an individually matched group of children without television sets in their homes. Two years later in 1959 a second survey was conducted to provide a comparison with the first one.

In Scotland, Brown et al. (1974) conducted a before-and-after study with three groups of children aged 5 to 11 years. The before-and-after television village was Arisaig, where 18 children were studied in May 1972 and May 1973, four months before and eight months after the arrival of television reception. The neighbouring district of Lochailort was the first control group, with 11 children who saw no television (except for daytime school broadcasts) in both 1972 and 1973. The second control group was the village of Furnace, where 18 children had television reception in both phases of the natural experiment. The research focused on functional similarities and differences in children's use of different media. Unfortunately the very small sample sizes limit the conclusions that can be drawn from this otherwise strongly designed study.

Perhaps the biggest pre-test/post-test naturalistic study occurred in Canada during the 1970s (Williams, 1986). Once again, this investigation took advantage of a media event, namely the introduction of television to a community for the first time, to explore the impact of the new medium on a wide range of behavioural and attitudinal measures taken from children in the community. The target community was compared with two others that were similar in size and already had television reception. In the case of one of these communities, however, its television reception was limited to one channel, while the other community had multiple-channel reception. These three towns were surveyed twice, two years apart.

During the first phase of data collection, in the autumn of 1973, then, one of the towns (labelled Notel) had no television reception but was due to begin receiving it when a new transmitter was installed about two months later, enabling television signals to reach the town for the first time. That transmitter brought one channel to Notel, the Canadian Broadcasting Corporation's (CBC) national English-language channel. The first control town, labelled Unitel, had been receiving one channel for about seven years at the time of the first wave of surveying. The second control town, labelled Multitel, had then been receiving three private national US networks (ABC, CBS and NBC), as well as CBC, for about 15 years. In the second phase of data collection, Notel residents had received CBC for two years and reception had not changed in Unitel and Multitel.

The research studied a wide variety of behaviours including fluent reading skill, creativity, aggression, gender role attitudes, and participation in community activities. Some studies focused only on school-aged children, some on adults, and some on both. For most behaviours, both longitudinal and cross-sectional data were obtained for comparisons of Phase 1 with Phase 2. The sample sizes ranged from 40 children in each town and phase for aggression, to 70–80 for creativity and reading skills, to more than 250 children and adults combined for participation in community activities.

One more recent naturalistic study has been launched during the 1990s in the USA using a pre-test/post-test design with controls. In the US study, Kubey et al. (1996) are studying a natural experiment on the east Coast of the USA, involving three small rural towns. Most residents of OldTVtown receive two to four channels, whereas residents of Cabletown receive a basic cable package of 20 to 25 channels. Dishtown residents used to receive the same channels as OldTVtown, and some still did when surveyed, but most Dishtown residents had gone from receiving two to four channels to receiving about 60 channels. Dishtown was surveyed twice, 3 months and 20 months after start-up of the satellite dishes. OldTVtown and Cabletown were each surveyed once, at the same time as the second survey in Dishtown. In this natural experiment, like many others, the researchers only learned about the situation after the dishes had been installed and so could not obtain prospective before-and-after data. They did, however, use some carefully worded retrospective measures, enabling them to make some longitudinal comparisons for some variables. Their data include hours of viewing; participation in various leisure, familial, and community activities; indicators of habitual or ingrained television habits; how parents deal with children's viewing; etc. The data were obtained using surveys mailed to residents aged 18 or over, with a 50 per cent to 65 per cent response rate for two mailings per wave of data collection.

The pre-test/post-test with one group

In television research of this type, observations would be made on individuals in a pre-existing group rior to their exposure to television (pre-test) and then again following exposure (post-test). The lack of any comparison group, either a no-treatment control or some other comparison, usually makes it impossible to rule out some alternative plausible explanations for any observed changes. In particular, the internal validity threats of history, maturation, and regression rarely are implausible, and so this type of design usually is not causally interpretable. Thus, MacBeth studied more than one community when conducting her investigation in Canada into the impact of television on a township which had previously had no television reception.

A long-term study of the displacement effects of television has been carried out in South Africa among a single group of respondents who were pre-tested before the introduction of television to their community, and then post-tested after the new medium had become available to them

(Mutz et al., 1993). Television was introduced in South Africa in January 1976 and permeated the white population very rapidly. Data were collected over an eight-year period from white school children aged between 10 and 17 years.

Two years before the introduction of television, a nationwide survey of 7,087 ten-year-olds established baseline data. In each of the following eight years the same children completed an extensive battery of questionnaires. Approximately nineteen hundred children participated in all eight surveys. These children constituted the panel element of the study. In addition, however, cross-sectional pre- and post-television data collected each year from samples of approximately fifteen hundred children also provide points of comparison.

Each year, the children estimated the amount of time they spent on hobbies, sports participation, clubs, out-of-school lessons, and homework. Media use items addressed time spent on radio, movies, and out-of-school reading as well as television viewing. According to Mutz and his colleagues, the design of the study provided a unique opportunity to examine the displacement hypothesis at both individual and aggregate levels of analysis. The cross-sectional pre-television samples enabled examination of aggregate change independent of children's general development trend, a particularly important consideration with respondents in this age range. Since post-television data were collected over six years, it is also possible to examine whether television's effects are short-term or long-term. Finally, the panel sample provided an opportunity to examine displacement using individual-level, longitudinal data.

In the panel analysis, changes were examined in activity levels for different activities in each of the six post-television years. Of course, changes in behaviour could be attributed to factors other than television, such as maturation. The time devoted to various activities is strongly related to age across the early years of life (Medrich, Roizen, Rubin and Buckley, 1982). Other activities may exert independent influences. For example, any change in time devoted to homework or sports (regardless of their cause) may influence change in other activities such as reading or movie attendance. Using data from the same populations during the same period of time, individual-level and aggregate-level analyses portrayed television's impact in a number of different ways.

Another recent study using a pre-test/post-test design with one group has been carried out on a remote island community in the south Atlantic. This study was launched in 1992 on the island of St Helena, more than two and a half years before satellite television transmissions to the island began in the early part of 1995. The focus of this study has been on the impact of television upon children. Each year, data have been collected on children's leisure activities, social behaviour and school performance. After television transmissions started, data were also collected on television viewing habits and the nature of the television output.

Post-television measures of leisure behaviour and social (antisocial and prosocial) behaviour, based on diaries, questionnaire self-reports and observations, can be compared with pre-television measures of the same activities (Charlton et al., 1995a; Charlton et al., 1995b; Gunter et al., 1998).

The post-test only with one group

In this design, participants are studied only once after the treatment of interest has occurred. Because there is no pre-test or control group, the design is generally uninterpretable causally, but the findings may nevertheless be of interest in certain circumstances.

Research conducted in New York City from 1976 to 1982 by Winick (1988) provides a good example. He interviewed families, each of which had only one television set, during the weeks following loss of the use of the set (because it broke down (81 per cent) or was stolen (19 per cent)). He obtained the names of such families from informal sources, repair services, stores, community groups, and law enforcement agencies. He conducted 1,614 interviews with individuals in 680 homes. When interviewed, the families had been living without television for an average of six weeks (range: 12 to 21) after having had their sets for at least three years. The sample was comparable in SES, ethnicity and education to census data for the area. All available persons in each home were interviewed. The focus was on pre- and post-loss use of media and the details, nature and intensity of participants' responses to the loss of their television sets.

Post-test only with more than one group

In some studies of the effects of television, comparisons have been made between individuals (or a community) who have acquired television reception and others who have not yet done so. There is no pre-test against which to compare the post-test findings, and that is the main flaw of the design (Cook et al., 1990). It may not be possible to decide whether differences between the post-test groups are due to television exposure or simply to other differences between the groups that might have been apparent had there been a pre-test.

The main survey in the study of the introduction of television to the UK, by Himmelweit et al. (1958), is a classic example of the post-test-only design with non-equivalent groups. In their main survey they tested children in England attending state schools in London, Portsmouth, Sunderland and Bristol. In their total sample of 4,500 children, there were 1,854 viewers (children with television at home). Himmelweit et al. matched each viewer on gender, age (10–11 and 13–14 years), IQ (115 or above, 100–114, and below 100) and SES. They used the term *working class* for children with parents in blue-collar jobs and *middle class* for those with parents in white-collar jobs. As far as possible, matching was done within the same classrooms to hold constant the influence of teachers, school, other children, and geographic factors. The four factors on which children were matched were chosen because in previous research they had been found to account for many of the important differences in children's outlook and leisure activities.

Having recognised the methodological limitations of their main survey because it lacked a pre-test, Himmelweit et al. (1958) conducted an additional study that took advantage of a natural experiment in which a new transmitter was opened in Norwich. They gave survey questionnaires to all the 10- to 11- and 13- to 14-year-olds (2,200 in total) in nearly every school in Norwich when very few families had television sets. A year later, they repeated their survey and at that point compared a group of 185 children whose families had not, by matching them as they had done in their main survey. The design on the Norwich study falls into the category described by Cook et al. (1990) as the untreated control group design with pre-tests.

The Norwich study had the methodological strengths associated with natural before-and-after studies, but the small sample size did not permit exploration of the roles of age, gender, IQ and SES in relation to the use and effects of television, as was done in the main survey. Moreover, the Norwich study assessed only the more immediate effects of television following its recent introduction, whereas in the main survey all viewers who had had television for less than three months were excluded.

A similar type of design was used in a study of early television audiences in North America. Schramm et al. (1961) conducted 11 studies between 1958 and 1960. Most were conducted in the USA on children, parents and families, with an emphasis on the use of television and other media in communities with television reception (San Francisco, Rocky Mountains, a metropolitan suburb, and Denver). Two of their studies were conducted in British Columbia, Canada, in two communities that were comparable except that one (Teletown) had television reception and one (Radiotown) did not. A total of 913 children in Grades 1, 6, and 10, as well as 269 parents, were studied.

Both Teletown and Radiotown had populations of about five thousand and were similar in industrial support, social structure, government and school system. But whereas Radiotown was four thousand miles from a major metropolitan area and two hundred miles from the nearest open-circuit television station, Teletown was within the television distance of a Canadian metropolitan area and also not far from the US border. Almost all adults and most of the children in Radiotown had seen television elsewhere but they could not watch it regularly at home. In Teletown, more than 75 per cent of the children had television sets at home, and others watched regularly at friends' homes. Most Radiotown residents were familiar with television and yearned for it. In Teletown, 25 per cent did not have television. As was the case for the Himmelweit et al. (1958) main survey, the lack of a pre-test in Teletown or a post-test in Radiotown makes it impossible to rule out the alternative possibility that any differences observed were due not to television but rather to pre-existing differences between the two communities.

A third example of a post-test only design using more than one group in which the groups were not pre-tested or matched in any way was conducted by Murray and Kippax (1977, 1978) in Australia. They studied three towns that were similar in size (populations of 2,000–3,000) and social structure but different in the duration, content and magnitude of their experience with television. They were located in rural areas, and 1971 census information indicated that they did not differ significantly in total population, housing conditions, ethnic composition or SES, although there were slight variations in educational level and family size.

The 'high-TV' town had had five years' experience with a commercial channel and two years' experience with the national public channel (ABC). The 'low-TV' town had had one year's experience with the public channel, and the 'no-TV' town did not receive a signal. An effort was made to obtain a random 50 per cent sample of families in each town with children under 12 years of age. Families were located using electoral rolls, town canvassing, school enrolments, and birth records. The towns were divided into geographic sectors, and interviewers contacted sequentially, without callback, all the families in each sector. There were no refusals by any family contacted, although there were some unsuccessful interviews because no one was home. The final sample sizes and their percentages of the estimated populations of families with children under 12 in each town were 82 (40 per cent) for the high-TV town, 102 (40 per cent) for the low-TV town, and 98 (52 per cent) for the no-TV town.

The problem that, when the penetration of a technology is less than near universal, it tends to vary with SES, did not apply to Murray and Kippax's Australian study. In addition, having three groups that vary on a continuum of exposure to television may make other pre-existing differences among the towns easier to detect or rule out (Cook et al., 1990). With three towns, one is looking for a sensible pattern of findings in relation to the different levels of television exposure. Some pre-existing differences that could account for differences between two towns that appear to be related to television probably would not map so well onto a three-town continuum. The caveat here, however, is that some pre-existing differences might co-vary with the levels of television exposure and indeed map well onto the continuum.

There are ways of overcoming the problem of a lack of pre-test data. A retrospective pre-test measure can be used. Retrospective reports may differ qualitatively from prospective ones because respondents are dependent on their memory for events, which can often prove to be inaccurate. A second technique is to form the treatment and control groups through matching on correlates of the pre-test. The potential hazard is under-matching, that is, not matching on enough or on the best variables.

A third suggestion is to measure proxies for respondents and then make statistical adjustments. Proxies are variables that correlate with the post-tests but are not measured on the same scale. They include demographic measures such as SES, age and gender which, along with IQ, were used as a type of pre-test proxy by Himmelweit et al. in the main survey.

Time series analyses

Quasi-experimental studies have been carried out on the impact of media events such as the introduction of television, widely publicized homicides, or major sports events, upon public behaviour. Such studies are *quasi*-experimental because the researchers do not actually apply direct manipulations or take advantage of a known event before it happens to conduct pre-test/post-test experimentation. Instead, it is necessary to use historical data from secondary sources to track changes or variations in public behaviour that are associated with specific media events. Data are analysed from before and after the period when the media event occurred. Using this approach, a number of studies have analysed apparent effects of television in general or specific televised events upon crime levels.

Arguments have been made about the role that the onset of television may have had in relation to crime levels in society. Hennigan et al. (1982) showed that the introduction of television to certain American cities in the early 1950s was not followed by any significant increase in violent crime, although at least one form of non-violent crime, larceny, did increase. The suggestion here was that although the introduction of television did not appear to promote the commission of crimes such as homicide and assault, it was associated with an increase in some other antisocial behaviours.

In another study of an alleged general impact of the presence of television in society, Centerwall (1989) analysed historical trend data on homicide rates, changes in television ownership, urbanization, economic conditions, age distribution of the population, alcohol consumption, civil unrest, use of capital punishment, and availability of firearms in the USA, Canada and South Africa between 1945 and 1975. Centerwall reported that following the initial introduction of television in the United States and Canada, there was a doubling of homicide rates in Canada and in white homicide rates in the USA over the next 10 to 15 years. None of the other factors measured over the same period were found to have accounted for this increase in the apparent aggressiveness of the population in these countries. In South Africa, over the period up to the introduction of television (which is the point at which Centerwall's analysis terminated) homicide rates were stable. The problem with this analysis is that the only television measure is penetration of television sets. No measures of actual levels of television exposure were used, whether of general viewing or viewing of specific (i.e. violence-containing) programmes.

Some researchers have used quasi-experimental designs to examine the potential effects of media violence on very harmful types of aggression.

Berkowitz and Macauley (1971) examined the potential role of several highly publicized homicides on violent crime. These researchers compared the month to month changes in violent crime rates (i.e. homicides, rape, robbery and aggravated assaults) in 12 US cities for several months prior to and following the assassination of President John F. Kennedy in 1963. In addition, the researchers contrasted the violent-crime rates in the months before and after Richard Speck and Charles Whitman had committed highly publicized mass murders. In July 1966, Speck killed seven student nurses in Chicago, and shortly afterward, Whitman, shooting from the University of Texas tower, killed or wounded a number of individuals below.

Using a time-series analysis procedure, Berkowitz and Macauley obtained evidence that these highly publicized crimes led to a short-term decrease and then a longer-term increase in violent crime. The time series statistical methods permitted the researchers to show that the increases and decreases in violent crime following these highly publicized crimes could not be explained as an artifact of the naturally occurring month-to-month fluctuations in violent crime.

The most ambitious and systematic attempt to account for real-world aggression with a hypothesis derived from experimental research has been made in a series of investigations by Phillips (1974, 1977, 1978, 1979, 1982, 1983; Phillips and Hensley, 1984). Dealing entirely with archival data, Phillips sought to show a causal connection between violence-related events shown on television, or reported in other news media, and increments in aggressive acts among the public in the immediate aftermath.

Phillips' original study (Phillips, 1974) was designed to show that incidence of suicides increases immediately after a suicide has been reported in the newspapers. Subsequent studies have addressed a presumed causal link between incidence of deaths due to car accidents and both reported suicides (Phillips, 1979) and suicides in episodes of soap operas (Phillips, 1982).

Phillips (1983) examined the impact of championship heavyweight prize fights on homicides in the USA. Eighteen such fights took place between 1973 and 1978, and the researcher analysed the number of homicides that occurred during the ten days following each fight compared with a computer-estimated expected number. The major result was that the number of homicides increased in days three, four, six and nine after a fight, with the major effect occurring on day three. Another analysis indicated that the increase occurred only if the fight took place outside the USA, if it was covered on network news, and if the expected number of homicides on day three was relatively high. In addition, if the loser of the fight was white, the number of young white men who were victims of homicide increased on the day of the fight and two and eight days later; if the loser was black, there was an increase in black homicides four and five days after the fight.

It is difficult to know how to make sense of this study because the pattern of results is odd. Certainly, the effect of a boxing match might be delayed for three days, but what would cause the effect to reappear six and nine days afterwards as well? Why does this effect only take place when the fight takes place outside the USA? Why were there differences in time lag between apparent effects of ethnicity of losers upon white and black victims of homicides?

Phillips and Hensley (1984) focused on daily patterns of homicide in the USA from 1973 to 1979 and examined the patterns of over 140,000 homicides before and after media publicity about prize fights, murder acquittals, life sentences, death sentences and executions. The researchers again used time series regression analyses and controlled fluctuations due to the day of the week, month or year as well as the effects of holidays.

After controlling for these factors, the researchers examined the incidence of homicides occurring during a three-week period following prize fights. They found significant effects of day of the week and holidays such that (a) homicides appeared most likely to occur on Saturday and (b) homicides tended to increase in number during holidays (particularly New Year's, independence day and Christmas). An examination of the effects of prize fights revealed that the number of homicides showed a significant increase on the third day after the fight.

Examining the effects of publicized accounts of the punishments of violent behaviour, the authors found a strong main effect of punishment such that the number of white murder victims significantly decreased on the fourth day after some form of highly publicized punishment took place. In their research, Phillips and Hensley (1984) first divided verdicts into four categories (life sentences, death sentences, acquittals, and executions). The researchers found some evidence that the number of homicides taking place after death sentences and executions was lower than the number of homicides taking place after life sentences, but these differences were not statistically significant. The non-significant findings were thought not to provide support for arguments suggesting that capital punishment had a greater deterrent effect than other forms of punishment (e.g. life sentences). Furthermore, the number of homicides did not appear to change significantly following an acquittal.

The Phillips research has been challenged by others. Baron and Reiss (1985) documented a number of potential problems in Phillips' research that could have arisen from small errors in specifications of the time-series model. These critics drew specific attention to the somewhat inexplicable finding that the publicized boxing matches seem to influence homicides only three to four days after the match. It was also noted that most of the fights employed in Phillips' research took place on a Tuesday or Wednesday. A three- to four-day lagged effect after the fight would appear on Friday, Saturday and Sunday. However, these days typically have a much higher homicide rate than other days of the week. Baron and Reiss reasoned that Phillips did not actually identify a three- to four-day lagged effect of prize fights. Instead, he was only measuring some subtle effect of weekends on homicide. In other words, the increase in homicides three to four days after the publicized fights might simply be due to the normal increases that occur on every weekend, regardless of whether a fight was scheduled in the middle of the week. In a re-analysis of Phillips' data, Baron and Reiss (1985) concluded that the results could be explained as little more than statistical artifacts. Other critics of this research argued that Phillips (1982) erred in his estimates of the transmission times of soap opera broadcasts featuring suicides, and that correction of this error eliminated the reported effect (Kessler and Stipp, 1984).

WHAT NEXT?

Concern about the behavioural effects of the mass media has existed throughout their history. Initially attention focused on the role the media could play in the political sphere as sources of propaganda that could shape public opinion and then ultimately influence voting behaviour. As the media became popular as sources, not just of information, but also of entertainment, however, attention shifted to the influences they could have upon social values and social conduct. In particular, there was concern about their potential effects upon young people whose impressionable minds could be particularly vulnerable to the behavioural examples presented by attractive mass-media role models. The popularity of media entertainment attracted the attention of another group – advertisers. Manufacturers of consumer goods and providers of services recognized the potential of the media for promoting their businesses and products. A further concern was that social behaviour might also be affected by the desires for attractive lifestyles promulgated by commercial messages.

Social scientists became involved in the investigation of the political and social impact of the early forms of modern media in earnest during the early years of the 20th century. Research into media effects was driven by the dominant theories of human behaviour that were in vogue at the time. Regardless of whichever paradigms were fashionable, research has always been limited by the capabilities of the available methodologies. As this book has shown, different paradigms have preferred methodologies. Much media research has been determined by the need to quantify behaviour in precise, numerical terms in an attempt to find out to what degree the media can shape public behaviour. This has meant that methodologies have been preferred that facilitate such measurement. Since research into media and audiences acquires data through a fairly limited number of routes – by asking people questions to which they verbally respond or by observing non-verbal, behavioural responses in different situations – it is essential that such measures are demonstrably valid indicators of the social phenomena they purport to measure. In so far as individuals are unable to provide accurate verbal reports on their own or other people's personalities, attitudes, values or behaviour, the validity of any research based on such measures is seriously undermined. If the behavioural responses that researchers measure fail to represent usual forms or patterns of behaviour that individuals display in everyday life, no amount of methodological rigour in the mounting of a research experiment will render its result truly indicative of naturally occurring behavioural reactions.

Other media researchers have exhibited preferences for methodologies that also rely on verbal responses of individuals about their media habits or on observations of non-verbal behavioural responses, but which place fewer restraints on the way people respond. Thus, verbal reports are open-ended and given in a respondent's own words rather than being constrained by the requirements of numerical scoring procedures. When investigating overt behavioural patterns, there is a preference for observing naturally-occurring behavioural sequences over the more precise, artificially controlled responses that can be quantified in degrees through some experimental apparatus.

Although, the open-ended or 'qualitative' approach allows individuals under investigation to respond freely using their own linguistic codes and displaying their natural behavioural forms, the advantages that accrue from this more liberal approach also contribute to its limitations as a research orientation. In its use of verbal reports, it is still reliant on accuracy and truthfulness of reporting. Although it permits respondents to converse at length about their media habits and related activities, it lacks the procedures necessary to determine causal agents. Despite its preference for observing naturally-occurring behaviour, such observations *per se* often lack the information necessary to explain why particular behavioural patterns occurred. Yet, being able to explain things is a fundamental aspect not just of scientific enquiry, but also of enhanced understanding about why social phenomena occur in the way they do.

Open-ended or focus group interviews have been promoted as a solution to the constrained and artificial question and answer format of the structured, questionnaire-driven interview. The focus group methodology is believed to model natural conversation, whereas the survey interview often proceeds on the prejudices of the researcher (Bertrand et al., 1992; Livingstone and Lunt, 1996). But are focus group interviews 'natural events'? Careful scrutiny of this qualitative methodology reveals that it is just as controlled in many respects as is a laboratory experiment. Participants are taken through a predefined series of questions, they interact with a moderator, whose personality can play a significant part in determining the results yielded from a group (Morgan, 1988). Focus groups can themselves produce unnatural effects on participants. One illustration of this is when participants are required to converse about topics they would not normally talk about, and display knowledge and opinions 'borrowed' from other group discussants on matters where they previously held no well-formed knowledge or opinions of their own (Morrison, 1992b).

Can these qualitative methodologies provide more effective predictors of behaviour than quantitative methodologies? Bristol and Fern (1993) used focus group research to investigate motives underlying consumer expenditure. Their analysis revealed that individuals interviewed in group discussions about intended consumer behaviour often displayed inconsistent attitudes and intentions. Indeed, in line with social psychological theory, evidence emerged that individuals exhibited intensified and polarized opinions on issues as a consequence of participation in conversations with others (Ickes et al., 1973; Kaplan, 1987). There are further social dynamics that occur within group discussion contexts that distort the opinions and behavioural intentions participants report. The way people behave towards each other in groups depends upon the social status they ascribe to the other participants. The nature of their participation and the kinds of disclosures they produce depend on whether they perceive the other participants to have a higher or lower social status than themselves (Goethals and Zanna, 1979). A further reason why a focus group creates an artificial setting in which to explore human behaviour is that the conversational interaction among group participants can lead individuals to consider facts they had not previously thought about in relation to the topic under discussion (Kaplan, 1987; Vinokar and Burnstein, 1974). This new information can result in attitude reinforcement or attitude change, and affect reported behavioural intentions. These effects may be especially likely to occur with weakly held attitudes or intentions (Bristol and Fern, 1993). These different dynamic processes can individually or jointly influence the way a focus group proceeds and the way individuals behave in that setting.

Morrison (1998: 183–4) offers some reassurance for qualitative research:

> The fact that 'influences' are at work in focus group research, not least the influence of the moderator, since it is he or she who directs proceedings, should not detract from their value as a qualitative method. All that is being said is that they are not as 'free' as some researchers would imagine, and that the very group dynamics that are its main strength over simple interviews also entail influences that ought to be taken into account in deciding the nature of the material collected.

In experimental research there is concern about 'experimenter demand'. In this case, an experimental subject's behaviour may be directly influenced by their assumptions or knowledge about the kind of responses it is believed the experimenter wants to see (Gauntlett, 1995). There is an equivalent concept of 'moderator demand' that some scholars have also attributed to focus group research (Morrison, 1998). Thus, whichever methodology – quantitative or qualitative – is considered, it is apparent that none is devoid of weaknesses or shortcomings. What is the way forward from this uncertain position?

The author's view is that the different social scientific paradigms referred to in this book and the quantitative and qualitative methodologies they have traditionally preferred all have something to offer in the quest for a better understanding of how people use and respond to the mass media. To assess causality, it is often necessary to set up artificial conditions or to intervene in some way in a naturally occurring phenomenon. But to understand how people become involved with the mass media and how they are affected by media content, simplistic, numerically-scored measures are unlikely to suffice. Individuals extract meaning from media content selectively and often in accordance with subjective perceptions of what is identified to be of personal relevance or significance. People extract meanings more often than specific behavioural examples, based on singular actions of media role models. That is not to say that crude imitation effects never occur – but they tend not to be the norm. The meanings extracted from media content will depend critically upon the social knowledge already held by the individual, and this is in turn affected by the particular community (group, organization, subculture, culture, society) to which that individual belongs or perhaps aspires to belong.

Significant advances have been made in research into the cognitive effects of the media, for example, that provide effective illustrations of a fruitful convergence of research perspectives. Qualitative data can be collected within experimental frameworks in which aspects of media exposure are systematically manipulated by the researcher (e.g. Rhee, 1997). The criterion variables, however, are more open-ended than is typical in such methodologies, with respondents being given an opportunity to respond to media content in their own words – perhaps by writing or conversing at length rather than by answering a few simple, multiple-choice questions. The media stimulus materials are also treated in a more sophisticated manner by the researcher, undergoing a complex linguistic analysis to identify meanings conveyed in the deep-structure of the content as well as in terms of what appears on the surface. Such approaches could be deployed in behavioural effects research in the future to assess not only the behavioural responses individuals display following exposure to media stimulus materials, but also to place these responses in a context of meaning as explicated by respondents themselves.

REFERENCES

Abel, T. (1930) Attitudes and galvanic skin reflex. *Journal of Experimental Psychology*, 13: 47–60.

Alexander, V.D. (1994) The image of children in magazine advertisements from 1950 to 1990. *Communication Research*, 21(6): 742–65.

Allen, C. (1965) Photographing the audience. *Journal of Advertising Research*, 5: 2–8.

Allen, J., Livingstone, S. and Reiner, R. (1997) The changing generic locations of crime in film: a content analysis of film synopses, 1945–1991. *Journal of Communication*, 47(4): 89–101.

Alperstein, G. (1980) The influence of local information on daily newspaper household penetration in Canada. (ANPA News Research Report No. 26). Reston, VA: ANPA News Research Center.

Altheide, D.L. (1985) *Media Power*. Beverly Hills, CA: Sage.

Altheide, D.L. (1987) Ethnographic content analysis. *Qualitative Sociology*, 10(1): 65–77.

Altheide, D.L. (1992) Gonzo justice. *Symbolic Interaction*. 15(1): 69–86.

Alwitt, L. (1985) EEG activity reflects the content of commercials. In L. Alwitt and A. Mitchell (eds) *Psychological Processes and Advertising Effects: Theory, Research and Application*. Hillsdale, NJ: Lawrence Erlbaum Associates. pp. 201–17.

Alwitt, L., Anderson, D., Lorch, E. and Levin, S. (1980) Preschool children's visual attention to television. *Human Communication Research*, 7: 52–67.

American Research Bureau/RKO General Broadcasting (1965) *The Individual Diary Method of Radio Audience Measurement*. New York: ARB.

Anderson, D. (1987) *Now you see them – now you don't: frequency and duration of exiting behavior in a home viewing environment*. Paper presented at the Association for Consumer Research, Boston.

Anderson, D.R. (1983) *Home television viewing by preschool children and their families*. Paper presented at the Society for Research in Child Development biennial meeting.

Anderson, D.R. (1985) Online cognitive processing during television viewing. In L. Alwitt and A. Mitchell (eds) *Psychological Processes and Advertising Effects: Theory, Research and Application*. Hillsdale, NJ: Lawrence Erlbaum Associates. pp. 177–200.

Anderson, D.R., Field, D.E., Collins, P.A., Lorch, E.P., and Nathan, J.G. (1985) Estimates of young children's time with television: a methodological comparison of parent reports with time-lapse video home observation. *Child Development*, 56: 1345–57.

Anderson, D.R. and Levin, S.R. (1976) Young children's attention to "Sesame Street". *Child Development*, 47: 806–11.

Anderson, D.R. and Lorch, E.P. (1983) Looking at television: action or reaction. In J. Bryant and D.R. Anderson (eds) *Children's Understanding of Television*. New York: Academic Press.

Andren, G., Ericsson, L.O., Oldsen, R. and Tannsjo, T. (1978) *Rhetoric and Ideology in Advertising*. Stockholm: Liber-Forlag.

Ang, I. (1990) *Desperately Seeking the Audience*. London: Routledge.

ARMS (1967) *All Radio Methodology Study*. New York: Audits and Surveys, Inc.

Armstrong, G.B. and Greenberg, B.S. (1990) Background television as an inhibitor of cognitive processing. *Human Communication Research*, 16(3): 355–86.

Atkin, C. and Gantz, W. (1978) Television news and political socialisation. *Public Opinion Quarterly*, 42: 183–97.

Babbie, E.R. (1990) *Survey Research Methods* (2nd edn). Belmont, CA: Wadsworth.

Bachrach, R.S. (1986) The differential effect of observation of violence on Kibbutz and city children in Israel. In R.L. Huesmann and L.D. Eron (eds) *Television and the Aggressive Child: A Cross-National Comparison*. Hillsdale, NJ: Lawrence Erlbaum Associates.

Baggaley, J. (1980) *The Psychology of the TV Image*. Aldershot, UK: Saxon House.

Baggaley, J. (1986) Developing a televised health campaign: I. Smoking prevention. *Media in Education and Development*, 19: 29–43.

Baggaley, J. (1988) Perceived effectiveness of international AIDS campaign. *Health Education Research*, 3(1): 7–17.

Bailey, K.D. (1994) *Methods of Social Research*. New York: The Free Press.

Bales, R.E. (1950) *Interaction Process Analysis*. Cambridge, MA: Cambridge University Press.

Bandura, A. (1965) Influence of model's reinforcement contingencies on the acquisition of imitative responses. *Journal of Personality and Social Psychology*, 1: 589–95.

Bandura, A. (1983) Psychological mechanisms of aggression. In R.G. Geen and C.I. Donnerstein (eds) *Aggression: Theoretical and Empirical Reviews, vol. I: Theoretical and Methodological Issues*. New York: Academic Press. pp. 1–40.

Bandura, A., Ross, D. and Ross, S.A. (1963a) Imitation of film-mediated aggressive models. *Journal of Abnormal and Social Psychology*, 66: 31–41.

Bandura, A., Ross, D. and Ross, S.A. (1963b) A comparative test of the status envy, social power and secondary reinforcement theories of identificatory learning. *Journal of Abnormal and Social Psychology*, 67: 527–34.

Barker, M. and Petley, J. (1997) *Ill Effects: The Media/Violence Debate*. London: Routledge.

Baron, J.N. and Reiss, P.C. (1985) Same time, next year: aggregate analyses of the mass media and violent behavior. *American Sociological Review*, 50: 347–63.

Barrow, L.C. and Westley, B.H. (1959) Comparative teaching effectiveness of radio and television. *Audio-Visual Communication Review*, 7: 14–23.

Bartlett, F.C. (1967) *Remembering: a Study in Experimental and Social Psychology*. London: Cambridge University Press.

Bartos, R. (1986) Qualitative research: what it is and where it came from. *Journal of Advertising Research*, 26: RC3–RC6.

Bausinger, H. (1984) Media, technology and everyday life. *Media, Culture and Society*, 6(4): 11–18.

Bechtel, R.B., Achelpohl, C. and Akers, R. (1972) Correlates between observed behavior and questionnaire responses on television viewing. In E.A. Rubinstein, G.A. Comstock and J.P. Murray (eds) *Television and Social Behavior*, vol. 4. Washington, DC: US Government Printing Office.

Behr, R.L. and Iyengar, S. (1985) Television news, real-world cues, and changes in the public agenda. *Public Opinion Quarterly*, 49: 38–57.

Belson, W. (1967) *The Impact of Television*. London: Crosby Lockwood & Son Ltd.

Belson, W. (1978) *Television Violence and the Adolescent Boy*. Westmead, UK: Saxon House.

Beniger, J.R. (1978) Media content as social indicators: the Greenfield Index of agenda-setting. *Communication Research*, 5: 437–53.

Bentele, G. (1985) Zeitstrukturen in den aktuellen informationsmedien. In W. Homberg and M. Sckmolke (eds) *Zeit, Raum, Kommunikations*. Munich, Germany: Olschlager. pp. 159–76.

Berelson, B. (1952) *Content Analysis in Communication Research*. New York: Free Press.

Berger, A.A. (1990) *Signs in Contemporary Culture: an Introduction to Semiotics*. New York: Sheffield Publishers.

Berger, A.A. (1993) *Media Analysis Techniques*. Newbury Park, CA: Sage.

Berkowitz, L. (1984) Some effects of thoughts on anti- and prosocial influences of media events: A cognitive-neo-association analysis. *Psychological Bulletin*, 59: 410–27.

Berkowitz, L. and LePage, A. (1967) Weapons as aggression-eliciting stimuli. *Journal of Personality and Social Psychology*, 7: 202–7.

Berkowitz, L. and Macauley, J. (1971) The contagion of criminal violence. *Sociometry*, 34: 238–60.

Berry, C. and Clifford, B. (1985) *Learning from television news: Effects of presentation factors and knowledge on comprehension and memory*. London: North East London Polytechnic and Independent Broadcasting Authority, Research Report.

Berry, C., Scheffler, A. and Goldstein, C. (1993) Effects of text structure on the impact of heard news. *Applied Cognitive Psychology*, 7: 381–95.

Bertrand, J.T., Brown, J.E. and Ward, V.M. (1992) Techniques for analysing focus group data. *Evaluation Review*, 16(2): 198–209.

Beville, H. (1985) *Audience Ratings*. Hillsdale, NJ: Lawrence Erlbaum Associates.

Biocca, F. (1991a) Models of a successful and unsuccessful ad: an exploratory analysis. In F. Biocca (ed.) *Television and Political Advertising, vol. 1: Psychological Processes*. Hillsdale, NJ: Lawrence Erlbaum Associates. pp. 91–124.

Biocca, F. (1991b) Viewers' mental models of political ads: towards a theory of the semantic processing of television. In F. Biocca (ed.) *Television and Political Advertising, vol. 1: Psychological Processes*. Hillsdale, NJ: Lawrence Erlbaum Associates. pp. 27–91.

Biocca, F. and David, P. (1990a) *How camera distance affects the perception of candidates during a presidential debate*. Unpublished manuscript, Center for Research in Journalism and Mass Communication, University of North Carolina at Chapel Hill.

Biocca, F. and David, P. (1990b) *Micro-shifts in audience opinion: a second-by-second analysis of the Omaha vice-presidential debate*. Paper presented at AAPOR, Lancaster, PA.

Biocca, F., David, P., Dion, A., Goodson, S., Lashley, M. and Tan, H.I. (1992) The effect of commercials on memory and perceived importance of news. *Mass Communication Review*, 19(2): 14–20.

Biocca, F., Neuwirth, K., Oshagun, H., Zhongdang, P. and Richards, J. (1987) *Prime-and-probe methodology: an experimental technique for studying film and television*. Paper presented at the meeting of the International Communication Association, Montreal.

Blank, D.M. (1977a) The Gerbner violence profile. *Journal of Broadcasting*, 21(4): 273–89.

Blank, D.M. (1977b) Final comments on the violence profile. *Journal of Broadcasting*, 21(4): 287–96.

Blankenburg, W.R. (1981) Structural determination of circulation. *Journalism Quarterly*, 58(4): 543–51.

Blankenburg, W.R. (1987) Predicting newspaper circulation after consolidation. *Journalism Quarterly*, 64(3): 585–7.

Bleyer, W. (1924) Research problems and newspaper analysis. *Journalism Bulletin*, 1(1): 17–22.

Blumer, H. (1933) *Movies and Conduct*. New York: Macmillan.

Blumler, J., Gurevitch, M. and Katz, E. (1985) Reaching out: a future for gratifications research. In K.E. Rosengren, L.A. Wenner and P. Palmgreen (eds) *Media Gratifications Research: Current Perspectives*. Beverly Hills, CA: Sage. pp. 225–74.

Blumler, J. and Katz, E. (1974) *The Uses of Mass Communications*. Newbury Park, CA: Sage.

Bogart, L. (1989) *Press and Public*. Hillsdale, NJ: Lawrence Erlbaum Associates.

Bogart, L. (1991) *Preserving the Press*. Hillsdale, NJ: Lawrence Erlbaum Associates.

Bohle, R.H. and Gracia, M.R. (1987) Reader response to color halftones and spot color in newspaper design. *Journalism Quarterly*, 64(4): 731–9.

Booth, C. (1889–1902) *Labour and Life of the People of London*. 17 volumes. London: Macmillan.

Bowley, A.L. and Barrett-Hurst, A.R. (1915) *Livelihood and Poverty: A Study in the Economic Conditions of Working Class Households in Northampton, Warrington, Stanley and Reading*. London: Bell.

Bowley, A.L. and Hogg, M.H. (1925) *Has poverty Diminished? A sequel to 'Livelihood and Poverty'*. London: King.

Bristol, T. and Fern, E.F. (1993) Using qualitative techniques to explore consumer attitudes: Insights from focus group theories. In *Advances in Consumer Research*, vol. 20. pp. 444–8.

Broadbent, D. (1958) *Perception and Communication*. London: Pergamon Press.

Brosius, H.B. and Kepplinger, H.M. (1990) The agenda-setting function of TV news. *Communication Research*, 17(2): 183–211.

Brown, M. (1994) Estimating newspaper and magazine readership. In R. Kent (ed.) *Measuring Media Audiences*. London: Routledge. pp. 105–44.

Brown, J.D., Bybee, L.R., Wearden, S.T. and Straughan, D.M. (1987) Invisible power: newspaper news sources and the limits of diversity. *Journalism Quarterly*, 64: 45–54.

Brown, J., Cramond, D.J. and Wilde, R. (1974) Displacement effects of television and the child's functional orientation to media. In J.G. Blumler and E. Katz (eds) *The Uses of Mass Communication*. Beverly Hills, CA: Sage. pp. 93–112.

Brown, J.D. and Schulze, L. (1993) The effects of race, gender and fandom on audience interpretation of Madonna's music videos. In B.S. Greenberg, J.D. Brown, and N.L. Buerkel-Rothfuss (eds) *Media, Sex and the Adolescent*. Cresskill, NJ: Hampton. pp. 263–76.

Bryant, J., Carveth, R. and Brown, D. (1981) Television viewing and anxiety: an experimental examination. *Journal of Communication*, 31: 106–19.

Bureau of Broadcast Measurement (1973) *Tests of Revised and Single Media Diaries*. Toronto: BBM.

Bureau of Broadcast Measurement (1974–75) *Research Programme 1974–5*. Toronto: BBM.

Burgess, J., Harrison, C. and Maiteny, P. (1991) Contested meanings: the consumption of news about nature conservation. *Media, Culture and Society*, 13: 499–519.

Burgoon, J., Burgoon, M. and Wilkinson, M. (1983) Dimensions of content readership in ten newspaper markets. *Journalism Quarterly*, 60(1): 74–80.

Burke, K. (1969) *A Grammar of Motives*. Berkeley, CA: University of California Press.

Byrne, N. (1978) Sociotemporal considerations of everyday life suggested by an empirical study of the bar milieu. *Urban Life*, 6: 417–38.

Calvert, S., Huston, A.C., Watkins, B.A. and Wright, J.C. (1982) The effects of selective attention to television forms on children's comprehension of content. *Child Development*, 53: 601–10.

Campbell, T., Wright, J. and Huston, A. (1987) Form cues and content difficulty as determinants of children's cognitive processing of televised educational messages. *Journal of Experimental Child Psychology*, 43: 311–27.

Cantril, H. and Allport, G. (1935) *The Psychology of Radio*. New York: Harper.

Cappella, J.N. and Street, R.L. (1989) Message effects: theory and research on mental models of messages. In J.J. Bradac (ed.) *Message Effects in Communication Science*. Newbury Park, CA: Sage. pp. 24–51.

Centerwall, B. (1989) Exposure to television as a cause of violence. In G. Comstock (ed.) *Public Communication and Behavior*, vol. 2. New York: Academic Press.

Ceulemans, M. and Fauconnier, G. (1979) *Mass Media: The Image, Role and Social Conditions of Women*, Report No. 84. Paris: UNESCO.

Chaffee, S. (1987) Assumptions and issues in communication science. In C. Berger and S. Chaffee (eds) *Handbook of Communication Science*. Newbury Park, CA: Sage.

Chaffee, S., McLeod, J.M. and Wackman, D. (1973) Family communication patterns and adolescent political participation. In J. Dennis (ed.) *Socialisation to Politics*. New York: John Wiley.

Chaffee, S. and Schleuder, J. (1986) Measurement and effects of attention to media news. *Human Communication Research*, 13(1): 76–107.

Chant, S. and Salter, M. (1937) The measurement of attitude toward war and the galvanic skin response. *Journal of Educational Psychology*, 28: 281–9.

Charlton, T., Abrahams, M. and Jones, K. (1995a) Rates and types of psychiatric disorder in pre-school pupils attending nursery classes in St Helena, South Atlantic. *Journal of Social Behaviour and Personality*, 10(1): 273–80.

Charlton, T., Lovemore, T., Essex, C. and Crowie, B. (1995b) Naturalistic rates of teacher approval and disapproval and on-task levels of first and middle school pupils in St Helena. *Journal of Social Behaviour and Personality*, 10(4): 1021–30.

Chatman, S. (1978) *Story and Discourse: Narrative Structure in Fiction and Film*. Ithaca, NY: Cornell University Press.

Cherry, C. (1953) Some experiments on the recognition of speech with one and two ears. *Journal of the Acoustical Society of America*, 23: 915–19.

Childers, T.L., Heckler, S.E. and Houston, M.J. (1986) Memory for the visual and verbal components of print advertisements. *Psychology and Marketing*, 3: 137–50.

Chomsky, N. (1965) *Aspects of the Theory of Syntax*. Cambridge, MA: MIT Press.

Click, J.W. and Baird, R. (1979) *Magazine Editing and Production*. Dubuque, IA: William C. Brown.

Click, J.W. and Stempel, R. (1982) *Reader Response to Front Pages with Modular Format and Color* (ANPA News Research Report No. 35). Reston, VA: ANPA News Research Center.

Clifford, B.R., Gunter, B. and McAleer, J. (1995) *Television and Children: Programme Evaluation, Comprehension and Impact*. Hillsdale, NJ: Lawrence Erlbaum Associates.

Coffin, T.E. and Tuchman, S. (1972) Rating television programs for violence: a comparison of five surveys. *Journal of Broadcasting*, 17(1): 3–20.

Cohen, B.C. (1963) *The Press and Foreign Policy*. Princeton, NJ: Princeton University Press.

Collett, P. and Lamb, R. (1986) *Watching People Watch Television*. Report to the Independent Broadcasting Authority, London.

Collins, W. (1983) Interpretation and inference in children's television viewing. In J. Bryant and D. Anderson (eds) *Children's Understanding of Television: Research on Attention and Comprehension*. New York: Academic Press. pp. 125–50.

Comstock, G. (1998) Television research: past problems and present issues. In J.K. Asamen and G.L. Berry (eds) *Research Paradigms, Television and Social Behavior*. Thousand Oaks, CA: Sage. pp. 11–36.

Converse, J.M. (1987) *Survey Research in the United States: Roots and Emergence, 1890–1960*. Berkeley: University of California Press.

Conway, M.M., Stevens, A.J. and Smith, R.G. (1975) The relation between media use and children's civic awareness. *Journalism Quarterly*, 8: 240–7.

Cook, T.D., Campbell, D.T. and Peracchio, L. (1990) Quasi-experimentation. In M.D. Dunnette and L.M. Hough (eds) *Handbook of Industrial and Organisational Psychology* (2nd edn), vol. 1. Chicago: Rand McNally. pp. 491–576.

Cook, T.D., Kendziersky, D.A. and Thomas, S.A. (1983) The implicit assumptions of television research: an analysis of the 1982 NIMH report on Television and Behavior. *Public Opinion Quarterly*, 47: 161–201.

Cooper, M. and Soley, L. (1990) All the right sources: a two-year study documents the bias in network reporting. *Mother Jones* (September), pp. 20–7, 45.

Corballis, M.C. (1980) Laterality and myth. *American Psychologist*, 35(3): 284–95.

Crigler, A.N., Just, M. and Neuman, W.L. (1994) Interpreting visual versus audio messages in television news. *Journal of Communication*, 44(4): 132–49.

Cumberbatch, G. and Howitt, D. (1989) *A Measure of Uncertainty: the Effects of the Mass Media*. London: John Libbey.

Curran, J. (1990) The "new revisionism" in mass communication research: a reappraisal. *European Journal of Communication*, 5(2–3): 135–64.

Curran, J., Gurevitch, M. and Woollacott, J. (1987) The study of the media: theoretical approaches. In O. Boyd-Barrett and P. Braham (eds) *Media, Knowledge and Power*. London: Routledge, pp. 57–79.

Currey, C.H. and Freeman, R.L. (1962) US Patent 3,056,135.

Dahlgren, P. (1980) TV news and the suppression of reflexivity. *Urban Life*, 9(2): 201–216.

Dale, E. and Chall, J.S. (1948) A formula for predicting readability. *Education Research Journal*, 27(1): 11–20.

Davies, M., Berry, C. and Clifford, B. (1985) Unkindest cuts? Some effects of picture editing on recall of television news information. *Journal of Educational Television*, 11: 85–98.

David, P. (1998) News concreteness and visual – verbal assumptions: do news pictures narrow the recall gap between concrete and abstract news? *Human Communication Research*, 25(2): 180–201.

Davis, F.J. (1952) Crime news in Colorado newspapers. *American Journal of Sociology*, 57: 325–30.

Dawson, M., Filian, D. and Schell, A. (1989) Is elicitation of the autonomic orienting response associated with allocation of processing resources? *Psychophysiology*, 26: 560–72.

De Fleur, M.L. (1964) Occupation roles as portrayed on television. *Public Opinion Quarterly*, 28: 57–74.

Deming, J. (1985) Hill Street Blues as narrative. *Critical Studies in Mass Communication*, 2: 1–22.

Diener, E. and DeFour, D. (1978) Does television violence enhance program popularity? *Journal of Personality and Social Psychology*, 36: 333–41.

Diener, E. and Woody, L.W. (1981) TV violence and viewer liking. *Communication Research*, 8: 281–306.

Dijk van, T. (1977) *Text and Context: Explanations in the Semantics and Pragmatics of Discourse*. London: Longman.

Dijk van, T. (1983) Discourse analysis: its development and application to the structure of news. *Journal of Communication*, 33(2): 20–43.

Dijk van, T. (1988) *News as Discourse*. Hillsdale, NJ: Lawrence Erlbaum Associates.

Dijk van, T. (1991) *Racism and the Press*. London: Routledge.

Dijk van, T. and Kintsch, W. (1983) *Strategies of Discourse Comprehension*. New York: Academic Press.

Dominick, J.R. (1972) Television and political socialisation. *Educational Broadcasting Review*, 6: 48–56.

Drew, D. and Grimes, T. (1987) Audio-visual redundancy and TV news recall. *Communication Research*, 14: 452–61.

Durand, J. (1987) Rhetorical figures in the advertising image. In J. Umiker-Sebeok (ed.) *Marketing and Semiotics*. Amsterdam: Mouton de Gruyter. pp. 295–319.

Durkin, K. (1985) Television and sex-role acquisition, 3: Counter-stereotyping. *British Journal of Social Psychology*, 24: 211–22.

Eaton, B.C. and Dominick, J.R. (1991) Product related programming and children's TV. *Journalism Quarterly*, 18: 67–75.

Edelstein, A.S. (1993) Thinking about the criterion variable in agenda setting research. *Journal of Communication*, 43(2): 85–99.

Edwardson, M., Grooms, D. and Pringle, P. (1976) Visualisation and TV news information gain. *Journal of Broadcasting*, 20: 373–80.

Edwardson, M., Grooms, D. and Proudlove, S. (1981) Television news information gain from interesting video vs talking heads. *Journal of Broadcasting*, 25: 15–24.

Edwardson, M., Kent, K., Engstrom, E. and Hofmann, R. (1992) Audio recall immediately following video change in television news. *Journal of Broadcasting and Electronic Media*, 36(4): 395–410.

Elliott, W.R. and Rosenberg, W.L. (1987) The 1985 Philadelphia newspaper strike: a uses and gratifications study. *Journalism Quarterly*, 64(4): 679–87.

Ericson, R.V., Baranek, P.M. and Chan, J.B. (1991) *Representing Order: Crime, Law and Justice in the News Media*. Milton Keynes: Open University Press.

Eron, L.D., Huesmann, L.R., Lefkowitz, M.M. and Walder, L.O. (1972) Does television violence cause aggression? *American Psychologist*, 27: 253–63.

Feshbach, S. (1961) The stimulating versus cathartic effects of a vicarious aggressive activity. *Journal of Abnormal and Social Psychology*, 63: 381–5.

Feshbach, S. and Singer, R.D. (1971) *Television and Aggression*. San Francisco: Jossey-Bass.

Feuer, J. (1986) *Dynasty*. Paper presented to International Television Studies Conference, London, July.

Fielding, R.V. and Lee, R.M. (eds) (1991) *Using Computers in Qualitative Research*. London: Sage.

Findahl, O. and Hoijer, B. (1976) *Fragments of Reality: an Experiment with News and TV Visuals*. Stockholm: Swedish Broadcasting Corporation, Audience and Program Research Department.

Findahl, O. and Hoijer, B. (1982) The problem of comprehension and recall of broadcast news. In J.F. Le Ny and W. Kintsch (eds) *Language and Comprehension*. Amsterdam: North-Holland. pp. 261–72.

Findahl, O. and Hoijer, B. (1984) *Comprehension Analysis: a Review of the Research and an Application to Radio and Television News*. Lund: Studentlitteratur.

Findahl, O. and Hoijer, B. (1985) Some characteristics of news memory and comprehension. *Journal of Broadcasting and Electronic Media*, 29(4): 379–96.

Fink, A. (1995a) *The Survey Handbook*. Thousand Oaks, CA: Sage.

Fink, A. (1995b) *How To Ask Survey Questions*. Thousand Oaks, CA: Sage.

Fiske, J. and Hartley, J. (1978) *Reading Television*. London: Methuen.

Flesch, R. (1943) *Marks of Readable Style*. New York: Columbia University Press.

Flesch, R. (1951) *How to Test Readability*. New York: Harper.

Fletcher, J. and Shimell, J. (1989) *Physiological indices of communication involvement and attention in the analysis of broadcast commercials*. Paper presented to Association for Consumer Research, New Orleans, LA.

Ford, P. (1934) *Work and Wealth in a Modern Port: An Economic Survey of Southampton*. London: Allen and Unwin.

Fowler, R. (1991) *Language in the News: Discourse and Ideology in the Press*. London: Routledge.

Fowler, G. and Smith, E. (1979) Readability of newspapers and magazines over time. *Newspaper Research Journal*, 1(1): 3–8.

Fowler, G. and Smith, E. (1982) Readability of delayed and immediate reward content in *Time and Newsweek*. *Journalism Quarterly*, 59(3): 431–4.

Fraczek, A. (1986) Socio-cultural environment, television viewing and the development of aggression among children in Poland. In L.R. Huesmann and L.D. Eron (eds) *Television and the Aggressive Child: A Cross-National Comparison*. Hillsdale, NJ: Lawrence Erlbaum Associates.

Franz, G. (1991) Methods of radio audience measurement comparing interview and diary techniques. In *The Expansion of the Broadcast Media: Does Research Meet the Challenge?* ESOMAR Seminar, Madrid, January. Amsterdam: ESOMAR.

Fraser, N. (1990) Rethinking the public sphere: A contribution to the critique of actually existing democracy. *Social Text*, 25/26, 56–80.

Frazier, P.J. and Gaziano, C. (1979) *Robert E. Park's Theory of News, Public Opinion and Social Control.* Lexington, KY: Journalism Monographs.

Freedman, J.L. (1984) Effect of television violence on aggressiveness. *Psychological Bulletin*, 96(2): 227–46.

Friedrich, L.K. and Stein, A.H. (1973) Aggressive and prosocial television programs and the natural behavior of preschool children. *Monographs of the Society for Research in Child Development*, 38(4), Serial No. 151.

Frost, W.A.K. (1969) The development of a technique for TV programme assessment. *Journal of the Market Research Society*, 11(1): 25–44.

Funkhouser, G.R. (1973) Trends in media coverage of the issues of the 60s. *Journalism Quarterly*, 50: 533–8.

Furnham, A. and Bitar, N. (1993) The stereotypical portrayal of men and women in British television advertisements. *Sex Roles*, 29(3/4): 297–310.

Furnham, A. and Gunter, B. (1985) Sex, presentation mode and memory for violent and non-violent news. *Journal of Educational Television*, 11: 99–105.

Furnham, A. and Voli, V. (1989) Gender stereotypes in Italian television advertisements. *Journal of Broadcasting and Electronic Media*, 33(2): 175–85.

Furu, T. (1962) *Television and Children's Life: a Before-After Study.* Tokyo: RTCRI (Radio and Television Culture Institute, Nippon Hogo Kyokai).

Furu, T. (1971) *The Functions of Television for Children and Adolescents.* Tokyo: Sophia University, Monumenta Nipponica.

Galen, D. and Ornstein, R. (1972) Lateral specialisation of cognitive mode: an EEG study. *Psychophysiology*, 9(4): 412–18.

Gauntlett, D. (1995) *Moving Experiences: Understanding Television Influences and Effects.* London: John Libbey.

Geen, R.G. and O'Neal, E.C. (1969) Activation of cue-elicited aggression by general arousal. *Journal of Personality and Social Psychology*, 11: 289–92.

Geiger, S. and Reeves, B. (1991) The effects of visual structure and content emphasis on the evaluation and memory for political candidates. In F. Biocca (ed.) *Television and Political Advertising*, vol. 1. Hillsdale, NJ: Lawrence Erlbaum Associates.

Geraci, P. (1984a) Comparison of graphic design and illustration use in three Washington DC newspapers. *Newspaper Research Journal*, 5(2): 29–40.

Geraci, P. (1984b) Newspaper illustration and readership: is USA Today on target? *Journalism Quarterly*, 21(2): 409–13.

Gerbner, G. (1972) Violence in television drama: trends and symbolic functions. In G.A. Comstock and E.A. Rubinstein (eds) *Television and Social Behavior, vol. 1: Media Content and Control.* Washington, DC: US Government Printing Office. pp. 28–187.

Gerbner, G. (1985) Children's Television: A National Disgrace *Pediatric Annals*, 14, 822–7.

Gerbner, G. (1992) Society's Storyteller: How television creates the myths by which we live. *Media & Values*, 59/60, 8–9.

Gerbner, G. and Gross, L. (1976) Living with television: the violence profile. *Journal of Communication*, 26: 173–99.

Gerbner, G., Gross, L., Eleey, M.E., Jackson-Beeck, M., Jeffries-Fox, S. and Signorielli, N. (1977) Television violence profile No. 8: the highlights. *Journal of Communication*, 27: 171–80.

Gerbner, G., Gross, L., Jackson-Beeck, M., Jeffries-Fox, S. and Signorielli, N. (1978) Cultural indicators: violence profile No. 9. *Journal of Communication*, 28: 176–207.

Gerbner, G., Gross, L., Signorielli, N., Morgan, M. and Jackson-Beeck, M. (1979) The demonstration of power: violence profile No. 10. *Journal of Communication*, 29: 177–96.

Gerbner, G., Gross, L., Morgan, M. and Signorielli, N. (1980) The "mainstreaming" of America: violence profile No. 11. *Journal of Communication*, 30: 10–29.

Gibbons, J., Anderson, D., Smith, R., Field, D. and Fischer, C. (1986) Young children's recall and reconstruction of audio and audiovisual narratives. *Child Development*, 57: 1014–23.

Giffard, A. (1989) *UNESCO and the Media*. New York: Longman.

Gitlin, T. (1978) Media sociology: the dominant paradigm. *Theory and Society*, 6: 205–53.

Glasgow Media Group (1976) *Bad News*. London: Routledge and Kegan Paul.

Goethals, G.R. and Zanna, M.P. (1979) The rule of social comparison in choice shifts. *Journal of Personality and Social Psychology*, 37: 1469–76.

Goldman, R. (1992) *Reading Ads Socially*. London: Routledge.

Goldman, R. and Papson, S. (1994) Advertising in the age of hypersignification. *Theory, Culture and Society*, 11(3): 23–54.

Gorney, R., Loye, D. and Steele, G. (1977) Impact of dramatized television entertainment on adult males. *American Journal of Psychology*, 134(2): 170–4.

Graber, D. (1984) *Processing the News*. New York: Longman.

Greenberg, B. (1975) British children and television violence. *Public Opinion Quarterly*, 39: 521–47.

Greenberg, B.S. and Brand, J.E. (1994) Minorities and the mass media: 1970s to 1990s. In J. Bryant and D. Zillmann (eds) *Media Effects: Advances in Theory and Research*. Hillsdale, NJ: Lawrence Erlbaum Associates. pp. 273–314.

Greenberg, B. and Gordon, T. (1972a) Perceptions of violence in television programs: critics and the public. In G.A. Comstock and E.A. Rubinstein (eds) *Television and Social Behavior, vol. 1: Content and Control*. Washington, DC: US Government Printing Office. pp. 244–58.

Greenberg, B. and Gordon, T. (1972b) Social class and racial differences in children's perceptions of televised violence. In G.A. Comstock and E.A. Rubinstein (eds) *Television and Social Behavior, vol. 5: Television's Effects: Further Explorations*. Washington, DC: US Government Printing Office.

Griffin, M., Hackett, R. and Zhao, Y. (1994) Challenging a master narrative: peace protest and the opinion/editorial discourse in the US press during the Gulf War. *Discourse and Society*, 5(4): 509–41.

Grimes, T. (1990) Audio-visual correspondence and its role in attention and memory. *Educational Technology Research and Development*, 38: 15–25.

Griswold, W.F. and Moore, R.L. (1989) Factors affecting readership of news and advertising in a small daily newspaper. *Newspaper Research Journal*, 10(2): 55–66.

Gunning, R. (1952) *The Techniques of Clear Writing*. New York: McGraw-Hill.

Gunter, B. (1979) Recall of television news items: effects of presentation mode, picture content and serial position. *Journal of Educational Television*, 5: 57–61.

Gunter, B. (1980) Remembering televised news: Effects of visual format on information gain. *Journal of Educational Television*, 6: 8–11.

Gunter, B. (1981) Measuring television violence: a review and suggestions for a new analytical perspective. *Current Psychological Reviews*, 1: 91–112.

Gunter, B. (1985a) *Dimensions of Television Violence*. Aldershot, UK: Gower.

Gunter, B. (1985b) News sources and news awareness: a British survey. *Journal of Broadcasting*, 29: 397–406.

Gunter, B. (1987a) *Television and the Fear of Crime*. London: John Libbey.

Gunter, B. (1987b) *Poor Reception: Misunderstanding and Forgetting Broadcast News*. Hillsdale, NJ: Lawrence Erlbaum Associates.

Gunter, B. (1988) The Perceptive Audience. In J.A.Anderson (ed.) *Communication Yearbook 11*. Beverly Hills, CA: Sage. pp. 22–50.

Gunter, B. (1995) Understanding the appeal of TV game shows. Media Psychologie, 7(2): 87–106.

Gunter, B. (1997a) An audience-based approach to assessing programme quality. In P. Winterhoff-Spurk and T.H.A. van der Voort (eds) *New Horizons in Media Psychology*. Opladen, Germany: Westdeutscher Verlag. pp. 11–34.

Gunter, B. (1997b) *Television and Gender Representation*, Luton, UK: John Libbey Media/University of Luton Press.

Gunter, B. (1998) *Understanding the Older Consumer: The Grey Market*. London: Routledge.

Gunter, B., Berry, C. and Clifford, B. (1981) Release from proactive interference with television news items: further evidence. *Journal of Experimental Psychology: Human Learning and Memory*, 7: 480–7.

Gunter, B., Clemens, J. and Wober, M. (1992) Defining television quality through audience reaction measures. In *Proceedings* of the ESOMAR/ARF Worldwide Broadcast Audience Research Symposium, Toronto, Canada, 1–3 June 1992.

Gunter, B., Charlton, T. and Lovemore, T. (1998) Television on St Helena: does the output give cause for concern? *Medien Psychologie*, 10: 184–203.

Gunter, B., Clifford, B. and Berry, C. (1980) Release from proactive interference with television news items: evidence for encoding dimensions within televised news. *Journal of Experimental Psychology: Human Learning and Memory*, 6: 216–23.

Gunter, B. and Furnham, A. (1984) Perceptions of television violence: effects of programme genre and physical form of violence. *British Journal of Social Psychology*, 23: 155–84.

Gunter, B. and Furnham, A. (1985) Androgyny and perceptions of male and female violence on television. *Human Factors*, 38: 353–9.

Gunter, B., Furnham, A. and Gietson, G. (1984) Memory for the news as a function of the channel of communication. *Human Learning*, 3: 265–71.

Gunter, B., Furnham, A. and Lineton, Z. (1995) Watching people watching television. *Journal of Educational Television*, 21(3): 165–91.

Gunter, B. and Harrison, J. (1998) *Violence on Television: an Analysis of Amount, Nature, Location and Origin of Violence in British Programmes*. London: Routledge.

Gunter, B., Harrison, J., Arundel, J., Osborn, R. and Crawford, M. (1996) *Violence on Television in Britain: A Content Analysis*. Report to the BBC, BSC, BSkyB, Channel 4, ITC and ITV. University of Sheffield, Department of Journalism Studies.

Gunter, B. and McAleer, J. (1997) *Children and Television* (2nd edn). London: Routledge.

Gunter, B., Svennevig, M. and Wober, M. (1986) *Television Coverage of the 1983 General Election*. Aldershot, UK: Gower.

Gunter, B. and Wober, M. (1983) Television viewing and public trust. *British Journal of Social Psychology*, 22: 174–6.

Gunter, B. and Wober, M. (1992) *The Reactive Viewer*. London: John Libbey.

Guthrie, T.L., Ludwin, W.G. and Jacob, S.B. (1988) A parsimonious regression model to predict metropolitan circulation in outlying counties. *Newspaper Research Journal*, 9(3): 59–60.

Habermas, J. (1989) *The Structural Transformation of the Public Sphere*. Cambridge, MA: MIT Press.

Haldane, I.R. (1970) Can attitudes be quantified? Measuring television audience reactions by multivariate analysis techniques. *Proceedings of the Market Research Society*, 39th Annual Conference, Brighton. pp. 59–86.

Hall, S. (1973) Encoding/decoding in television discourse. Stencilled Paper 7. Birmingham: Centre for Contemporary Cultural Studies, University of Birmingham.

Hall, S. (1980) Cultural studies: two paradigms. *Media, Culture and Society*, 2.

Hallonquist, T. and Peatman, J. (1947) Diagnosing your radio program. *Education on the Air, 1947 Yearbook of the Institute for Education by Radio*. Columbus: Ohio State University Press. pp. 463–74.

Hallonquist, T. and Suchman, E. (1944) Listening to the listener: experiences with the Lazarsfeld–Stanton Program Analyzer. In P. Lazarsfeld and F. Stanton (eds) *Radio Research 1942–43*. New York: Duell, Pearce and Sloan. pp. 265–334.

Halloran, J., Elliott, P. and Murdock, G. (1970) *Communications and Demonstrations*. Harmondsworth, UK: Penguin.

Handel, L. (1950) *Hollywood Looks at its Audience*. Urbana: University of Illinois Press.

Hansen, C.H. (1989) Priming sex role stereotypic event schemas with rock music videos: effects on impression favourability, trait inferences and recall of a subsequent male and female interaction. *Basic and Applied Social Psychology*, 10: 371–91.

Hansen, C.H. and Hansen, R.D. (1988) How rock music videos can change what is seen when boy meets girl: priming stereotypic appraisal of social interactions. *Sex Roles*, 19: 287–316.

Hansen, C.H. and Krygowski, W. (1994) Arousal-augmented priming effects: rock music videos and sex object schemas. *Communication Research*, 21: 124–37.

Harris, A. and Feinberg, J. (1977) Television and ageing: is what you see what you get? *Gerontologist*, 17: 464–8.

Hart, H. (1991) *Critical Communication Studies*. New York: Routledge.

Hartley, J. (1982) *Understanding News*. London: Methuen.

Hartnagel, T.F., Teevan, J.J. and McIntyre, J.J. (1975) Television violence and violent behaviour. *Social Forces*, 54(2): 341–51.

Harwood, J. and Giles, H. (1992) Don't make me laugh: age representations in a humorous context. *Discourse and Society*, 3(3): 403–36.

Haskins, J.B. and Flynne, L. (1974) Effects of headline typeface variation on reader interest. *Journalism Quarterly*, 51(4): 677–82.

Hawkins, R.P. and Pingree, S. (1990) Divergent psychological processes in constructing social reality from mass media content. In N. Signorielli and M. Morgan (eds) *Cultivation Analysis: New Directions in Media Effects Research*. Newbury Park, CA: Sage. pp. 35–50.

Hayes, T.J. and Tathum, C.B. (1989) *Focus Group Interviews: a Reader (2nd edn)*. Chicago: American Marketing Association.

Hennigan, K.M., Del Rosario, M.L., Heath, L., Cook, T.D., Wharton, J.D. and Calder, B.J. (1982) Impact of the introduction of television on crime in the United States: empirical findings and theoretical implications. *Journal of Personality and Social Psychology*, 42: 461–77.

Herman, E.S. and Chomsky, N. (1988) *Manufacturing Content*. New York: Pantheon Books.

Herzog, H. (1944) What do we really know about daytime serial listeners? In P.F. Lazarsfeld and F.N. Stanton (eds) *Radio Research 1942–43*. New York: Duell, Pearce and Sloan.

Heuvelman, A., Peeters, A. and d'Haenens, L. (1998) *The relationship between appreciation and retention of television news*. Paper presented at Television News Research: Recent European Approaches and Findings: an International Colloquium, Department of Communication, University of Nijmegen, The Netherlands, 22–24 October.

Hijmans, E. (1996) The logic of qualitative media content analysis: a typology. *Communications: The European Journal of Communication Research*, 21(1): 93–108.

Himmelweit, H., Oppenheim, A. and Vince, P. (1958) *Television and the Child*. London: Oxford University Press.

Hirsch, P. (1980) The 'scary' world of the non-viewer and other anomalies: a reanalysis of Gerbner et al's findings on cultivation analysis: Part I. *Communication Research*, 7: 403–56.

Hodge, B. and Tripp, D. (1986) *Children and Television*. Cambridge: Polity Press.

Hoffner, C., Cantor, J. and Thorson, E. (1988) Children's understanding of a televised narrative. *Communication Research*, 15: 227–45.

Hoijer, B. (1989) Television-evoked thoughts and their relation to comprehension. *Communication Research*, 16(2): 179–203.

Hoijer, B. (1990) Studying viewers' reception of television programmes: theoretical and methodological considerations. *European Journal of Communications*, 5: 29–56.

Hoijer, B. (1992a) Socio-cognitive structures and television reception. *Media, Culture and Society*, 14: 583–603.

Hoijer, B. (1992b) Reception of television narration as a socio-cognitive process: a schema-theoretical outline. *Poetics*, 21: 283–304.

Hopkins, R. and Fletcher, J.E. (1994) Electrodermal measurement: particularly effective for forecasting message influence on sales appeal. In A. Lane (ed.) *Measuring Psychological Responses to Media*. Hillsdale, NJ: Lawrence Erlbaum Associates. pp. 113–32.

Horton, D. and Wohl, R. (1956) Mass communication and parasocial interaction. *Journal of Psychiatry*, 19: 215–29.

Hoskins, R. (1973) A readability study of AP and UPI wire copy. *Journalism Quarterly*, 50(2): 360–2.

Hovland, C.I., Lumsdaine, A.A. and Sheffield, F.D. (1949) *Experiments in Mass Communication*. Princeton, NJ: Princeton University Press.

Huber, G.L. (1989) Qualitat versus Quantitat in der Inhaltsanalyse. In W. Bos and C. Tarnai (eds) *Angewandte Inhaltsanalyse in Empirischer Padagogik und Psychologie*. Munster: Waxmann. pp. 32–47.

Huesmann, L.R., and Eron, L.D. (eds) (1986) *Television and the Aggressive Child: a Cross-National Comparison*, Hillsdale, NJ: Lawrence Erlbaum Associates.

Huesmann, L.R., Eron, L.D., Lefkowitz, M.M. and Walder, L.O. (1984) Stability of aggression over time and generations. *Developmental Psychology*, 20(6): 1120–34.

Hughes, M. (1980) The fruits of cultivation analysis: a re-examination of the effects of television in fear of victimisation, alienation and approval of violence. *Public Opinion Quarterly*, 44: 287–302.

Hughes, D. (1992) Realtime response measures redefine advertising wearout. *Journal of Advertising Research*, 32: 61–77.

Hunziger, P. (1988) *Medien, Kommunikation und Gesellschaft*. Darmstadt: Wiss, Buchgemeinschaft.

Husson, W.G. and Hughes, C. (1981) *A time series analysis of children's attention to television in a naturalistic environment*. Paper presented to the Association for Education in Journalism, East Lansing, MI.

Huston, A.C. and Wright, J.C. (1983) Children's processing of television: the informative functions of formal features. In J. Bryant and D.R. Anderson (eds) *Children's Understanding of Television: Research on Attention and Comprehension*. New York: Academic Press. pp. 35–68.

Huston, A.C., Wright, J.C., Wartella, E., Rice, M.L., Watkins, B.A., Campbell, T. and Potts, R. (1981) Communicating more than content: formal features of children's television programmes. *Journal of Communication*, 31: 32–48.

Hvistendahl, J.K. (1977) Self-administered readership surveys: whole copy vs clipping method. *Journalism Quarterly*, 65(2): 511–14.

Ickes, W.J., Wickland, R.A. and Ferris, B.C. (1973) Objective self awareness and self esteem. *Journal of Experimental Psychology*, 9: 202–19.

Iyengar, S. (1987) Television news and citizens' explanations of national issues. *American Political Science Review*, 81, 1099–1120.

Iyengar, S. (1991) *Is Anyone Responsible? How Television Frames Political Issues.* Chicago: University of Chicago Press.

Iyengar, S. and Kinder, D.R. (1985) Psychological accounts of agenda-setting. In R. Perloff and S. Kraus (eds) *Mass Media and Political Thought.* Beverly Hills, CA: Sage.

Iyengar, S. and Kinder, D.R. (1987) *News that matters: Television and American Opinion.* Chicago: University of Chicago Press.

Iyengar, S., Peters, M.P. and Kinder, D.R. (1982) Experimental demonstration of the "not-so-minimal" consequences of television news programmes. *American Political Science Review*, 76: 848–58.

Iyengar, S., Kinder, D.R., Peters, M.P. and Krosnick, J.A. (1984) The evening news and presidential evaluations. *Journal of Personality and Social Psychology*, 46: 778–87.

Jabine, T., Straf, M.L., Tamur, J.M. and Tourangeau, R. (eds) (1984) *Cognitive Aspects of Survey Methodology: Building a Bridge Between Disciplines.* Report of the Advanced Seminar on Aspects of Survey Methodology, Washington DC.

Jay, M. (1973) *The Dialectical Imagination: A History of the Frankfurt School and the Institute of Social Research 1923–50.* London: Heinemann.

Jensen, K-B. (1986) *Making Sense of the News: Towards a Theory of an Empirical Model of reception for the Study of Mass Communication.* Aarhus: Aarhus University Press.

Jensen, K-B. (1987) News as ideology: economic statistics and political ritual in television network news. *Journal of Communication*, 37: 8–27.

Jensen, K-B. (1988) News as social resource. *European Journal of Communication*, 3(3): 275–301.

Jensen, K-B. (1991) Reception analysis: mass communication as the social production of meaning. In K.B. Jensen and N.W. Jankowski (eds) *A Handbook of Qualitative Methodologies for Mass Communication Research.* London: Routledge.

Jensen, K-B. and Rosengren, K. (1990) Five traditions in search of an audience. *European Journal of Communications*, 5(2–3).

Johnson, H. (1992) Audience reaction information: its use, its measurement and its future in the UK. In ARF/ESOMAR Worldwide Broadcast Audience Research Symposium, Toronto, 1–3 June. pp. 553–68.

Johnson, J.M. (1975) *Doing Field Research.* New York: Free Press.

Johnson, W. (1944) Studies in language behaviour. *Psychological Monographs*, 56(2).

Jordin, M. and Brunt, R. (1988) Constituting the television audience – a problem of method. In P. Drummond and R. Paterson (eds) *Television and Its Audience: International Research Perspectives.* London: British Film Institute.

Josephson, W.L. (1987) Television violence and children's aggression: testing the priming, social script and disinhibition predictions. *Journal of Personality and Social Psychology*, 53, 882–90.

Kahneman, D. (1973) *Attention and Effort.* Englewood Cliffs, NJ: Prentice Hall.

Kaplan, M.F. (1987) The influencing process in group decision making. In C. Hendrick (ed.) *Group Process.* Newbury Park, CA: Sage.

Kaplan, S.J. (1992) A conceptual analysis of form and content in visual metaphors. *Communication*, 32: 144–61.

Katz, E. (1959) Mass communications research and popular culture. *Studies in Public Communication*, 2: 10–19.

Katz, E. (1980) On conceptualising media effects. *Studies in Communications*, 1: 119–41.

Katz, E. (1988) On conceptualising media effects: another look. In S. Oskamp (ed.) *Applied Social Psychology Annual, vol. 8., Television as a Social Issue.* Newbury Park, CA: Sage. pp. 361–74.

Katz, E., Blumler, J. and Gurevitch, M. (1974) Utilisation of mass communication by the individual. In J.G. Blumler and E. Katz (eds) *The Uses of Mass Communications: Current Perspectives on Gratifications Research.* Beverly Hills, CA: Sage.

Katz, E. and Lazarsfeld, P. (1955) *Personal Influence.* New York: Free Press.

Katz, E. and Liebes, T. (1986) Mutual aid in the decoding of Dallas: preliminary notes from a cross-cultural study. In P. Drummond and R. Patterson (eds) *Television in Transition.* London: British Film Institute. pp. 197–8.

Kelly, G. (1955) *The Psychology of Personal Constructs.* New York: Norton.

Kelly, J.D. (1985) The data-ink ratio and accuracy of newspaper graphics. *Journalism Quarterly,* 66(3): 623–39.

Kenny, D.A. and Judd, C.M. (1984) Estimating the nonlinear and interactive effects of latent variables. *Psychological Bulletin,* 96: 201–210.

Kenney, D., Milavsky, J.R., Kessler, R.C., Stipp, H.H. and Rubens, W.S. (1984) The NBC study and television violence. *Journal of Communication,* 34(1): 176–88.

Kepplinger, H.M. (1989) Content analysis and reception analysis. *American Behavioral Scientist,* 33(2): 175–82.

Kepplinger, H.M. and Roth, H. (1979) Creating a crisis: German mass media and oil supply in 1973–74. *Public Opinion Quarterly,* 43: 285–96.

Kepplinger, H.M. and Staab, J.F. (1992) *das Aktuelle in RTL plus. Analysemethoden-Untersuchungsergebnisse – Interpretationsmuster.* Munchen: Reinhard Fischer.

Kerlinger, F.N. (1986) *Foundations of Behavioural Research* (3rd edn). New York: Holt, Rinehart and Winston.

Kinder, M. (1991) *Playing with power on Movies, Television and Video Games: From Muppet Babies to Teenage Mutant Ninja Turtles.* Berkeley: University of California Press.

Kinsbourne, M. (1982) Hemispheric specialisation and the growth of human understanding. *American Psychologist,* 37(4): 411–20.

Kintsch, W. (1974) *The Representation of Meaning in Memory.* New York: Wiley.

Kintsch, W. and van Dijk, T. (1978) Toward a model of text comprehension and production. *Psychological Review,* 85: 363–94.

Kirkham, M.A. and Wilcox, P. (1994) Measuring what is being watched. In ESOMAR/ARF Worldwide Electronic and Broadcast Audience Research Symposium, Paris, 1–4 May. pp. 85–90.

Klapper, T. (1960) *The Effects of Mass Communication,* Glencoe, IL: Free Press.

Knight, G. and Dean, T. (1982) Myth and the structure of news. *Journal of Communication,* 32(2): 144–61.

Kosicki, G.M. (1993) Problems and opportunities in agenda setting research. *Journal of Communication,* 43(2): 120–7.

Kracauer, S. (1952) The challenge of qualitative content analysis. *Public Opinion Quarterly,* 16: 631–42.

Krippendorf, K. (1980) *Content Analysis: an Introduction to its Methodology.* Beverly Hills, CA: Sage.

Krull, R. (1983) Children learning to watch television. In J. Bryant and D.R. Anderson (eds) *Children's Understanding of Television: Research on Attention and Comprehension.* New York: Academic Press. pp. 103–23.

Krull, R. and Husson, W. (1979) Children's attention: the case of TV viewing. In E. Wartella (ed.) *Children Communicating*. Sage Annual Reviews of Communication Research, vol. 7. Beverly Hills, CA: Sage.

Krull, R. and Watt, J.H. (1975) *Television program complexity and ratings*. Paper presented to the American Association for Public Opinion Research, Itasca, IL.

Krull, R., Watt, J.H. and Lichty, L.W. (1977) Entropy and structure: two measures of complexity in television programmes. *Communication Research*, 4: 61–86.

Kubey, R. (1980) Television and ageing: past, present, future. *Gerontologist*, 20: 16–25.

Kubey, R. and Csikszentmihalyi, M. (1990) *Television and the Quality of Life: How Viewing Shapes Everyday Experience*. Hillsdale, NJ: Lawrence Erlbaum Associates.

Kubey, R., White, W., Saphir, M., Chen, H. and Appiah, O. (1996) *Social effects of direct broadcast satellite television: from 3 to 60 channels overnight*. Symposium presented at the meeting of the Speech Communication Association, San Diego.

Lacy, S. and Fico, F. (1991) The link between content quality and circulation. *Newspaper Research Bureau*, 12(2): 46–56.

Lacy, S., Fico, F. and Simon, T.F. (1991) Fairness and balance in the prestige press. *Journalism Quarterly*, 68(3): 363–70.

Lacy, S. and Sohn, A. (1990) Correlations of newspaper content with circulation in the suburbs. *Journalism Quarterly*, 67(4): 785–93.

Lagerspetz, K.M., Vlamero, V. and Akademi, A. (1986) Television and aggressive behavior among Finnish children. In L.R. Huesmann and L.D. Eron (eds) *Television and the Aggressive Child: a Cross-national Comparison*. Hillsdale, NJ: Lawrence Erlbaum Associates. pp. 81–117.

Lagerspetz, K.M., Wahlroos, C. and Wendelin, C. (1978) Facial expression of pre-school children while watching televised violence. *Scandinavian Journal of Psychology*, 19: 213–22.

Lang, A. (1994) What can the heart tell us about thinking? In A. Lang (ed.) *Measuring Psychological Responses to Media*. Hillsdale, NJ: Lawrence Erlbaum Associates. pp. 99–112.

Lang, P., Bradley, M. and Cuthbert, B. (1992) A motivational analysis of emotion: reflex-cortex connections. *Psychological Science*, 3: 44–9.

Larkin, E. and Hecht, T. (1979) Research assistance for the non-metro newspaper, 1979. *Newspaper Research Journal*, prototype edition: 62–6.

Lasorsa, D. and Reese, S. (1990) News source use in the crash of 1987: a study of four national media. *Journal Quarterly*, 67: 60–71.

Lasswell, H.D. (1949) The structure and function of communication in society. In L. Bryson (ed.) *The Communication of Ideas*. New York: Glencoe. pp. 37–51.

Lazarsfeld, P., Berelson, B. and Gaudet, H. (1944) *The People's Choice*. New York: Columbia University Press.

Lazarsfeld, P. and Merton, R. (1948) Mass communication, popular taste, and organised social action [Reprinted in W. Schramm (ed.) *Mass Communication* (2nd edn)]. Urbana: University of Illinois Press.

Lazarsfeld, P. and Obershall, A.R. (1965) Max Weber and empirical research. *American Sociological Review*, April, 185–99.

Lazarsfeld, P. and Stanton, F. (1941) *Radio Research*. New York: Duell, Pearce and Sloan.

Lefkowitz, M.M., Eron, L.D., Walder, L.O. and Huesmann, L. R. (1972) Television violence and child aggression: a follow-up study. In G.A. Comstock and E.A. Rubinstein (eds) *Television and Social Behavior, vol. 3: Television and Adolescent Aggressiveness*. Rockville, MD: National Institute of Mental Health. pp. 35–135.

Lefkowitz, M.M., Eron, L.D., Walder, L.O. and Huesmann, L.R. (1977) *Growing Up to be Violent.* New York: Pergamon.

Lévi-Strauss, C. (1963) *Structural Anthropology.* New York: Penguin.

Levy, M.R. (1978) The audience experience with television news. *Journalism Monographs,* No. 55.

Levy, M.R. (1982) The Lazarsfeld – Stanton programme analyzer: an historical note. *Journal of Communication,* 32(4): 30–8.

Leyens, J-P., Herman, G. and Durand, M. (1982) The influence of an audience upon the reactions to filmed violence. *European Journal of Social Psychology,* 12: 131–42.

Leyens, J-P. and Parke, R.D. (1975) Aggressive slides can induce a weapons effect. *European Journal of Social Psychology,* 5: 229–36.

Leyens, J-P., Parke, R., Camino, L. and Berkowitz, L. (1975) Effects of movie violence on aggression in a field setting as a function of group dominance and cohesion. *Journal of Personality and Social Psychology,* 32: 346–60.

Leymore, V.L. (1975) *Hidden Myth: Structure and Symbolism in Advertising.* London: Heinemann.

Libresco, J.D. (1983) Focus groups: Madison Avenue meets public policy. *Public Opinion,* August/September: 51–3.

Liebes, T. (1992) Decoding television news: the political discourse of Israeli hawks and doves. *Theory and Society,* 21: 357–81.

Liebes, T. and Katz, E. (1986) Patterns of involvement in television fiction: a comparative analysis. *European Journal of Communication,* 1(2): 151–72.

Liebes, T. and Katz, E. (1989) Critical abilities of TV viewers. In E. Seiter, H. Borchers, G. Kreutzmer and E.M. Warth (eds) *Remote Control.* London: Routledge and Kegan Paul. pp. 204–29.

Liebes, T. and Katz, E. (1990) *The Export of Meaning.* New York: Oxford University Press.

Liebes, T. and Livingstone, S. (1994) The structure of family and the romantic ties in soap opera: an ethnographic approach. *Communication Research,* 21(6): 717–41.

Lindlof, T. (1988) Media audiences as intrepretive communities. In J.A. Anderson (ed.) *Communication Yearbook 11.* Newbury Park, CA: Sage. pp. 81–107.

Lindlof, T. (1995) *Qualitative Communication Research Methods.* Thousand Oaks, CA: Sage.

Lindlof, T. and Meyer, T.P. (1987) Mediated communication as ways of seeing, acting, and constructing culture: the tools and foundations of qualitative research. In T.R. Lindlof (ed.) *Natural Audiences: Qualitative Research of Media Uses and Effects.* Norwood, NJ: Ablex. pp. 1–30.

Lindlof, T., Shatzer, M.S. and Wilkinson, D. (1988) Accommodation of video and television in the American family. In J. Lull (ed.) *World Families Watch Television.* Newbury Park, CA: Sage. pp. 158–92.

Linsky, M. (1986) *Impact: How the Press Affects Federal Policymaking.* New York: W.W. Norton.

Lipschultz, J.H. (1991) The nonreader problem: a closer look at avoiding the newspaper. *Newspaper Research Journal,* 8(4): 59–70.

Littlejohn, S.W. (1983) *Theories of Human Communication.* (2nd edn) Belmont, CA: Wadsworth.

Livingstone, S. (1989) Interpretive viewers and structured programmes. *Communication Research,* 16(1): 25–57.

Livingstone, S. (1990) The meaning of domestic technologies: a personal construct analysis of familial gender relations. In R. Silverstone and E. Hirsch (eds) *Consuming Technologies: Media and Information Technologies in Domestic Spaces.* London: Routledge. pp. 113–30.

Livingstone, S. and Green, G. (1986) Television advertisements and the portrayal of gender. *British Journal of Social Psychology,* 25: 149–54.

Livingstone, S. and Lunt, P. (1996) *Talk on Television: Audience Participation and Public Debate.* London: Routledge.

Loftus, E.F., Fienberg, S. and Tamur, J.M. (1985) Cognitive psychology meets the national survey. *American Psychologist*, 40: 175–80.

Long, M. and Simon, R. (1974) The roles and statuses of women and children on family TV programmes. *Journalism Quarterly*, 51: 100–10.

Lorch, E., Bellack, D. and Augsbach, L. (1987) Young children's memory for televised stories: effects of importance. *Child Development*, 58: 453–63.

Lorch, E.P. (1994) *Measuring children's cognitive processing of television.* In A. Lang (ed.) *Measuring Psychological Responses to Media.* Hillsdale, NJ: Lawrence Erlbaum Associates, pp. 209–26.

Loye, D., Gorney, R. and Steele, G. (1977) Effects of television: an experimental field study. *Journal of Communication*, 27: 206–16.

Lu, D. and Kiewit, D.A. (1987) Passive people meters: a first step. *Journal of Advertising Research*, 23: 9–14.

Lull, J. (1978) Choosing television programmes by family vote. *Communication Quarterly*, 26: 53–7.

Lull, J. (1980) The social uses of television. *Human Communication Research*, 6: 197–209.

Lull, J. (1982) How families select television programmes: a mass observational study. *Journal of Broadcasting*, 26: 801–11.

Lull, J. (1985) Ethnographic studies of broadcast media audiences: notes on method. In J. Dominick and J. Fletcher (eds) *Broadcasting Research Methods.* Boston: Allyn and Bacon.

Lull, J. (1988) Critical response: the audience as nuisance. *Critical Studies in Mass Communication*, 5: 239–43.

Lull, J. (1990) *Inside Family Viewing.* London: Routledge.

Lunt, P. and Livingstone, S. (1996) Rethinking the focus group in media and communication research. *Journal of Communication*, 46(2): 79–98.

Lynn, J. and Bennett, E. (1980) Newspaper readership patterns in non-metropolitan communities. *Newspaper Research Journal*, 1(4): 18–24.

MacBeth, T. (1996) Indirect effects of television: creativity, persistence, school achievement, and participation in other activities. In T.M. Macbeth (ed.) *Tuning in to Young Viewers: Social Science Perspectives on Television.* Thousand Oaks, CA: Sage. pp. 149–219.

MacBeth, T. (1998) Quasi-experimental research on television and behavior. In J.K. Asamen and G.L. Berry (eds) *Research Paradigms, Television and Social Behavior.* Thousand Oaks, CA: Sage. pp. 109–51.

McCarthy, E.D., Langner, T.S., Gerstein, J.C., Eisenberg, V.G. and Orzeck, L. (1975) Violence and behavior disorders. *Journal of Communication*, 25(4): 71–85.

McClure, R. and Patterson, T. (1973) *Television News and Voter Behavior in the 1972 Presidential Election.* Unpublished paper, American Political Science Association.

McCombs, M. (1977) *Newspaper Readership and Circulation* (ANPA News Research report No. 3). Reston, VA: ANPA News Research Center.

McCombs, M. (1981) The agenda-setting approach. In D.D. Nimmo and K.R. Sanders (eds) *Mass Communication Review Yearbook 2.* Newbury Park, CA: Sage. pp. 219–24.

McCombs, M., Mullins, L.E. and Weaver, D. (1974) *Why People Subscribe and Cancel: A Stop-Start Survey of Three Daily Newspapers.* (ANPA News Research Bulletin No. 3). Reston, VA: ANPA News Research Center.

McCombs, M.E. and Shaw, D.L. (1972) The agenda-setting function of the press. *Public Opinion Quarterly*, 36(2): 176–87.

McIntyre, J.J., Teevan, J.J. and Hartnagel, T. (1972) Television violence and deviant behavior. In G.A. Comstock and E.A. Rubinstein (eds) *Television and Social Behavior, vol. 3: Television and Adolescent Aggressiveness.* Washington, DC: US Government Printing Office.

McLaughlin, H. (1969) SMOG grading: a new readability formula. *Journal of Reading*, 22(4): 639–46.

McLaughlin, L. (1991) Discourse of prostitution/discourses of sexuality. *Critical Studies in Mass Communication*, 8: 249–72.

McLeod, J., Atkin, C. and Chaffee, S. (1972) Adolescents, parents and television use: adolescent self-report measures from Maryland and Wisconsin samples. In G.A. Comstock and E.A. Rubinstein (eds) *Television and Social Behavior, vol. 3: Television and Adolescent Aggressiveness*. Washington, DC: US Government Printing Office.

McLeod, J.M., Becker, L.B. and Byrnes, J.E. (1974) Another look at the agenda setting function of the press. *Communication Research*, 1: 131–66.

McQuail, D. (1985) With the benefits of hindsight: reflections of uses and gratifications research. In M. Gurevitch and M.R. Levy (eds) *Mass Communication Review Yearbook*, vol. 5. Beverly Hills, CA: Sage. p. 131.

McQuail, D. (1994) *Mass Communication Theory: An Introduction*. London: Sage.

Mead, G.H. (1934) *Mind, Self and Society*. Chicago: University of Chicago Press.

Meadowcroft, J. and Watt, J. (1989) *Fourier analysis as a method of observing children's attention spans*. Paper presented to the International Communication Association, San Francisco, CA.

Meadowcroft, J.M. and Reeves, B. (1989) Influence of story schema development on children's attention to television. *Communication Research*, 16(3): 352–74.

Medrich, E.A., Roizen, J.A., Rubin, V. and Buckley, S. (1982) *The Serious Business of Growing Up: a Study of Children's Lives Outside School*. Berkeley: University of California Press.

Merten, K. (1995) *Inhaltsanalyse: Eine Einfuhrung in Theorie, Methode und Praxis*. Opladen: Westdeutscher Verlag.

Merten, K. (1996) Reactivity in content analysis. *Communications: The European Journal of Communication Research*, 21(1): 65–76.

Merten, K. and Teipen, P. (1991) *Empirische Kommunikationsforschung. Darstellung, Kritik, Evaluation*. Munchen: Olschlager.

Merton, R. (1946) *Mass Persuasion*. New York: Free Press.

Merton, R.K. (1987) The focused interview and focus groups: continuities and discontinuities. *Public Opinion Quarterly*, 51: 550–66.

Merton, R. and Kendall, P.L. (1946) The focused interview. *American Journal of Sociology*, 51: 541–57.

Merton, R., Fiske, M. and Kendall, P.L. (1956) *The Focused Interview*. A Report of the Bureau of Applied Social Research, Columbia University, New York: Free Press.

Meyer, T.P. (1995) Integrating information technologies in the household: using case studies to understand complex and rapidly changing processes. In D. Torten (ed.) *Living and Working in Cyberspace: New Technologies at Home and Work*. Kingston: University of Rhode Island Press.

Meyer, T.P. and Meyer, K.A. (1994) The videocassette recorder: an historical analysis of consumer expectations and post-purchase uses and satisfaction. In R. King (ed.) *Research in Retailing: the Future Agenda*. Richmond, VA: Academy of Marketing Science. pp. 75–9.

Meyrowitz, J. (1985) *No Sense of Place: the Impact of Electronic Media on Social Behavior*. New York: Oxford University Press.

Mielke, K. (1983) Formative research on appeal and comprehension in 3-2-1 CONTACT. In J. Bryant and D.R. Anderson (eds) *Children's Understanding of Television: Research on Attention and Comprehension*. New York: Academic Press. pp. 241–64.

Milavsky, J.R., Kessler, R., Stipp, H. and Rubens, W.S. (1982) *Television and Aggression: Results of a Panel Study*. New York: Academic Press.

Milgram, S. and Shotland, R.L. (1973) *Television and Antisocial Behavior: Field Experiments*. New York: Academic Press.

Millard, W. (1989) *Research using the Millard System (Televac)*. (Research report) Alexandria, VA: W.J. Millard.

Millard, W. (1992) A history of handsets for direct measurement of audience response. *International Journal of Public Opinion Research*, 4(1): 1–17.

Miller, M.M. and Reeves, B. (1976) Dramatic TV content and children's sex-role stereotypes. *Journal of Broadcasting*, 20: 35–50.

Mills, Wright, C. (1951) *White Collar*. New York: Oxford University Press.

Mills, Wright, C. (1956) *The Power Elite*. New York: Oxford University Press.

Mills, Wright, C. (1959) *The Sociological Imagination*. New York: Oxford University Press.

Morgan, D.L. (1988) *Focus Groups and Qualitative Research*. Newbury Park, CA: Sage.

Morgan, D.L. (1993) *Successful Focus Groups: Advancing the State of the Art*. Newbury Park, CA: Sage.

Morley, D. (1980) *The 'Nationwide' Audience: Structure and Decoding*, London: British Film Institute.

Morley, D. (1981) The 'Nationwide Audience': a critical postscript. *Screen Education*, 39.

Morley, D. (1985) Cultural transformations: The politics of resistance. *Mass Communication Review Yearbook*, 5: 237–50.

Morley, D. (1986) *Family Television: Cultural power and Domestic Leisure*. London: Comedia Publishing Company.

Morley, D. (1992) *Television, Audiences and Cultural Studies*. London: Routledge.

Morley, D. and Silverstone, R. (1990) Domestic communications. *Media, Culture and Society*, 12(1).

Morrison, D. (1992a) *Television and the Gulf War*. London: John Libbey.

Morrison, D. (1992b) *Conversations with Voters*. (1992 General Election) Report to the British Broadcasting Corporation and Independent Television Commission, Institute of Communications, University of Leeds.

Morrison, D. (1998) *The Search for a Method: Focus Groups and the Development of Mass Communication Research*. Luton: University of Luton Press.

Morrison, D., MacGregor, B. and Millwood-Hargrave, A. (1994) Beyond focus groups: understanding audience response to programmes through interactive methodology. Paper in *Proceedings of the ESOMAR/ARF Worldwide Electronic and Broadcast Audience Research Symposium*, 1–4 May, 1994. pp. 359–76.

Morrison, D. and Tumber, H. (1988) *Journalists at War*. London: Sage.

Moser, C.A. and Kalton, G. (1971) *Survey Methods in Social Investigation*. Aldershot: Gower.

Murdock, G. (1989) Critical inquiry and audience activity. In B. Dervin et al. (eds) *Rethinking Communication, vol. 2: Paradigm Exemplars*. London: Sage. pp. 226–49.

Murray, J.P. (1972) Television in inner-city homes: viewing behavior of young boys. In E.A. Rubinstein, G.A. Comstock and J.P. Murray (eds) *Television and Social Behavior, vol. 4: Television in Day-to-Day Life: Patterns of Use*. Washington, DC: US Government Printing Office.

Murray, J.P. (1973) Television and violence: implications of the Surgeon General's research program. *American Psychologist*, 28: 472–8.

Murray, J.P. and Kippax, S. (1977) Television diffusion and social behaviour in the community: a field experiment. *Australian Journal of Psychology*, 29(1): 31–43.

Murray, J.P. and Kippax, S. (1978) Children's social behaviour in three towns with different television experiences. *Journal of Communication*, 28: 19–29.

Mustonen, A. and Pulkkinen, L. (1997) Television violence: a development of a coding scheme. *Journal of Broadcasting and Electronic Media*, 41: 168–89.

Mutz, D.C., Roberts, D.F. and van Vuuren, D.P. (1993) Reconsidering the displacement hypothesis: Television's influence on children's time use. *Communication Research*, 20(1): 51–75.

Nestvold, K. (1972) Cloze procedure correlation with perceived readability. *Journalism Quarterly*, 49(3): 592–4.

Neuchterlain, K., Goldstein, M., Ventura, J. and Dawson, M. (1989) Patient – environment relationships in schizophrenia: information processing, communication deviance, autonomic arousal and stressful life events. *British Journal of Psychiatry*, 165 (Suppl. 5): 84–9.

Neuman, W.L. (1994) *Social Research Methods: Qualitative and Quantitative Approaches*. Boston: Allyn and Bacon.

Newcomb, W.R. (1976) *Television: The Most Popular Art*. Garden City, NY: Doubleday/Anchor.

Newcomb, H. (1978) Assessing the Violence Profile of Gerbner and Gross: a humanistic critique and suggestion. *Communication Research*, 5(3): 264–82.

Newcomb, H. (1981) One night of prime time: an analysis of television's multiple choice. In J. Carey (ed.) *Media, Myths and Narratives*. Beverly Hills, CA: Sage. pp. 88–113.

Nielsen, A.C. (1992) *Nielsen Media Research: The Quality Behind the Numbers*. New York: A.C. Nielsen.

O'Carroll, M., O'Neal, E.C. and Macdonald, P.J. (1977) Influence upon imitative aggression of an imitating peer. *Journal of Social Psychology*, 101: 313–14.

Olson, J. and Ray, W. (1983) Brain wave responses to emotional versus attribute oriented television commercials. Working paper No. 83–108, Marketing Science Institute, Cambridge, MA 02138.

Omanson, R.C. (1982) An analysis of narratives: identifying central supportive and distracting content. *Discourse Processes*, 5: 15–28.

O'Neal, E.C., Macdonald, P.J., Cloninger, C. and Levine, D. (1979) Coactor's behaviour and imitative aggression. *Motivation and Emotion*, 3: 313–14.

Oppenheim, A.N. (1992) *Questionnaire Design, Interviewing and Attitude Measurement*. London: Pinter Publishers.

ORC (1972) News and current affairs. London: Opinion Research Centre, 10477.

Osborn, D.K. and Endsley, R.C. (1971) Emotional reactions of young children to TV violence. *Child Development*, 42: 321–31.

Osgood, C., Suci, G.J. and Tannenbaum, P. (1957) *The Measurement of Meaning*. Urbana: University of Illinois Press.

Palmer, E.L. (1974) Formative research in the production of television for children. In D.E. Olson (ed.) *Media and Symbols: the Forms of Expression, Communication, and Education* (Seventy-Third Yearbook of the National Society for the Study of Education). Chicago: University of Chicago Press.

Palmer, E.L., Crawford, J.J., Kielsmeier, C.J. and Inglis, L. (1968) *A comparative study of current educational television programs for preschool children*. Monmouth: Oregon State System of Higher Education.

Palmer, P. (1986) *The Lively Audience: a Study of Children Around the TV Set*. Sydney: Allen and Unwin.

Parke, R., Berkowitz, L., Leyens, J-P., West, S. and Sebastian, R. (1977) Some effects of violent and non-violent movies on the behavior of juvenile delinquents. In L. Berkowitz (ed.) *Advances in Experimental Social Psychology*, vol. 10. New York: Academic Press.

Parry-Giles, T. (1994) Ideological anxiety and the censored text: real lives – at the edge of the union. *Critical Studies in Mass Communication*, 11: 54–72.

Parsons, T. (1968/1937) *The Structure of Social Action, vol 2*. New York: Free Press.

Pasternak, S. and Utt, S.H. (1990) Reader use and understanding of newspaper infographics. *Newspaper Research Journal*, 11(2): 28–41.

Patterson, T. and McClure, R. (1976) *The Unseeing Eye*. New York: G.P. Putnam's.

Payne, G.A., Severn, J.J. and Dozier, D.M. (1988) Uses and gratifications motives as indicators of magazine readership. *Journalism Quarterly*, 65(4): 909–13.

Penrose, J., Weaver, D., Cole, R. and Shaw, D. (1974) The newspaper non-reader ten years later. *Journalism Quarterly*, 51(4): 631–9.

Perloff, R., Wartella, E. and Becker, L. (1982) Increasing learning from TV news. *Journalism Quarterly*, 59: 83–6.

Phillips, D. (1974) The influence of suggestion on suicide: substantive and theoretical implications of the Werther effect. *American Sociological Review*, 39: 340–54.

Phillips, D. (1977) Motor vehicle fatalities increase just after publicised suicide stories. *Science*, 196: 1464–5.

Phillips, D. (1978) Airplane accident fatalities increase just after stories about murder and suicide. *Science*, 201: 148–50.

Phillips, D. (1979) Suicide, motor vehicle fatalities, and the mass media: evidence toward a theory of suggestion. *American Journal of Sociology*, 84: 1150–74.

Phillips, D. (1982) The impact of fictional television stories on US adult fatalities: new evidence on the effect of the mass media on violence. *American Journal of Sociology*, 87: 1340–9.

Phillips, D. (1983) The impact of mass media violence on US homicides. *American Sociological Review*, 48: 560–8.

Phillips, D. and Hensley, J.E. (1984) When violence is rewarded or punished: the impact of mass media stories on homicide. *Journal of Communication*, 34: 101–16.

Philport, J. (1980) The psychology of viewer program evaluation. In J. Anderson (ed.) *Proceedings of the 1980 Technical Conference on Qualitative Television Ratings*. Washington, DC: Corporation for Public Broadcasting. pp. B1–B17.

Pierce, C. (1931) *Collected Papers*. Cambridge, MA: MIT Press.

Pitiela, V. (1992) Beyond the news story: news as discursive composition. *European Journal of Communication*, 7(1): 37–67.

Poindexter, P. (1978) *Non-Readers, Why They Don't Read*. (ANPA News Research Report No. 9). Reston, VA: ANPA News Research Center.

Porter, W.C. and Stephens, F. (1989) Estimating readability: A study of Utah editors' abilities. *Newspaper Research Journal*, 10(2): 87–96.

Posner, M. (1982) Cumulative development of attention theory. *American Psychologist*, 37: 168–79.

Potter, W.J., Linz, D., Wilson, B.J., Kunkel, D., Donnerstein, E., Smith, S.L. Blumenthal, E. and Gray, T. (1996) *Content Analysis of Entertainment Television: New Methodological Developments*. Paper presented at the Duke University Conference on Media Violence and Public Policy in the Media, Durham, NC, 27–29 June.

Potter, J. and Wetherell, M. (1994) Analysing discourse. In A. Bryman and R. Burgers (eds) *Analyzing Qualitative Data*. London: Routledge. pp. 47–66.

Potter, J., Wetherell, M. and Chitty, A. (1991) Quantification rhetoric – cancer on television. *Discourse and Society*, 2(3): 333–65.

Potts, R., Doppler, M. and Hernandez, M. (1994) Effects of television content on physical risk-taking in children. *Journal of Experimental Child Psychology*, 58: 321–31.

Powers, E., Goudy, W. and Keith, P. (1978) Congruence between panel and recall data in longitudinal research. *Public Opinion Quarterly*, 42(3): 380–9.

Propp, V. (1975[1928]) *Morphology of the Folk Tale*. London: Austin.

Purdye, K. and Harvey, B. (1994) TV audience measurement around the world. In ESOMAR/ARF *Worldwide Electronic and Broadcast Audience Research Symposium*, Paris, 1–4 May. Amsterdam: ESOMAR. pp. 1–15.

Qualter, T.H. (1985) *Opinion Control in the Democracies.* New York: St Martin's Press.

Radway, J. (1984) *Reading the Romance.* Chapel Hill: University of North Carolina Press.

Radway, J. (1988) Gendered technology, gendered practice. *Critical Studies in Mass Communication,* 5.

Recnkstorff, K. and McQuail, D. (1996) Social action perspectives in mass communication research. *Communication,* 21(1): 5–26.

Reeves, B., Lang, A., Thorson, E. and Rothschild, M. (1989) Emotional television stories and hemispheric specialisation. *Human Communication Research,* 15(4): 494–508.

Reeves, B., Rothschild, M. and Thorson, E. (1983) *Evaluation of the Tell-Back Audience Response System* (Research Report for ABC). Madison, WI: Mass Communication Research Center, University of Wisconsin–Madison.

Reeves, B., Thorson, E., Rothschild, M., McDonald, D. and Hirsch, J. (1985) Attention to television: intrastimulus effects of movement and scene changes on alpha variation over time. *International Journal of Neuroscience,* 25: 241–55.

Rentz, J., Reynolds, F. and Stout, R. (1983) Analysing changing consumption patterns with cohort analysis. *Journal of Marketing Research,* 20: 12–20.

Rhee, J.W. (1997) Strategy and issue frames in election campaign coverage: a social cognitive account of framing effects. *Journal of Communication,* 47(3): 26–48.

Rice, M.L. (1979) *Television as a medium of verbal communication.* Paper presented at the meeting of the American Psychological Association, New York.

Roberts, M.S. (1992) Predicting voting behavior via the agenda-setting tradition. *Journalism Quarterly,* 69(4): 878–92.

Robertson, L.S., Kelley, A.B., O'Neill, B., Wixon, C.W., Eisworth, R.S. and Haddon, W. (1974) A controlled study of the effect of television messages on safety belt use. *American Journal of Public Health,* 64(11): 1071–80.

Robinson, J.P. (1967) World affairs information and mass media exposure. *Journalism Quarterly,* 44: 23–40.

Robinson, J.P. (1969) Television and leisure time: yesterday, today and (maybe) tomorrow. *Public Opinion Quarterly,* 33: 210–23.

Robinson, J.P. (1977) *How Americans Use Time.* New York: Praeger.

Robinson, J.P. and Bachman, J.G. (1972) Television viewing habits and aggression. In G.A. Comstock and E.A. Rubinstein (eds) *Television and Social Behavior, vol. 3: Television and Adolescent Aggressiveness.* Washington, DC: US Government Printing Office.

Robinson, J.P., Davis, D., Sahin, H. and O'Toole, T. (1980) *Comprehension of Television News: How Alert is the Audience?* Paper presented to the Association for Education in Journalism, Boston.

Robinson, J.P. and Sahin, H. (1984) *Audience Comprehension of Television News: Results from Some Exploratory Research.* London: British Broadcasting Corporation, Broadcasting Research Department.

Rogers, E.M. and Dearing, J.W. (1988) Agenda-setting research: where has it been and where is it going? In J.A. Anderson (ed.) *Communication Yearbook 11.* Beverly Hills, CA: Sage. pp. 555–94.

Rosenberg, B. and White, D.M. (1957) *Mass Culture.* New York: Free Press.

Rosengren, K.E. (1985) Culture, media and society. *Mediacommunicatie,* 13(3–4): 126–44.

Rosengren, K.E., Palmer, P. and Rayburn, J. (eds) (1985) *Media Gratification Research: Current Perspectives.* Beverly Hills, CA: Sage.

Rosengren, K.E. and Windahl, S. (1989) *Media Matter: TV Use in Childhood and Adolescence.* Norwood, NJ: Ablex.

Rothschild, M.L., Hyon, Y.J., Reeves, B., Thorson, E. and Goldstein, R. (1988) Hemispherically lateralized EEG as a response to television commercials. *Journal of Consumer Research,* 15: 185–98.

Rothschild, M.L., Thorson, E., Reeves, B., Hirsch, J.E. and Goldstein, R. (1986) EEG activity and the processing of television commercials. *Communication Research,* 13(2): 102–220.

Rowntree, B.I. (1906) *Poverty: A Study of Town Life.* London: Longmans.

Rubin, A.M. (1984) Ritualized and instrumental television viewing. *Journal of Communication,* 34(3): 67–77.

Rubin, D.M. (1987) How the news media reported on Three Mile Island and Chernobyl. *Journal of Communication,* 37(2): 42–57.

Rust, L. (1985) Using test scores to guide the content analysis of TV materials. *Journal of Advertising Research,* 25: 17–23.

Rust, L., Price, L.L. and Kumar, V. (1985) EEG response to advertisements in print and broadcast media. Working Paper No. 85–111, Marketing Science Institute, Cambridge, MA 02138.

Salomon, G. (1983) Television watching and mental effort: a social psychological view. In J. Bryant and D.R. Anderson (eds) *Children's Understanding of Television: Research on Attention and Comprehension.* New York: Academic Press.

Salomon, G. and Leigh, T. (1984) Predispositions about learning from print and television. *Journal of Communication,* 34: 119–35.

Salwen, M.B. (1986) Effect of accumulation of coverage on issue salience in agenda setting. *Journalism Quarterly,* 65(1): 100–6.

Saussure, F. de (1966[1915]) *Course in General Linguistics.* New York: McGraw-Hill.

Savage, P. (1992) Measures of quality in Canadian broadcasting: the CBC audience panel. In ARF/ESOMAR *Worldwide Broadcast Audience Research Symposium,* Toronto, Canada, 1–3 June. Amsterdam: ESOMAR. pp. 635–48.

Scannell, P. (1988) Radio times: the temporal arrangements of broadcasting in the modern world. In P. Drummond and R. Patterson (eds) *Television and its Audience.* London: British Film Institute.

Schlesinger, P., Dobash, R.E., Dobash, R.P. and Weaver, C.K. (1992) *Women Viewing Violence.* London: BFI.

Schramm, W. (1957) Twenty years of journalism research. *Public Opinion Quarterly,* 21(1): 91–108.

Schramm, W., Lyle, J. and Parker, E. (1961) *Television in the Lives of Our Children.* Stanford, CA: Stanford University Press.

Schroder, K. (1987) Convergence of antagonistic traditions. *European Journal of Communications,* 2.

Schudson, M. (1978) *Discovering the News.* New York: Basic Books.

Schudson, M. (1984) *Advertising: The Uneasy Persuasion.* New York: Basic Books.

Schudsinger, F., Mednick, S. and Knop, J. (1981) *Longitudinal Research.* Boston: Nijhoof Publishing.

Seiter, E., Borchers, H., Kreutzmer, G. and Warth, E-M. (1989) *Remote Control: Television, Audiences and Cultural Power.* London: Routledge.

Shannon, C.E. and Weaver, W. (1949) *The Mathematical Theory of Communication.* Urbana: University of Illinois Press.

Shapiro, M.A. (1994) Signal detection measures of recognition memory. In A. Lang (ed.) *Measuring Psychological Responses to Media.* Hillsdale, NJ: Lawrence Erlbaum Associates, pp. 133–48.

Shapiro, M., Dunwoody, S. and Friestad, M. (1987) *Criterion shift in recognition memory for news stories about risk: the use of signal detection measures of memory in mass communication.* Paper presented to the Annual Meeting of the International Communication Association, Montreal.

Sharot, T. (1994) Measuring television audiences in the UK. In R. Kent (ed.) *Measuring Media Audiences.* London: Routledge. pp. 42–81.

Shaw, D.L. (1977) The press agenda in a community setting. In D.L. Shaw and M.E. McCombs (eds) *The Emergence of American Public Issues: the Agenda-setting Function of the Press.* St Paul, MN: West. pp. 19–31.

Shaw, I. and Newell, D. (1972) *Violence on Television: Programme Content and Viewer Perception.* London: British Broadcasting Corporation.

Sheehan, P.W. (1986) Television viewing and its relation to aggression among children in Australia. In L.R. Huesmann and L.D. Eron (eds) *Television and the Aggressive Child: a Cross-National Comparison.* Hillsdale, NJ: Lawrence Erlbaum Associates.

Shoemaker, P.J. and Reese, S.D. (1991) *Mediating the Message: Theories of Influences on Mass Media Content.* New York: Longman.

Shrum, L.J. (1996) Psychological processes underlying cultivation effects: further tests of construct accessibility. *Human Communication Research,* 22(4): 482–509.

Shrum, L.J. and O'Guinn, T.C. (1993) Processes and effects in the construction of social reality: construct accessibility as an explanatory variable. *Communication Research,* 20: 436–71.

Siegelman, L. and Bullock, D. (1991) Candidates, issues, horse races and hoopla. *American Political Quarterly,* 19(1): 5–32.

Signorielli, N. (1989) Television and conceptions about sex roles: maintaining conventionality and the status quo. *Sex Roles,* 21: 341–60.

Signorielli, N. (1993) Television, the portrayal of women, and children's attitudes. In G. Berry and J.K. Asamen (eds) *Children and Television: Images in a Changing Sociocultural World.* Newbury Park, CA: Sage. pp. 229–42.

Silverstone, R. (1990) Television and everyday life: towards an anthropology of the television audience. In M. Ferguson (ed.) *Public Communication: the New Imperatives.* London: Sage. pp. 173–89.

Silverstone, R., Morley, D., Dahlberg, A. and Livingstone, S. (1989) *Families, technologies and consumption: the household and information and communication technologies.* CRICT Discussion paper, Brunel University.

Silvey, R. (1974) *Who's Listening? The Story of BBC Audience Research.* London: George Allen and Unwin.

Simmons Market Research Bureau (1991) *Page Opening and Reading Style.* New York: Simmons Market Research Bureau.

Singer, J.L. (1980) The power and limitations of television: a cognitive-affective analysis. In P.H. Tannenbaum (ed.) *The Entertainment Functions of Television.* Hillsdale, NJ: Lawrence Erlbaum Associates.

Singer, J.L., Singer, D.G. and Rapaczynski, W. (1984) Children's imagination as predicted by family patterns and television viewing: A longitudinal study. *Genetic Psychology Monographs,* 110: 43–69.

Siskind, T. (1979) The effect of newspaper design on reader preference. *Journalism Quarterly,* 56(1): 54–62.

Smith, H.L. (ed.) (1930–35) *The New Survey of London Life and Labour.* 9 volumes. London: P.S. King.

Smith, R. (1984) How consistently do readability tests measure the difficulty of newswriting? *Newspaper Records Journal,* 5(4): 1–8.

Smith, E.J. and Hajash, D.J. (1988) Information graphics in 30 daily newspapers. *Journalism Quarterly,* 65(3): 714–18.

Smythe, D. (1954) *Three Years of New York Television: 1951–1953.* Urbana, IL: National Association of Educational Broadcasters.

Sneed, L. (1991) *Evaluating Video Programs: Is It Worth It?* White Plains, NY: Knowledge Industry Publications.

Sobal, J. and Jackson-Beeck, M. (1981) Newspaper nonreaders: a national profile. *Journalism Quarterly*, 58(1): 9–13.

Soderland, W.C., Surlin, S.H. and Romanow, W.I. (1989) Gender in Canadian local television news. *Journal of Broadcasting and Electronic Media*, 33(2): 187–96.

Sorenson, J. (1991) Mass media and discourse on famine in the Horn of Africa. *Discourse and Society*, 2(2): 223–42.

Stamm, K., Jackson, K. and Jacoubovitch, D. (1980) Exploring new options in newspaper readership methods. *Newspaper Research Journal*, 1(2): 63–74.

Stauffer, J., Frost, R. and Rybolt, W. (1980) Recall and comprehension of radio news in Kenya. *Journalism Quarterly*, 57: 612–17.

Stauffer, J., Frost, R. and Rybolt, W. (1983) The attention factor in recalling network television news. *Journal of Communication*, 33: 29–37.

Stempel, G.H. (1952) Sample size for classifying subject matter in dailies. *Journalism Quarterly*, 29: 333–4.

Stern, A. (1971) Presentation to the Radio-Television News Directors Association, Boston. Unpublished paper, University of California at Berkeley, Graduate School of Journalism.

Steuer, F.B., Applefield, J.M. and Smith, R. (1971) Televised aggression and the interpersonal aggression of pre-school children. *Journal of Experimental Child Psychology*, 81: 442–7.

Stipp, H. and Milavsky, R. (1988) US television programming effects on aggressive behavior of children and adolescents. *Current Psychology: Research and Reviews*, 7: 76–92.

Surbeck, E. and Endsley, R.C. (1979) Surbeck, E. and Endsley, R.C. Children's emotional reactions to TV violence: Effects of film character, reassurance, age and sex. *Journal of Social Psychology*, 109: 269–81.

Sussman, S., Burton, D., Dent, C.W., Stacy, A.W. and Flay, B.R. (1991) Use of focus groups in developing an adolescent tobacco use cessation program: collection norm effects. *Journal of Applied Social Psychology*, 21: 1772–82.

Swanson, C. (1955) What they read in 130 daily newspapers. *Journalism Quarterly*, 32(3): 411–21.

Tannenbaum, P.H. (1954) Effect of serial position on recall of radio news stories. *Journalism Quarterly*, 31: 319–23.

Taylor, W. (1953) Cloze procedure: a new tool for measuring readability. *Journalism Quarterly*, 30(4): 415–33.

Television Audience Assessment, Inc. (1983) *The Audience Rates Television*. Cambridge, MA: Television Audience Assessment, Inc.

Television Audience Assessment, Inc. (1984) *Program Impact and Program Appeal: Qualitative Ratings and Commercial Effectiveness*. Boston, MA: Television Audience Assessment, Inc.

Thorndyke, P. (1977) Cognitive structures in comprehension and memory for narrative discourse. *Cognitive Psychology*, 9: 77–110.

Thorndyke, P. (1979) Knowledge acquisition from newspaper stories. *Discourse Processes*, 2: 95–112.

Thorson, E. (1994) Using eyes on screen as a measure of attention to television. In A. Lang (ed.) *Measuring Psychological Responses to Media*. Hillsdale, NJ: Lawrence Erlbaum Associates. pp. 65–84.

Thorson, E. and Reeves, B. (1986) Effects of over-time measures of viewer liking and activity during programmes and commercials on memory for commercials. In R.J. Lutz (ed.) *Advances in Consumer Research*, vol. 13. Provo, UT: Association for Consumer Research. pp. 549–53.

Thorson, E., Reeves, B. and Schleuder, J. (1985) Message complexity and attention to television. *Communication Research*, 12(4): 427–54.

Thorson, E., Reeves, B. and Schleuder, J. (1986) Attention to local and global complexity in television messages. In M. McLaughlin (ed.) *Communication Yearbook 10*. Newbury Park, CA: Sage. pp. 368–83.

Thorson, E. and Zhao, X. (1988) *Memory for TV commercials as a function of onset and offsets in watching.* Paper presented at the Mass Communication Division of the Annual Meeting of the International Communication Association, New Orleans.

Thorson, E. and Zhao, X. (1989) *Predicting attention and memory for TV commercials using Relevance, Originality and Impact scores.* Paper presented to the Advertising Division of the Annual Meeting of the Association for Education in Journalism and Mass Communication, Washington, DC.

Tichenor, P.J., Donohue, G.A. and Olien, C.N. (1970) Mass media flow and differential growth of knowledge. *Public Opinion Quarterly*, 34: 159–70.

Tillinghast, W. (1981) Declining newspaper readership: impact of region and urbanisation. *Journalism Quarterly*, 58(1): 14–23.

Traudt, P.J. and Lont, C.M. (1987) Media-logic-in-use: the family as locus of study. In T.R. Lindlof (ed.) *Natural Audiences.* Norwood, NJ: Ablex. pp. 139–60.

Treisman, A. (1969) Strategies and models of selective attention. *Psychological Review*, 76: 282–99.

Trenaman, J. (1967) *Communication and Comprehension.* London: Longman.

Trujillo, N. and Ekdom, L.R. (1987) A 40-year portrait of the portrayal of industry on prime-time television. *Journalism Quarterly*, 64(2): 368–75.

Tuchman, G. (1978) The symbolic annihilation of women by the mass media. In G. Tuchman, A. Daniels and J. Benet (eds) *Hearth and Home: Images of women in the mass media.* New York: Oxford University Press.

Turner, C.W. and Goldsmith, D. (1976) Effects of toy guns on children's anti-social free play behaviour. *Journal of Experimental Child Psychology*, 21: 303–15.

Twyman, T. (1994) Measuring audiences to radio. In R. Kent (ed.) *Measuring Media Audiences.* London: Routledge. pp. 88–104.

Upton, C. (1969) *Broadcast program analysers: a century of no progress in instrument design.* Unpublished masters thesis, University of Wisconsin – Madison.

Utt, S. and Pasternak, S. (1989) How they look: an updated study of American newspaper front pages. *Journalism Quarterly*, 66(3): 621–27.

Van der Voort, T.H.A. (1986) *Television Violence: A Child's Eye View.* Amsterdam, Holland: Elsevier Science Publishers.

Veraguth, O. (1907) Das psycho-galvanische reflex-phenomenon. *Monatschrift für Psychiatrie und Neurologie*, 21: 387–424.

Vinokar, A. and Burnstein, E. (1974) Effects of partially shared persuasive arguments on group induced shifts: a group problem solving approach. *Journal of Personality and Social Psychology*, 29: 305–15.

Wakshlag, J., Day, K.D. and Zillmann, D. (1981) Selective exposure to educational television programmes as a function of differently paced humorous inserts. *Journal of Educational Psychology*, 73: 23–32.

Wakshlag, J., Vial, V. and Tamborini, R. (1983) Selecting crime drama and apprehension about crime. *Human Communication Research*, 10: 227–42.

Walizer, M.H. and Wienir, P.L. (1978) *Research Methods and Analysis: Searching for Relationships.* New York: Harper and Row.

Walker, J.L. (1980) Changes in EEG rhythms during television viewing: preliminary comparisons with reading and other tasks. *Perceptual and Motor Skills*, 51(1): 255–61.

Walma van der Molen, J. and van der Voort, T.H. (1997) Children's recall of television and print news: A media comparison study. *Journal of Educational Psychology*, 89(1): 82–91.

Waples, D., Berelson, B. and Bradshaw, F.R. (1940) *What Reading Does to People.* Chicago: University of Chicago Press.

Ward, L.M. and Eschwege, K. (1996) *Would that really happen? Adolescents' perceptions of television's tales of dating and romance.* Unpublished manuscript, University of California, Los Angeles.

Ward, D.B. (1992) The effect of sidebar graphics. *Journalism Quarterly,* 69(7): 318–28.

Ward, L.M. and Greenfield, P.M. (1998) Designing experiments on television and social behavior: Developmental perspectives. In J.K. Asamen and G.L. Berry (eds) *Research Paradigms, Television and Social Behavior.* Thousand Oaks, CA: Sage. pp. 67–108.

Warner, W. and Henry, W. (1948) The radio daytime serial: a symbolic analysis. *Genetic Psychology Monographs,* 37: 3–71.

Watt, J.H. and Krull, R. (1974) An information theory measure for television programming. *Communication Research,* 1: 44–68.

Watt, J.H. and Krull, R. (1975) *Arousal model components in television programming: form activity and violent content.* Paper presented to the International Communication Association, Chicago.

Watt, J.H. and Krull, R. (1976) An examination of three models of television viewing and aggression. *Human Communication Research,* 3: 991–1112.

Watt, J.H. and Welch, A.J. (1983) Effects of static and dynamic complexity on children's attention and recall of televised instruction. In J. Bryant and D.R. Anderson (eds) *Children's Understanding of Television: Research on Attention and Comprehension.* New York: Academic Press. pp. 69–102.

Weaver, D. (1977) Political issues and voter need for orientation. In M. McCombs and D. Shaw (eds) *The Emergence of American Political Issues.* St Paul, MN: West.

Weaver, D., Wilhoit, C. and Reide, P. (1979) *Personal Needs and Media Use.* (ANPA News Research Report No. 21). Reston, VA: ANPA News Research Center.

Webb, P.H. and Ray, M.L. (1979) Effects of TV clutter. *Journal of Advertising Research,* 19: 7–12.

Weber, M. (1907) *Wirtschaft und Gesellschaft.* Tubingen: Mohr.

Weber, H. and Laux, L. (1985) Der begriff "Stress" in Publikumszeitschriften. Ergebnisse einer Inhaltsanalyse. *Publizistik,* 30(1): 25–34.

Wesley, W. (1978) *The use of the psychogalvanometer in testing the effectiveness of advertising.* Paper presented at the American Marketing Association 16th Annual Advertising Research Conference, Los Angeles, CA.

West, M. and Biocca, F. (1992) *What if your wife were murdered: Audience responses to a verbal gaffe in the 1988 Los Angeles presidential debates.* Paper presented at the annual conference of the American Association for Public Opinion Research, St Petersburg, FL.

White, N.R. and White, P.B. (1982) Vietnamese refugees in Australia: press definitions of reality. *Media Asia,* 9(2): 68–79.

Wiegmann, O., Kuttschreuter, M. and Baarda, B. (1992) A longitudinal study of the effects of television viewing on aggressive and prosocial behaviours. *British Journal of Social Psychology,* 31: 147–64.

Wilhoit, C. and deBock, H. (1978) Mass Communication Review Yearbook. Beverly Hills, CA: Sage. pp. 73–112.

Williams, D.C., Paul, J. and Ogilvie, J.L. (1957) The mass media, learning and retention. *Canadian Journal of Psychology,* 11: 157–63.

Williams, T.M. (ed.) (1986) *The Impact of Television: A Natural Experiment in Three Communities.* Orlando, FL: Academic Press.

Williams, T.M., Zabrack, M.L. and Joy, L.A. (1982) The portrayal of aggression on North American television. *Journal of Applied Social Psychology,* 12(5): 360–80.

Williams, W. and Semlak, W. (1978a) Campaign '76: agenda setting during the New Hampshire primary. *Journal of Broadcasting*, 22(4): 531–40.

Williams, W. and Semlak, W. (1978b) Structural effects of TV coverage on political agendas. *Journal of Communication*, 28(1): 114–19.

Wilson, B.J. and Cantor, J. (1985) Developmental differences in empathy with a television protagonist's fear. *Journal of Experimental Child Psychology*, 39: 284–99.

Wilson, B.J., Smith, S.L., Linz, D., Potter, J., Donnerstein, E., Kunkel, D., Blumenthal, E. and Gray, T. (1996) *Content Analysis of Entertainment Television: The 1994–95 Results.* Paper presented at the Duke University Conference on Media Violence and Public Policy in the Media, Durham, NC, 27–29 June.

Wilson, B.J. and Weiss, A.J. (1993) The effects of sibling co-viewing on preschoolers' reactions to a suspenseful movie scene. *Communication Research*, 20(2): 214–56.

Wilson, C.E. (1974) The effect of medium on loss of information. *Journalism Quarterly*, 51: 111–15.

Wimmer, R.D. and Dominick, J.R. (1994) *Mass Media Research: An Introduction* (4th edn). Belmont, CA: Wadsworth Publishing Company.

Winick, C. (1988) The functions of television: life without the big box. In S. Oskamp (ed.) *Television as a Social Issue.* Newbury Park, CA: Sage. pp. 217–37.

Wober, J.M. (1990) *The Assessment of Television Quality: Some Explorations of Methods and Their Results.* London: IBA Research Department, Research Paper, July.

Wober, M. and Gunter, B. (1982) Television and personal threat: fact or artifact? A British view. *British Journal of Social Psychology*, 21: 43–51.

Wober, M. and Gunter, B. (1988) *Television and Social Control.* Aldershot, UK: Avebury.

Wonsek, P. (1992) College basketball on television: a study of racism in the media. *Media, Culture and Society*, 14: 449–61.

Zabor, D., Biocca, F. and Wren, J. (1991) How to determine whether your video is a winner or a wild card. In R. Roehr (ed.) *Electronic Advancement: Student Recruiting.* Chicago: Council for Advancement and Support of Education. pp. 57–73.

Zechmeister, E.B. and Nyberg, S.E. (1982) *Human Memory.* Monterey, CA: Brooks/Cole.

Zillmann, B. and Bryant, J. (eds) (1985) *Selective Exposure to Communication.* Hillsdale, NJ: Lawrence Erlbaum Associates.

Zipf, G.K. (1932) *Selected Studies of the Principle of Relative Frequencies in Language.* Cambridge: Cambridge University Press.

INDEX

academic research, 135, 136, 155–61
actional theory, 2, 3
Action-Evaluation Matrix, 60
active audiences, 164
advertising, 86–7, 107–8, 112, 177, 182, 184, 186
affective responses, 135–62
ageing, 205
agenda-matching, 200
agenda-setting, 56, 192–203
aided recall, 105
Allen, C., 170
All Radio Methodological Study, 116
alpha waves, 181–2
Alwitt, L., 182
Amount of Invested Mental Effort (AIME), 167
Anderson, D., 171–2
Ang, I., 127–9
anxiety, 212–13
appreciation, 233
Appreciation Index, 137–8
Arbitron, 118, 121
attention, 163–89
    children, 167
    divided, 179
    experiments, 164, 166–7, 189
    phasic, 180
    selective, 185
    tonic, 180
Audience Reaction Assessment (AURA), 141
audiences, 22–54, 55
    affective responses, 135–62
    appreciation, 136–8
    behavioural impact, 236–79
    cognitive impact, 190–235
    cognitive responses, 163–89
    interpretation, 234
    key measures, 95–6
    media usage and exposure, 93–134
    perception, 78–81
    radio, 113–16
    research paradigms, 9–21
    retention, 218–19
audimeter, 118

Bachman, J.G., 242
Baird, R., 71–2
Bales, R.E., 60
Bandura, A., 15, 53, 254–5
Baron, J.N., 275–6
Bechtel, R.B., 170–1
behavioural effects, 15, 36–7, 190–1

behavioural impact, 236–79
behavioural measures, 15, 175–9
behaviourist perspective, 3–4, 13, 16–17
beliefs cultivation, 192, 203–15
Belson, W., 249–50
Berelson, B., 56
Berger, A.A., 83, 84
Berkowitz, L., 15, 53, 256, 274
Berry, C., 222
bias, 37, 102–3, 104
Blumler, J., 9
Bogart, L., 109–10
Booth, C., 239
brain wave measures, 181–2
British Broadcasting Corporation, 79–80, 122,
    137–8, 158
Broadcasters' Audience Research Board (BARB),
    120, 122, 141
Brown, J., 267
Bryant, J., 212–13
Bureau of Broadcast Measurement, 116

Canadian Broadcasting Corporation, 143
Canadian enjoyment index, 143–4
cardiac response curve (CRC), 180–1
carry-over effects, 34–5
Castle, V., 185
catch-up panel design, 245–7
causation, 29, 30, 31, 32, 35, 36, 51, 237
    agenda-setting, 199, 200
    cultivation analysis, 212
    focus groups, 47
    surveys, 250
census, 238–9
Centerwall, B., 273
characters, 153, 154
children, 216–17
    attention measurement, 167
    environmental distractions, 177–8
    eyes on screen, 176–7
    field experiments, 258–9
    news retention, 225
    panel studies, 245–50
    secondary reaction time, 185
    TV control, 132
    TV programmes, 76–8
    violence, 80–1, 155–8, 160
    vulnerability, 14
circulation research, 111–12
Click, J.W., 71–2
clipping method, 105–6

Cloze Procedure, 73–4
cluster analysis, 140–1
coders' perception, 78–81
codes, 83, 85–6
cognitive elements, 13
cognitive impact, 190–235
cognitive responses, 163–89
coherence, 154, 229
cohort studies, 27–8, 244
coincidental interviewing, 115
coincidental surveys, 118
Collett, P., 173
Collins, W., 74–5
communication flow, 15, 78, 194
community contexts, 226
complexity, 178
comprehension, 72, 73–4, 163–89, 234
Computer Assisted Telephone Interviewing, 103
Comstock, G., 37
Comte, A., 4
concept-oriented families, 131
confusion control, 102
construct accessibility test, 214
constructivism, 2
content analysis, 55–92, 194
    cultivation theory, 206–7
    experimental research, 201, 202
    media agendas, 197
    media news output, 216
continuous panel studies, 28
continuous response measurement, 147–51
contrast, 154
Cook, T.D., 41
correlational surveys, 215, 242
correlations, 202, 216, 246
crime perception, 214–15
crime reporting, 68
critical perspective, 6–8, 9, 17–19, 20, 22, 45, 53, 230–5
critical theorists, 128, 226
cross-cultural research, 247
cross-lagged correlational techniques, 196
cross-sectional analyses, 196, 200, 217
cross-sectional surveys, 27, 240–3
cultivation analysis, 205–6, 207–8
cultivation differential, 206
cultivation effects, 69, 210
cultivation theory, 203–15
Cultural Indicators, 204, 205, 206
cultural studies perspective, 18–19
Curran, J., 10, 20, 47–8

data capture, 95–9
day-after recall (DAR), 114, 116, 122
Dearing, J.W., 193, 194–5, 199, 200
decoding, 19, 227, 228

De Four, D., 158–9
delayed-reward content, 74
demographic factors, 206, 211–12, 216, 234
dependent variables, 31
de Saussure, F., 83–4, 86–7
descriptive analysis, 62–3
descriptive surveys, 24
developmental differences, 39
diachronic studies, 84
diaries, 96–7, 105, 108, 218
    AURA, 141
    enjoyment, 142–4
    radio, 114–15, 116
    readership, 103, 105
    television, 117, 118, 120, 124
    video comparison, 171–2, 173
Diener, E., 158–60
direct observation, 50
discourse analysis, 87–8
discourse comprehension model, 231
Distractor Method, 178–9
divided attention problem, 179
double-blind procedure, 37
drama, 153
Durkheim, E., 4

ecological validity, 40, 46
economic welfare, 201–2
Edelstein, A.S., 196
editor-reader comparisons, 109–10
Edwardson, M., 222–3
electrocardiograms, 180
electrodermal measurement, 183–4
electroencephalogram, 181
electronic media usage, 112–26
electronic recording devices, 97, 117–18
embedded meaning, 5
emotional responses, 135–62
empirical research, 2, 228, 230–5, 237
enjoyment, 142–4, 152–4, 156, 158, 173–4
environmental distractions, 177–80
epistemology, 2–3
equivalent time series design, 35
establishment surveys, 124
ethnography, 50, 127, 129, 188
evaluative broadcast ratings, 136–8
evaluative ratings, 141–2, 155–6
event analyses, 74–5
evoked response curve (ERC), 181
experience sampling, 97–8
experiments, 29–41, 51, 52, 53, 201–3, 220, 251–76
    attention, 164, 166–7, 189
    behaviour impact, 237
    cultivation analysis, 212–13, 214
    early research, 14–15

experiments, *cont.*
  media output, 70–82
  retention, 219–20
exposure effects, 216–17
extended focus groups, 43
external validity, 36, 40, 214, 259, 260
eyes on screen (EOS), 175–7

factorial designs, 34, 255–6
factual learning, 192, 215–35
false consciousness, 7, 10
familiarity, 80
feminist research, 8
field studies, 40–1, 201, 202, 218–19, 257–66
film observation, 169, 170–5
filters, 102, 104, 184
First Reading Yesterday (FRY), 103, 104
Flesch Reading Ease Formula, 73
Flynne, L., 71
focus groups, 35, 42–7, 51, 54, 226–8, 277, 278
  extended, 43
  off-line measurement, 164–5, 167–8
  on-line responses, 150
  programme analyzer, 151, 152
  viewers as editors, 161
Fog Index, 73
follow back panel, 249
framework, 82–3
Frankfurt School, 10, 11–12, 18, 226
Frost, W.A.K., 139, 140, 141
Furu, T., 266–7

galvanic skin response (GSR), 156, 157, 183
Geiger, S., 186
gender
  differences, 234
  roles, 38–9, 68
  stereotypes, 205
  TV dominance, 130–2
  violence appeal, 215
General Programme Rating Battery (GPRB),
    140–1
General Social Survey, 211
Gerbner, G., 63, 66, 69–70, 203–4, 205–6,
    207, 208–9, 210–11
Gitlin, T., 17, 18
Gordon, T., 155–6
Graber, D., 218
Greenberg, B., 155–6
Greenfield, P.M., 37–40
group administration, 26–7
group effect, 44
Gunning, R., 73
Gunter, B., 67, 156, 174, 217–18, 225
  familiarity, 80
  General Election, 216

Gunter, B., *cont.*
  programme analyzer, 151–4
  scales, 143
  story grouping, 221

Haldane, I.R., 138, 140
Hall, S., 19, 85–6
Hansen, C.H., 254
Hansen, R.D., 254
Haskins, J.B., 71
heart rate, 157, 179–81
Heidegger, M., 8
Hennigan, K.M., 273
Hensley, J.E., 275
hermeneutics, 2, 4, 5
hidden agendas, 67
Hijmans, E., 82, 83
Himmelweit, H., 270–1
Hirsch, P., 208–9
Hoijer, B., 47
Hughes, M., 211–12
Hunziger, P., 3
Huston, A.C., 77
hypodermic model, 10, 11, 17

immediate-reward content, 74
Independent Broadcasting Authority, 141
Independent Television Authority, 138, 139, 141
independent variables, 31, 252
indirect observation, 50–1
industry-driven affective research, 136–55
informational redundancy, 223
information-processing measures, 184–8
Information Theory, 75
infrared, 126
interactional perspective, 3–4
interaction process analysis, 60
internal validity, 214
interpersonal relations, 15, 16–17
interpretative analysis, 90–1
interpretive communities, 232–3, 235
interpretivist perspective, 5–6, 7–8, 20, 22, 45
interrupted time series, 35
interval panel studies, 28
intervening variables, 17
interviews, 58
  coincidental, 115
  in-depth, 35, 54, 99, 130, 228–30
  open-ended, 277
  personal, 26
  structured, 26
  survey, 164, 165–6
  telephone, 103
  television ratings, 117
  unstructured, 26
involvement, 153

issue-framed campaign, 231–2
item-association analysis, 106
item selection studies, 105–6
Iyengar, S., 201

Jensen, K.-B., 9, 18–19, 228–30
Johnson, H., 142
Josephson, W.L., 263–4

Katz, E., 9, 10, 12, 15, 16–17, 53, 194
Kelly, G., 130, 139
Kendall, P., 43
Kepplinger, H.M., 60
Kerlinger, F.N., 56–7
Kintsch, W., 231
Kippax, S., 272
Klapper, T., 13, 14
knowledge-gap hypothesis, 217
Kosicki, G.M., 199
Krippendorf, K., 82–3
Krull, R., 75, 177–8
Kubey, R., 268

laboratory experiments, 253–6
Lamb, R., 173
language, 77–8, 87
law and order, 201–2
Lazarsfeld, P., 12, 53, 54, 193, 240
    continuous response measurement, 148–9
    focus groups, 42
    interpersonal relations, 16–17
    mass culture, 10
    presidential election, 14
    two-step flow, 15, 194
learning, factual, 192, 215–35
Lefkowitz, M.M., 245
Levy, M.R., 165–6
Leymore, V.L., 86–7
Liebes, T., 9
Life, 101
linguistic codes, 77–8
Littlejohn, S.W., 2–3
Livingstone, S., 47
logic, 82–3
longitudinal research, 27–9, 217, 237, 241, 243–50
long-term agenda analyses, 198
Lorch, E., 185
Loye, D., 265–6
Lull, J., 9, 131, 169
Lunt, P., 47

Macauley, J., 274
macro-level learning, 221
magazines *see* print media
mail survey technique, 110
manipulation, 10, 13, 196
Marx, K., 6, 18

mass culture, 10
McCarthy, E.D., 242–3
McClure, R., 216
McCombs, M., 194, 195, 196, 199
McLaughlin, H., 73
McLeod, J., 242
McQuail, D., 9
Meadowcroft, J.M., 185
meaning, 3, 5, 85, 86–7
media agendas, 197
media dependency, 193
Mediamark Research Inc, 110
memory response latencies, 186–7
Merten, K., 57, 58, 59–60
Merton, R., 12, 42–3, 44, 54, 150, 193
message system analysis, 205
meta-theoretical scheme, 2
meter systems, 122–5
Meyer, T.P., 133
Mielke, K., 178–9
Milavsky, J.R., 248
misrepresentation, 39
modal complexity, 76
modernism, 8
Morley, D., 45, 46, 99, 127–8, 130, 226–8, 234
Morrison, D., 160–1, 278
multiple regression, 246
multiple-scale studies, 151
Murray, J.P., 272
Mustonen, A., 63
Mutz, D.C., 269

narrative analysis, 74–5, 86, 89–90
narrative construction, 221–2
National Broadcasting Company (NBC) study, 247–9
National Television Violence study, 63–4, 65, 67
Nationwide study, 45, 226–8
natural experiments, 40, 41, 257, 266–76
Neuman, W.L., 4, 5
news
    awareness, 217–18
    comprehension, 234
    diffusion, 217
    formats, 231–2
    packaging effects, 220–1
    retention, 221, 223, 224–5
    stories coherence, 229
Newspaper Readership Project, 100–1
Newspaper Research Council, 101, 106
newspapers *see* print media
Nielsen, 117–18, 121
Nielsen Radio Index, 115
Nietzsche, F.W., 8
nominal scales, 151
nomothetic explanation, 4

non-actional theory, 2–3
non-participant observation, 49, 52, 98
non-selective viewing, 204
NORC, 211

observation, 48–53, 58, 98–9, 126–7, 168–75, 188
  direct, 50
  indirect, 50–1
  non-participant, 49, 52, 98
  participant, 5, 49, 52, 98, 131, 169–70
  photographic, 169, 170–5
  structured, 49, 50–1
  unstructured, 49, 50, 51
off-line measurement, 136, 141–7, 155,
  161, 164–8, 191, 237
one-group, post-test-only design, 33, 270
one-group, pre-test-post-test design, 33, 266–8
one-off surveys, 217, 236
one-shot studies, 196, 200
on-line measurement, 136, 147–55, 161–2, 168–88, 191
ontology, 2–3
open-ended interviews, 277
opinion cultivation, 192
opinion polls, 24, 194, 198, 243
opinions cultivation, 203–15
orienting response, 180
output, 55–92
over-time condition, 196

packaging effects, 220–1
page makeup research, 70–2
panel studies, 28–9, 240, 244–7, 249–50, 269
paradigmatic analysis, 85
paradigms convergence, 231
Parke, R., 261–2
participant observation, 5, 49, 52, 98, 131, 169–70
passive audiences, 164
passive measurement, 124–5
Patterson, T., 216
Payne Fund, 14
people meters, 97, 118–20, 123–5
personal constructs, 130–1, 139
personal experience, 200
personal interviews, 26
phasic attention, 180
Phillips, D., 274–6
photographic observation, 169, 170–5
physiological measures, 179–84
physiological response, 156–7
picture-sampling technique, 119
plot, 153, 154
policy decisions, 194
politics, 24, 186, 190, 201–2, 215–16, 217
positivism, 4–5, 6–8, 12, 16, 20–1, 22, 35, 53, 252
postal surveys, 25, 144–5
postmodern research, 8–9

post-test only, 252
  with control group, 33, 254–5, 264–6
  with more than one group, 270–3
  with one group, 33, 270
  with two groups, 33, 254
post-tests, 31
pre-experimental designs, 32–3
pre-school studies, 258–9
presidential campaign, 14, 194, 216
pre-test, 31, 34, 223
pre-test/post-test, 252, 253–4, 258, 260
  with control group, 32, 257, 266–8
  with one group, 33, 268–70
Principal Components Analysis, 139
print media, 70–4, 88, 99–112, 197, 224–5
profiles, readers, 105
programme analyzer, 151–5
propaganda, 12
Propp, V., 84–5
prosocial behaviour, 236
psychographics, 112
public agendas, 197–8, 200
Pulkkinen, L., 63

qualitative research, 22, 53–4, 134, 277–9
  audiences, 23, 41–54, 126–33, 154, 163, 164
  behavioural impact, 237, 251–2
  cognitive impact, 225–30
  content analysis, 82–92
  convergence, 9
  interpretivism, 5
  print media, 100
  TV viewing, 132
  see also focus groups; interviews; observation
quality, 142–3
quantitative research, 134, 278–9
  attention, 188–9
  audiences, 23–41, 54, 127–8, 154, 163, 164
  behavioural impact, 237, 251–76
  content analysis, 57, 81–2, 91–2
  convergence, 9
  positivism, 4–5
  print media, 100
  see also experiments
quasi-experiments, 33, 40–1, 259, 273
questionnaires, 25, 26–7, 28, 52, 53, 58, 95–6
  extended focus groups, 43
  political knowledge, 217
  television ratings, 117
  viewing behaviour, 171
  violence, 160
quiz shows, 151–3

radio, 112–16, 224–5
Radway, J., 46
randomized experiments, 263–4

rationalism, 2
Reaction Indices, 138
reactivity, 57, 58–9
readability, 73–4
reader/non-reader studies, 107
reader profiles, 105
readership
    diary, 103, 105
    frequency, 107–8
    research, 101–10
real-world indicators, 200
recent-reading survey, 102–3, 104
reception analysis, 18–19, 231, 232, 233
recognition memory tests, 187
recognition response latency, 187
recording devices, 115
Reese, S.D., 186
Reeves, B., 185, 186
Reiss, P.C., 275–6
relativism, 7
repeated measures, 34–5
Repertory Grid, 139
replication, 4
research paradigms, 9–21
responsibility, 201–2
retrospective panels, 249–50
reward dimension, 153
rhetorical analysis, 89
Rice, M.L., 78
Risk Ratios, 69–70, 206
ritualized viewing, 204
Robertson, L.S., 262–3
Robinson, J.P., 167, 242
Rogers, E.M., 193, 194–5, 199, 200
Rosengren, K.E., 16, 17, 18–19
Rothschild, M.L., 181–2
Rowntree, B.I., 239

Sahin, H., 167
Salomon, G., 167
Salwen, M.B., 200
sampling, 66–7, 97–8, 239
Sartre, J-P., 8
Savage, P., 144
scales, 143, 151
schema, 233–4
Schramm, W., 100, 271–2
Schudsinger, F., 249
secondary reaction time, 184–6
selective attention, 185
selectivity, 15
semiology, 83–7
semi-structured study, 51
set complexity, 75–6
Shaw, D.L., 194, 196, 199

Shoemaker, P.J., 186
shot complexity, 75
Shrum, L.J., 214
signal detection, 187–8
signifiers, 83, 84
Silvey, R., 137–8
Simmons Market Research Bureau, 110
Singer, J.L., 245
single-scale studies, 151
Siskind, T., 71
skin resistance level, 183
SMOG Grading, 73
soap operas, 151–2, 153–4, 214–15
social action theory, 18
social cognitive model, 231
social reality, 57–8, 59, 69, 203, 209–11
social science paradigm, 237
social welfare, 201–2
socio-oriented families, 131
Solomon four-group design, 34
sonar systems, 125–6
Staab, J.F., 60
Stanton, F., 148–9
Stauffer, J., 219, 225
Stempel, G.H., 66
stereotypes, 38, 39, 68, 205, 254
Stern, A., 218–19
Stouffer, S., 240
strategy-framed campaign, 231–2
structuralism, 86–7
structuralist-semiotic analysis, 83–7
structured interviews, 26
structured observation, 49, 50–1
subjective meanings, 3
super-themes, 230
survey model, 46
surveys, 23–9, 35, 51, 52, 53, 238–50
    agenda-setting, 202–3
    causation, 250
    coincidental, 118
    correlational, 215, 242
    cross-sectional, 27, 240–3
    descriptive, 24
    establishment, 124
    General Social Survey, 211
    interviews, 164, 165–6
    limitations, 237
    mail technique, 110
    National Readership
        Surveys, 100
    one-off, 217, 236
    politics, 24, 216
    postal, 25, 144–5
    public agendas, 197
    reader/non-reader, 107

surveys, *cont.*
   recent-reading, 102–3, 104
   telephone, 25–6, 105, 118, 120, 218–19
   violence, 24, 241–3
synchronic studies, 84
syntagm, 84
systematic recall, 114

Taylor, W., 73–4
technical professionalism, 154
telephone surveys, 25–6, 105, 118, 120, 218–19
telescoping, 104
television audience assessment (TAA), 146–7
television qualitative ratings (TQR), 145–6
tension, 153
text-based data, 54
theatre tests, 219
thermal infrared, 126
through-the-book technique, 101, 102, 104, 108
time series analyses, 35, 273–6
time span, 27
tonic attention, 180
tracking, 106, 196
transactional perspective, 3–4
transmissional perspective, 3–4
trend analysis, 198
trend studies, 27, 243, 244
TVQ service, 144–5
two-group, post-test-only design, 33, 254
two-shot studies, 200
two-step flow, 15, 194
Twyman, T., 113, 117, 120
typography, 70–2

underrepresentation, 39
universal laws, 4
University of Sheffield study, 64
unpredictability, 152
unstructured interviews, 26
unstructured observation, 49, 50, 51
USA Today, 72
uses and gratification research, 15–16, 108–9, 231

validity, 36, 40, 46, 47, 214, 259, 260
Van der Voort, I.H.A., 160
van Dijk, T., 231
versimilitude, 153
victimization, 204, 205, 213
video cameras, 98, 125, 127, 169, 170–5
viewers as editors, 160–1
violence, 14–15, 16, 204
   affective response, 155–61
   beliefs cultivation, 207, 210–12
   content analysis, 62–7, 69–70, 79–82
   definitions, 62, 63–4, 81–2
   experiments, 29, 32, 33, 34, 37, 53
   factorial designs, 255–6
   field experiments, 258–66
   gender differences, 215
   longitudinal research, 245–50
   perception, 158–9
   quasi-experiments, 41
   surveys, 24, 241–3
Violence Index, 69, 206, 207
Violence Profile, 69, 206–7
visual interaction complexity, 76
visual presence, 76
visual-verbal congruence, 76
VOXBOX, 150

Wakshlag, J., 213
Ward, L.M., 37–40
Watt, J.H., 75, 178
Weber, M., 5, 56, 239
Welch, A.J., 178
whole copy method, 105, 106
Williams, T.M., 63, 267–8
Wittgenstein, L., 8
Wober, J.M., 142
Woody, L.W., 159–60
World Views I & II, 2, 3
Wright Mills, C., 11

Printed in the United Kingdom
by Lightning Source UK Ltd.
106524UKS00001BA/22